Research Methods in Public Administration and Nonprofit Management

Research Methods in Public Administration and Nonprofit Management

Quantitative and Qualitative Approaches

David E. McNabb

M.E. Sharpe
Armonk, New York
London, England

Library of Congress Cataloging-in-Publication Data

McNabb, David E.
  Research methods in public administration and nonprofit management : quantitative
and qualitative approaches / David E. McNabb.
    p. cm.
  Includes bibliographical references and index.
  ISBN 0-7656-0957-6 (alk. paper)
    1. Public administration—Research—Methodology. 2. Nonprofit
organizations—Management. I. Title.

JF1338.A2 M38 2002
001.4′2—dc21   2001057689

Printed in the United States of America

The paper used in this publication meets the minimum requirements of
American National Standard for Information Sciences
Permanence of Paper for Printed Library Materials,
ANSI Z 39.48-1984.

BM (c)   10   9   8   7   6   5

Dedicated, with love, to Meghan, Michael, and Sara.

Special thanks to the faculty and staff
of the Masters in Public Administration Program
at The Evergreen State College for allowing me to be a part of your very
special team. Without you, this would not have been possible.
Finally, I wish to thank Harry Briggs who believed in the book and made it
happen, and Susan Rescigno, who made sure it met expectations.

Table of Contents

List of Tables and Figures

Tables

Figures

Part 1

Foundations of Research

1 Introduction to Research Methods

Research is an important skill required of all managers in public and nonprofit organizations. "Research" means *gathering*, *processing*, and *interpreting* data, then intelligently and cogently communicating the results in a report that describes what was discovered from the research. Knowing how to interpret and evaluate research that has been done by academics, administrators, or contract research organizations is another important skill. To learn the skills needed both to conduct and evaluate research, students of public administration are often required to take one or more courses in *research methodology*. Designing and conducting a research project is usually a requirement in those courses. This book has been developed to help students and practicing public and nonprofit organization administrators successfully complete their research projects.

When beginning researchers embark on what too often seems to be an extremely daunting and thoroughly confusing task, they find themselves faced with such questions as these:

- What is the purpose of doing this research?
- What is a "research problem?"
- Who has the needed information?
- What is the best way to ask questions?
- Which research design should be followed in this situation?
- How should the data be gathered?
- How should data be processed?
- What does all this processed data mean?
- What is the best way to communicate these findings?

Equally important, they must decide what questions *not* to ask; what questions cannot be readily answered; and how much research can be conducted in the time allotted and with the people and money available.

This book has been written to provide answers to both sets of questions. It is organized around a discussion of the major approaches taken in research: *quantitative* and *qualitative* research strategies. A few studies employ a strategy that *combines* elements of both approaches; these are mentioned throughout the work. The book defines and explains some of the major variations and processes found in these three strategies, focusing on the different research methods used today in public administration research.

Why Develop Research Skills?

There are at least five very good reasons for developing or expanding the skills needed to use research methods and prepare written research reports. The first reason is that it will develop and hone analysis and communication skills. Government and nonprofit organization employers have long identified these skills as the most important characteristics of successful leaders and managers. Employees able to gather information, to analyze and interpret data, and to communicate their findings effectively to others are valuable assets in any organization.

A second reason is that by engaging in the research process, the public administrator can become aware of what others in the career field are doing and saying about common problems. Every edition of the relevant periodical literature contains one or more articles about topical issues in public and nonprofit organization administration. In research terminology, the process of examining the literature of the field is called "reviewing the literature," and it is a critical early step in every research project or program.

Conducting a literature review involves finding and studying information contained in both textbooks and journals. Textbooks are a good way to become introduced to a subject and to gain a broad awareness of an issue or a discipline; they are, however, often outdated by the time they reach library shelves. It can take as long as four years for a textbook to move from the author's first draft to finally being published, and some texts are used year after year with little or no revision.

On the other hand, professional journals usually present the most current information available; they try to publish information on the cutting edge of the discipline. In this way, journals provide the "new" information needed for success in a discipline or career field. It is important to know which are the best publications in a field, why they are better than others, and what they stand for.

A third reason for learning how to do research has to do with *credibility*— which itself is founded on *replicability* and the scientific method. Any theory that is developed according to the scientific method must first be testable and, if necessary, correctable. Furthermore, conclusions that are derived from such theories must be repeatable, predictable, and supportable. Thus, conducting "scientific research" means that anyone reading a report of the research must be able to achieve the same or similar results by following the same research design. If not, the work may simply not be believed.

A fourth reason is the way new information is passed on to future generations: the findings of research studies are published in scientific and professional journals. Research findings are also written up as papers presented at professional conferences and scholarly or professional meetings. Scientists and educated people with an interest in the report of an author's research tend to consider the research incomplete or unfounded unless the findings are published (Gubanich 1991). Other researchers and people working in the field read or hear these reports. Following long-established guidelines for research and report writing makes verification through publishing easier and more likely to take place.

Finally, in this era of superfast change and uncertainty, a key skill needed by public and nonprofit agency administrators is the ability to make quick, intelligent *decisions*. The best decisions are almost always made after all the available information pertaining to the outcomes of the decisions is gathered, read, and weighed. This usually involves some research activity, whether it is formal or informal.

The Research Activity

Research is the activity administrators do to gain a better understanding of how their world works. More formally, research can be defined as *the process of systematically acquiring data to answer a question or solve a problem* (Strauss and Corbin 1998). *Research methodology*, on the other hand, refers to the steps involved in a given approach.

Research has also been defined as a set of easily understood procedures and as a philosophical *mind-set* that people bring to any research activity. Achinstein (1997) used this set of procedures and the mind-set that it requires as his definition of the *scientific method*. Rosenthal and Rosnow (1991) noted that the scientific method should not be considered simply a fixed procedure. Rather, it is a philosophical way of approaching all research, regardless of the problem addressed and approaches and methods employed.

This scientific method means approaching a research problem without any preconceived answers; it requires avoiding any hint of subjective bias. It includes preparing comprehensive operational definitions, forming hypotheses and theories, and applying the appropriate quantitative or qualitative method of data analysis.

The goals of all scientific research should be: (1) to *describe* some event, thing, or phenomenon, (2) to *predict* future behavior or events based on observed changes in existing conditions, and (3) to provide for greater *understanding* of phenomena and how variables are related (Shaughnessy and Zechmeister 1994). Today there is a growing awareness of the need to use research to better *understand* as well as to describe human events and phenomena. Description has been the traditional domain of quantitative methods, whereas understanding involves the researcher in qualitative methods as well.

Research—the Scientific Way

The first activity in researching the scientific way is the *recognition of a problem*. Either an administrator or the researcher must recognize that there is something not known or understood about a problem or situation. An administrator or a researcher must believe that the unknown information is important enough that an effort should be taken to determine what it is.

Next, the researcher makes some type of observations and/or measurements of the "things" (variables) associated with the problem. The researcher then arranges the data in some meaningful order, looking for similarities and dissimilarities. This process of gathering or accumulating data may mean asking people to complete a survey questionnaire, interviewing a number of people, observing events or reading about them, or preparing an in-depth study of a case. However gathered, these data must be coded, tabulated, arranged and classified, and analyzed and interpreted if they are to become *information*.

The researcher may then formulate a hypothesis or set of hypotheses. Hypotheses can be tentative explanations of a solution, interpretations of the variables or of a potential relationship, or cause-and-effect perception of a situation. The researcher may employ *inductive reasoning*, which means moving from the specific to the general. This reasoning process is involved in the act of making an *inference*; that is, using data from a sample for describing the characteristics or behaviors of larger populations. Or the researcher may use *deductive reasoning*, concluding that the facts in the case or situation speak for themselves. In this way, using deductive reasoning means moving from the general to the specific.

The researcher may then test the hypothesis or hypotheses. In quantitative designs, *objective* statistical tests are used for this purpose. In qualitative designs, the researcher makes a *subjective* determination of the validity of the hypothesis. After determining that the hypothesis is valid, the researcher may then see if there are other applications to which the hypothesis can be applied. The researcher proposes, for example, that, "In this study, such and such was true; therefore, in further applications, the same must occur and also be true."

The final activity in this scientific approach to research is the verification of conclusions derived from the research. This may entail replication of the design with a different sample. For example, the researcher asks, "If X occurred once, will it occur in similar circumstances?" If it does, then the researcher may propose a *theory.* And if others accept the theory, the researcher may attempt to have it accepted as a *law.*

While there are other ways to go about conducting research, this scientific approach underlies them all. This approach emerged during the Enlightenment, the explosion in scientific investigation and artistic creativity that began in Europe beginning in the seventeenth century. Early scientific investigators proposed the scientific approach to research as a way of maintaining rigor in scientific investigation. The method, simply put, meant coming to a conclusion based not on preformed beliefs alone, but instead on only what can be observed or tested by the senses. Authority, custom, or tradition—the stuff of metaphysics—should not be the source of knowledge and understanding. Instead, these should come from the reality of objects themselves (Richardson and Fowers 1998).

Bernard Phillips (1976, 4) described this method of looking at the growth of knowledge and understanding this way:

> [It is] an effort to achieve increasing understanding of phenomena by (1) defining problems so as to build on available knowledge, (2) obtaining information essential for dealing with these problems, (3) analyzing and interpreting these data in accordance with clearly defined rules, and (4) communicating the results of these efforts to others.

Out of this scientific outlook emerged the idea that the world and everything in it was a giant collection of objects that could be mapped and understood by empirical observation. Scientists developed a faith in the formal, objective, or *positivist* method. Richardson and Fowers have described that faith as "an almost boundless confidence." The positivists saw this "faith in method" as the only path to true knowledge. They concluded that this faith is exemplified by "mainstream social sciences' insistence on the use of correlational and experimental methods regardless of the subject matter being investigated."

Logic and Reasoning

Logic is the subfield of philosophy that relates to how people make judgments. The word evolved from the Greek *logos,* which in its translation to English is generally used to refer to the activity of *reasoning.* Reasoning refers to how people come to various conclusions. In the fourth century B.C., Aristotle concluded that humans employ two types or methods of reasoning: deductive and inductive. Deductive reasoning means arriving at a conclusion on the basis of something that you know or that you assume to be true—a general law. Deductive reasoning is usually demonstrated with a *syllogism*. A syllogism is an argument that has three parts: a major premise, a minor premise, and a conclusion. In deductive reasoning, the conclusion must be true if the premises are true. A 'syllogism' is often used to illustrate this concept. For example: (1) Socrates is a man; (2) all men are mortal; therefore, Socrates is mortal (conclusion).

Deductive reasoning requires only that the premises be accepted as true in their own terms—that is, as they are defined or assumed to be so. Truth is what the researcher decides it is or what it has always been; it is based on a *faith* that does not have to be empirically tested or proved. For example, a cultural anthropologist might gather as much information as possible about the mating habits of young islanders in a primitive society by observing their actions over time. The researcher may then conclude that these are the mating habits of all young people in that society. This may not, in truth, be the case; it may be true only for the subjects observed by the researcher. Thus, it can be seen only as a conclusion (or faith) of the researcher, not "truth." Deductive reasoning is the paradigm that underlies qualitative research.

Inductive reasoning, on the other hand, is the quantitative paradigm of *positivism*—the approach normally followed in research in the natural sciences. When following the scientific approach, researchers identify a problem, gather data from observation or through an experiment, then draw an inductive conclusion from (and only from) the data. In this model an inductive conclusion is never thought to be final; it is always open to further question (verifiability). In inductive reasoning, the researcher uses a set of established facts (research data) to draw a general conclusion, but that conclusion remains open to revision if new facts are discovered.

The positivist tradition that dominated research methods until the late 1970s emerged in the early twentieth century in Vienna, Austria (Dusche 1994). A group of philosophers—the Vienna Circle—were concerned with what they saw as a rash of theoretical speculation in the new sciences that were appearing. These speculative concepts included evolution, natural selection, thermodynamics, and molecular theory. The Vienna Circle philosophers were worried that science was returning to its early metaphysical foundations. Their reaction was to propose a philosophy of science—*positivism*—that stressed the need for the researcher to follow a process that moves from observable evidence to accurate predictions. This approach is the standard scientific method; it occurs through the following steps:

- Selection of a hypothesis
- Observation
- Data collection
- Hypothesis testing
- Acceptance or rejection of the hypothesis

It is important to know that today most public and nonprofit administration researchers agree that no single method is the only appropriate way to conduct research. Rather, there is a place and a purpose for all approaches and methods.

Purpose of the Book

The purpose of this book is to provide in one location information about how to design, conduct, interpret, and report on research projects. It has been written to serve as a tool for reading and writing on any administrative or social science discipline or topic. Its emphasis, however, is on research methods for students of public administration and those persons already embarked on their careers. It can also aid all students who have little or no experience in writing a scholarly paper for publication in a journal in their disciplines. Graduate students will find the book useful for designing and completing assignments in their research methods course and for preparing their degree dissertation or thesis. Managers now employed in administrative and managerial positions may use the book as a step-by-step guide for designing and conducting a research project with their available internal staff.

In addition to a review of the basic features of a research project and its written report, a number of discipline-specific requirements and examples are provided, including portions of published papers.

Scope of the Book

This book has been written to help students and practicing administrators in public administration and all types and forms of nonprofit organizations successfully complete both simple and complex research projects. The book covers such important topics as research design, specifying research problems, designing questionnaires and writing questions, designing and carrying out four classes of qualitative research approaches, and analyzing both quantitative and qualitative research data. Also covered is the evolution of the research philosophy from the positivist approach to postpositivist theory and critical research.

The book was developed to fill a need for a research methods book that incorporates the latest thinking in public administration and nonprofit organization management. It includes discussions and examples of research topics and research methods found in the current professional literature.

An additional key advantage of this book is that it integrates *both* the quantitative and qualitative approaches to research within one cover. It also provides specific instructions in the use of available statistical software programs like Excel and SPSS. It also incorporates the latest developments in social science research, management and organizations research, and research in the social and administrative sciences.

Structure of the Book

The book is organized into seven major sections, each with two or more chapters. The first section, "Foundations of Research," contains three chapters. Chapter 1, "Introduction to Research Methods," begins with an overview of the two important philosophical approaches to research and science: the *objectivist* and the *humanist* approaches (also known as the *positivist* and *postpositivist* approaches). This discussion is followed by an overview of the purpose and rationale of social science research in general, and research in the public administration discipline specifically. It concludes with this descriptive overview of the structure of the book.

Chapter 2, "Research in Public Administration," is a review of the state of research as it is used in public administration today. It includes a discussion of the use of research for theory building, and of research in its practical, applied approach. Chapter 3, "Research Ethics," begins with an overview of the fundamental moral principles upon which ethical decisions are founded and concludes with a discussion of the key moral concerns and ethical dilemmas encountered by researchers. Special emphasis is placed on research with human subjects.

Part 2, "Introduction to the Research Process," is designed to give readers a thorough grounding in the necessary steps to be taken when conducting a research project. Chapter 4, "The Research Process," introduces the reader to the eight steps that make up the research process. This set of steps begins with a discussion of the importance of thoroughly defining the problem before beginning the research and concludes with a review of different ways to organize reports of research findings.

Chapter 5, "The Research Problem," provides a more in-depth discussion of the first step in the research process: clearly and thoroughly defining the research problem. It also provides suggestions on how and where to begin the literature search. This includes carrying out detailed examination of textbooks, journals, electronically stored and retrieved articles, and other materials in sources inside and outside of the researchers' organization. Most researchers' early research proposals tend to be far too broad for the resources at hand (particularly time and money). Therefore, a discussion of the importance of *focus* is included in this chapter.

Chapter 6, "Research Designs," is a discussion of several different ways to design and conduct research projects. Three types of strategies are used in public administration: quantitative, qualitative, and combination strategies. Combined designs include parts of both quantitative and qualitative strategies and methods.

Part 3, "Quantitative Designs," contains three chapters that together provide an overview of the fundamentals of *quantitative* research. Chapter 7, "Quantitative Research Fundamentals," begins with a discussion of the characteristics of measurements and includes an explanation of the types or categories of statistics used in research. Chapter 8, "Introduction to Sampling," is a discussion of the process of sampling and the nature of distributions. Chapter 9, "Questionnaires and Questions," is a practical guide to writing the many types of questions and scales that are used to measure attitudes, opinions, lifestyles, preferences, concerns, and other data. The chapter also includes instruction on how to put these questions into a logical sequence in the formal data-gathering instrument called the *questionnaire*.

In Part 4, "Quantitative Analysis Methods," readers are introduced to ways to conduct the major types of quantitative research strategies, including surveys and experiments. Chapter 10, "Using Descriptive Statistics," describes the four different types of descriptive measurements in a data set, including measures of central tendency, variability, relative position, and correlation. It concludes with an introduction to elementary concepts of statistical distributions.

Chapter 11, "Using Tables, Charts, and Graphs," reveals how these graphic tools can improve the readability of research reports and describes specific software steps needed to produce tables, charts, and graphs. In Chapter 12, "Research Hypotheses," readers are shown how and why statistical tests are used to communicate information that relates to the validity of the results of the research. This is the first of several chapters dealing with *inferential statistics*, that is, statistical tests used with samples rather than entire populations and in which probabilities play an important role. Chapter 13, "Testing Hypotheses About Two or More Groups," is the second chapter dealing with hypothesis tests. It reviews the *t*-test and analysis of variance (ANOVA) procedures for measuring statistically significant differences between two or more groups or subgroups.

Chapter 14, "Looking for Relationships," discusses two statistical tests used in association analysis: correlation and regression. These tests can now be quickly processed with modern statistical software for desktop and laptop personal computers. Chapter 15, "Experiments and Experimental Design," covers the principles and methods associated with experimental or cause-and-effect research designs. Included are single-factor, multiple-factor, and regression analysis methods. It is the last chapter in this section on quantitative research strategies and methods.

Chapter 16, "Using SPSS to Process Statistical Data," describes how to use Versions 9 and 10 of this powerful statistical software package to conduct most if not all of the statistical tests used in public administration research.

Part 5, "Qualitative Research Strategies," is the first of two sections on qualitative research strategies and methods. Chapter 17, "Introduction to Qualitative Research," describes the development and purpose of qualitative research strategies. It also discusses how qualitative designs can contribute to understanding public organizational culture and its impact upon employees and the public. Chapter 18, "The Case Study in Public Administration Research," describes both the single- and multicase approach to research. The case method is considered by many to be the most-used qualitative design in public administration and nonprofit organization research.

Chapter 19, "Grounded Theory in Public Administration Research," looks at a strategy that is becoming increasingly popular among researchers in education, sociology, and social psychology. This design is slowly being applied in public administration research as well. In these studies, researchers approach a situation, event, or relationship with little or no preconceived theoretical bias. The researcher seeks to construct a theory only after the in-depth analysis of the study data. Chapter 20, "Ethnography in Public Administration Research," is a discussion of some ways that this culture-based strategy is used in public administration. Ethnography was developed by anthropologists originally to describe and explain phenomena in distant and what were considered to be "primitive" societies. It has been successfully adapted to research on modern cultures and subcultures.

The final chapter in this section, Chapter 21, "Action Research in Public Administration," is an introduction to five different models of this approach and how they are being used in public administration research.

Part 6, "Qualitative Analysis Methods," contains two chapters on methods used for analyzing qualitative data. The first, Chapter 22, "Analyzing Qualitative Data," provides important general instruction in this often cumbersome task. Analysis involves probing for the symbolic meaning people place on things, and on how events are gathered, analyzed, and interpreted. The chapter also includes a brief introduction to the use of computers to analyze qualitative data. Chapter 23, "Analyzing Texts, Documents, and Artifacts," looks at a number of nontraditional research and analysis approaches—nontraditional in public administration, that is—including hermeneutics, content and narrative analysis, archival and artifact analysis, and the analysis of signs and symbols.

Part 7, "Preparing and Presenting Research Findings," contains two chapters that provide detailed instruction on how to structure and write a final research report, and looks at such special considerations as research ethics. Chapter 24 provides tips on how to organize and structure the report, including the use of graphics, while Chapter 25 is a discussion of the importance of following ethical procedures and dealing with ethical issues in research.

Summary

This book includes a variety of examples and exercises designed to move the reader beyond simple familiarization with the topic to achievement of full understanding. The goal of the book is for students and professionals alike to know when and how to use a given research strategy and data-gathering method for a given information-need situation.

Research and writing are important skills required of all public administrators. Researching means gathering, processing, and interpreting data of some kind. Research results must be communicated in intelligently and cogently written reports. Public administrators also must interpret and evaluate research reports that have been produced by academics, administrators, or contract-research organizations. Producing clear, cogent reports is an important ingredient in producing effective research.

There are at least five very good reasons for developing or expanding the skills needed to use research methods and prepare written research reports. The first reason is that it will develop and hone analysis and communication skills. Second, the research process helps the public administrator remain aware of what others in the career field are doing and saying about common problems. The third reason has to do with *believability*. Anyone reading a research report must be able to achieve the same or similar results by following the same research design. Fourth, following long-established guidelines for research and report writing makes verification through publishing easier and more likely to take place.

Finally, public and nonprofit agency administrators need to know how to make quick, intelligent decisions. The best decisions are almost always made after all the available information pertaining to outcomes of the decisions is gathered, read, and evaluated. This usually involves some type of formal or informal research activity. The research activity can be defined as *the process of systematically acquiring data to answer a question or solve a problem.* Research methodology refers to the steps involved in a given approach.

Two philosophical approaches underlie public administration research: *positivism* and *postpositivism.* The positivist approach is the standard scientific method that involves the following steps: selection of a hypothesis, observation, data collection, hypothesis testing, and acceptance or rejection of a hypothesis. The postpositivist approach is associated with qualitative research methods; it emphasizes understanding as well as description of phenomena.

Suggested Reading

Couvalis, George. 1997. *The Philosophy of Science: Science and Objectivity*. London: Sage.

Hughes, John, and Wes Sharrock. 1990. *The Philosophy of Social Research*. 3d ed. London: Longman.

Neuman, W. Lawrence. 2000. *Social Research Methods: Qualitative and Quantitative Approaches*. 4th ed. Boston: Allyn and Bacon.

2 Research in Public Administration

Many new scientific disciplines were born during the last half of the nineteenth century when the study of human sciences was separated from that of the natural sciences. Among the first of the "new" human or "social" sciences to emerge were anthropology, economics, psychology, and sociology. Combinations and derivatives of these, such as cultural anthropology and social psychology, soon followed. The disciplines of communications, industrial psychology, organizational behavior, and administrative and management science appeared at about the same time. As these disciplines grew in emphasis and scope, specific research methods were developed to embrace the expanding level of knowledge in each. Some of these research methods focused on quantitative analysis of research data, while others adopted various qualitative approaches to data analysis.

Public administration is one of the newest disciplines to come on the scene, evolving out of antecedents in political science and management. It was recognized as a legitimate field of study in the late 1880s, but the first university education program in public administration did not appear until 1926. From its beginnings, there has been a continuing debate on what should be the nature of public administration: Should it be considered a social science, along with sociology and psychology? Or should it be considered an administrative science, akin to professional education such as business administration? The debate is important because it influences the scope and direction of research in the field.

A nagging problem with the approaches and methods used in public administration research sprang from the argument over the nature of the discipline. Researchers asked, what is the most appropriate methodology for research—quantitative or qualitative methods? As the discipline continued to grow in scope and acceptance, early researchers argued that the *positivist* approach, with its emphasis on quantitative methods, was the only valid way to conduct research. However, others found that positivism was not able to answer many of the human problems facing public administrators. They turned to the body of qualitative research methods for help with those problems. Richardson and Fowers (1998, 471) described emerging attitudes calling for a shift in methodological emphasis this way:

> [I]n spite of tremendous effort, enormous methodological sophistication, and many decades of efforts, [mainstream social science, including public administration] has failed to achieve anything even resembling the kind of explanatory theory that counts as truth and is needed for precise prediction and instrumental control. Just describing interesting patterns of variables—which always have many exceptions—does not yield the sort of technical control over events we associate with modern physics, biology, or engineering.

Research Emphasis

There is both a practical and a theoretical side to public administration, and researchers have naturally developed an interest in both aspects of the discipline. However, the emphasis in public administration research has long been on the practical side (Rutgers 1997). It has primarily been concerned with resolving issues and problems in practical administration. That research has focused on ways to improve the *practice* of administration. Specifically, most public administration research has been on finding practical solutions to problems facing administrators in urban and local government agencies (Garson and Overman 1983).

While maintaining a largely practical focus, public administration researchers have looked at a wide variety of topics (Garson and Overman 1983; Stivers 2000; Lan and Anders 2000). In addition, many different research methods have been used. Research in public administration has involved most if not all of the methods developed by the natural, social, human, and administrative sciences. The focus has not changed, however; it is still *applied research* for the resolution of practical problems faced by public and nonprofit organization administrators. Academicians or practitioners have conducted very little "pure" or theoretical research, although interest in theoretical research is increasing.

In recent decades a growing number of researchers have directed their attention toward research aimed at establishing or building on a *theory* of public administration. This research has not proved to be particularly rewarding, however, as Stivers (2000, 134) has noted:

> In my view, the field of public administration has been marked since the early twentieth century by a largely fruitless search for scientific truth. I say "fruitless" because the attempts to identify generalizations about administrative practice that hold

across all or even most situations inevitably runs up against what seems to me to be an undeniable aspect of our subject matter—that is, any particular situation is simultaneously similar to and different from any other situation (134).

Public Administration Research Today

A number of studies on the scope and focus of public administrative research have been published. Most of these studies have criticized the published research. For example, Perry and Kraemer (1986) found that public administration research has been deficient in the following three important methodological areas. First, little theory testing is performed. Second, the research lacks cumulativeness—little attention is given to earlier studies and little effort is given to build upon that earlier work. And third, the published research has seldom been funded by outside sources.

Some observers believe that much if not most of the research conducted in public administration has been of low quality (McCurdy and Cleary 1984; Perry and Kraemer 1986; Stallings and Ferris 1988; Houston and Delevan 1990; Cleary 1992; Cozzetto 1998; Brewer et al. 2000; Lan and Anders 2000). Brewer et al. (2000, 374) put it this way:

> Over the past fifteen years, scholars have sought to address the quantity and quality of research in the field of public administration by examining dissertations written by public administration students and articles published in public administration and related journals. The results have been most discouraging.

Research Topics and Themes

What sorts of topics and themes do public administration students, practitioners, consultants, and academics research? In an early answer to this question, all public administration research was grouped into just two broad categories: *generic* research and *mission-specific* research. Generic research is conducted in order to advance knowledge or understanding of management processes and is likely to have wide applicability. Mission-specific research, on the other hand, focuses on a specific purpose, program, agency, or policy and is likely to have only limited applicability to the field in general.

Garson and Overman (1983) established a list of topics (displayed in Table 2.1) from their examination of sources published during the 1970s. Those topics were mostly concerned with management and administrative concerns and covered all organizational functions. The focus of the approach was almost entirely on how these problems affected local and state government administration.

Table 2.1

Topics in Published Public Administration Research

- Policy output
- Adaptation to scarcity
- Local attitudes and leader opinion
- Licensure effectiveness
- Policy outcomes
- Organizational costs
- Attitudes, beliefs, and values
- Cash-management strategy
- Tax limitations
- (Research) validity and reliability

- Manpower-modeling methods
- Productivity measures
- Effects of federal aid
- Public participation
- Cooperative management style
- Job managing effectiveness
- Staff burnout
- School effectiveness
- Risk-management practice
- Affirmative-action effectiveness

Source: Adapted from Garson and Overman 1983, 89.

Houston and Delevan (1990) examined a sample of 218 papers published in six different public administration journals between 1984 and 1989. Most were written primarily to develop conceptual themes for further research. Most of the remaining (28 percent) were categorized as empirical efforts to examine relationships between variables. A very small number were reports of public policy evaluations.

Houston and Delevan concluded that descriptive statistics (frequency distributions, measures of central tendency, and variability) are the most commonly used statistical techniques used in reported public administration research. These statistical methods served three main functions in the sixty-one papers coded by Houston and Delevan as "relationship studies." These functions were *description*, *inference*, and *control*. Nearly 69 percent of the papers used statistical hypothesis testing, suggesting that inferential statistical methods are widely understood and applied. Table 2.2 contains a breakdown of the statistical techniques found in the quantitative methods papers.

Richard Box (1992) examined 230 articles published in just one journal, *Public Administration Review* (PAR), over the five-year period from 1985 to 1989. The majority (67 percent) of the papers published in PAR dealt with issues pertaining to the practice of public administration. The remaining were almost equally divided between public administration *theory* and assorted specific issues, such as the research task itself. Eight papers dealt with politics and/or administration, four papers each were concerned with the public/private dichotomy, and four dealt with reorganization issues. Motivation, regulation, and conflict resolution were the subjects of three papers each. Eleven papers were on public administration theory in general; six each were on either public administration research or theory in the public/private issue. Another five were on the politics/administration issue, and two dealt with

Table 2.2

Statistical Techniques in a Sample of Published Articles ($n = 218$)

Statistic(s)	Frequency
Univariate	37
Bivariate correlation	20
Multiple regression	25
Cross-tabulations	22
Factor analysis	5
Chi square	4
ANOVA	3
Path analysis	3
Bivariate regression	1
MANOVA	1
Nonlinear regression	1
Other	3

Source: Adapted from Houston and Delevan 1990, 678.

bureaucracy. According to Box, none of the articles contained complex or sophisticated statistical techniques.

A comprehensive analysis by Lan and Anders (2000) reviewed 634 research papers published in eight academic and professional journals over a three-year period (1993–95). The authors found that most published public administration research dealt with managerial issues relating to federal, state, or local government, with the emphasis on state and local levels. A lesser number dealt with public sector issues in general, while only a small portion addressed international issues. The primary emphasis of the research examined was on government in general or issues that concern the executive branch (at all levels). The topics were almost all focused on solving managerial or administrative problems.

Lan and Anders also found that researchers in their sample studied a wide variety of administration and function topics within this applied framework. Most focused on such organizational management issues as personnel management and human resources planning, political/legal institutions and processes, finance and budgeting, administration theory, policy design and analyses, social and economic issues, and research methodology. Less than 2 percent addressed ethics issues.

A Void in Public Administration Research

An analysis of the published public administration literature reveals that very little research has been conducted on topics relating to *culture* or *climate* in public and nonprofit organizations. Despite the emphasis on applied research focusing on solving real problems, there has been very little research on how internal culture and operating climate influence public policy and public agency operations. According to Edgar H. Schein (1996), public administration researchers—and social scientists in general—have incorrectly underestimated the importance of culture (shared norms, values, and assumptions) in their analyses of how organizations function. When managers fail in their efforts to build what is called "a learning organization," this failure can be better understood by examining the organization's culture and its various occupational subcultures. "The implication is that culture needs to be observed, more than measured, if organization studies is to advance" (Schein 1996, 229).

Research Methods

No single research method has overwhelmingly dominated the articles investigated by any of the authors who surveyed published public administration literature, including doctoral dissertations. At best, a majority of these studies favored a *qualitative* approach. Quantitative approaches were followed in a little less than 41 percent of the papers; qualitative approaches were followed in 59 percent.

Of the quantitative papers, 15.4 percent used simple descriptive statistics and/or simple correlation analysis. Another 15 percent applied some intermediate statistics, which included hypothesis testing and some inferential statistics. More advanced statistical tests, including regression analysis, time series, and more sophisticated inferential statistics added another 13 percent.

Lan and Anders concluded that nearly all the qualitative methods used in social science research were represented in the sample of articles they investigated. The case study was the preferred qualitative research method (it was not clear if these were single case or multiple case studies). A small number used ethnography methods. The remaining third were grouped into the category of "others" which included literature reviews, reports of interviews, and other qualitative approaches. Slightly more than 44 percent used existing literature (other than government statistical reports) as the basis of their analysis; 27 percent used self-collected data; and almost 21 percent used data from government publications.

Research Strategies

A philosophical split exists between those who hold that the *quantitative* method is the only valid, truly scientific approach to follow and those who "reject mathematics" in favor of a *qualitative* or "empathic" research approach (Phillips 1976). Some researchers argue strongly on the side of the positivist approach for public administration (Houston and Delevan 1990). They hold that the best approach to use when studying public administration problems is a quantitative strategy. Today, however, many researchers believe that both the qualitative and quantitative models, with either deductive or inductive reasoning, are valid approaches for research in the social and administrative sciences (White 1986).

The qualitative/quantitative characteristic of information refers to different ways of describing and processing research data. Qualitative data are subjective (verbal) data. They usually do not entail the use of statistics; that is, responses or things or events may be counted, but no analysis is carried out on the distribution of the numbers. As a result of this difference of opinion, three different research strategies are possible: qualitative, quantitative, and combined.

Qualitative Strategies

Broadly speaking, qualitative strategies fall into one or more of three types of study techniques. These are explanatory, interpretive, and critical (White 1999). Any of these approaches can be applied to many different study approaches, including ethnography, kinetics (the study of movement), atmospherics, phenomenology, proxemics (the study of space in social settings), and three other methods: focus group and elite group interviewing and the use of unobtrusive measures. Data are typically gathered using interviewing, participant or unobtrusive observation, or by analysis of documents and/or artifacts.

The two qualitative research methods used most often in the social and administrative sciences are *ethnography* and the *case study* approach. Ethnographic methods were developed by researchers in anthropology, then picked up and expanded upon by sociologists and public administration researchers, among others. The method has a long history of use in business and government studies, but is seldom used in economics research. Case studies are used extensively in public administration and business management research.

Ethnography allows the researcher to gather information while acting as a participant in the situation. This approach is used primarily to identify *patterns* in human activity. According to Gill and Johnson (1991), it focuses on the way that people interact and cooperate. Ethnographic research is often considered to be "unobtrusive" in that subjects' behaviors are observed but not manipulated or adulterated by exposure to research methods.

Two types of case studies are used in the social and administrative sciences—the single case approach and one that uses a limited number of closely related cases. For both approaches, Van Evera (1997) has identified five main uses for case studies in political science and public administration as well.

- To create theories
- To test previously established theories
- To identify antecedent conditions
- To test the importance of these antecedent conditions and
- To explain cases of intrinsic importance

Quantitative Strategies

Quantitative research involves the use of *numbers* to describe things. Statistical analysis of data is usually employed, if only used for a description of the measures of central tendency (averages) for the responses of a group (sample) of individuals. Interpretations are based on principles of *probability*. Statistical tests are also used to establish whether the differences in the way different groups respond to a stimulus are "real" (that is, statistically significant) or whether they are due only to naturally occurring variation. Experiments to identify relationships between variables (such as testing the relationship between spending on advertising and the degree of citizen involvement in recycling programs by varying the amount spent on advertising in different communities) are another uncommon study design in public administration research.

The quantitative approach to research owes its growth in popularity during the 1920s and 1930s to the reemergence at the time of *logical positivism* as a requisite principle of scientific inquiry (Phillips 1987). The positivist (sometimes called the *objectivist*) approach holds that a thing, idea, or concept is meaningful only if it can be seen or measured. An example of the positivist approach can be seen in this statement in Kaplan and Norton's (1996, 21) book on organizational management, *The Balanced Scorecard*: "Measurement matters: 'If you can't measure it, you can't manage it.'" The qualitative argument can be summarized in the obverse of that statement: "If you can count it, that ain't it" (Holsti 1969, 11).

The quantitative approach was initially an attack on metaphysical reasoning. Positivists based their argument on what they saw as the inability to verify metaphysical phenomena—the principle of *lack of verifiability*. During the first half of the twentieth century, it was extended to bring all qualitative research methods into disrepute. Recently, however, this argument against qualitative approaches has lost much of its acerbity, although it still appears periodically in the social and administrative sciences and still retains its old ability to rally supporters to opposing camps. Such statements as "In all fields there is a growing tension between the so-called 'qualitative' and 'quantitative' paradigms" seem to show up on a regular basis in the philosophy of science and research methodology literature (Phillips 1987, 27).

Combined Strategies

Combined studies employ both qualitative and quantitative methods. The three broad classes of combined studies are archival, media, and artifact studies. Techniques used in these types of studies include hermeneutics and content analysis in document analysis, in situ analysis, and at least three types of multivariate statistical tools: correlation, cluster analysis, and factor analysis.

Hermeneutics

The analysis of documents and texts often employs both qualitative and quantitative study components in the study design. The most appropriate *qualitative* technique in such designs is *hermeneutics*. Hermeneutics is the science of subjective interpretation of the content in printed texts and documents. It was originally an approach to the study of biblical texts, but has been expanded greatly in scope and is now adopted as a fundamental method underlying all learning. According to Richardson (1995, 8):

> Hermeneutics has come forward as that comprehensive standpoint from which to view all the projects of human learning. For those of us who have been puzzled by the new intellectual dominance of hermeneutics, the key is that the term no longer refers to the interpretation of texts only but encompasses all the ways in which subjects and objects are involved in human communication. From "theories of everything" in natural science, to the textualizing of every act of communication, hermeneutics has become an essential reflection upon knowledge claims and a recategorization of the act of making knowledge claims. Under this conceptuality, hermeneutics or interpretation has come to be regarded as shorthand for all the practices of human learning.

This definition of hermeneutics includes an underlying philosophy of science and a particular way of analyzing textual material (Myers 1997). In its philosophical role, hermeneutics provides the foundations for the concept of *interpretivism*. As a method of analysis, its focus is on answering the question: What is the meaning of this text (or language)? In what is called "a hermeneutic circle," it involves first developing an understanding of the text as a whole and then moves to the interpretation of its parts, in themselves and as they are determined by the whole.

As a caveat, it is important at this point to mention that by itself, the hermeneutic approach to document analysis does not result in the establishment of any fundamental "truth." Rather, it is truth as the author of the text intended it to be. As Maas (1999, 2) has noted:

> Though the influence of hermeneutics is far-reaching, its efficiency must not be overstated. Hermeneutics does not . . . rectify false philosophical principles or per-

verse passions . . . of itself, hermeneutics does not investigate the objective truth of a writer's meaning . . . it does not inquire what is true or false, but only what the writer intended to say. Hence, a hermeneutic truth may be an objective falsehood.

Content Analysis

Content analysis is the quantitative component of document analysis. It is used to describe attributes contained in documents and other forms of messages, but is not intended to determine the intentions of the sender. The process involves breaking the written material down into researcher-selected categories or units. The researcher then prepares an "item dictionary" in order to clearly define measured constructs. Measurements of the occurrence of these items in the text make statistical analysis of the data possible.

Holsti (1969, 14) defined the process as "any technique for making inferences by objectively and systematically identifying specified characteristics of messages." The point he was making is that content analysis does not illuminate "truth." It can only measure *usage*.

Holsti did not limit analysis of data gathered by the process only to quantitative analysis, stating that he believed that a "rigid qualitative-quantitative distinction seems unwarranted." He concluded that researchers using content analysis should use both qualitative and quantitative methods in order to supplement each other. In this way, Holsti can be said to have combined aspects of hermeneutics with the traditional quantitative interpretation of content analysis.

Bernard (1995, 339) has remained closer to the quantitative traditions of the content analysis process. He defined content analysis as a "catch-all term" used to describe a variety of techniques for making inferences from textual material: "The idea [of content analysis techniques] is to reduce the information in a text to a series of variables that can then be examined for correlations." He noted that the major difficulty with the process is the subjectivity inherent in identifying the original codes and categories that are to be counted. It is nearly impossible to avoid interjecting some researcher bias into this step of the analysis. Bernard recommends use of a multistep, independent jury process to reduce the potential for category-selection biases.

In-Situ Analysis

This is the process of examining the artifacts and inventions of human and organizational cultures in the environment in which they exist. The current interest in urban archeology incorporates this technique. Example studies include examining refuse sites to determine such things as product usage, waste generation, and consumption rates. The technique has great potential for public administration research, but has not been widely adopted.

Like content analysis, *in situ* analysis involves both interpretive and quantitative analyses. The researcher must go beyond simply counting phenomena, for this provides only a partial picture of the concept under study. For full understanding, the researcher must also determine the meaning or meanings underlying the event or behavior under study.

A number of conclusions can be drawn from these reports. First, there is an emphasis on research topics that address practical, organizational administrative issues over theory building. Second, there seem to be few if any restrictions on the nature of the study problem addressed in public administration —public administration research seems to be concerned with many of the same issues that are found in private sector organizations. Third, public administration researchers use qualitative and quantitative research methods in generally equal proportions, although today a small majority favors qualitative approaches.

Summary

Research in public administration is conducted by students, academicians, people working in public agencies, and consultants. Most public administration research is concerned with problem-solving issues at all levels of government and nonprofit organization management.

Three types of research strategies are used in public administrative research: qualitative, quantitative, and combined. Qualitative research strategies are marginally preferred over quantitative strategies. Qualitative strategies involve such mainstream social science research methods as ethnography, phenomenology, case studies, and the like. They may be explanatory, interpretive, or critical designs. Quantitative strategies are statistical designs. They may be exploratory, descriptive, or causal, or they may involve all three approaches in a more comprehensive, large sample design. Most quantitative studies did not go much beyond the use of simple descriptive statistics. Combined strategies employ components of both qualitative and quantitative methods.

Hermeneutics is emerging as a major direction in the philosophy of science and is, hence, influencing the manner in which qualitative research in public and nonprofit organization administration is conducted. Content analysis is the process of breaking written material down into researcher-selected categories or units for statistical analysis. In situ analysis is similar to content analysis in that it involves both interpretive and quantitative analyses. Simply counting phenomena provides only a partial picture of the concept under study; for full understanding, the researcher must also determine the meaning that underlies the event.

Suggested Reading

Holsti, Ole R. 1969. *Content Analysis for the Social Sciences and Humanities*. Menlo Park, CA: Addison-Wesley.

Hughes, John, and Wes Sharrock. 1997. *The Philosophy of Social Research*. 3d ed. London: Longman.

Miller, Gerald J., and Marcia L. Whicker, eds. 1999. *Handbook of Research Methods in Public Administration*. New York: Marcel Dekker.

Schwab, Donald P. 1999. *Research Methods for Organizational Studies*. Mahwah, NJ: Lawrence Erlbaum, 1999.

White, Jay D. 1999. *Taking Language Seriously: The Narrative Foundations of Public Administration Research*. Washington, DC: Georgetown University, 1999.

3 Research Ethics

Why do some people select careers in public administration over work in the private sector? Why do others elect to devote their working life to helping others by laboring in nonprofit agencies and organizations—what are now known collectively as *nongovernment organizations* (NGOs)? Pay in government and NGO service is often much less than in industry; the hours are often longer; the personal rewards, such as expense accounts, company cars, and attractive retirement programs are often fewer and of less monetary value.

There are many answers to these questions, of course. Some people choose government or NGO service because it is the best place to exercise their particular skills. The military, public safety, wastewater management, and child welfare are just a few of many examples that come to mind. Others do it by accident; they might have begun as an intern during college and stayed on after graduation. And still others do it because of a sincere desire to serve. Their own quality of life is enhanced because they know that every day they are doing something to make life better or easier for others, people less fortunate than themselves. Finally, some do it specifically to lie, cheat, and steal.

No matter how honorable, how thoroughly upstanding and professional we would like to think our public servants are, the truth is that some public administrators are no more immune to unethical pressures than are other professionals. Bad choices can be made by anyone—and often are. This is not to make an excuse for unethical behavior in the public sector. Rather, recognizing the *universality* of the potential for unethical behavior is the necessary first step in ensuring a climate of ethical operations in government and NGO bodies.

Academics, administrators, and the popular press are alike in their increasingly strident calls for moral reform, passage of ethics laws and codes, and greater education and training in ethical behavior for public employees.

Calls for ethics reform have been directed at every level of government, from the Office of the President to the smallest local special service district.

Ethical problems in government run the gamut from sexual harassment to embezzlement of millions. And when they happen, they are loudly pointed out by the press as examples of the poor quality of public servants in general. In one week, for example, newspapers contained stories about the alleged sale of presidential pardons and diplomatic passports (*New York Times*, June 17, 2001, A1+), charges that the town president (i.e., mayor) and nine others stole $10 million in taxpayer money in Cicero, Illinois, and the conviction of the former mayor of Camden, New Jersey, on charges of laundering drug money and accepting bribes from racketeers (*San Francisco Chronicle*, June 16, 2001, A2 and A5, respectively). Citing a recent Gallup poll, *USA Today* reporter Karen Peterson (2001) wrote that, for only the second time in half a century, ethics and morality are near the top of a list of the major problems that people believe are facing the nation. She reported that 78 percent of the public feels that the nation's moral values are somewhat or very weak.

Those were not isolated, seldom seen instances. There has long been an ethical, political aspect to public administration. It has been, in fact, one of the major reasons for developing a *profession* of public administration and separating administration from politics (Rohr 1998, 4). It is becoming increasingly important today.

According to one widely cited author on the topic, Terry Cooper (1998), interest in administrative ethics appears to have mushroomed. This has resulted in a growing demand for in-service training, publication of many ethics articles, and professional conferences devoted solely to ethics problems in government. In addition, more and more public administration graduate education programs are requiring or offering courses in ethical behavior.

This heightened interest in public administration ethics has also included the practice of research. For example, J. Mitchell (1998, 305) described the growing interest in ethics in public administration research as follows:

> Public administration research and analysis involves ethics. This is evidenced by newspaper headlines questioning the veracity of government reports and by legislative hearings on research misconduct in public agencies.

Mitchell included most types of research in his analysis, including "pure" social science, as well as more "applied" studies such as policy analyses, and program evaluations. He considered ethics to be an issue in research whether it is conducted to describe problems, predict outcomes, evaluate solutions, or measure agency performance.

The Meaning of "Ethics"

Ethics, a branch of philosophy, is the study of the *moral* behavior of humans in society. It has also been defined as the set of principles that govern the conduct of an individual or a group of persons, and briefly as the study of morality or moral behavior (Velasquez 1998). *Morality* refers to the standards that people have about what is right, what is wrong, what is good, and what is evil; these standards are the behavior norms of a society. *Moral behavior* is acting in ways that follow the moral standards that exist in society. *Moral standards* are the rules by which a society functions. Examples of moral standards include the moral commandments: *Do not kill*; *do not steal; do not lie;* and so forth. They tell us what behavior is acceptable, what is 'right' and what is 'good' in society, and their opposites, of course. While moral standards differ from time to time, they remain relatively constant for at least a generation or more. When they do change, they tend to do so very slowly.

Moral standards vary from society to society; there are few absolutes in ethics. However, the fundamental standards of behavior tend to be quite similar throughout the industrialized nations of the world. This is so because, if standards were wildly different, nations would have a difficult time cooperating in such value-laden areas as international relations, commerce, and other global activities. China's difficulty in achieving most favored nation (MFN) status—valued in international trade because it provides lower tariffs—is a case in point. Some say that a key barrier has been the Chinese government's behavior on certain human rights issues, a moral standard that is considered unacceptable in the West.

What distinguishes moral standards from standards that are not moral? Velasquez (1998) has identified five characteristics of moral behavior that make this distinction. First, moral standards are concerned with matters that people think can seriously injure or benefit human beings. Second, people absorb their moral standards as children and revise them as they mature. Therefore, moral standards are neither established nor changed by the decisions of authoritative bodies; ethics cannot be legislated.

Third, by their very nature as fundamental norms of behavior in a society, moral standards are preferred over other values, including self-interest. Fourth, moral standards are based on impartial considerations; they apply equally to all persons in society.

Finally, moral standards evoke special emotions, including guilt and shame, and are associated with a special vocabulary; words such as "good," "bad," "honesty," "justice," and "injustice" are examples.

Scientific research of all types is beset with ethical dilemmas, paradoxes, and ambiguities (de Laine 2000). This is particularly true with research with humans and in social settings, as the following statement illustrates:

> Ethical and moral dilemmas are an occupational work hazard of fieldwork that the researcher cannot plan for, but nonetheless must be addressed on the spot, by drawing

on the values, ideals, ethical codes, moral and professional standards, intuition and emotions (de Laine 2000, 16).

Ethicists have identified a number of different theoretical foundations for the values, ideals, ethical codes, and moral standards that researchers draw upon when faced with these dilemmas; the foundations of our moral principles that have gained the widest acceptance are discussed in the next section of this chapter.

Foundations of Our Moral Standards

Moral standards have evolved from a number of different philosophical traditions, some of which are as old as recorded time. Similar codes of behavior evolved some 5,000 years ago in both Egypt and Babylonia (present-day Iraq), for example. A key concept in those early codes was the idea of *justice*. It continues to underlie moral standards in many modern societies. In the United States and Europe, codes of ethics have roots in the Judeo-Christian tradition. In the Middle East, behavioral standards are founded on writings in the Koran. In parts of Asia, moral standards spring from either Confucius or Buddha. In the last half of the twentieth century, a renewed interest in the *rights* of human beings has emerged as an integral part of modern ethical standards—and expanded to include the rights of animals as well, a point with great implications for medical researchers.

Today, at least five different ways to approach an ethical situation have evolved from these earliest guidelines for moral behavior. These include: *utilitarian, rights, justice, caring, and virtue ethics* (Velasquez 1998).

Utilitarian Ethics

Utilitarian ethics are based on the view that the "right" action or policy is the one that will result in the greatest benefit (or the lowest costs) to society. Thus, decisions on actions and policies must be evaluated according to their net benefits and costs. Utilitarianism is concerned with the consequences of an action, not the means to achieve the results. Today's cost-benefit analysis is based on this principle. Because it supports the value of efficiency, utilitarianism is often used in the resolution of public administration dilemmas.

A key characteristic of utilitarianism is that the benefits need not be equally distributed; some people may not benefit at all, and some may be negatively impacted. What counts is the greatest good for all concerned—but the moral dilemma is determining who is to decide what is good (Malhotra 1999).

Rights Ethics

Rights ethics are another approach often seen in public administration. A right is often defined as a person's entitlement to something. Because of this focus on the individual rights, ethics differ from the utilitarian approach, where the focus is on the greater good of a society. Two types of rights are included in ethics, legal rights and human rights. Legal rights are based upon laws; consumer protection and contract rights are examples. Human rights, on the other hand, are culturally based; they provide people with a way of justifying their actions; they are also associated with duties.

Today's basis for rights ethics comes from the writings of philosopher Immanuel Kant (1724–1804). Kant believed that all human beings possess some rights and duties, which exist regardless of any utilitarian benefit or detriment they might have for others in a society.

Kant proposed moral principles he called *categorical imperatives* to make this point. Kant's first categorical imperative states that an action is morally right if—and only if—the reason for doing it is one that the person would be willing for everyone to act upon in a similar situation. There are two parts to this concept: (1) *Universality* (it applies to everyone), and (2) *reversibility* (a person would be willing to have others use the concept in the way they treat him or her). Kant's second imperative holds that an action is morally right if—and again, only if—a person performing the action does not use others as a means for improving his or her own interests. When making a decision, administrators must respect the right of others to choose freely for themselves.

Several key concepts in public administration are founded upon Kantian rights theories, including the idea that all people have positive rights to work, clothing, housing, and medical care; that everyone has a negative right to freedom from injury or fraud; and that humans have the right to enter into contracts.

Justice Ethics

Moral standards based on the idea of justice include the concept of fairness. Together, these ideas contribute to three fundamental bases for moral behavior: distributive justice, retributive justice, and compensatory justice. Distributive justice is concerned with the "fair" distribution of society's benefits—and burdens. A just distribution based on a person's contribution to society is the value behind the capitalist system, whereas distributive justice based on needs and abilities underlies socialism, and justice, defined as freedom to do as a person chooses, is the idea behind libertarianism. Retributive justice is concerned with providing punishments and penalties that are just. Thus, a person should not be considered to be morally responsible under conditions of ignorance or inability. This principle is the idea behind the standard of enlightened consent for participation in research studies. Compensatory justice supports the idea of compensating people for what they lose when they are wronged by other individuals or by society (including government itself).

Caring Ethics

The ethics of caring means making a decision in the face of an ethical dilemma based upon a genuine caring for the best interests of another individual. Key virtues of the caring administrator include friendship, kindness, concern, and love for fellow human beings. As might be expected, these ethical standards are often employed in describing decisions made in social welfare agencies and NGO activities.

The care ethic emphasizes two moral demands (Velasquez 1998, 122). First, because everyone lives in their own web of relationships, people should preserve and nurture the valuable relationships they have with others. Second, they must care for those with whom they are related by attending to their particular needs, values, desires, and concrete well-being as seen from their perspective. This also means responding to the needs, values, desires, and well-being of those who are vulnerable and dependent on our care.

Three different types of care ethics come into play in social situations: caring *about* something, caring *after* someone, and caring *for* someone. In public and NGO administration, the applicable ethic is caring for someone. It focuses on people and their well-being, not on things.

Virtue Ethics

Based upon the writings of Aristotle and others, virtue ethics refers to the idea of using society's virtues as the basis for making ethical decisions. Aristotle identified four "pivotal" virtues: courage, temperance, justice, and prudence. St. Thomas Aquinas added the following "Christian" virtues: faith, hope, and charity. In today's society, the virtues considered most important include honesty, courage, temperance, integrity, compassion, and self-control—terms often used to describe the "ideal" public servant. Vices are the opposite of virtues; they include such examples of "bad" behavior as dishonesty, ruthlessness, greed, lack of integrity, and cowardice. These are considered to be undesirable because of the way they can destroy human relationships.

Velasquez (1998, 137) described the thinking that shapes decision making in virtue theory in the following way:

> An action is morally right if in carrying out the action the agent exercises, exhibits, or develops a morally virtuous character, and is morally wrong to the extent that by

carrying out the action the agent exercise, exhibits, or develops a morally vicious character.

Which Approach to Follow?

Which, if any, of these ethical principles should guide the researcher when preparing, conducting, and reporting the results of research studies? Some of the underlying principles have resulted in the passage of laws that define specifically what a researcher can and cannot do. However, it is not enough to simply do what is legal; researchers have a moral responsibility that goes far beyond adhering to the letter of the law. Because there is no one comprehensive moral theory that is capable of stating exactly when a utilitarian consideration should take precedent over a right, a standard of justice, or the need for caring, the public administration researcher is forced to follow his or her conscience when faced with an ethical dilemma.

Ethical dilemmas that cause most difficulty for public administrators and researchers in public administration are not those associated with what Orlans (1967) described as outright "knavery—lying, bad faith, conscious misrepresentation to get money, or the deliberate breach of the terms on which it was obtained (i.e., research grants)." These are practical problems of a legal nature rather than problems of ethics. Although he attributed the problems specifically to funded or sponsored researchers, Orlans's description is applicable to all research:

> The persistent ethical dilemmas in . . . research are those in which the right course of action is *not* clear, in which honorable [researchers] may differ and no consistent rule obtains. They involve issues in which what is reasonable to one [person] is ignoble to another; in which honesty must be reconciled with tact and effectiveness; in which the disinterested pursuit of innocent truth can abet the interested selection of useful knowledge; in which the judgment of the pragmatic [person] of affairs confronts that of the academic moralist. (4)

Reynolds (1979, 43) identified five problem areas where research dilemmas occur most often; researchers should include answers for each of these problematic areas in the research proposal:

- *Research program effects:* the positive and negative effects of an overall research program
- *Research project effects:* the positive and negative effects that result from a specific research project
- *Participation effects*: the effects of participation in the research project upon each participant
- *Overall distribution effects*: the even distribution of the key positive

and negative effects of research among different social groups (stakeholders)

- *Consideration of participants' rights and welfare*: the features of the research program and project that ensure that the rights and welfare of participants are, or will be, respected

Physicist Richard Feynman has been given credit for providing the following final summary guiding principle for all researchers (paraphrased): The key to research is scientific integrity, a principle of scientific thought that corresponds to utter honesty; for example, if you're doing an experiment, you should report everything that you think might make it invalid and not only what you think is right about it.

What Are Public Administration Ethics?

Is there a distinct ethics for public administration? Most professionals like to think that their profession is in someway unique, that it has an ethics or a morality of its own, and that their ethics takes precedence over the ethics of ordinary people (Goss 1996). Of course, public and NGO administrators feel the same about their professions.

What Administrators Think Is Important

How do public administrators perceive the ethical climate of their profession? Goss (1996) compared the attitudes of 378 public administrators with 100 elected state officials and a random sample of 250 voting citizens. Attitudes were measured across twelve dimensions arranged in two scales of six items each. One set of items covered the professional (bureaucratic) ethos; the second set of six items covered the service or democratic ethos. Public administrators valued professional competence above the other eleven value characteristics and rated being an advocate of the public interest as the least important characteristic. Clearly, practicing administrators were more concerned with their professional skills than with service to the public.

Both the state legislator and general public samples rated *trustworthiness* as the most important behavioral characteristic for public servants. If Goss's one-state case study is valid—if his results can be considered representative of administrators everywhere—it appears that administrators are out of touch with the publics they serve. They apply their skills to the job at hand in ways that are different from the ways in which the public and their elected legislators would have them do so; they are less sensitive to the public interest and individual rights than the public, directly or through their elected representatives, would prefer them to be.

This difference in moral focus has important implications for public administration and NGO researchers. Administrators value competence, including knowledge, experience, and skill, above all other things. They believe that it is most important to conduct or purchase research that is competently conducted, informative, and skillfully presented. These are abilities that can be readily learned. What is not so easily learned is the ability to do research that is compassionate, caring, thoughtful, and, above all, ethical. However, caring, compassionate research may not be funded, and if it is, it may not reach its intended audience. It is critical, therefore, for researchers to strike a balance between the two points of view—but erring always on the side of ethics over expediency.

The Two Ethos of Public Administration

Ethics in public administration functions on two dominant levels or *ethos* (Garofalo and Geuras 1999; Goss 1996; Denhardt 1988). The term ethos refers to the characteristics that distinguish a particular person or group. First, public administrators are faced with a professional or bureaucratic ethos. This has to do with the way people perform their jobs. According to Garofalo and Geuras (1999, 48), it is based "on hierarchical control and obedience to political superiors." In some ways, the ethics of public administration are not much different from the ethics of any profession; the major distinguishing characteristic is the lack of a profit factor that motivates behavior in the private sector.

The second defining moral standard of public and NGO administrators is the underlying belief and commitment to public service. This is the *democratic ethos*—possibly an unfortunate selection of names since it can exist in nondemocratic societies as well; a better choice might have been a *service ethos*. The democratic ethos deals with such values as liberty, justice, human rights, and equality (Garofalo and Geuras 1999).

Managers in public and nonprofit organizations face ethical questions in both of these areas of morality. For example, while maintaining a sense of fiscal responsibility and professional competence across the principle areas of administrative activity, administrators are also expected to live up to several distinctive values of the service ethos in order to retain the public's trust. These include: (1) avoiding conflicts of interest, (2) maintaining impartiality toward the public and stakeholders with conflicting interests, (3) avoiding any appearance of impropriety, and (4) regularly submitting to public disclosure in almost every detail of their existence (Petrick and Quinn 1997).

Because research projects are carried out for all levels and functions of public administration, the ethical conduct of research is extremely important. There are dual responsibilities involved. First, research must be done ethically by the researcher, who must be concerned with the ethical treatment of respondents. In addition, the sponsoring agency has a moral obligation to be honest, to do research that is complete, and to be supportive of ethical methodological choices. Morality, public administration functions, and research ethics are closely interconnected. This is illustrated in Figure 3.1.

How people behave in their roles as public administrators depends in large part upon the core beliefs and values that they bring to their position. Some of these are moral in nature; they reflect the administrator's sense of moral duty. Ethics may not be able to be taught, but it is clearly apparent that people can be made aware of the ethical principles that underlie the organizations. Administrators must also be informed of the potential consequences of unethical behavior.

Establishing and maintaining a climate of ethical behavior in an organization begins with an overtly communicated commitment by the chief executive. Workers take their behavior cues from their leaders.

What Are Research Ethics?

Research ethics refers to the application of moral standards to decisions made in planning, conducting, and reporting the results of research studies. The fundamental moral standards involved focus on what is right and what is wrong. Beyond these, however, J. Mitchell (1998) has identified the following four practical ethical principles that shape morality in public administration research: *truthfulness*, *thoroughness*, *objectivity*, and *relevance*.

The *truthfulness principle* means that it is unethical for researchers to purposefully lie, deceive, or in any way employ fraud. Deliberately misrepresenting the purpose of a study, not informing subjects of the dangers of participation, hiding the identity of the sponsor of the study, or inflating or understating the findings of a research project are all examples of research that fails the truthfulness principle.

Despite the belief that truthfulness is a fundamental standard for all human endeavors, it sometimes gives way to expediency in research applications. When it does, a rationale for not telling the truth is usually provided. For example, some researchers believe that certain research could not be conducted without deception of some sort or that disclosing the true sponsor of a study would unnecessarily bias the findings. Researchers who use deception use two arguments to justify their actions: (1) they assume that participants

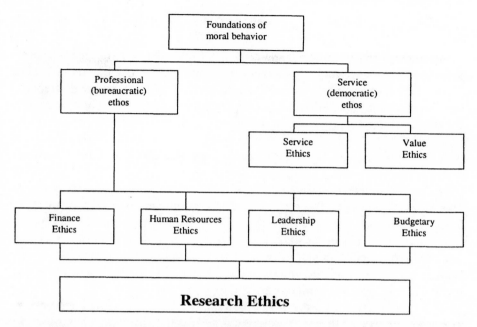

Figure 3.1 A Hierarchy of Public Administration Research Ethics

will not suffer any physical or mental harm as a result of the deception, and (2) they take on the responsibility of informing the participants about the deception after the research study is completed (Zikmund 1994).

The *thoroughness principle* demands that researchers not "cut corners" in their designs. It means being "methodologically thorough" (Mitchell 1998, 312). It means "doing good science" by following all steps in a study. Researchers are morally obligated to include the following in the study reports:

- Definitions for all key concepts used in the study
- Selection of appropriate samples or group participants, including full descriptions
- Identification of all limitations of the research design
- A description of the analysis design

Furthermore, remaining methodologically thorough means that all results and findings are reported—good news and bad. It means guaranteeing that participants will not be physically harmed or emotionally distressed. Thoroughness is not a simple concept, however, and can cause a great deal of difficulty for a researcher. Mitchell (1998, 313) summarized this difficulty in the following way: "In short, thoroughness is evidently at the core of methodology;

the ethical problem is defining exactly what thoroughness means in the actual conduct of research."

The *objectivity principle* refers to the need for the researcher to remain objective and impartial throughout all aspects of the study. Objectivity is one of the cornerstones of the positivist scientific tradition. "Doing good science" means that the researcher does not bias the study in any way. The researcher should avoid interjecting personal feelings or biases into the design of a study, using probability methods to select a sample, word questions in such a way as to avoid any hint of leading the subject to give a desired answer, and not allow the researcher's own values to color the results.

Not all researchers believe that remaining neutral is the proper role for a researcher to take in conducting research for public and NGO organizations. Some say that it is impossible to do so. These researchers object to the positivist philosophy of science and instead purposefully place themselves as one with the study participants. Following a postpositivist approach, these researchers employ such qualitative methods as ethnography, case analysis, grounded theory, and action or participatory research methods.

The final ethical research principle discussed by Mitchell is *relevance*. Research should never be frivolous or done because the researcher wants to punish the persons or groups involved in the subject organization. According to Mitchell, research, in a democracy, has a moral responsibility to be understandable to people and useful. Research that fails this test can be open to ridicule and worse. From 1975 to 1988, Wisconsin senator William Proxmire often used the press to disclose what he deemed to be wasteful, irrelevant, and often childish government-funded research projects. He awarded the sponsoring government agencies his Golden Fleece Award. An example was a $27,000 study to determine why inmates want to escape from prison (TFCS 2001).

Senator Proxmire's public ridicule of federally funded research that he called a "wasteful, ridiculous or ironic use of the taxpayers' money" should serve as a warning signal to all researchers in public and NGO organizations. The phrase, "if it sounds ridiculous, people will think it is" applies to all research. Kumar (1996, 192) has summarized the need for relevance in the following way: "If you cannot justify the relevance of the research you are conducting, you are wasting your respondents' time, which is unethical."

Research with Human Subjects

The acceptance of ethical standards as a guiding principle for research involving all human subjects is based upon decisions made during the Nuremberg Military Tribunal on Nazi war crimes held after the end of World War II. The standards that emerged from those trials resulted in adoption of what is known as the *Nuremberg Code* (Neuman 2000; Neef, Iwata, and Page 1986). Although originally applied to medical experiments only, the principles in the code are today used in all research that involves human subjects, including the social and administrative research employed in public administration. Included in the code are the following principles:

- Participants must be fully informed of the experiment and its effects
- Subjects' participation must be completely voluntary
- Participation must not cause injury or disablement to subjects
- The experiment must cease immediately if injury or death is possible
- Experiments should be conducted only by highly qualified researchers
- The results of the experiments must benefit society
- The experiment should not occur if the information is attainable by any other method

A sample of a human subjects research application for use at the Evergreen State College in Olympia, Washington, is included in Figures 3.2 through 3.4. Figure 3.2 describes the college policy and its history; Figure 3.3 is the form required for all research involving human subjects; Figure 3.4 is a sample human subjects review committee application form.

The following instructions are included with consent forms distributed with each human subjects research application:

- Prepare an *abstract* of your research project by summarizing the nature and purpose of your research.
- List the *procedures* to which humans will be subjected, that is, questionnaires, interviews, audio or video recordings, etc.
- Explain when, where, and how these procedures will be carried out. In the case of questionnaires or interviews, please attach a copy of the questions you will be asking.
- Explain how *subjects* will be recruited for the proposed work, including your recruitment criteria and procedures.
- List the possible *risks to the human subjects*. Outline precautions that will be taken to minimize these risks, including methods to ensure confidentiality or obtaining a release to use attributed material. *Note*: The concept of risk goes beyond obvious physical risk. It could include risk to the subject's dignity and self-respect, as

The Evergreen State College
USE OF HUMAN SUBJECTS

Background. The Human Subjects Review policy at Evergreen took effect in January 1979 to protect the rights of humans who are participants in research activities. If you are conducting a study using information from people or if you are recording them is some way for that study, you must complete this application with the collaboration of your faculty sponsor.

General Principles. All students, staff, and faculty conducting research at the college which involves the participation of humans as subjects of research must ensure that participation is *voluntary*, that *risks are minimal*, and that the *distribution of your study is limited.* All potential physical, psychological, emotional, and social risks should be considered, and explained to the participants in the study. This explanation must be clear, in letter form, and accompanied by a written consent form, which the participants sign. Similarly, the researcher must explain the benefits to the participant, the course of study, and intellectual inquiry. Participants must not be asked to expose themselves to risk unless the benefits to the participants or society are commensurate.

Please note that in most cases, keeping the participants' names confidential significantly minimizes risk.

Figure 3.2 Background and Requirements for Human Subjects Review Form
Source: Forms and instructions are used with permission from the Evergreen State College.

well as emotional, psychological, and behavioral risk. Risk could also include a potential for jeopardizing one's employment or standing in an academic program.
- List specific *benefits* to be gained by completing the project, which may be at an individual, institutional, or societal level.
- Describe how the information gained from this study is to be used, to whom the information is to be *distributed*, and how promise of confidentiality, if made, will be carried out in the final project.
- Prepare an *Informed Consent Affidavit* and a cover letter.

Ethics in the Research Process

Public administration and NGO researchers are most concerned with ethics at four times in the research process: (1) when they are planning to gather data, (2) while they are gathering data, (3) when they are processing and interpreting data, and (4) when they are disseminating the results of their research. The interrelated nature of these four situations is displayed in Figure 3.5.

Ethics When Planning Research

A key activity in planning a research project is deciding who will be the participants in the study. In a positivist design—what most people call a quan-

---

The Evergreen State College
Sample Informed Consent Affidavit

I, _____, hereby agree to serve as a subject in the research project entitled
_____ . It has been explained to me that the purpose of
this study is _____and that the
proposed use for the research obtained, now and in the future, is _____ .
I understand that the possible risks to me associated with this study are:
_____ .

Medical treatment and/or compensation is _____ / is not _____ available for projects presenting
physical risks; if available, treatment or compensation consists of _____ .
I may not receive any direct benefit from participation in this study, but my participation may help
_____
_____ has offered to answer any questions I may have about the study
and provide me with access to the final report or presentation.

I understand that the person to contact in the event I experience problems as a result of my
participation is _____ at _____ .

I hereby agree to participate as a subject in the above-described research project. I
understand that my participation in the project is voluntary, that I am free to withdraw from
participation at any time, and that my choice of whether or not to participate in this project
will not jeopardize my relationship with the Evergreen State College. I have read,
understood, and agree to the foregoing.

Participant's Signature: _____ Date: _____

Parents' Signature (required if subject is a minor): _____

Figure 3.3 **Sample Informed Consent Form**

titative study design—this typically entails the use of sampling. Use of the
proper sampling design is a critical decision factor in these designs. If the
study is an interpretive design, participants may be as few as one person in a
case study or, in an action research study, everyone in a group, organization,
or a community. The most commonly used probability sampling design is
what is called a simple random sample (SRS). In an SRS, every subject in the
population has an equal chance of being selected for the sample.

In all designs, special care must be taken to ensure that participants voluntarily agree to participate, that their privacy is protected, and that they are not
physically or mentally harmed in any way.

When researchers follow a positivist (or quantitative) research approach,
they often use the information gathered from a representative *sample* drawn
from a larger *population* to imply or infer that the results apply to the larger
body as well. Samples can be one of two basic types (with many variations): *probability* or *nonprobability*. Both have a place in research, but they
are not interchangeable. In a probability sample, all participants have an
equal or known chance at being selected for the study. This is not the case
with a nonprobability sample, where participants are usually selected for

---

Human Subjects Review Application
Please return this application to:

The Evergreen State College, Olympia WA 98505
The Evergreen State College (Revised Application 1/12/00)

Research project title: _____

Name of project director(s): _____

Mailing address or mailstop: _____

Phone number: _____

Proposed project dates: _____

Date application submitted: _____

Immediate supervisor, faculty sponsor, or dean: _____

Funding agency/research sponsor (if applicable): _____

INDICATE IF THE PROJECT INVOLVES ANY OF THE FOLLOWING:

___ Minors   ___ Pregnant women   ___ Developmentally disabled
___ Prisoners   ___ Abortuses   ___ Random sample
___ New drugs   ___ Fetuses   ___ A cooperating institution

Certification: We understand that the policies and procedures of the Evergreen State College apply to all research activities involving human subjects which are being performed by persons associated with the college and, therefore, that these activities cannot be initiated without prior review and approval by the appropriate academic dean and, as required, by the Human Subjects Review Board.

X _____
   Signature of the project director   *Date*

X _____
   Signature of the supervisor or project coordinator   *Date*

Figure 3.4 Sample Application for Human Subjects Review Board Approval

the convenience of the researcher or simply to fill a quota. Therefore, the results of a nonprobability sample study should not be used for inference; it is unethical to do so. Nonprobability samples provide information for insights and ideas or for use in the design of a larger study that does use probability-sampling methods.

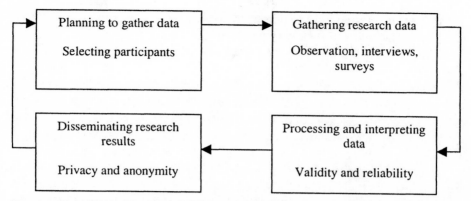

Figure 3.5 **A Model Illustrating When Ethics Are Particularly Important in Research**

Sampling is also used in some postpositivist or interpretive designs, although typically not for inferential purposes. In case studies, for example, the sample might be a single person, some or all members of a group or organization, or people from two or more groups or organizations. Thus, the sample ethics question may not be as critical; case study results are traditionally used not to extend the results to entire populations but, instead, to be a description of the case itself. Six questions must be answered before involving a subject in the study:

1. Has the participant given his or her *informed consent* to be included in the study?
2. Has the subject *voluntarily agreed* to participate, or has some form of coercion been used to force the subject's participation?
3. Has the subject been *fully informed* of his or her right not to participate and of any risks and/or benefits that might accrue from the study?
4. Will the subject be *harmed, either physically or mentally*, in any way as a result of participation in the study?
5. Is it necessary to use *deception*, to disguise the research, or use covert research methods in order to collect the data?
6. Will a jury of external professional peers *validate* the study?

Informed consent. The idea of informed consent is based upon Western society's ideas of individual freedom and self-determination, as spelled out in the body of common law (Neef, Iwata, and Page 1986). A person's right to be free from intrusion by others is supported by a number of court decisions, among which is the 1973 *Roe v. Wade* decision. From this and other court actions, the following components of the concept of informed consent have been of particular interest:

- The capacity of the person to consent to participation
- The free and voluntary giving of consent
- Consent that is informed and knowledgeable

Courts have held that the capacity to consent requires that the person giving consent knowingly and rationally understand the nature of the experiment or study, any associated risk, and other relevant information. At the same time, researchers are not permitted to decide whether the subject is competent enough to make the decision; all people retain the right to manage their own affairs.

In research involving children, parents have traditionally been allowed to give consent on their behalf, but Neef, Iwata, and Page (1986) noted that the courts have not always accepted that as a right. Therefore, researchers are advised to acquire the consent of parents and the child, as well as that of relevant organizations (such as schools).

Voluntary consent. There are two aspects to the concept of voluntary consent. First, the agreement must be entirely free of any coercion. Second, the subject must understand that the consent can be withdrawn at any time without any harmful consequence (Neef, Iwata, and Page 1986). Often, academic researchers use the students in their classes as participants in research studies. Students are not required to participate, and must be assured that their performance in the class will not suffer as a result of their not participating.

Knowledgeable consent. All potential research participants must be made aware of all aspects of the study. This means that they must be told (1) that they have the right not to participate, (2) that they can withdraw at any time, (3) what risks might be involved, and (4) what the potential benefits of the study are, if any. If the study is an experiment, participants must also know the risks and benefits of any alternative treatments.

Freedom from harm. A fundamental ethical principal that must be followed in all research studies is that no harm shall fall on the participants as a result of their participation in the research (Neuman 2000; Oppenheim 1992). *Harm* is broadly defined; for example, it can mean physical, cultural, social, or psychological distress as well as physical pain.

Ethics When Gathering Data

Kumar has identified five key points in the research when an ethical concern for respondents is particularly important: (1) when seeking consent from the subject, (2) when providing incentives to participate, if any, (3) when seeking sensitive information or information that might embarrass or otherwise cause discomfort to the subject, (4) when there is a possibility of causing harm, and (5) when maintaining confidentiality for the respondent.

Data-gathering methods used most often in public administration and NGO research include observation, interviewing, and survey questionnaires. Deciding which subjects to include in a research study and which to exclude is also affected by which of these methods is chosen. For example, personal interviews can take two or more hours to complete. As a result, sample sizes may be quite small; researchers must be very selective in their choice of participants. However, if the design calls for use of a self-administered questionnaire, it is often relatively easy to add more subjects to the mailing list.

A number of ethical issues come into play when conducting interviews or writing questionnaires. The ethics of data gathering in all forms continue to raise controversial questions among researchers (Oppenheim 1992). The two problems that cause most difficulty are the potential for *bias* on the part of the interviewer or in the wording of the question, and the *response distortion* that such biases can cause. Most researchers concede that it is impossible to eliminate all interviewer bias; conscientious training of interviewers is the only way to reduce it.

Ethics in Processing and Interpreting Data

Researchers are sometimes asked to design and conduct a research study and analyze the collected data in order provide "scientific credence" to preestablished conclusions. Other researchers have been asked to compromise their ethical standards as a condition for receiving a contract to conduct research. Both of these situations present ethical dilemmas. The researcher has three options in these situations (Neuman 2000): (1) Feeling loyalty to an employer or group overrides any ethical considerations, the researcher may quietly go along with the request; (2) he or she may overtly oppose the request, making the opposition a part of the public record, placing the researcher in the role of whistle-blower, and possibly causing loss of credibility in the agency, elimination of future research opportunities, or even loss of a job; (3) he or she can simply refuse to make compromises and walk away from the request, aware that another researcher may be found to do the work.

Making the right moral decision in such situations is not an easy choice. Opting for the first path may not only cause the researcher undue personal stress, but also open the door to criminal prosecution. On the other hand, refusing to go along with the request exposes the researcher to accusations of disloyalty to the organization and disregard for the well-being of fellow workers.

Many ethicists often encourage selecting the path of becoming a whistle-blower; it is clearly the most "moral" of the three options. However, whistle-blowers are seldom rewarded for their willingness to publicize unethical activity. They must be in a position to prove their allegations in a court of law, where deliberations may take years to complete. In the intervening time, they are often ostracized by fellow workers, removed from any meaningful work in the organization, eliminated from potential promotion, and ultimately forced to suffer loss of a job. The popular press has aired many reports of whistle-blowers who have lost not only their job but their home and other possessions as well. It takes a brave person to adopt this role; fortunately, many still do.

Refusing to do the study may be the easiest way out of the dilemma. If morality can exist on a continuum, this path is less immoral than going along with the request and less moral than publicly disclosing the request. This does not mean that it is an easy solution. Choosing to not do the research may mean loss of income or professional standing. On the other hand, complying with the request because someone else will do it anyway is never an acceptable justification. Neuman (2000, 103), discussing the conflict that often appears in such situations, concluded, "Whatever the situation, unethical behavior is never justified by the argument that 'If I didn't do it, someone else would have.'"

Ethics in Disseminating Research Results

Researchers are faced with two broad classes of ethical considerations when disseminating their findings. First, ethical considerations come into play with the distribution and/or publication of the findings. Second, researchers have the moral obligation to protect the privacy of the participants in the research.

Researchers must consider several factors when communicating the results of their research. These include (1) telling the entire story rather than just a few significant portions, (2) presenting insignificant, adverse, or negative findings, and (3) contributing to the general storehouse of disciplinary knowledge. Telling the entire story relates to the idea of methodological completeness discussed earlier. The obligation to include findings that reflect negatively on the sponsoring agency, the research method, or the researchers themselves is based on the ethical standard of honesty. Telling only part of the truth is little different from not telling the truth at all. Contributing to knowledge in the field refers to the researchers' obligation to the ethos of the profession, both as administrators and as researchers.

In addition to the ethical obligation to be truthful when preparing the research report, the researcher must also protect the rights of participants. Three issues are of particular importance when disseminating the results of a research study: (1) protecting the privacy of participants, (2) ensuring the anonymity of participants, and (3) respecting the confidentiality of individuals involved in the study. Protecting participants' privacy is a fundamental moral standard as well as a legal requirement affecting all researchers. While this is primarily a concern during the sample selection and data-gathering steps, the researcher must take great care to ensure that participants' identity cannot be deciphered from the findings. Participants must know that their privacy will not be invaded as a result of dissemination of the findings.

Ensuring the anonymity of participants is closely related to the privacy standard, except that it is primarily a concern during the preparation of the findings stage. An integral part of every study is, or should be, a description of the sample participants. This description should always be done in the aggregate, focusing on characteristics of the group, such as measures of central tendency, variation, and the like. The results related to any single participant should never be made known, except in interpretive studies, which can focus on a single case.

The confidentiality standard means that no one other than the primary researcher should know sample members' names and addresses. A single list must be kept by the researcher.

Researchers also have a moral obligation to avoid reporting incomplete research results, issuing misleading reports, and issuing biased reports (Malhotra 1999). Incomplete reports are more likely to be disseminated when the researcher uncovers adverse or negative information. Misleading results are released to intentionally mislead an audience, even if they are not an actual lie. For example, say that 90 percent of the citizens of a community prefer that a ten-acre parcel at the edge of town be left undeveloped, 5 percent want a new shopping center on the site, 3 percent want an industrial park, and 2 percent want a park with softball and soccer fields. It is unethical for the city planning commission to announce that more of the citizens prefer a shopping center to any other development scheme for the parcel without also saying that 90 percent want no development at the site at all. It is misleading not because it is false, but because it does not give all the facts.

Biased research is often conducted to justify a preconceived result or solution. It also occurs when researchers do not follow the required steps in a research process, when the problem is incorrectly defined, when the questionnaire is not pretested, when questions are written that almost force respondents to answer in a particular way, or when respondents are asked questions that they are unable to answer.

Finally, ethical decisions during dissemination of research findings arise regarding disclosure of the limitations of the study. The sponsoring agency, respondents, and the recipients of the research report are justified in their right to know how much credence they can give to the findings.

Summary

The potential for unethical behavior is a universal problem; it affects administrators at all levels of government and nonprofit nongovernment organizations (NGOs). Academics, administrators, and the popular press have called for moral reform, passage of ethics laws and codes, and greater education and training in ethical behavior for public employees. These calls for reform have been directed at every level of government, from the Office of the President to the smallest local special service district.

Ethics, a branch of philosophy, is the study of the *moral* behavior of humans in society. *Morality* refers to the standards that people have about what is right, what is wrong, what is good, and what is evil. *Moral behavior* is acting in ways that follow the moral standards that exist in society. *Moral standards* are the rules by which a society functions.

Moral standards have evolved from a number of different philosophical traditions. Today, at least five different ways to approach an ethical situation have evolved from these earliest guidelines for moral behavior. These include *utilitarian, rights, justice, caring, and virtue ethics.* Researchers draw upon these traditions when faced with ethical dilemmas.

No one approach is more correct than any other. For example, because no one comprehensive moral theory is capable of stating exactly when a utilitarian consideration should take precedence over, say, a right, a standard of justice, or the need for caring, public administration researchers are forced to follow their conscience.

Ethics in public administration function on two dominant levels or *ethos*. First, public administrators are faced with a professional or *bureaucratic ethos*. The second defining moral standard of public and NGO administrators is the underlying belief and commitment to public service. This is the *democratic ethos*—possibly an unfortunate selection of names since it can exist in nondemocratic societies as well; a better choice might have been a *service ethos*. This ethos deals with such values as liberty, justice, human rights, and equality.

Research ethics refers to the application of moral standards to decisions made in planning, conducting, and reporting the results of research studies. The fundamental moral standards involved focus on what is right and what is wrong. Four additional, practical ethical principles that shape morality in public administration research are *truthfulness, thoroughness, objectivity,* and *relevance.*

Although originally applied to medical experiments only, the principles spelled out in the Nuremberg Code are today used in all research that involves human subjects, including the social and administrative research employed in public administration. The key clauses of the code ensure that participants have the right not to participate, that they are informed of all risks, and that they will not be intentionally physically or mentally harmed.

Public administration and NGO researchers are most concerned with ethics at four times in the research process: (1) when they are planning to gather data, (2) while they are gathering data, (3) when they are processing and interpreting data, and (4) when they are disseminating the results of their research.

Suggested Reading

Cooper, Terry L. 1998. *The Responsible Administrator: An Approach to Ethics for the Administrative Role.* 4th ed. San Francisco: Jossey-Bass.

De Laine, Marlene. 2000. *Fieldwork, Participation and Practice: Ethics and Dilemmas in Qualitative Research.* London: Sage.

Elliott, Deni, and Judy E. Stern, eds. 1997. *Research Ethics.* Hanover, NH: University Press of New England.

Garofalo, Charles, and Dean Geuras. 1999. *Ethics in the Public Service: The Moral Mind at Work.* Washington, DC: Georgetown University Press.

Neuman, W. Lawrence. 2000. "The Ethics and Politics of Social Research." In *Social Research Methods: Qualitative and Quantitative Approaches*, ch. 5, pp. 89–120. Boston: Allyn and Bacon.

Rohr, John A. 1998. *Public Service, Ethics, and Constitutional Practice.* Lawrence: University Press of Kansas.

Part 2

Introduction to the Research Process

4 The Research Process

All research activity takes place in a sequence of fundamental steps. First, someone is faced with a problem circumstance, event, or situation (a *study problem*). That person or someone else is instructed to design a method of collecting information that pertains to the problem (planning a *research strategy*). Information is then collected (a *data-gathering* activity). Once the information is collected, its meaning must be found (*data processing*, *analysis*, and *interpretation*). Finally, all the pieces are put together in a report that brings about resolution of the problem. *How* these steps are put together is the subject matter of this book; the process is called *research strategy and methods*.

There is no limit to the variety of choices of study questions, research strategies, data collection methods, and data processing and evaluation approaches. There are also many different ways of interpreting the results. It is possible to put these together in many different combinations—no one of which is inherently more correct than another. Today, these different combinations are all seen as valid research strategies. Their selection and application are based upon the nature of the study question, the objectives for the study, and the researcher's level of skill and comfort with the research method.

Steps in the Research Process

Today, both quantitative and qualitative research strategies are considered legitimate designs for research in public administration and all other social and administrative sciences; they simply serve different purposes. Whichever approach is taken, all research takes place over the eight-step process shown in Figure 4.1.

Tested and refined over decades of scientific investigation, today this eight-step process is used to guide research activities in all the social, administrative, and natural sciences.

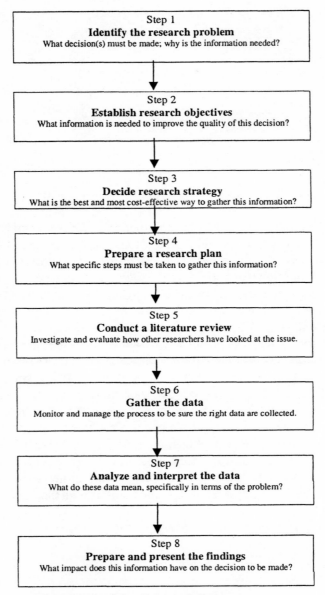

Figure 4.1   The Eight Steps of the Research Process

Identify the Research Problem

The first step in research is to *identify the research problem clearly and succinctly*. There is unanimous agreement that this is the most important step in the entire research process. If the first step is not done correctly, the remaining activities will be a waste of the researcher's time and labor. Data will be gathered, but the meaning of that data will be lost.

The label *research problem* is not always used to describe this activity. In the social sciences, it is often replaced with the phrase *defining the study question*. Other authors refer to it as a process of establishing a *rationale for the study*. It has also been called the *research topic*, the *research situation*, the *information need*, and other things. They all mean the same: establishing what it is you want to know, and why.

Establish Research Objectives

Step two in the research process is to spell out in advance what is to be accomplished by the research. These are the objectives for the study. This step is closely allied to the first step, identifying the research problem. Both look at the reasons for doing the research. At this stage, however, the objectives may still be tentative; a final set of objectives may not emerge until after a review of the literature pertaining to the study question has been completed.

The research problem is a statement of the reason for doing the research; research objectives are statements of what you want the research to accomplish. Say, for example, that you manage a statewide program to improve high school students' awareness of the prevention of sexually transmitted diseases. A study question might be to determine the best way to accomplish this task. Specific research objectives might include first determining the students' current level of awareness of the diseases, their cause, spread, and methods of prevention.

A second objective might be to determine where the students received their information. Another might be to establish their preferred medium of communication and its ability to effectively convey persuasive messages. The researcher will also want to know who makes up the population at greatest risk. There are usually no simple answers to study questions; instead, each involves many subcomponents and antecedent factors.

Decide on a Research Strategy

Step three of the research process is deciding on the research strategy that provides the most cost-effective way of gathering the needed information, and the strategy that produces the best possible answer for the research question. The three broad classes of research strategies are qualitative, quantitative, and combined. Each of these strategies provides the researcher with a wide variety of data-gathering approaches and specific methods and data processing and analysis techniques. The researcher's selection must be based on the first two steps in the research process.

Prepare a Research Plan

In step four, the researcher prepares a plan for the subsequent research activity. This means identifying in advance the research subjects or sample, the methods planned for gathering and processing data, and a timeline for completing the project. Thus, designing an effective research plan requires decisions on (1) the data sources, (2) the research approaches, (3) the data-gathering instruments, (4) a sampling plan, and (5) methods of contacting study subjects. Each of these steps will be discussed in detail in subsequent chapters.

Conduct a Literature Review

An important part of any research project is an activity called a literature review. This is nothing more than a review of prior research on the topic at hand. It typically involves reading and analyzing material in published books, professional and academic journals, government documents, and other sources.

The literature builds on the work already done by other investigators. The focus of the literature review should always be on the key ideas that may function as leads for further investigation. Previous investigators may have already stated and tested hypotheses about your topic. Your task is to gather these previously published ideas, to evaluate their usefulness as they relate specifically to your research, and to determine whether they suggest new ways of looking at the problem that you might have missed (Selltiz, Wrightman, and Cook 1976).

Gather the Data

Step five, an action step, involves gathering the data needed for meeting the study objectives and answering the study question. Depending on the research strategy selected, data may be gathered by: (1) participating in a social situation and recording the findings, (2) passively observing subjects, (3) interviewing subjects one at a time or in groups, (4) preparing a questionnaire to survey a sample, or 5) reviewing documents of other information sources. The researcher may gather primary data, secondary data, or both. These data can come from internal sources, external sources, or both. A classification of data sources is displayed in Table 4.1.

Primary data are original data that the researcher gathers from original sources. Examples of primary data include responses to a questionnaire, an interview, or some other type of measurement. Secondary data are data that have been collected by someone else for another purpose. Examples of secondary data include government statistical reports, articles in professional

Table 4.1

A Classification of Data Sources

I. Qualitative data sources
  A. Existing documents
    1. Books, periodicals, published reports, domestic and foreign
    2. Local, state, and federal government documents
    3. Trade and professional association reports
    4. College and university documents
    5. Minutes of meetings
    6. Commercial databases
    7. Other
  B. Primary sources
    1. Interviews
    2. Life histories
    3. Case analyses
  C. Internal sources
    1. E-mail
    2. Memorandums
    3. Reports and other documents
II. Quantitative data sources
  A. Surveys (in-person, mail, telephone, interactive)
    1. Questionnaires
    2. Attitude and lifestyle surveys, psychographics
  B. Experiments and field studies
    1. Laboratory experiments
    2. Field experiments
    3. Observation studies
    4. Interviews
    5. Videotaping and audio recordings
  C. Internal sources
    1. Company or organization annual reports
    2. Company or organizational invoices and/or accounts payable records
    3. Production and services records
    4. Human resources records

journals, and city or agency records. Neither data type is inherently better than the other, but care must always be taken in the interpretation of secondary data to ensure that it meets the specific research objectives.

Analyze and Interpret the Data

Step six is the payoff step; it is also the activity that may be the most difficult for beginning researchers to master. Once the data are in hand, the researcher must establish some order in the data and determine its meaning and/or implications. This interpretation must be carried out so that the findings can be related to the original study question and research objectives.

Researchers are typically interested in knowing the following things about a mass of data. First, they want to know what is "typical" in the sample. This means getting some idea of the central tendency of the responses. In everyday language, they want to know what are the averages.

Second, they want to know how widely individuals in the sample vary in their responses. In a community economic development study, for example, the director might want to know whether local citizens have similar or widely diverse attitudes about the proposed development of a ten-acre parcel on the city limits.

Third, researchers want to see how subjects are distributed across the study variables. For example, is the number of people who prefer a new park for the ten–acre site the same as or greater than the number preferring a new shopping center or new single-family housing on the site. A good way to display this type of information is to use charts or graphs showing the frequency of responses. What is the shape of the graph? Is one response category very much greater or smaller than the others?

Four, the analyst will want to show how the different variables relate to one another. It may be important to know, for example, that the preferences for different types of uses for the parcel seem related to certain characteristics of the population, such as age, gender, occupation, or annual income.

And, five, the researcher will want to describe any differences among the two or more groups or objects. It might be important to know, for example, whether males in the sample respond differently about their preferences for the site than do females in the sample. This type of understanding is important because much public administration research focuses on the comparisons of groups of citizens (Selltiz, Wrightman, and Cook 1976).

Tabulating Responses

The first step in data analysis is to tabulate the responses to all items in the study. In a quantitative study, this could mean counting all the answers to each question or schedule item. This counting of responses is often referred to as *frequency distributions*, after the statistical software process that counts responses and prepares summary data for the researcher.

Frequency distributions and summaries are prepared for one variable at a time, producing *univariate statistics* for each variable. Counts of how many subjects answered "yes" to a question and how many answered "no" and the distribution of males and females in a sample are both examples of univariate

Table 4.2

A Simple Univariate Table ($n = 70$)

Gender	Count	Percent
Females	40	57.1
Males	30	42.9

Table 4.3

A Bivariate Cross-Tabulation Example

Gender	Yes response		No response	
	Number	Percent	Number	Percent
Females	47	38.2	81	60.4
Males	76	61.8	53	39.6
Totals	123	100.0	134	100.0

frequencies. Univariate statistics often include one or more of the following: measures of central tendency, variation, and/or location. Table 4.2 is an example of a typical frequency table with counts and percentages shown.

Once univariate statistical tabulations are prepared, the researcher then begins *bivariate* tabulations. In this process, responses to one variable are tabulated with a second variable. The information is usually presented in a table (called *cross-tabulations* or *cross-tabs* for short). For example, responses to a yes-no question are displayed broken down for males and females in Table 4.3.

In addition to simple counts of responses, cross-tabulations can also display some summary information for each of the responses. The individual boxes with counts displayed are called *cells*; *rows* run across the page; and *columns* run down the page. Summary statistics include the percentage of the total represented by the number of responses in each cell, the cell's percentage of the row total, and the cell's percentage of the column. Row, column, and total percentage values are provided along the sides of the cross-tabulation table. Finally, a wide variety of statistical tests for nominal, ordinal, and interval/rations data can also be produced with cross-tabulation software.

After analyzing relevant bivariate data, the researcher turns next to either an analysis of variable correlations or hypothesis tests. Analysis then proceeds to any of the many multivariate statistical processes needed to meet the objectives of the study.

For a qualitative study, the researcher often begins the analysis by reviewing the data to establish a structural skeleton that will provide for meaningful interpretation and discussion. For qualitative research, the typical data analysis has been the *narrative text* (Miles and Huberman 1984). This is often a comprehensive rewrite of the researcher's field notes, with the researcher's verbal interpretation and conclusions from the data. There are few agreed-upon styles and formats for the broad scope of qualitative analysis methods. Selection is left up to the researcher. According to Miles and Huberman (1984, 79):

> Valid analysis requires, and is driven by, displays (i.e., narrative text and graphic presentations of qualitative research findings) that are as simultaneous as possible, are focused, and are as systematically arranged as the questions at hand demand. While such displays may sometimes be overloading, they will never be monotonous. Most important, the chances of drawing and verifying valid conclusions are very much greater. . . . The qualitative analyst has to handcraft all such data displays . . . each analyst has to invent his or her own.

Prepare and Present the Findings

Step seven is preparing the research report and presenting the findings. It is the final step in the process, but is second in importance only to clearly defining and focusing on a research problem/study question. An outline for the research report follows the same outline developed during the fourth step, preparation of a research plan. Some portions of the report, such as a description of the research problem, delineation of research objectives, the review of the literature, and the rationale for selecting the strategy employed, may have been written as the researcher completed the earlier steps in the process.

There are many different ways to gather data—that is, conduct a research project—and many different ways of communicating the research findings. Ultimately, however, someone must sit down and write out the results of the study. These results must then be passed on to a supervisor, a fellow employee, or members of a funding organization or, if possible, even published in a brochure, report, or professional journal.

Doing good research means more than using good scientific methods to select the sample, gather data, and tabulate the results. It also means interpreting what the data mean in terms of the study objectives and writing research reports that clearly and effectively communicate the findings of the research effort. Using an appropriate *style* is critical in all research writing. Style refers to the words, syntax, and punctuation that are used or not used. It includes the way these components are placed into sentences and paragraphs. It involves the structure and organization of the report and whether it conforms to the traditions of the discipline. It also refers to the way that the author's sources are cited, identified, and credited.

An administrator—present or future—should remember that there is no one best style. One or more may be more appropriate for a given discipline, but often that fact seems arbitrary. The best style to use in all research reports and organizational papers is writing that is *clear, concise,* and *readable.*

The processes necessary for producing a research report for the social and administrative sciences are similar to those that are used for research in chemistry, physics, biology, or any other natural science. Slightly different research, analysis, interpretation, and presentation processes are involved, however.

Following an accepted style enhances the readability of the research report, regardless of its discipline. Academicians (teachers) and practitioners (managers) are typically pressed for time. If a paper is written in a familiar format (style), it will be easier to read—and take less of the reader's time. This often results in greater acceptance of the research findings—an extremely important point for research that comes up with negative findings. This benefit alone should be a desired outcome.

One problem that makes professional writing difficult for researchers and students is the *lack of conformity* in formats required by different disciplines and their journals. The format demanded by the editors of a journal sponsored by the Academy of Management, for example, will probably result in rejection of the paper by the editors of a public administration, finance, accounting, or economics journal. Researchers must determine which style is required in their field and which styles are unacceptable. The only thing consistent about writing styles is inconsistency!

Summary

The research process can be defined as *the process of systematically acquiring data to answer a question or solve a problem.* Research is done to help managers, administrators, and academics achieve a better understanding of how the world works. Research *methodology* refers to the approach researchers take as they examine their study questions or problems. It includes a philosophical mind-set that researchers bring to the research activity as well as a set of procedures. This mind-set is what we now call *the scientific method.*

Humans employ two types or methods of coming to conclusions about things: deductive reasoning and inductive reasoning. Deductive reasoning means arriving at a conclusion on the basis of something that you know or that you assume to be true—a general principle or *law.* Inductive reasoning, on the other hand, is the logic model or paradigm normally followed in scientific research.

The research process involves eight steps, beginning with establishing what and why the research is necessary and ending with a comprehensive report of the findings that emerge from the research process. These steps are (1) identify the research problem, (2) establish research objectives, (3) decide on a research strategy, (4) prepare a research plan, (5) conduct a comprehensive review of the literature, (6) gather the data, (7) analyze and interpret the data, and (8) prepare and present the findings.

Suggested Reading

Bernard, H. Russell. 1995. *Research Methods in Anthropology*. 2d ed. Walnut Creek, CA: AltaMira Press.

Kumar, Ranjit. 1996. *Research Methodology*. London: Sage.

White, Jay D. 1999. *Taking Language Seriously: The Narrative Foundations of Public Administration Research*. Washington, DC: Georgetown University.

5 The Research Problem

Beginning researchers often find themselves at the start of the research process struggling for answers to basic questions: *What shall I research? How shall I do it?* And *Once I've gathered my information, how can I make any sense of it? What does it really mean?* For some, simply choosing a subject to research and write about can be the most difficult part of the entire project. These questions and others will be addressed in this chapter.

The research conducted in public and nonprofit organizations is done to provide information needed to make better administrative and managerial decisions. For example, an administrator of a program to provide financial assistance education to welfare recipients might find that the number of applicants for aid has declined precipitously in the last quarter. She would need to conduct research to find out the cause of the decline.

Another administrator might need to determine the most cost-effective way to communicate information about sexually transmitted diseases to teens and subteens in the central city. And another might need to help a new manager determine whether the morale, attitudes, and beliefs of the agency's personnel are affecting their job satisfaction and job performance.

These are all examples of research projects conducted by employees for the organizations in which they were employed. These were real problems that needed resolution. But how does a student determine what topic to research?

Research topics can come from questions discovered in texts, in the professional literature, from classroom discussions, from hobbies and other outside interests, and, of course, from the life experience of the researcher. An example is the study of a hearing-impaired graduate student who learned that Native American children are more likely to have hearing problems than are children of other ethnic groups with similar socioeconomic characteristics. Determining why this is so and what can be done to alleviate the problem became the student's graduate-program research project.

This is what Sylvan Barnet said about choosing a topic: "No subject is undesirable," and "No subject is too trivial for study" (1993, 177–178). Barnet might have added: *No subject is inherently uninteresting.* It is the way subjects are researched and reported that makes them desirable or undesirable, interesting or uninteresting. Here are a few guidelines to think about when choosing a research project topic:

- Research and write about something that interests you
- Be sure enough material about the topic is available to allow you to do a good job
- Make sure that the topic is not so big that it is overwhelming
- Be sure the topic fits your abilities and understanding
- Make sure you take good notes once you start reading about the topic
- Ask your reference librarian for guidance on your research topic
- Get assistance from your instructor
- Focus, focus, and focus!

Defining the Problem

A key requirement for all research is the clear, concise, and thorough definition of the problem for which the research will be carried out. This doesn't mean that answers are known before the questions are asked. Rather, it means that the researcher has a specific goal in mind for the research—before getting started. It must be admitted, however, that this is hardly ever an easy process. Here are some examples:

Administrators are experiencing a decline in enrollments in programs designed to help welfare recipients gain the skills necessary for successful full-time employment. A recent state law mandates that all able-bodied recipients of public assistance receive aid for a maximum of five years. At the end of that period, they must be removed from the program, regardless of their employment or dependent status. The administrators of the program do not know the reason for the decline in the skill-development program, although they have some assumptions. Nor do they know what should be done to reverse the trend. Considering that people's lives are involved, making the wrong decision may be extremely costly.

Another example is the difficulty faced by administrators of substance-abuse programs and law-enforcement agencies as they seek to halt growth in the use of controlled substances. Despite billions of dollars spent on public education and abatement programs, drug use continues to be a major problem across the nation. Demand for treatment facilities far outstrips the availability of tested, effective programs. Federal and state legislators, program administrators, and local law-enforcement agencies are all looking for the most effective way to apply their limited resources to deal with the problem. Each agency involved has a different mission, different information needs, and different objectives. Defining the research problem is a difficult task for every agency involved. The following process of problem definition can help everyone who faces this difficult task.

Tasks in the Problem Definition Process

The process displayed in Figure 5.1 has been designed to help administrators identify and define research problems.

Relate the Problem to Program Mission and Objectives

The first step in the problem definition process is determining whether the proposed research project will produce information that is commensurate with the purpose, goals, and objectives of the organization, program, or agency. The research project must be worth the effort, time, and money it will consume. The researcher and administrator requesting the research must be absolutely sure of the relevance of the project.

An organizational problem can usually be translated into many different types of study problems. Many of these may be intuitively interesting, but beyond the scope of the agency or ability of the administrator to change or influence. This does not mean that administrators should not "stretch" to increase their level of awareness of their agency, its client population, and the problems associated with both. It means only that they should first do what can be done. Answers to such questions as these must be found before proceeding with the program:

- What is it specifically that we do?
- Whom do we serve, and why?
- What information do we need to improve the way we function?
- Does what I want to know fit these functions, programs, or operations?
- Do we need this information for personal reasons or is it for our operations?
- Is this something I really need to know, or is it something I think I would like to know?
- Has someone else already researched this question—that is, am I just repeating something that has already been done?
- Could these resources be put to better use elsewhere?

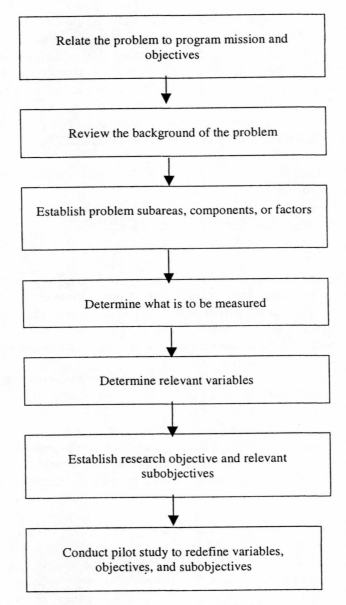

Figure 5.1 **Tasks in the Problem Definition Process**

Answers to such questions can often be found by conducting a thorough review of the background and published literature on the topic. Another way is to conduct a series of interviews with several key informants, who have a greater than average familiarity with the problem and its associated antecedents or consequences.

Review the Background of the Problem

There are two aspects to a problem's background. The first is the nature of the problem within the organization; this is called the internal background. This is the total body of knowledge on the topic that exists within the organization or its larger administrative body. It may exist as published reports, operations records, or accounting data, it may reside in the memories of other participants in the organization, or it may be in the historical archives of the organization. It is usually easier to access than external literature. It should always be the first place a researcher looks when conducting organizational research.

The second aspect is the body of work that already exists on the problem, its causes and cures, its extent and impact, and the way that other researchers have approached the issue. This is the *external background*. External information exists in the body of literature on the topic; accessing this earlier work is referred to as a *review of the literature*. It includes all the published and unpublished-but-available material on the question.

What happens when the researcher is unable to pinpoint a specific research problem before turning to the literature? Not surprising, this is often the case when students begin their research projects. The answer to the question is for the budding researcher to use the literature review to achieve a greater focus for the research.

It is a good idea to begin with an idea about some aspect of the general topic that seems particularly interesting—for example, something from the student's life experience or the experiences of friends or family members. It could be an article in a newspaper or a story on a television news or opinion program. It could be something seen in a textbook or an issue discussed in a classroom. It could be a topic as broad as taxation, unemployment, the impact of technology on family life, workplace diversity, gender issues, disproportionate distribution of resources, or environmental degradation. All that is is an interest in a topic.

The first step in the literature review is to examine a relevant index of articles or a library catalog. The researcher should then scan the several journal articles or books to see what parts of the broad topic are of most interest. It will not take long to go from just having a tentative interest in an unfocused topic to becoming focused on an interesting problem that can be researched.

Searching the literature to break the larger problem down into subproblems can facilitate the remaining steps in the research process.

Establish Problem Subareas, Components, or Factors

Once the researcher has settled on a problem or circumstance that requires more information, the next step is to break that broad problem into as many parts or subproblems as are feasible. Say, for example, the researcher decides upon this problem: "How can the level of service provided to outpatient disabled veterans be improved without raising hospital operating costs?" Here is a partial list of some relevant subproblems of this question:

- The type of organization (e.g., hospital, outpatient clinic, field provider, etc.)
- Type of service that patients require
- Staffing levels
- Queuing system in effect or not
- Location of facility (urban, suburban, rural)
- Prescreening system
- Attitudes of provider staff
- Attitudes of service users
- Expectations of service users
- Operating and other costs

Normally, not all of the possible subareas can or should be included in the research study. Instead, they are prioritized, and only the most important are included. Limiting the final choice of factors to be included in the study are (1) what the researcher can do in the time allowed, and (2) what will give the greatest payback for the time and labor resources expended.

Determine What Is to Be Measured

Once the researcher has identified the problem to study, the next step is to determine which relevant components should be measured. For example, say that a researcher is confronted with a problem pertaining to school dropouts. Should the researcher collect data on local economic conditions, neighborhoods, schools, ethnic groups, families, peer groups, students who drop out, students who do not drop out, or students below a certain age, students above that age? Each option will produce very different information.

In another example, say that the research problem is gender abuse. Should the researcher gather data on men, women, children, family dyads, parents, or some other combination of subjects? If the research topic deals with problems faced by persons with hearing disabilities, should the researcher study society in general, employers, service providers, persons with hearing disabilities, or persons without hearing disabilities?

Related to this question is one of *accessibility*. If the element or subject to be measured is a person, that subject must have the needed information, be willing to share the information with the researcher, speak the researcher's language, and be able to put into words why the person behaved in a certain way. The same problems exist for all possible measurement elements.

Determine Relevant Variables

Researchers investigate and test variables. A variable is anything that changes in value or varies in some way. Thus, variables are phenomena that can be "measured" in some way. Said another way, variables are study questions that have been rephrased into testable statements.

For example, the high school dropout phenomenon is a *study question*, whereas the annual rate of dropouts is a *variable* that can be measured. Another variable is the gender of the dropout; others are the dropout's age, ethnic group, the level of education of the dropout's parents, the location of the dropout's residence, and many more.

Another variable relating to this issue is the dropout's attitudes or opinions about education in general. Other variables are the effectiveness of the dropout's teachers, the dropout's need to work in order to help support a family, and any similar measurement. A listing of some of the types of variables researchers use is displayed in Figure 5.2.

There are several ways to identify variables. One way is to divide variables into two categories based on the type of numerical measurements they provide. These are *categorical* and *continuous* variables. Categorical variables identify a limited number of possible categories. Gender is an example, with just two categories possible: female or male.

Continuous variables, on the other hand, can have an unlimited number of values. Values for continuous variables can be measured on a continuous scale (such as weights or height in inches). They are not restricted to specific, discrete categories or values, as are categorical variables. Attitude scales that provide continuous data are used often in public administration research. Researchers are concerned with mean (average) scores on a scale, not the response category (score) of any single subject.

Variable:
> A characteristic, quantity, or anything of interest that can have different values. Examples include saving account amounts, stock prices, package designs, weight, monthly sales, gender, and salaries. The values of variables may be said to be either *continuous* or *categorical.*

Independent variable:
> A variable that functions as the causal element in a hypothesis. A change in the value of an independent variable is said to "cause" a positive or negative change in a dependent variable. An example is the independent variable "poverty" in the hypothesis "Poverty causes crime."

Dependent variable:
> The second part of a causal hypothesis, a change in the value of a dependent variable is hypothesized to have been "caused" by a change in the level of the independent variable. In the hypothesis "Poverty causes crime," the level of crime is the dependent variable.

Intervening variable:
> Sometimes referred to as a *control variable,* an intervening variable lies between an independent and a dependent variable. A change in the intervening variable must be "caused" by the independent variable; this change then "causes" the change in the dependent variable. For example, in the hypothesis "Workplace stress causes physical illness, which causes absenteeism," physical illness is the intervening variable.

Conditional variable:
> This variable establishes the antecedent conditions necessary for change in the dependent variable. The values of a conditional variable influence the level of impact that the independent and intervening variables have on a dependent variable. In the example "Poverty causes substance abuse, causing HIV-positive rates to increase wherever needle-exchange programs are proscribed," the existence of needle exchange programs is the conditional variable.

Study variable:
> A variable whose cause or effect status the researcher is trying to discover through research. The study variable can be an independent variable, a dependent variable, an intervening variable, or a conditional variable.

Continuous variable:
> Quantities that can take any value within a range of measurements, such as weight or percentage of increase in the price of a stock, are said to be continuous.

Categorical variable:
> Categorical variables (sometimes called *discrete* variables) have values that can vary only in specific steps or categories.

Figure 5.2 **A Classification of Types of Variables**

A second way of looking at variables is whether they are *dependent* or *independent*. This dichotomy is important in causal research designs. Dependent variables are variables that are influenced in some way by another variable or variables. Independent variables are the variables that act upon the dependent variables. For example, the dependent variable *voting behavior* can be influenced by many different factors, such as the type of political contest involved or the income, education, occupation, or age of the voters and nonvoters.

Establish Research Hypotheses

The *hypothesis* is the fundamental building block of all scientific research. It defines the research topic and the researcher's ideas about it. Hypotheses can be defined in many different ways. One way is to look at the hypothesis as the researcher's ideas about a relationship between two phenomena (variables). Shaughnessy and Zechmeister (1994) defined a hypothesis as nothing more than a "tentative explanation for something."

Hypotheses are tentative answers to the "How?" and "Why?" questions about the research problem. No research should be started before one or more testable hypotheses have been written.

There are two types of hypotheses: *causal* or *noncausal*. With causal hypotheses, the researcher proposes that *event or activity A causes C to happen*. An example is: "Poverty *causes* juvenile crime." In this sense, the hypothesis is suggested as the reason for the occurrence of the phenomenon called "juvenile crime."

In a noncausal hypothesis, the researcher surmises that *A and B are caused by C*. In this example, A and B can be said to be *correlated* (associated). However, in the absence of any further proof, it is not possible to say that either A or B "causes" the other (Van Evera 1997). An example of this type of hypothesis is: "High rates of high school dropouts and high rates of teenage pregnancies are caused by poverty." This hypothesis does not say that dropping out of high school causes increases in the rate of pregnancies among teenage females. The high school dropout phenomenon and teen pregnancies are related, but neither "causes" the other.

Hypotheses must be written so no questions can be raised about the concepts that underlie them. This requires preparing clear and concise *definitions* for all variables, constructs, and concepts and spelling out all assumptions relating to the study. Hypotheses must always be written in ways that allow for their scientific testing. Such metaphysical concepts as beliefs or faith should never be used as the basis for a hypothesis because they cannot be empirically tested.

Establish Research Objective and Relevant Subobjectives

Research objectives are statements of what the researcher wants to accomplish by completing the research activity. They are related directly to the study question. For example, the director of a program designed to help single parents receiving public assistance make the move to full-time employment might be concerned that the program participation rate is declining while the numbers of parents receiving assistance is not declining. Why enrollment is declining is a key study question. Identifying ways to reverse the decline might be the program director's main research objective. Subobjectives might include the following:

- Identifying characteristics of clients who participate in the program
- Determining reasons why they elected to participate
- Identifying characteristics of clients who do not participate in the program
- Determining reasons why they elected not to participate
- Identifying barriers to participation
- Identifying what incentives might entice more qualified people to participate
- Determining what successes other programs have had and whether they may be transplanted to the local program

Clearly, the above subobjectives are only a partial list of the possible factors the director may wish to include in the study.

Conduct Pilot Study to Redefine Variables, Objectives, and Subobjectives

Pilot-testing the study instrument or discussion guide is a critical step in the research process. No matter how close they might be to a problem, program, or issue under study, researchers are very different from their research subjects. They do not look at variables in the same way. The working definitions of variables and issues are also different. Without a thorough pretest of the data-gathering scheme, the probability of encountering a study error is significantly greater than it would be with a pretest.

An example of the value of a pretest occurred when the author designed a questionnaire to gather information about commercial fishermen for the manufacturer of rainwear. In exploratory discussions with key informants, the phrase "In what area of the industry do you work?" was used to differentiate fishermen from fish processors, suppliers, bankers, and others. The open-ended question was included in the draft instrument. Most respondents assumed that the question to implied a geographic location; their answers were "Alaska," "Washington," "Oregon Coast," and so on. The question was changed to a checklist of possible occupational areas before the survey was administered to the full sample. Without the pretest, this question would have provided neither the researcher nor the client with the information desired.

Finding a Research Focus

The second problem researchers often face is this: *What part of this problem should I study, and what parts should I ignore?* This is a question of *focus*. Making a few relatively easy decisions about the focus of the study early will make it easier to gather the data, interpret what's in the data, and then organize ideas into a meaningful research report later.

One way to address the issue of *research focus* is for the researcher to establish the *point of view* proposed for the topic and the research project. Making this determination early in the study establishes the method of gathering the required information. Narrowing the study's focus also makes it easier to organize the final report. *Organizing* the report means deciding what goes first in the paper, what goes second, and so on.

Once the researcher has decided on a topic, there are many options on how to approach the study of the topic. According to Seech (1993), research studies and their reports can follow one of five different approaches:

- Thesis or "position" studies
- Compare-and-contrast studies
- Analysis studies
- Summary studies
- Basic research studies

A *thesis* or *position* study is one in which the researcher begins by stating a position, either his or her own or some other person's or group's. This is then followed by arguments for or against the point of view. Various types of evidence are presented to support one viewpoint and/or refute the others. Political candidates regularly issue position papers in which they spell out their support or lack of support for such things as tax increases, school budgets, and welfare expenditures. The evidence presented in such papers is usually the product of a research project. It can be acquired by using qualitative research methods to gather anecdotes, testimonials, or analogies or by using quantitative research methods involving statistical analysis.

Compare-and-contrast studies are used to compare two or more ideas, methods, proposals, or positions. First, each approach is defined and discussed. Research is usually necessary to fully develop each position. This is followed by a section in which key points or threads are pointed out. This is then followed by a more detailed discussion of the differences. The researcher then selects one argument and uses supportive evidence to explain to readers why that argument is best. Again, research is used to come up with the evidence.

Analysis studies are closely related to generic research reports, often following a similar structure. These studies require the researcher to carry out an in-depth analysis of an *idea*. Examples include such public administration issues as privatizing services, adopting user fees for services, and spending limitations. The researcher's opinions are typically included in analysis reports.

The investigator reviews and summarizes existing literature on a topic, then writes an analytical summary interpreting the information for the reading audience. For example, a researcher might be assigned to research and write a report about how passage of a people's initiative putting a cap on state automobile excise taxes affects the state highway department's plans to reinforce bridges to comply with federal earthquake damage requirements. The researcher will first go to the published literature to review trends and developments on all the topics. This review could be followed by a series of interviews with department and budget administrators to establish their opinions about delaying work on some bridges, finding cheaper ways to do the required work, or identifying other revenue sources.

Summary studies are detailed summaries of a topic or issue. They are much like an expanded version of the *review of the literature* section of other types of studies. These summary report studies include a brief introduction defining and describing the topic, then move immediately into a summary of what other researchers or practitioners have said about the topic. Unlike analysis studies, summary reports often do not require the author to subjectively interpret the previous research, but only to summarize what others have reported.

Seech's last style or approach to research studies is the *basic research* study. The form followed in research studies is rooted in the earliest traditions of scientific research. The scientific method approach to research evolved out of this tradition. Social science and administrative research, therefore, usually follows a structure similar to research for such disciplines as chemistry or biology.

When conducting a basic research study, the researcher designs and conducts a data-gathering project. The researcher may elect to follow a qualitative or a quantitative approach. In either approach, the data is either *primary data* or *secondary data*. Collecting *primary data* means the researcher gathers "new" information. This might mean conducting a survey with a questionnaire, carrying out a series of personal interviews, employing content analysis on published documents, or conducting an experiment. Afterward, the gathered primary data are processed (often with computers) and interpreted. The researcher can then draw relevant conclusions and make recommendations

Research to collect *secondary data* means getting most of the information from already published sources. However, these data can be found in libraries, on the Internet, or in internal publications, among other sources. Because this material has already been published, the researcher must use extreme care to report all the sources of material used in the report. The report must not be just a repeat of what others have written. Rather, the research report must include the researcher's *interpretation* of what others have written. In his book on writing about art, Barnet (1993, 176) said this about using secondary data in research reports:

> A research report is not merely an elaborately footnoted presentation of what a dozen scholars have already said about a topic; it is a thoughtful evaluation of the available evidence, and so it is, finally, an expression of what the author thinks the evidence adds up to.

Finding Information About a Topic

Writing a research report means that the researcher must first do research. There is no way to get out of it. However, there are a number of different ways to go about this task. The researcher can work in a library, examining written, recorded, or filmed sources. Or the researcher can sit in front of a computer screen and do the research electronically. The researcher can interview subjects at work, at play, shopping, or anywhere it is possible to gain access to them. The researcher can sit with a telephone in a central location and ask respondents questions from a survey questionnaire. Or the researcher can design and conduct either a laboratory or field experiment, or both.

Assuming that the topic has been narrowed down to something that sounds interesting, the researcher gathers preliminary information by conducting a comprehensive review of the published literature on the topic and its various subtopics. There are three ways to locate this literature:

1. Dive straight into the library stacks and begin the search by pulling out books, periodicals, reference materials, government documents, and other reference works that just might seem interesting.
2. Examine computerized, *on-line library catalogs*. These list most library materials, including books, journals, videos, and CD-ROMS,

filing items by subject, author, and title. (Although highly unlikely, some or all of this information might still be stored in card catalog form. If so, the concepts and methods to follow are the same as if the data were available on-line.)

3. Refer to a *commercial database*; almost all will be found on-line. For example, *ABI/INFORM*, the business periodical CD-ROM database, is now available via the Internet, allowing access to information from any networked computer.

Traditional Library Research

Researchers call all previously published information secondary literature—regardless of the form in which it is recorded. It is called secondary because it is information that has been gathered by someone else. Published government statistics on aging, for example, are secondary data. Accounting information in an agency's annual report is secondary data. A report on regional economic conditions published by the federal government or a local bank is secondary data. Tables, charts, and graphs from textbooks or city, county, and federal government documents or international organizations such as the United Nations are secondary sources. All information contained in previously published reports, magazines, and journals are secondary data.

It is the nature of academic research to find that, usually, more than one person is or has been interested in the same topic. As with fashions, researchers often follow fads. This means that there will often be many possible sources of information about the chosen topic—sometimes more sources than the researcher can deal with. Therefore, one of the researcher's first tasks is to narrow the topic down to a manageable scope. For example, for an eight-page report on economics, a researcher cannot cope with 200 sources. Instead, examining eight to a dozen at most is manageable.

In summary, researchers are encouraged to do what Lester and Lester (1992) recommended: "Start your research with a narrowed or *focused* topic—and begin with a *plan*."

Begin with a Research Plan

Efficient library research always begins with a plan. This means starting with a general topic, then focusing on relevant parts of that topic. The researcher must decide on what key words to begin with. Say that a student has been given a general assignment to research and write something about how computers have impacted ethical standards and practices in business. The student might start the search in the library catalog (cards or electronic) or in a special index of articles in a discipline, looking up a general subject, such as business ethics. The Business Periodicals Index is an example of a comprehensive list of articles in a discipline; similar sources are compiled for nearly every discipline. These indexes (also called indices) are available either in CD-ROM or on-line databases.

Despite the phenomenal increase in the availability of information from electronic sources, libraries are still filled with books and add hundreds if not thousands of new books to their collections each year. And, they still subscribe to many printed periodicals and other resource materials. Accessing much—but not all—of the information in the library has been made easier and faster through the use of computers and on-line databases.

It is important to remember that a large database might return hundreds or even thousands of titles on a topic. The researcher should narrow the search down by using *qualifiers*. These limit the search to only topics that match the focus of the study. For example, a researcher could narrow down a broad topic like *ethics* to something like *ethics in government*, or *ethics and computers*. The topic can be focused even more this way: *government ethics and computers in Michigan*. Restricting the search to a specific year could make it even narrower.

Most library research begins with periodical literature. Periodicals are scholarly journals, magazines, or newspapers that are published *periodically* (daily, weekly, monthly, quarterly, etc.). Journals contain articles and research reports on relatively narrow topics, written by people who work in or know a lot about a particular career field. They are an excellent source of background information on most topics.

Once the researcher has found an interesting article listing and its abstract (if available), the full article can usually be accessed from either the library stacks, microfilm, interlibrary loan, or the full-text provisions of many databases. Whatever else is done, it is always good to start the research with a visit to a reference librarian!

Research Using Electronic Sources

Electronic sources of information for research studies are often erroneously grouped under the single label, the Internet. The Internet is just one of a wide variety of electronic sources. Other important electronic sources include on-line databases, CD-ROM databases, local area networks, and library networks. Another important part of the Internet is the cooperative education and research network called Bitnet (today, Bitnet is used primarily for e-mail and electronic discussion groups or conferences, which are called listservs).

The Internet is a vast international network of computer networks. Hardware ranges in size from individual desktop computers to supercomputers used for complex scientific modeling. All kinds of information have been made available through the connecting of this huge network of computers; not all of it is true; not all of it is acceptable for research.

Anyone, including private citizens, universities, research laboratories, companies, and government agencies, can place information on the Internet, change it at any time, or take it off. The information stored on those computers is accessed through the *World Wide Web* (WWW, or simply the Web). It is this complete accessibility that creates potential problems for users of the Internet.

The committee on new technologies for research of the Modern Language Association (MLA) had this to say about problems with Internet sources:

> We want researchers to look at more than the Web, for the sake of historical concerns. Many important things aren't on the Web. Also, researchers must learn how to cite Web sites. And we have to learn how to read Web sites critically. . . . How do you know if what you're reading is fact? What are the credentials of the person who posed the information? The very quality that makes the Internet an attractively egalitarian tool—anybody can say anything and send it anywhere—makes it problematic for researchers. (Keller 1998, C 2)

Search Tools

Researchers use two tools to search for information on the Web. The first is known as an *Internet directory*. These directories index information from many different sources, which is then stored in various databases. There are many different such collections of information; each deals with some particular aspect of research information. For example, one database indexes only economics literature; another index lists articles and papers from 375 life-science journals. For topical information about anything in the news, an on-line news, and current affairs database is also available.

The second way to search for information on the Web is using *search engines*. Search engines allow you to search the Web for information on any subject, such as companies, products, agencies and organizations, by using keywords.

If these search engines cannot find the desired information, more powerful programs can often be accessed. They are particularly effective for search on obscure topics because they search multiple search engines at the same time, retrieving as many documents as possible with one search. Most eliminate duplicate listings as they search. A reference librarian can direct the researcher to these tools.

On-Line Databases

Today, most literature search information is accessed using on-line databases. Until very recently, many if not most of these were available only as CD-ROM databases. Now, CD-ROMs are used almost exclusively for such resources as encyclopedias and special-interest compilations of sight and sound.

A number of different databases may be found in each of several different categories of information. For example, the business and economics areas are served by at least ten different databases, sixteen on-line databases are available in the natural and health sciences disciplines, and eight databases index articles and other information in the news and current events collection.

The following databases contain citations and full-text listings of scholarly and popular articles on public administration, economics, and business administration (Note: Not all libraries subscribe to every possible source).

- *EBSCOhost (Academic Search Full Text Elite)*: This is a comprehensive index to more than 3,100 scholarly (academic) journals and general periodicals in all subject areas.
- *EconLit*: This is the key database for economics information; it also includes reports on public administration and public policy issues.
- *ABI/INFORM Global*: This database covers U.S. and international professional publications, academic journals, and trade magazines.
- *Business & Industry*: This database indexes leading trade magazines, newsletters, the general business press, and international business newspapers.
- *Organizations, Agencies, and Publications Directory*: This is a global directory of new and established organizations, agencies, and publications.

Summary

Information about a research topic can come from already published sources—what is called *secondary data*—or it can be gathered directly from the first or primary source by the researcher or research team in what is called *primary data*. Most research involves a combination of these approaches. The researcher first identifies a study topic, looks to the published literature to gain more information or additional insights into the problem or issue, and then gathers primary data as needed.

A seven-step process can aid the researcher in defining the research problem. These steps are: (1) relate the problem to the program mission and objectives; (2) review the background of the problem, usually by conducting a literature review; (3) break down the problem into its subareas, components, or factors; (4) determine what should be measured; (5) select the most relevant variables; (6) establish testable research hypotheses; (7) establish an objective for the research and relevant subobjectives; (8) conduct a pilot study to check on the validity of the variables, measurements, and hypotheses. The pilot study is also used to redefine any or all variables and hypotheses, if necessary, and to determine whether the objectives and subobjectives can be achieved.

Once the literature review is completed, the researcher decides which factors or components of the study question require more information. Then the researcher either delves deeper into the published literature or designs a research project for acquiring the needed additional information.

Suggested Reading

Adams, Gerald R., and Jay D. Schvaneveldt. 1985.*Understanding Research Methods.* New York: Longman.

Anastas, Jeane W., and Marian L. MacDonald. 1994. *Research Design for Social Work and the Human Services.* New York: Lexington Books.

Shaughnessy, John J., and Eugene B. Zechmeister. 1994. *Research Methods in Psychology.* 3d ed. New York: McGraw-Hill.

Wildavsky, Aaron. 1993. *Craftways: On the Organization of Scholarly Work.* 2d ed. New Brunswick, NJ: Transaction.

6 Research Designs

Researchers in the social and administrative sciences are no longer required to follow a single design for their investigations. Instead, today many different approaches are possible. To clarify this great variety of options in research designs, they can be grouped into just three broad categories: *qualitative*, *quantitative*, and *combined* designs. Each design supports a variety of methods for gathering data, and each allows the researcher a variety of analysis and interpretation approaches. A key task of the director of the research project is selecting the appropriate strategy for the research problem and study objectives. This selection task is known as the process of developing a *research design.*

An important thing to remember about research design selection is that the researcher is never locked into using any one "best" design. There are many acceptable ways to conduct research; the only selection criterion that makes sense is that the method chosen must provide the best possible conclusions. Phillips (1976, 5) described the research process as a Magna Carta for the researcher; he added:

> [The researcher] is not chained to a set of techniques simply because they have worked adequately in the past, nor must [he or she] defer to the supposedly superior methodological knowledge of other investigators because of their research reputation. It is not necessary for [researchers] to continually look back over [their] shoulder, wondering if others would consider [the] procedure to be "correct" or incorrect. . . . What counts is not what others think of those procedures but how well they work.

The key to good research results is always to do "good science." As Eisner (1997, 261) noted:

> Increasingly, researchers are recognizing that scientific inquiry is a species of *research*. Research is not merely a species of social science. Virtually any careful, reflective, systematic study of phenomena undertaken to advance human understanding can count as a form of research. It all depends on how that work is pursued.

Researchers spend considerable time and effort selecting their design. As always, the nature of the problem to be researched and the data to be acquired will establish the researcher's options. For now, all that is necessary is for researchers to understand what their options are. Therefore, the following pages are devoted to an introductory discussion of the three basic forms of research designs: *quantitative*, *qualitative*, and *combined*. The relationship of three strategies, together with some of the approaches used in each design, is displayed in Figure 6.1.

Quantitative Research Designs

Quantitative research strategies are employed in a sequence of steps (Figure 6.2). Until recently, many research traditionalists maintained the opinion that quantitative research methods used in most physical or natural sciences research were the only appropriate approach to follow with any scientific research problem. Among these traditionalists, the watchword for "good science" is measurement: "If it can't be measured, it can't be studied."

While this may no longer be the dominant opinion in research, quantitative studies still outnumber other approaches by far. For proof, a glance at any social or administrative science professional journal will usually support the contention.

Questions and Statistical Tests

In deciding what strategy to follow in a quantitative design, public administration researchers usually seek answers to these six basic questions (Miller 1991):

1. What characteristics of the people in my sample (such as demographic differences) distinguish them from other groups or subgroups of people whom I might have included in my study?
2. Are there any differences in the subgroups contained in this sample that might influence the way the questions are answered or the opinions that are offered?
3. Is there any statistically significant difference in the answers of any groups or subgroups in this sample, or did they all answer the questions in roughly the same way?
4. What confidence can I have that any difference that I do find did not occur by chance?
5. Is there any association between any two or more variables in my study? Is it relevant? Is it significant?

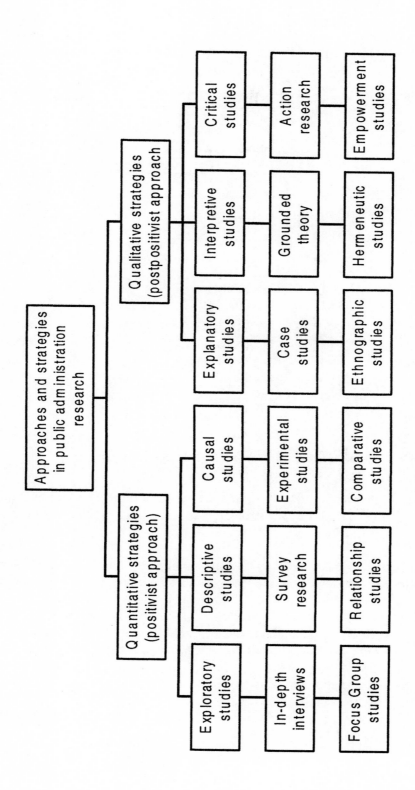

Figure 6.1 A Brief Introduction to the Variety of Possible Research Approaches

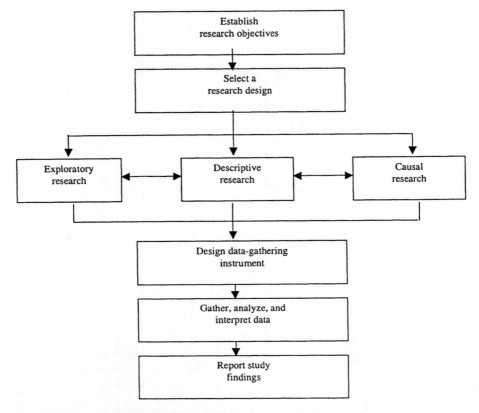

Figure 6.2 **Quantitative Strategies in the Research Process**

6. If there is any relationship between two or more variables, is it possible to measure how strong it is and whether it is a positive or negative relationship?

The statistical tests typically used in quantitative public administration research to answer questions such as these include, but are not limited to, the following:

- Measures of central tendency, variability, and/or dispersion
- Graphic methods, such as tables, charts, and graphs
- Hypothesis tests
- Association (correlation) tests
- Regression analysis
- A few tools for specific purposes, such as *time series* and *quality tests*

Three Types of Quantitative Designs

Depending on their research objectives, researchers select from three types of quantitative research designs: exploratory, descriptive, or causal. In each of these approaches, one or more of a variety of statistical tools are used to test ideas and to communicate research findings. The researcher may begin with a small-sample, exploratory study designed to provide the information needed for developing a questionnaire (also called a survey instrument or simply an instrument) for carrying out a large-sample, descriptive study.

The exploratory study may be used to identify the key dependent and independent variables that will be tested in an experiment (a *causal design*). Or the researcher may elect to use all three approaches, beginning with an exploratory study for insights and ideas, then going to a descriptive study to define the salient variables, and concluding with a causal study to test the variables for cause-and-effect relationships.

For more complex studies, a host of powerful multivariate statistical tools have been developed to aid the researcher. Some of these will be discussed in later chapters.

Exploratory Designs

Exploratory studies are small-sample designs used primarily for gaining insights and ideas about research problems and the variables and issues associated with those problems. These types of studies are sometimes referred to as "pilot studies."

Exploratory studies are often employed as the first step in a multipart research project. Because of their limited scope, however, they seldom stand alone. Exploratory studies help the researcher gain greater understanding of the problem for which more information is needed. They also help the researcher identify variables that may be only tangentially or marginally related and thus that should not be included in a more extensive research effort.

Data gathering in exploratory research may involve quantitative, qualitative, or a combination of strategies. The data may come from either primary or secondary sources; that is, it may be gathered directly by the researcher, or it may be data gathered by someone else for a different purpose. Both data types have similar validity in exploratory research.

Exploratory research designs often involve conducting personal interviews with knowledgeable individuals from within and/or outside of the organization. These individuals are called "key informants," and the process is known as *key informant interviews*. These subjects are selected because they are likely to be well informed about the study problem and the issues associated with that problem. For example, the author was part of a team engaged to design and conduct an extensive community needs analysis for a regional general hospital. The team's first step in the study was to conduct a series of in-depth interviews with key local employers, community leaders, hospital administrators, and senior medical staff. These data were then developed into a comprehensive needs-analysis questionnaire administered throughout a three-community region. The hospital administrative staff in its presentation to the hospital district board of directors also used the findings of the exploratory study. The report provided evidence that a larger, in-depth survey was needed to complete the district's ten-year development plan.

Focus-group interview sessions with groups of six to ten representative subjects are another common exploratory research strategy. A major benefit of group interviews is the potential interaction among participants, which is impossible to achieve in one-on-one interviews. Focus groups are also more efficient than a series of individual in-depth interviews. A major disadvantage of focus groups is the fear of public embarrassment, which sometimes makes it difficult, if not impossible, to bring up sensitive issues.

A third approach used in exploratory research studies is to survey a small random sample drawn from the same population of interest—what is called a "pilot survey." A commonly used purpose of a pilot study is for pretesting a draft of a survey questionnaire. Results of the exploratory study are used only to test the validity and reliability of the study design and the instrument questions. Problem words, phrases, and entire questions may be edited, deleted, or replaced. Results of such pilot studies should never be included with the findings of the final study.

Another purpose of exploratory research studies is to provide the researcher with greater insight into the study problem and ideas about the variables that should be included in a larger or more comprehensive study to follow. In addition, the findings of an exploratory study can be used to train data gatherers and help the researcher design and test a data-processing plan. Equally important, the findings of an exploratory study can provide guidance to the researcher in rephrasing the study question. They can also require the imposition of totally new variables into the study.

Descriptive Designs

Descriptive research designs are used to develop a snapshot of a particular phenomenon of interest. Descriptive studies typically involve large samples. They provide a description of an event or define a set of attitudes, opinions, or behaviors that are observed or measured at a given time and in a environment. The focus of descriptive research is the careful mapping out of a circumstance, situation, or set of events to describe what is happening or what has happened (Rosenthal and Rosnow 1991).

Descriptive studies may be either *cross-sectional* or *longitudinal*. The snapshot study is called a cross-sectional design. It is a one-shot assessment of a sample of respondents. Time is an important consideration because the "picture of the sample" usually varies—sometimes substantially—if the research is repeated at a later date or conducted with another sample taken from the same population. Descriptive research that is repeated with the same sample over two or more time intervals is known as longitudinal *research*. Studies using panels of participants are longitudinal studies. The purpose of a longitudinal study is to identify and measure *change* in the subjects' responses.

Researchers use two related but different types of descriptive research approaches, *field studies* or *field surveys*. Field studies tend to go into greater depth on a smaller number of issues or items. They may use face-to-face or telephone interviewing techniques for data gathering. The survey instruments often include "branching questions" that require a different set of questions for subjects who respond differently at a given place or "branch" in the instrument. They may also involve one or more open-ended questions. Such questions require far more effort for coding and tabulating than is needed for the fixed response items found in field surveys.

Field surveys are the most commonly encountered approach in the administrative, social, and human sciences; they make up more than 80 percent of all quantitative research. Surveys are popular because they are relatively easy to design and administer. The wide availability of powerful desktop computers and statistical software today makes them easy to tabulate and interpret.

Both field studies and field surveys produce data that are used as numeric *descriptions*. These descriptions may be of a *sample* of subjects or from an entire *population*. Many different types of variables can be used, including but not limited to demographic characteristics, attitudes, opinion, intentions, characteristics of organizations, groups, families, subgroups, and so on. In essence, almost anything that can be measured can be a descriptive variable.

Causal Designs

Causal research studies are often the last step in a three-part approach to research into a problem in the administrative and social sciences. They require designing and conducting *experiments*. In experiments, researchers must control for confounding or intervening variables while testing hypotheses about differences and/or relationships. Because they are usually difficult to arrange with human subjects, experiments are used far more often in laboratory conditions than in practical or applied public administration research.

Causal studies may be either *relational* or *experimental*. The purpose of relational studies is to identify how one or more variables are related to one another. They are sometimes called *correlation* studies. The purpose of an experimental causal study is to identify the cause or causes of *change* in a variable or event—that is, to determine "what leads to what" (Rosenthal and Rosnow 1991).

Designing an experiment is the key activity in a causal research project. Experiments involve subjecting two or more samples or subsamples to different treatments. Researchers may manipulate one, two, or more independent variables in the same treatment experiment. "Treatments" can be any relevant characteristic or phenomena:

- Different teaching methods (lecture vs. experiential)
- Testing the efficacy of a new drug vs. a placebo
- Tests of the impact of two different levels of expenditures on a social program
- Different communications media

Researchers must be careful in the design of experiments and interpretation of the findings so that potential intervening or confounding variables do not muddy the results of the study. The set of experiments conducted at the Western Electric manufacturing facility at Hawthorne, New Jersey, illustrates the need for careful attention to experimental design. They also reveal how experiments can themselves affect the behavior that they are supposed to measure.

A random sample of assembly workers was selected, moved to a special location, and subjected to variations of working conditions. These included changes in the speed of the production line, lighting levels, rest periods, and others. Researchers measured workers' performance under normal conditions—the *pretest*. They then changed a working condition characteristic (i.e., a *variable*). Worker performance was then measured again after the change—the *posttest*.

To their surprise, production increased with negative environment changes just as much as it did with positive changes. The design had not considered the effect on workers of being singled out for attention. This unplanned change is what is known as an *intervening* or *confounding* variable.

Experiments can involve manipulating (making changes to) a single independent variable or two or more variables. The changes are referred to as *different treatments*. For example, a park administrator might want to know whether increasing the fee for campsite use will reduce or increase the need for maintenance personnel at the campground. Two or three similar sites with comparable usage levels could be selected, with different fees charged in each test site (the treatment is the different fee). The administrator might use damage to campsites over the test period as a measurement of the need for more or fewer maintenance personnel. At the end of a designated test period, results at the three sites would be compared.

Manipulating two or more variables is also possible. For example, agricultural researchers often vary amounts of both fertilizer and irrigation, measuring the effects of different combinations on crop production. In a three-factor experiment, the researcher might also include different types of soil (such as clay, sandy loam, etc.) as another of the test variables.

Qualitative Research Designs

Qualitative research is not based on a single, unified theoretical concept, nor does it follow a single methodological approach. Rather, a variety of theoretical approaches and methods are involved (Flick 1999). All of these approaches and methods have one common underlying objective: understanding of the event, circumstance, or phenomenon under study. Thus, description is less important than the researcher's interpretation of the event, circumstance, or phenomenon. To achieve qualitative study objectives, researchers analyze the interaction of people with problems or issues. These interactions are studied in their context and then subjectively explained by the researcher.

Figure 6.3 displays the interconnected nature of the qualitative process. In all three approaches, several different techniques may be employed for gathering data, including *observation*, *participation*, *interviewing*, and *document analysis*. In each, data are coded, placed in some intelligent order, interpreted, and used for explaining and/or predicting future interrelationships in similar circumstances.

Flick (1999) has identified the following features of qualitative research that help to differentiate these methods from positivist quantitative approaches:

- Diverse theories underlying the approach
- Diverse perspectives of the participants
- Reflexivity of the researcher and the research (i.e., responses to each other)
- Variety of approaches and methods
- Reconstructing cases as a starting point
- Construction of reality as a basis for the research
- Use of text as empirical data

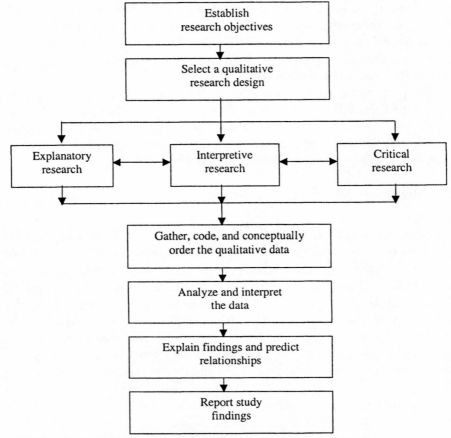

Figure 6.3 Qualitative Strategies in the Research Process

Three Types of Qualitative Designs

Broadly speaking, qualitative strategies fall into three categories of study techniques. These are *explanatory*, *interpretive*, and *critical* designs (White 1999). These approaches can be applied to many different types of studying, including *ethnography*, *kinetics* (the study of movement), *atmospherics*, *phenomenology*, and *proxemics* (the study of space in social settings). Qualitative research also includes the use of such data-gathering methods as focus groups and elite-group interviewing and the use of unobtrusive measures.

Explanatory Research

Explanatory research is the approach taken in most mainstream qualitative research. Its goal is to go beyond the traditional descriptive designs of the positivist approach to provide meaning as well as description. The purpose of explanatory research is also broader than descriptive research; it is conducted to *build theories* and *predict events*. According to White (1999, 44):

> Explanatory research strives to build theories that explain and predict natural and social events. Theory building requires the development of a collection of related and testable law-like statements that express causal relationships among relevant variables. The ultimate goal of explanatory research is the control of natural and social events.

Typical objectives for explanatory research include explaining why some phenomenon occurred, interpreting a cause-and-effect relationship between two or more variables, and explaining differences in two or more groups' responses. The design is similar to the traditional positivist approach, and some numerical description and simple statistical analysis may be involved.

Interpretive Research

Interpretive research is characterized by a strong sense of connection between the researcher and the subjects who are a part of an interpretive study. The goal of interpretive research is to build *understanding* between the participants and the researcher. Therefore, interpretive research often focuses on standards, norms, rules, and values held in common, and how these all influence human interactions (White 1999).

The primary objective of interpretive research is to establish the *meaning* of a circumstance, event, or social situation. It goes beyond simple description or explanation in aiming to enhance people's understanding of the symbols, artifacts, beliefs, meanings, feelings, or attitudes of the people in the study situation (White 1999).

Interpretive research has much in common with the study of phenomenology in philosophy and the phenomenological approach to sociological research. Public administration theorist Camilla Stivers (2000, 132) provided this view:

> To me, interpretation entails sense-making: taking a more or less inchoate bundle of events and processes—what might be thought of as a situation or group of situations—and putting a frame around them based on more or less conscious assumptions about what is likely to be important, significant or meaningful.

Interpretive research also plays an important role in the third approach, critical research, and provides the common understanding that is necessary for successful attitude change. In this way, the interpretation of ideas that are associated with Freudian psychoanalysis has become an integral part of critical research.

Critical Research

Critical research is the least-used approach in qualitative research in general and public administration in particular. The subjective nature of critical analysis makes it difficult for students to adopt in meaningful ways. Although it has potential for application in public administration, it has not yet been widely adopted. According to White (1999, 57):

> Criticism is the most radical of the three modes of [qualitative] research because it calls into question our most basic assumptions and asks us to evaluate them as a basis for action. Critical research does not always satisfy the critic, nor does it always change beliefs and values, but it has the potential to do so.

Critical research in public administration has been adopted mostly from sociology research methodology. It also has roots in the criticisms of social structures and the capitalist economic system that emerged in reaction to the excesses of the Industrial Revolution. It reached its highest influence in studies of society's acceptance of tyrannical governments and reactions to propaganda. This research was greatly influenced by the social scientists who fled Nazi-dominated Europe in the 1930s and later helped found the New School for Social Research in New York City.

The purpose of the critical research tradition that emerged from those early foundations was to help citizens overcome the constraints that an oppressive government placed on their freedom and development. "Thus, critical research assumes that people can misunderstand themselves and their situations and that people can be deceived about what is in their own interests" (White 2000, 54).

The overriding objective of critical research is to change people's beliefs and actions in ways that the investigator believes will better satisfy their needs and wants. The criticism points out inconsistencies between what is true and false and what is good and bad. It aims to bring people to actions that are commensurate with accepted truth and goodness. According to White (1999), the "truth" of critical research is only realized when people (through a process of self-reflection) finally take action to change their situation.

Gathering Qualitative Data

The three methods used most often for gathering qualitative data in public administration research are *observation, participation,* and *interviewing.* A fourth method, *document analysis,* is also used, but less often than the first three approaches. However, a variation of document analysis—*hermeneutics*—is rapidly becoming one of the most popular approaches in qualitative research.

Observation Studies

Observation research studies are the least intrusive of all research methods. In this approach, the researcher simply watches and records the social behavior of subjects. This method came into wide acceptance with the growth of *cultural anthropology* for the study of the behavior, beliefs, and customs of primitive cultures. It is still the predominant data-gathering method in anthropological ethnographic studies and is also common in sociological field studies.

With data gathered by observation, researchers must interpret what they see in the light only of the conditions that exist in a culture at a given time. They cannot interpret the data in terms of their own experiences with their own modern culture. The method is gaining increasing acceptance in the study of organizations in both the private and the public sectors (Gummesson 1987). For example, today public administration researchers are using the method to come to a better understanding of the role organizational culture plays in organizational effectiveness.

Observation has very low impact on the social setting because the researcher only watches and records events in the study group or setting, remaining uninvolved in the group's activities or actions. The researcher's goal is to produce an unbiased record of events and behaviors. Extensive field notes must be maintained, however, including what has been described as the "systematic noting and recording of events, behaviors, and artifacts [objects] in the social setting chosen for the study" (Marshall and Rossman, 1999, 107). Analysis of these descriptive records often occurs as an integral part of the data-gathering process (Miles and Huberman 1984).

Participation Studies

Participation research studies are more intrusive than observation approaches. The researchers' involvement in the culture, subculture, clan, group, or organization under study cannot help but have some influence on the study target. Participation requires that the researcher become wholly immersed in the activities and environment of the study group, thereby experiencing and sensing the same reality that members of the study group do.

The goal of a participation research study is to understand what individuals in the group *see, feel,* and/or *hear.* While acting as a participant, the researcher prepares field notes that include a description of the group members' experiences, reactions, and feelings (Marshall and Rossman 1999). For greater understanding, the researcher often includes his or her own experiences in the analysis.

Interviewing Studies

Interviewing is the third method of gathering primary data method used by researchers pursuing qualitative research strategies. Interviewing research is the most intrusive of all qualitative research approaches.

Face-to-face or voice-to-voice (i.e., telephone) interviews may be *structured* or *unstructured.* Structured interviews follow a planned discussion guide in which answers are sought for specific questions. Unstructured interviews are more like conversations between friends. Respondents are left free to bring up whatever topic they wish. The researcher may then probe for more detailed information, but is careful to avoid leading questions or communicating any value judgments. The researcher may, however, ask questions when the responses are terse or the respondent is unable to express needed information.

Face-to-face interviews typically take two or more hours to complete. The researcher must not allow the respondent to ramble excessively or use the interview to continually vent frustration or anger (some such information is valuable, of course, but continual repetitions waste time and other resources).

Combination Research Designs

Combined designs entail using both qualitative and quantitative methods. The three broad classes of combined studies are archival, media, and artifact studies. Techniques used in these types of studies include content analysis, document analysis, and in situ analysis (also known as within-site analysis). Several types of multivariate statistical tools are also used in these designs, including canonical correlation and cluster and factor analysis. These statistical tools all require some subjective (qualitative) interpretation of the data.

Flick (1999, 634) is one of many who now report that good research often requires the use of a combination of quantitative and qualitative approaches:

> It is well known that the juxtaposition "qualitative—quantitative" has sometimes led to not very fruitful controversies and is sometimes used as a schematic demarcation. But the combination of approaches is often truthful as well.

Data-Gathering Methods

Archival studies involve the study of historical records and documents in order to establish an understanding of the circumstances that characterized an event or period. Researchers review the published and unpublished records of an organization, a community, or a culture. McNabb (1968) used this design for a thesis study in mass communications history and persuasive communication. The design required analysis of historical documents dealing with the battle for public acceptance by private power firms and public utilities from 1909 to 1939. Documents included pamphlets, press releases, annual reports, and newspaper articles published during the period.

Media analysis is a similar process, although in media analyses the items studied tend to be current rather than historical. Like archival studies, media analysis often employs *content analysis*, which is a way of organizing content into desired categories and weighing the results. In another example, the author once designed and led a study that involved comparative analysis of London's eight daily newspapers for editorial-content emphasis on the then-controversial plan of Britain's joining the European Union.

In a media analysis study, McNabb (1991) surveyed two hundred years of publications in the newspaper section of the British Library. These included actual and microfilm copies of seventeenth- and eighteenth-century newspapers and other periodicals. The research resulted in a published report on the first one hundred years of publication of one of Great Britain's first daily newspapers and consumer magazines as part of a larger description of the birth and development of the modern consumer society.

Artifact studies (also called *object studies*) owe their emergence to the transposition of archeological methods to the study of modern societies and cultures. An example of a modern use of the method is the investigation and cataloging of items discarded in modern landfills. Researchers use this method to gain a greater understanding of the culture and values of groups.

Summary

This chapter has discussed the various different types of research designs used by researchers in the social, administrative, and natural sciences.

Quantitative research strategies are employed in a sequence of steps. They usually begin with a small-sample, exploratory study to provide information for developing a questionnaire (also called a *survey instrument* or simply an *instrument*). The questionnaire is then used in a large-sample, descriptive study. Or the exploratory study may be used to identify the key dependent and independent variables to be tested in an experiment (a *causal design*). Or the researcher may elect to use all three approaches, gaining insights into the problem with an exploratory study, following with a descriptive study to define the salient variables, and concluding with a causal design to test for cause-and-effect relationships.

Broadly speaking, qualitative strategies fall into three categories of study techniques. These are *explanatory*, *interpretive*, and *critical*. These approaches can be applied to many different study approaches, including ethnography, kinetics, atmospherics, phenomenology, and proxemics.

The three methods used most often for gathering qualitative data in public administration research are unobtrusive observation, participant observation, and personal interviewing. A fourth method, document analysis, is used less frequently.

Some of the methods that combine parts of both quantitative and qualitative approaches include archival studies, media analysis, and artifact studies. Content analysis is the quantitative methods used in these studies, and hermeneutics is the predominant qualitative method.

Suggested Reading

Adams, Gerald R., and Jay D. Schvaneveldt. 1985. *Understanding Research Methods*. New York: Longman.

Folz, David H. 1996. *Survey Research for Public Administration*. Thousand Oaks, CA: Sage.

Kumar, Ranjit. 1996. *Research Methodology*. London: Sage.

Miller, Gerald J., and Marcia L. Whicker, eds. 1999. *Handbook of Research Methods in Public Administration*. New York: Marcel Dekker.

Schwab, Donald P. 1999. *Research Methods for Organizational Studies*. Mahwah, NJ: Lawrence Erlbaum.

Van Evera, Stephen. 1997. *Guide to Methods for Students of Political Science*. Ithaca, NY: Cornell University Press.

White, Jay D. 1999. *The Narrative Foundations of Public Administration Research*. Washington, DC: Georgetown University Press.

Part 3

Quantitative Designs

7 Quantitative Research Fundamentals

The objective of most public administration research is to provide the information needed to improve the quality of the decisions that must be made by managers and administrators. Among their many tasks and responsibilities, administrators of public and nonprofit organizations must establish priorities, identify alternatives and choose options, set and manage budgets, and hire, motivate, and, when necessary, fire employees. They receive, give, or pass on instructions, develop and write plans with objectives and strategies, monitor their staff's performance, and inform higher-level managers about the progress in achieving their objectives. Higher-level managers are often called upon to communicate the organization's progress to outside stakeholders, including voters, bankers, financial analysts, and the general public.

In every one of these tasks, administrators make decisions. They compare two or more alternatives, weigh the costs and benefits of each, and then select and implement the better alternative. To improve the quality of their decisions, administrators often conduct research. In the past, most of this research followed a *quantitative* paradigm, and much still does.

To make effective administrative decisions, managers must know how to conduct quantitative research and how to interpret quantitative data. The proper use of numbers makes communicating easier, faster, and far more effective than the use of words alone.

Statistics and statistical methods cannot be applied, however, until the fundamental nature of measurement is understood. Beginning with a discussion of the four types of measurements, the next several chapters are an introduction to some of the most-used quantitative research designs. The emphasis is on how to use and interpret statistical methods, rather than on the theoretical side of statistical analysis.

Measurement Fundamentals

The key to ensuring that everyone who reads a research report understands the measurements lies in the consistent use of the measurement scale appropriate for the task at hand. In the following discussion, the terms *measurement scale* and *data type* will often be used interchangeably to refer to the numbers used to signify variables and their relevant classes or levels. Quantitative variables are things that can be counted. When different values are assigned to categories of a variable—such as female and male in the variable *gender*—different, but specific, meanings are established.

Four Levels of Measurement

Researchers use four different types of measurement data: (1) nominal, (2) ordinal, (3) interval, and (4) ratio. Statisticians have produced different statistical tests in order to analyze data of each different type.

In differentiating between the scale types, each level or type must meet one or more rules. Moving beyond nominal scales—considered to be the least powerful of the four scales in terms of meaning conveyed—toward higher or more powerful scales requires more rules that must be applied to each type of measurement.

Nominal Data

Nominal data, the least powerful, must pass just one test: *Different numbers must mean different things.* A nominal scale, as the term implies, is simply a *naming* or *classification* number. With these scales, the differences in categories to which a number may be assigned are qualitative differences. This means they are not counts of something but a number that is subjectively assigned to one category in a class that contains more than one group.

With nominal-level data, numbers or labels are used only to differentiate between things. The numbers or labels serve no other purpose or function and supply no additional information. Furthermore, once a number has been assigned to a given category, all other items with the same characteristics must receive the same number label. Just one attribute is singled out, such as gender, and that attribute and only that attribute dictates further classification. Typical examples of nominal or categorical scales include the following:

- The values of 1 and 2 arbitrarily assigned to the categories of female and male
- The values 0 and 1 assigned to service user and nonuser groups
- Numbers used to denote different types of occupations, political party membership, class in college (freshman, sophomore, etc.), newspapers or magazines read

To repeat, for nominal data, the only rule which the data must meet is that different numbers mean different things. The counts of how many times a naming variable appear can only be processed with statistical tests developed for this lowest level data.

Ordinal Data

An ordinal scale supplies more information than does a nominal scale; rules apply as opposed to just one with nominal data. The nominal scale rule—different numbers mean different things—must first be passed. But the second rule is new. It states that *the things being measured can be ranked or ordered along some dimension.* Now, with ordinal data (often simply referred to as *ranked* data), the differences between measures are *quantitative* rather than just qualitative. When things are ordered, they are arranged in some logical sequence or have more or less of a particular characteristic than others in the set. The limitation with ordinal data is that the numbers never state precisely how much more or less difference exists in the scores of the two groups; only *more* or *less* is communicated by these numbers, not *how much* more or less.

A typical use for ordinal scales is to measure people's preferences or rankings for services or things. Much of the data collected by public administrators is based upon ordinal scales. Examples include political opinion questionnaires and citizens' preference ranking.

Interval Data

The third type of measurement data is *equidistant interval*—more commonly referred to simply as *interval.* To qualify as an interval scale, the measurements must now pass three tests. First, the different numbers must mean different things. Second, the things measured can be ranked or ordered on some appropriate dimension. And third—the most important rule—is that *the differences between adjacent levels on the scale are* (or are assumed to be) *equal.*

With interval data, in addition to determining that one scale item falls above or below another, it is now possible to determine exactly *how much* one item differs from another. The differences between levels on the scale can be any size. The zero-point on the scale can be set anywhere on the scale that the researcher wants it to be. The key requirement is that a single-unit change *always* measures the same amount of change in whatever is being measured. The unit gradations within the scale may be as broad or as fine as need be. For example, on a five-point scale, the distance between 3 and 4 or between 4 and 5 might be measured in tenths, in hundreds, thousands, or even finer, but they apply to every part of the scale equally. Thus, one might see *mean* (average) measurements of 3.3, 3.33, or 3.333, depending on the accuracy desired. The distance between 3 and 4, or 1 and 2, never changes, however. Only the fineness of the measurement is changed.

Measuring temperature using the Fahrenheit scale is a good example of interval-scale data. Fahrenheit scales have a zero point, but it is no more important that any other number on the scale. Other examples are grade point averages, dimensions, and IQ scores. Attitude scales using different levels of agreement are assumed to provide interval-level data. This makes attitude scales a highly desired measurement tool for all social and administrative science researchers.

Interval scales provide more information than either nominal or ordinal scales because of the equal distance between measurement points. There are, however, still limitations to the information provided by interval data. For example, because the zero point is set arbitrarily, it is not possible to say that one measure is exactly twice as great or twice as small as another. We cannot say that 100 degrees Fahrenheit is exactly twice as warm as 50 degrees, nor that 35 degrees is half as warm as 70 degrees. Nor can we say that "Strongly Agree" is twice as strong a response as its neighbor, "Agree." We can only say that the differences between single points on the scale are equal. We must turn to the fourth level, *ratio scales*, to make such qualifying statements.

Some analysts decry the practice of calling attitude scales interval data, emphasizing that they are really ordinal. One criticism they put forward as a "law" is: *Do not make interval-level conclusions on ordinal-level data.* Despite this criticism, much published social and administrative science research continues to report statistical processing of attitude scales and their interpretations using statistical tests that assume the data are interval rather than ordinal.

Ratio Data

As with the other three scales or data types, lower-level rules also apply to *ratio* scales. Different numbers must still mean different things, the data can still be ranked or ordered on some dimension, and the intervals between adjacent points are of equal value. The ratio-required fourth rule is that *the measurement scale has an absolute or fixed zero point*—even if it is not used in the specific range of items being measured. Examples of ratio scales are time, distance, mass, and various combinations of these; units sold; number of purchasers; and temperature according to the Celsius scale. In applications of statistics in public administration research, the distinction between interval and ratio is of little practical value. The same statistical tests can be used for either type of data; they are also interpreted in the same manner. As a result, statistical software packages like the Statistical Package for the Social Sciences (SPSS) have combined the two into a single category called scale data, which includes statistical tests for both interval and ratio data.

Applications

Nominal and ordinal data have their own statistics tests; they are considered to provide "nonparametric" data. This means that they do not depend upon the normal distribution of the characteristics of a population, such as the mean. They are said to be "distribution free."

It is inappropriate to use lower-level statistical tests on data from higher-level scales of measurement. However, higher-level tests may be used on lower-level data, although there is seldom any reason to. Using higher-level tests on lower-level data will always provide less information than could be gained using a more appropriate-level test. It is much easier to play by the rules.

Defining "Statistics"

The term *statistics* is used in a number of different ways. It is used to mean the numerical data in a report. Examples include the number of clients served each day, week, or month; hours worked and employees' earnings; costs per unit; turnover rates; performance ratios; age and gender of citizens in the community; and many, many more. The term *statistics* is also used to define the many mathematical techniques and procedures used for collecting, describing, analyzing, and interpreting data. Statistical processes include simple counts of events, the determination of the central values of a group of counts, conducting hypothesis tests, and determining relationships between two variables.

In summary, statistics must be considered as both *numerical data* and the variety of *tools* or techniques that administrators and researchers use to process raw data to make it more meaningful.

Some Important Statistical Terms and Concepts

As in every discipline or management function, a variety of concepts and terms not part of our common language experience are to be found in the study of management statistics. Here are definitions for some of these concepts:

- *Descriptive statistics*: Measurements or numbers used to summarize or describe data sets.
- *Inferential statistics:* Statistical techniques used to make estimates or inferences about the characteristics of interest for a population using the data from a sample data set.
- *Sample:* A portion of a population. The sample is chosen as representative of the entire population.

- *Population:* The set of all elements for which measurements are possible. A population can consist of products, workers, customers, firms, prices, or other items about which the decision maker or manager is interested. Another word used to identify a population is a *universe.*
- *Statistic:* A number used as a summary measure for a sample. For example, "The mean age for the 20 students in the sample is 20.3 years."
- *Parameter:* A numerical value used as a summary measure for a population or universe. For example, in the statement "The mean age for all entering college or university freshmen is 19.1 years," the age of all entering freshmen is a *parameter.*
- *Variable:* A characteristic or quantity that can have different values. Examples include saving account amounts, stock prices, package designs, weight, monthly sales, gender, salaries, and so on. The values of variables may be said to be either *continuous* or *discrete.*
- *Continuous variables:* Quantities that are measured, such as weight or percentage of increase in the price of a stock, are said to be continuous. Values for continuous variables can be measured on a continuous scale, such as weights, and are not restricted to specific, discrete categories or values.
- *Discrete variables:* Discrete variables have values that can vary only in specific steps or categories (they are sometimes called *categorical*). Assuming that we assign in advance the value of 1 for female and 2 for male, the variable *gender* is an example of a discrete variable.
- *Univariate statistics:* Univariate statistics are the statistics describing a single variable. They include such measures as the valid number of responses (frequencies), the mean, median, and mode, and standard deviation.
- *Bivariate statistics:* These are measurements with which two variables are described or compared at the same time. A cross-tabulation table is an example of bivariate statistics in use. Counts, percentages, correlations, difference tests, and many other statistical tests can be carried out with bivariate statistics.
- *Multivariate statistics:* Multivariate statistics, such as *multiple regression analysis*, are statistics used when more than one independent variable influences one dependent variable. For example, public acceptance of a piece of sculpture for a public park is probably influenced by aesthetics, price, fame of the artist, and the like.

Statistics Applications

Statistics can be categorized in several different ways. One way is according to how they are applied. Statistics can be used to describe something or to infer similar measurements in another, larger group. The first of these applications is called *descriptive statistics*; the second application is called *inferential statistics*. *Descriptive statistics* are used to numerically *describe* events, concepts, people, work, and many other things.

Another use of descriptive statistics is for *summarizing* a set of data. A *data set* is simply a collection of a distinct set of measurements. A data set can be as large as the combined total of all measurements of all United States residents taken every ten years for the Census of Population. Or it can be as small as a dozen or so test scores from a midterm examination.

Inferential statistics describe a class of statistics that are used for one or more of the following three purposes:

- To make generalizations about a larger group—called a *population*—from which the sample was taken
- To make estimates or draw conclusions about the characteristics of a population or
- To make predictions about some future event or state of affairs

Note that all of these uses employ measurements of a smaller group (a *sample*) for making *inferences* about a larger group (a *population*). This is why they are known as "inferential" statistics. The term *sample* is used to mean some portion of a population. Samples are usually chosen to be representative of some larger population. A *population*, on the other hand, is the set of all elements for which measurements are possible. A population can consist of products, workers, customers, firms, prices, or anything else about which the decision maker is interested. A survey of every unit in a population is called a *census*. Individually, each person, item, or thing in the sample, population, or universe is called a *population unit*.

Another label sometimes used to identify a population is a *universe*. The labels *population* and *universe* are often used interchangeably to mean a complete set or group of people, items, or events, from which a sample is or can be drawn.

Is It a Parameter or Is It a Statistic?

Another way that statisticians categorize measurement data is based on whether they apply to a sample or to its parent population. Differences in these applications result in two types of statistics: *parametric statistics* and *nonparametric statistics.*

A *parameter* is a numerical value used as a summary measure for a population or a universe. For example, consider the statement, "The mean age for all entering college or university freshmen in California is 18.8 years." Because 18.8 years is the average of all entering freshmen—the population—it is a *parameter.*

A *statistic*, on the other hand, is a number used as a summary measure for a sample. For example, consider the statement, "The mean age for a sample of thirty Benson College freshmen is 20.3 years." The mean for this sample is a *statistic.* In this case, the mean for the sample is larger than it was for the population of all college and university freshmen in the country, and statistical techniques have been developed to determine whether the two mean values are "statistically different" or not.

Parametric Statistics

Parametric statistics require that measurements come from a population in which the distribution of variances is normal. This doesn't mean that all the measurements are the same. Rather, it means that the differences vary in what we call a "normal" way. Take the measurements of the incomes of a randomly drawn sample of a thousand households for an example. If each of the measurements were plotted, it would be expected that the distribution of incomes for members of the sample would come close to the same distribution that occurred in the population—and this distribution would be expected to be "normal."

Plotting this distribution would result in a typical bell-shaped curve. There would be a few values at either end of the curve, but the bulk would fall around the middle value—near what would be the mean for the sample. When discussing measures of central tendency, it would be appropriate to refer to the average or *mean* income of the group with this measurement. Inferential statistical tests could be used as well.

Nonparametric Statistics

Nonparametric statistical procedures must be used when working with nominal- and ordinal-level data. No assumptions can be made about the distribution of these measurements; nor can any assumptions be made about the larger population. Rather, with nonparametric statistics, the distribution must be assumed *not* to be normal.

Testing a sample of new parts coming off a manufacturing line can be used as an example. The parts are examined to see if they work or don't work—often called a "pass or fail" test. Only one of two possible outcomes is possible. There is no way to establish if the distribution of "passes" and "fails" is normal or not. A mean or average score is no longer possible; instead, the researcher can only say something like "three out of a hundred failed" or that "ninety-seven out of a hundred passed." Both the "three" and the "ninety-seven" are nonparametric statistics.

With this nonparametric example, the means must be replaced by the mode. The *mode* is the value that comes up most often. Here, the mode is ninety-seven. It is meaningless to talk about a "mean" score on a two- or three-category item. Rather, the category appearing most often, the "mode," is the relevant information.

Using Statistics to Communicate

One of the great advantages of using numbers instead of words to describe something is that numbers often make it easier for both the sender and receiver to agree on what is being said. For example, one person might be described as being six feet tall and a second person as being five feet, nine inches tall. Clearly, when both people are standing on the same level surface, one is taller than the other. But how great is the difference? It is hard to tell by just looking at the two people. By *measuring* the differences in height, it becomes possible to know for sure.

Because numbers are used instead of just saying "one person is taller," it is now possible to know that one person is precisely three inches taller than the other person. Furthermore, in the English language, the word "three" and the symbol "3" refer to the same amount. Three inches or three bananas are the same number as three oranges.

The same communication concept is true for fractions and percentages. Most people will comprehend the idea behind the phrase "one-third" and will know that 33.3 percent is very nearly the same thing as one-third. One-third of a gallon is the same *share* of the whole as is one-third of a liter or one-third of a pound, even though the absolute quantities are different. One-third of anything is always one-third of whatever is the unit of measurement. Numbers make it possible to communicate these ideas.

The same goes for other percentages. One hundred percent of anything can only mean all of it, a totality. One hundred and ten percent, on the other hand, is all of something plus 10 percent more. And every time you use it or say it, it is the same. That's the beauty of using statistics when communicating; little or nothing is lost in translation. Because things can be measured, they can be described.

Using Descriptive Statistics

The term *descriptive statistics* refers to the set of measurements (numbers) that are used to *summarize* a set of larger numbers and that *have the same meaning for everyone*. Here is an example of how an administrator might use descriptive statistics:

A public assistance program manager might be interested in knowing the size (amount) of clients' allotments. In today's age of desktop computers, it would be a relatively simple task for the manager to call up a list of all client monthly totals, when the last payment occurred, and a host of other information about each client. However, the volume of data that such requests can quickly provide would soon become overwhelming. By themselves, the numbers for any individual would most likely provide little information about the total. What the manager could use instead is a simple set of numbers that *summarized* specific features of all clients' accounts—in a word, a *summary* of the data set. Such a summary uses descriptive statistics.

Using Inferential Statistics

As stated earlier, a major component of statistics is the body of tests that are used to make *inferences*. With these tools, researchers assume or infer that measurements of some characteristics of a smaller group (the sample) are held in common by some larger group (the population). One example of inferential statistics is in the periodic testing of small portions of a production run (a sample or samples) to *estimate* the failure or error rate of the entire day's production (a population).

Another example of how inferential statistics are used is the now famous experience of administrators who determined statistically that taking one aspirin a day might greatly decrease the likelihood of having a heart attack. In the aspirin experiment, some 10,000 medical doctors were recruited to participate in a ten-year experiment. Half were to take one aspirin a day; the other half, an inert placebo (colored chalk).

Participants were assigned to their group randomly so that no one knew to which group he or she belonged. After just a few years, the incidence of heart attacks among the aspirin takers was found to be so much lower than among the placebo group that the experiment was called to a halt and the results announced. Taking one aspirin a day was deemed to be highly likely to reduce one's chance of (that is, lower the probability of) having a heart attack. Thus, the assumption (or inference) was made that the results (measurements) of the sample applied to the overall population as well.

Statistics in Action

Statistics is the collective term used to denote the numbers used to communicate the *measurements* of something. The measurements of a particular *sample* are typically drawn from a larger body called the *population* or *universe*. As we have seen, only the numerical values that apply to the sample are known as "statistics," whereas the values of the population are known as "parameters." In learning about applying statistics to public administration situations, this difference is seldom a problem; managers rarely deal with entire populations.

In statistics, the term *measurement* refers to numeric values that researchers read from some measuring device, such as a ruler, a thermometer, and lists of questions or attitude scales. Lists of questions or scales are arranged together in questionnaires. Numeric values are assigned to each different answer or level of response to a variable in the questionnaire.

The term *scale* can refer to at least three different statistical concepts. First, it is used to describe a device to measure a continuous set of values. Examples include bathroom scales, postage scales, rulers, gauges, and the like. Second, questions that are developed to measure such abstract concepts as attitudes or personal opinions are referred to as scales by social science researchers. Third, the set of increments in a measurement system is often referred to as a scale. Examples include a scale of inches and increments of inches, a set of millimeters or centimeters, foot-pounds of pressure, miles per hour or mileage traveled, and many others.

Following the lead of the social sciences, public administration expanded the concept of a scale to include such phenomena as responses to questions on a consumer attitude or lifestyle questionnaire. Scales have also been established to measure levels or increments of awareness, agreement, desirability, rank order, preference, and many other similar concepts. In all applications, numbers have also been assigned to various "things" such as events, objects, characteristics, responses, and qualities.

In manufacturing or processing operations, the recordings of the rate of occurrence of various events or happenings are regularly carried out. Examples of such measurements include the number of products in a production run that fail to meet specifications and the number of consumers who use a particular government-provided service. Measurements are used to produce data. Only when analyzed and interpreted does *data* become *information*.

Some Examples of the Use of Statistics

More likely than not, managers in all departments and functions of public and nonprofit organizations have a use for statistics. Some examples of statistics used by public and nonprofit organization managers and administrators are displayed below.

- *Program management and administration:* New program planning, acquisition, and distribution administrators use statistical analyses of environmental trends, detailed cost accounting, budgeting, inventory control and similar systems—all of which are measurements.
- *Planning and forecasting:* Managers of public health and welfare agencies are regularly required to forecast community needs for their services; managers must determine service-provider staff requirements; client trends and demographics for planning and budget preparations are established with statistical studies.
- *Decision making:* Decision making includes a broad variety of studies, demand tests, and concept evaluations that involve collection, evaluation, and interpretation about consumer preferences, habits, lifestyles, demographic trends, and the like.
- *Process controls:* Statistical record keeping and analysis aid quality control managers to maintain standards and efficient production schedules. Medical administrators and hospital staffs maintain statistical records to monitor patients' reactions to pharmaceutical products.
- *Human resources:* Today more than ever, human resources managers use statistics to track and predict workplace diversity trends, staff turnover, absenteeism, appraisals, and so on. Many more such business applications require statistical record keeping, analysis, and interpretation.

Statistics in Public Administration Research

Public administrators use both *descriptive* and *inferential statistics*. In each application, the numerical information may be presented in tables, charts, and graphical illustrations. The most important of these statistics and some of the more commonly encountered uses of descriptive and inferential statistical tests are discussed in the following sections.

Descriptive Statistics

These are the four basic types of descriptive statistics used by managers most often (Lang and Heiss 1994):

- *Measures of central tendency:* These include the *mean*, the *mode*, and the *median* values of a data set.
- *Measures of variability in the data set:* The three variability values to be discussed are the *standard deviation* (SD), the *range*, and the *interquartile range*.
- *Measures of relative position in the set:* Included are *percentiles* and *standard scores*. The most commonly used standardized score is the *z score*.
- *Measures of correlation between two or more variables:* Correlation tests are used to show how strongly and in what direction two variables are related, if at all.

A wide variety of inferential statistical tools have been developed for use in these four applications. Naturally, not all of these are relevant to the majority of decisions that face managers or administrators. The tests included here have been selected for their extensive use in organization and organizational management literature, their relative ease of use and clear interpretation characteristics, and their availability in most general statistical software packages.

Inferential Statistics

These are the basic types of inferential statistics (i.e., procedures) used in public administration research:

- The *t*-test for significant differences between means of dependent (uncorrelated) groups
- The *t*-test for significant differences between the means of paired or correlated groups
- Simple regression analysis for measuring the strength and the direction of relationships between variables
- Analysis of variance (ANOVA) tests for differences on one variable for two or more groups
- Analysis of variance (ANOVA) tests for differences on two or more variables between two or more groups, and for any *interaction* that might result from the two variables
- Analysis of covariance (ANCOVA), which is used in pre- and posttest experimental applications

In addition to these easy-to-apply-and-interpret statistical tests, other commonly encountered statistical applications include the following:

- The use of probability in decision making
- Concepts and applications of sampling
- Prediction and forecasting tools
- Statistical applications for managing quality

Computer Applications

Managers of public and nonprofit organizations use statistical tools to carry out the decision-making and communication tasks of their position. However, it is no longer necessary for anyone to memorize confusing statistical formulas or to work complex statistical calculations by hand. Today, most administrators have access to a personal computer. While powerful statistical software has been available almost from the desktop computer's introduction, much of the early statistical software was limited in scope because of hardware restrictions that resulted in slow processing speed. Another limitation was that statistical processing of large data sets required far more memory than available on early desktop computers.

However, most desktop and laptop computers today are powerful enough for managers to analyze large data sets and to conduct sophisticated statistical tests on that data. Throughout the remainder of this book, a variety of statistical software for desktop computers will be referred to, including Microsoft Excel and the Statistical Package for the Social Sciences (SPSS).

Summary

Administrators use words and statistics to communicate with their staffs, supervisors, and with people and groups outside of the organization. Statistics, presented in tables, graphs, and other illustrations, ensure mutual understanding of the data at hand. Statistics are used for two main purposes: (1) as *descriptive statistics*, they are used to summarize a larger set of numbers, called a data set; (2) as *inferential statistics*, the measurements of a smaller group—a *sample*—are used for making assumptions about a larger group—the *population* or *universe* of interest.

The numerical values in statistics are typically measurements taken with some type of scale or measuring device. These scales provide different levels of information, based upon the type of data they are intended to measure. The four types or levels of data (the terms apply to the data-gathering scales as well) from the lowest in power to the highest are nominal, ordinal, interval, and ratio. Each data type has a body of statistical tests that are appropriate for that level; lower-level tests should not be used on higher-level data.

When the term "statistics" is used, it can mean one or more specific measures or values describing some thing, a sample of some type. Or the word can be used to refer to a body of mathematical tools and techniques invented for analyzing and giving meaning to sets of numbers. This latter use of the word is called *statistical analysis*.

Statistics may be *parametric* or *nonparametric*. Parametric statistics require that certain assumptions be made of the host population, such as a normal distribution. With nonparametric statistics, no such assumptions need be made.

Suggested Reading

Berenson, Mark L., and David M. Levine. 1996. *Basic Business Statistics: Concepts and Applications*. 6th ed. Upper Saddle River, NJ: Prentice Hall.

Einspruch, Eric L. 1998. *An Introductory Guide to SPSS for Windows*. Thousand Oaks, CA: Sage.

Green, Samuel B., Neil J. Salkind, and Theresa M. Akey. 2000. *Using SPSS*. Upper Saddle River, NJ: Prentice Hall.

Lapin, Lawrence. 1993. *Statistics for Modern Business Decisions*. New York: Harcourt Brace Jovanovich.

Neufeld, John L. 1997. *Learning Business Statistics with Microsoft Excel*. Upper Saddle River, NJ: Prentice Hall.

Phillips, John L. 1996. *How to Think About Statistics*. 5th ed. New York: Freeman, 1996.

8 Introduction to Sampling

Unless they are working with a census, researchers seldom find themselves measuring entire populations. Rather, they draw *samples* from populations and measure the elements in that sample. Sample measurements are called *statistics*. These results are then assumed to apply to the entire population as well; the researchers conclude that similar results would be found if every element in the sample were measured. Population measurements are called *parameters*. Researchers acquire sample *statistics* to estimate a larger population's unknown *parameters*. The process is known as *inference*, and the statistical tests that are used for this purpose are called *inferential statistics*.

This section begins with a discussion of why sampling is important. This is followed by a comparative description of several different types of samples, the meaning of bias and error in sampling, sample distributions, and concepts of sample size. It concludes with a review of several statistical procedures relating to sampling.

If all possible information needed to solve a business problem could be collected, there would be no need to sample. Decision makers, however, seldom have this luxury. They are typically limited in time and money. Therefore, they use samples and make decisions based on probabilities (Fitz-Gibbon and Morris 1987).

For example, the author once conducted a series of focus groups in ten different cities across the United States for an international sport-shoe manufacturer. The objective of the study was to determine which features of running shoes male and female recreational runners preferred. Obviously, the study did not require that all runners in the United States or even in a single town be interviewed. Instead, a series of samples were interviewed in each of the ten cities. The results provided an opinion consensus that greatly reduced the potential loss that would have resulted from including less desirable features in new shoe models.

It must also be noted that sometimes it is, indeed, possible to take a census. The term *census* means that every element in the group or population of interest is measured. Surveys of industrial consumers or of consumer product distributors are frequently conducted as a census.

For example, in order to determine preferences for rainwear brands among commercial fishermen, a manufacturer of commercial rainwear purchased from the U.S. Coast Guard a list of all registered owners of commercial fishing vessels. The firm mailed a questionnaire to every name on the list. This turned out to be a costly mistake, which became apparent when the firm learned that the owners of commercial fishing vessels are not always fishermen. Banks and other investors own a majority of the boats. These owners did not return the questionnaires sent to them—less than 10 percent of the surveys were returned. Because of this small response rate, the firm found little helpful information for its marketing program. On the other hand, this same firm later surveyed a sample of just 165 active commercial fishermen to learn their preferences in waterproof footwear. Subjects were randomly selected from participants at an off-season trade show. That information enabled the firm to earn more than $1.5 million in sales of waterproof footwear in less than a year.

Why We Sample

Research subjects learn from being questioned about things. To anwer, they are required to think about things that they might not have considered important before the questioning. Because of this "residue of learning," subsequent measurements of the subject on the same characteristic may not produce exactly the same results. Therefore, the act of measuring—particularly with attitude scales—is said to be *destructive in nature.*

The main reasons that samples are used in place of a census of a population involve considerations of cost, time, accuracy, and the destructive nature of the measurement process. Costs and time are closely related. In planning a statistical study budget, the researcher must address these key concerns:

- How accurate must the final results be in order to make the type of decision required in the particular business situation?
- What is the cost to the organization if the wrong decision is made?
- How much more information must be added to reach the desired level of accuracy?
- What kinds of data are needed? How much do they cost to acquire?
- Can we afford the extra cost to collect the data?

Sampling Precision

Administrators, managers, and researchers often use measurements of the characteristics of a sample for forecasting similar characteristics about larger samples or populations. In a sense, they use the sample data to *predict* how a population will act or react under the same conditions in some future situation or event. However, researchers can control few if any of the intervening variables that might affect that future event; they are asked to "measure the unknowable." The idea of *sampling precision* refers to how confident the researcher feels about the ability of the sample to allow the researcher to make inferences. The idea of *sampling* is rooted in the fundamental concepts of probability. Confidence is typically stated in terms of probability, that is, as either a 0.10, 0.05, or 0.01 level of confidence. In the language of probability, a value of 1.0 indicates that the researcher is 100 percent confident about statistical result; 0.10 indicates that the researcher is 90 percent sure about the results; 0.05 means 95 percent sure, and 0.01 means 99 percent sure.

Predictably, a high degree of precision is often difficult—if not impossible—to attain without greatly increasing the size of a sample. This is not the problem that it might seem to be, however. In most research in the social and administrative sciences, it is seldom necessary to achieve very high degrees of precision or reliability. Instead, decision makers can often deal very well with information that is only *relative*.

The cost of acquiring additional information in order to improve the precision of a measurement is often prohibitive. Precision and, hence, reliability increase at a much slower rate than sample size does. Reliability grows at the rate of the square root of the increase in sample size. Thus, to double reliability requires making the sample four times as large.

Using very large samples can have other drawbacks as well. One is the *destructive nature* of the survey process. Simply by being asked questions, subjects begin to think about them. This can result in changes in their attitudes. Exposure to a survey questionnaire may help the subject to verbalize deeply seated attitudes that had lain dormant, but were brought to the fore during the study.

Sampling Methods

There are a number of techniques that researchers can use to achieve greater reliability in a sample study. Among the most important of these is the type of *sampling method* employed. Sampling method refers to the way the sample units are selected from a parent population. When deciding which combination of sampling characteristics to use, researchers must make decisions in

- Probability or nonprobability sample?
- Single unit or cluster of units?
- Stratified sample or unstratified?
- Equal unit probability or unequal probability?
- Single stage or multistage?

Figure 8.1 **A List of Sampling Decision Considerations**

five basic areas. These, when combined, allow for thirty-two different possible choice combinations. The five basic concerns are displayed in Figure 8.1.

Probability or Nonprobability Sample?

A *probability* sample is one in which the sample units (people, parts, groups, homes, cities, tribes, companies, etc.) are selected at random and all have an equal chance at being selected. Examples include simple random samples (SRS) and systematic samples. A *nonprobability* sample is one in which chance selection techniques are not used. Examples include *convenience samples* (selected at the convenience of the manager) and *quota samples*, where only subjects with specific characteristics are added until some predetermined mix is achieved.

A third example of a nonprobability sample often used in practical public administration research is the *judgment sample*. This entails substituting experience or the judgment of an administrator or researcher for a more scientific approach at randomization. It often means deliberately picking a sample that is nonrepresentative of a population.

The choice between a probability and a nonprobability sample is often based on the cost-versus-value principle. The researcher will pick the method that provides the greatest margin of value over cost. A worthwhile rule of thumb to follow in sample selection is that, the more diversified the population, the greater the need to guarantee representativeness by following a probability sampling method.

Single Unit or Cluster Sampling?

A *sampling unit* is the basic element of the population—such as a person or a thing—being sampled. When choosing whether to use single unit or cluster sampling methods, the deciding factor is the nature of the sampling unit. In single unit sampling, each sampling unit is selected independently. In cluster sampling, the units are selected as groups. If sampling units are households, single unit sampling requires that all households in the population of interest be selected without reference to any other characteristic. A cluster sample might change the sampling unit to the random selection of city blocks, with some or all households on each selected block then surveyed. Cluster sampling usually costs less per sampling unit than does single unit sampling. As a rule of thumb, whenever a study involves a low tolerance for error with a high expected cost of errors, and a highly heterogeneous population, single unit sampling is favored over cluster sampling.

Stratified or Unstratified Sampling?

A third consideration is whether to use a *stratified* or *unstratified* sample. A sample *stratum* is a portion of a population that has one or more characteristics of interest to the analyst. Examples include political party membership, income level, and age. The final sample is selected so that it reflects the same percentages of the characteristic that are found in the larger population. A stratified sample may help to ensure representativeness and, thus, reduce potential for sampling error. Finally, to obtain the same level of sampling error, a smaller sample size is needed with a stratified sample than would be needed if a nonstratified sample were used.

Equal Unit or Unequal Unit?

The question of *equal unit* or *unequal unit* probability sampling (that is, a greater or lesser likelihood of a sampling element's being included) is closely associated with strata in the population. The final sample drawn will include a disproportionately larger (or smaller) percentage of the characteristic of interest.

For example, a furniture retailer conducting a survey of local furniture buying patterns will probably include fewer persons older than 50 years of age in the sample because this group spends a disproportionately small amount on furniture items. At the same time, the retailer's sample will more than likely be heavily weighted in favor of the 24- to 34-year-old and 35- to 44-year-old demographic groups because they spend disproportionately more on furniture than other age groups.

Single Stage or Multistage Sampling?

The final consideration has to do with *single* or *multistage sampling*. The number of stages included in a sampling process is usually dictated by the nature of the population and the sample frame (source of units). For example, sampling food products in a canning or packaging process is typically a single stage process; items are randomly selected from the production process.

In a comprehensive survey of consumer attitudes across a large area, a multistage process will often be used. Multistage sampling is the method of choice for needs analysis studies when sampling large populations and with population elements dispersed over a wide area. This type of multistage sampling would involve the three-stage process displayed in Figure 8.2.

Sample Bias and Sampling Error

The ultimate objective of all sampling is to select a set of elements from a population in such a way that the measurements of that set of elements accurately reflect the same measurements of the population from which they were selected.

A number of potential pitfalls make achieving this objective difficult. Among these are bias and several different types of potential error. These are characterized as *sampling error* and *nonsampling error*. Several types of nonsampling error can occur, including sampling frame error, nonresponse error, and data error.

Sample Bias

Bias in sampling refers to the sampling process itself; it is sometimes referred to as *systematic bias*. Bias can be intentional or unintentional. *Intentional* bias is used when a researcher has a particular point to prove and uses statistics to support the preestablished conclusion. For example, an agriculture decision maker might intentionally select a better piece of ground to show more dramatic yield improvements from a new plant seed.

Unintentional bias can occur as a result of a researcher's best efforts to include relevant elements in the final sample. For example, in decision making to determine whether voters might approve a special bond issue for library construction, the researcher might telephone only registered voters. This results in a *double* bias. First, it includes only people with telephones, and second, it ignores the library users who have not voted in the past, but would in order to improve the library system. The best way to avoid or reduce any and all bias is to maintain random selection procedures.

Sampling Error

Sampling error occurs when a sample with characteristics that do not reflect the population is studied. It is almost impossible to specify a sample that

---

A THREE-STAGE SAMPLING PROCESS

- The first stage is random selection of census tracts in the various socioeconomic sections of the region.

- This is followed by the random selection of residential blocks in the selected census tracts.

- The third stage is the random selection of individual households in each selected block.

Figure 8.2   An Example of a Multistage Sampling Process

exactly matches the parameters of a given population. Nor will the results of a second sample exactly match the first. More samples taken will not increase the likelihood of a perfect match.

Two "laws of numbers" affect sampling error. First, the *law of large numbers* suggests that increasing sample size will reduce the size of the sampling error encountered. However, the *law of diminishing returns* also applies to this error reduction method. Recall that to reduce error by half requires making the sample *four* times as large. Using a statistically efficient sampling plan is clearly the best way to control sampling error.

Dealing with Nonsampling Error

Nonsampling error can result from many different sources, including problems with the *sampling frame*, with subjects' *nonresponse*, and errors in the *data* itself.

Sampling Frame Error

The sampling frame is the source from which the sample is drawn (such as a list or a telephone directory). If the study is a test of components provided by an outside supplier, the sampling frame is the collected total of all parts provided by the supplier.

If the sample is to be drawn from customers who enter a particular facility, the sample frame consists of the actual premises; the population in this example is all persons who enter the facility during the survey period.

For example, a sociologist conducted a study of the attitudes and concerns about terrorism among a group of regional airline passengers. The sampling frame for the study consisted of the list of passengers with reservations to fly on a specific route on a specific day. Individual passengers were randomly selected from those waiting in the boarding lounge before boarding their aircraft.

The key to reducing *sampling frame error* is to start with as complete a sampling frame as possible. If the sampling frame is a list of clients, it should be up-to-date and include everyone. If the sample frame is all the products produced by a given machine, it should include all products produced during all shifts, under the control of all supervisors, over the entire time period in question.

A way to adjust for potential sample frame error has been developed by researchers who gather data by telephone. Increasingly, private telephone numbers are not included in printed telephone directories. To deal with this problem, the survey operators modified their telephone book sample frames to include unknown, nonlisted numbers. In a process that is called *plus-one dialing*, they do this by adding one number to the numbers taken at random from the directory.

Nonresponse Error

Nonresponse error is another problem encountered in survey decision making. When only small proportions of subjects respond, there is a strong probability that the results are not characteristic of the population. This type of error may be reduced through the use of incentives for completing and returning the survey instrument and through follow-up telephoning, although there is no guarantee error reduction will occur.

Data Error

Finally, *data error* can occur because of distortions in the data collected or from mistakes in data coding, analysis, or interpretation of statistical analysis. Several different ways to reduce data error in research projects are displayed in Figure 8.3.

Sample Distributions

When researchers talk about *sampling distributions*, they are referring to the way a statistic would be distributed if computed for a series of samples taken from the same population. This concept has several uses. First, it provides the researcher a quick estimate of the validity of the results of the study. Second, it enables the researcher to estimate the values of some variable in a popula-

- Ensure that survey instruments (questionnaires) are well prepared, simple to read, and easy to understand.

- Avoid any internal bias (such as the use of leading or value-laden words).

- Properly select and train interviewers to control data-gathering bias or error.

- Use sound editing, coding, and tabulating procedures to reduce the possibility of data-processing error.

Figure 8.3 **Some Ways to Reduce Data Error**

tion of interest. Third, it produces a value that is associated with determining sample size.

Sampling distributions represent a fundamental concept in statistics (Zikmund 1994). It is a difficult concept to grasp, however, because it refers to a *hypothetical* distribution of something that will never take place: randomly selecting a very large number of samples (such as 50,000 or more) from a specified population, computing a mean for every sample, then examining the distribution of those means. The mean of all the means is called the *expected value* of that statistic, and the standard deviation of the sampling distribution is the *standard error of the mean.*

When decision makers draw two or more random samples of subjects or items from a given population, the statistics computed for each sample will almost always vary. Such variation is natural and expected. Drawing samples from the same population will produce summary measures that are also different from the first sample or samples drawn. Drawing more and more samples will also produce varying measurements. From this point on, assume that the statistic is the mean value on any relevant question, characteristic, or scale item.

If the mean score for each of the group of samples were displayed as a frequency distribution, the individual sample measurements will be distributed in such a way that they would present a picture of a normal, symmetrical distribution. Most of the values would cluster around the center of the range, with smaller and smaller amounts drifting off toward the edges. This pictorial representation of the frequency distribution would be what is called a traditional *bell-shaped curve.* A key requirement of many statistical tests is that the data be normally distributed.

The Sampling Error of the Mean

It is important to remember that the standard error of the mean is only an estimated standard deviation of a hypothetical series of samples. Still, it does provide an indication of how close the sample mean probably is to the mean of the population. It is an estimate of the sampling variability in the sample mean.

For example, in a study of public agency organizational climate, scale items consisted of such statements about the organization as "Red tape is kept to a minimum in this organization." The mean score on this seven-point agreement scale was 3.50; the standard deviation for the sample was 1.512. A standard error of .535 indicated that the sample mean was within a little more than half a point of what could be expected as the mean for the population from which the sample was drawn.

Central Limit Theorem

A rule of statistics called the central limit theorem states that as the number of samples drawn from a population gets larger, the distribution of the sample statistic will take on a normal distribution. The number of samples necessary for this to occur is thirty. What is a "normal" distribution? This term describes a frequency distribution that follows a bell-shaped, symmetrical shape. The two sides of the curve are the same, with the *mean* and *median* both falling at the peak of the curve. Distributions that are not symmetrical are said to be *skewed*. Skewed distributions that have fewer values at the high end (right side) are said to be *positively skewed*, or *skewed to the right*. When the values taper off toward the left side of the distribution, it is said to be *negatively skewed*, or *skewed to the left*. Distributions can also have more than one peak (in what is called a *bipolar* distribution).

The central limit theorem applies for all sample statistics, but is usually applied to the value of the mean. The *sampling distribution of the mean* (sometimes referred to as the sampling distribution of the *average*) is nothing more than a distribution of the means of each of the samples that could be drawn from a population. The phrase "could be" is used instead of "is" because this is a theoretical concept; decision makers typically deal with just one sample. The problem at hand is how to know that the distribution of that sample statistic accurately reflects the same measurement that might be found in a census of the population.

No single sample is likely to produce measurements that *exactly* mirror the measurement of population. In addition, the measurements of another sample taken from the same population will produce values that are different from every other possible sample. The same is true for the third, fourth, fifth, and more samples. Researchers are concerned that the measurements of the sample fall within an accepted *range* of possible values.

Summary

Sampling in public administration research is used because it is more efficient than studying a full population. Sampling can lower the cost and improve the efficiency of measurement activities. Studying a sample rather than an entire population saves time and money. It is also thought to be less destructive of underlying attitudes (the process of measuring may influence future measurements).

The five fundamental considerations of the sampling process result in many different possible combinations in sample design. Sample design is based on these five choices: (1) probability or nonprobability, (2) single unit or unit clusters, (3) stratified or unstratified, (4) equal unit probability or unequal probability, and (5) single stage or multistage sampling.

Decision makers must avoid introducing bias and sampling or nonsampling error into the sample design and selection process.

Sampling distributions—the way each individual measurement clusters around some statistic—tend to reflect distinct patterns, with most following what is referred to as the *normal distribution*. In a normal distribution, the bulk of the measurements cluster around the mean value, with a few trailing off above and below the mean. When plotted, they appear in the shape of the familiar *bell-shaped curve*. Most inferential statistics require that the data be from a normal distribution.

According to the *central limit theorem*, as the size of the sample increases, the distribution of the sample measurements tends to take on the shape of normal distribution, whereas small-sample studies may result in data that do not reflect the parameters of the larger population.

Suggested Reading

Eddington, Eugene. 1987. *Randomization Tests*. New York: Marcel Decker, 1987.

Mattson, Dale. 1984. *Statistics: Difficult Concepts, Understandable Explanations*. Oak Park, IL: Bolchazy-Carducci.

Sincich. Terry. 1996. *Business Statistics by Example*. 5th ed. Upper Saddle River, NJ: Prentice Hall.

Warwick, Donald P., and Charles A. Lininger. 1975. *The Sample Survey: Theory and Practice*. New York: McGraw-Hill.

9 Questionnaires and Questions

Researchers use two different approaches when gathering primary data in quantitative research studies; they may collect data by *observing* and counting overt acts of behavior, or they may use a *questionnaire* to generate responses to specific questions. Questionnaires are the most popular way to gather primary data—it has been estimated that questionnaires are used in 85 percent or more of all quantitative research projects. They are particularly appropriate when the research problem calls for a *descriptive* design.

For both approaches, the researcher must first prepare or acquire either a list of topics to cover or a number of questions to ask. The observation method uses what is known as a *schedule*, which is nothing more than a list of items, events, characteristics, or behaviors that the observer wants to be sure are counted. A questionnaire, as might be expected, is a set of questions that respondents are asked to answer. This chapter will discuss the process of questionnaire preparation, including the nature, limitations, and wide variety of ways to write survey questions. Observation methods will be discussed in some detail in the qualitative methods section.

Questionnaires can be used to gather information about large numbers of respondents (populations) and from small groups (samples). Most of the time, public administration research is conducted with *samples*. The sample method used most often is the *probability* or random *sample*. Samples that are representative of the population are surveyed; the researcher then makes inferences about the population from the sample data. Within some known margin of error, the sample *statistics* are assumed to be a reflection of the population's *parameters*. Careful planning and construction of the questionnaire is, therefore, a critical step in research.

Advantages of Using Questionnaires

Questionnaires have many advantages. The greatest of these is the considerable *flexibility* of the questionnaire. Questionnaires can be custom designed to meet the objectives of almost any type of research project. Public administration researchers can also purchase the rights to employ many different types of prepared questionnaires. These are instruments that have been developed by other researchers and thoroughly tested with a variety of different samples. They have therefore been applied enough times to warrant strong belief in their ability to effectively measure some phenomenon. These prepared questionnaires are called *standardized instruments* and may be ordered from a variety of test catalogs. At one time, they were used extensively in human resources applications, but their popularity has waned in recent years.

Questionnaires can be designed to gather information from any group of respondents. Questionnaires can be short or long, simple or complex, straightforward or branched. They can be rigidly structured or a loosely organized list of topics to discuss. They can be administered face to face, over the telephone, by mail, and over computer networks. Usually, respondents' answers are relatively easy to code and tabulate. This can reduce turnaround time and lower project costs.

Questionnaires can be designed to determine what people know, what they think, or how they act or plan to act. They can measure subjects' factual knowledge about a thing or an idea, or people's opinions, attitudes, or motives for behaving in certain ways. They can be used to measure the frequency of past behaviors or to predict future actions. When subjects are children or persons from different cultures, response alternatives in the form of pictures or symbols may be substituted for words.

Because of the flexibility of the questionnaire, there are very few absolute rules to follow in development of the instrument. However, constructing an effective questionnaire does demand a high degree of skill. Questions must be arranged in a logical order; they must be worded in such a way that their meaning is clear to people of all backgrounds, ages, and educational levels. Particular care must be taken when asking questions of a potentially controversial or personal nature not to embarrass or offend respondents. Folz (1996, 79–80) has summarized the concerns associated with questionnaire construction this way:

> Know what you want to ask and why you want to ask it; compose clear, unambiguous questions; keep the survey [questionnaire] as brief as possible; and have a plan for analyzing the result before the instrument is administered.

Questionnaire Construction Procedure

Researchers have developed many different ways to construct questionnaires. Broadly speaking, most seem to follow the systematic process outline by Malhotra (1999). The questionnaire must:

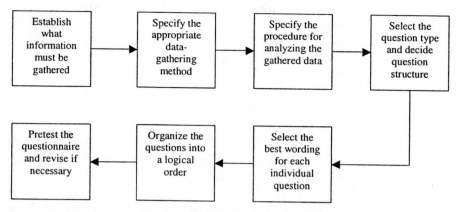

Figure 9.1 **The Seven-Step Questionnaire Construction Procedure**

- Successfully gather information that answers each study question.
- Motivate respondents to answer all questions to the best of their ability.
- Keep all potential error to a minimum.

The following seven-step procedure (Figure 9.1) has been designed to help in the preparation of effective questionnaires and questions. Because questionnaire construction is as much an art as it is a science, the chart should be considered as a guide, rather than a checklist of steps that must be followed in the order presented.

Determine What Information Is Needed

Before any questions are written, the researcher must be absolutely certain that the objectives for the research are clearly spelled out. It is never enough for a researcher to just think that he or she has an idea of what it would be nice to know. Rather, only questions that contribute to the overall research objective should be asked. The researcher must understand the scope of the proposed research: Is the research being done to solve a particular problem in a public administration or nonprofit organization, or is it "pure" research designed to identify or test some theory? This is the dichotomy between applied and theoretical research that appears periodically in the literature on public administration research.

The bulk of public administration research is applied research. However, over the past several decades, a growing body of research on public administration theory has emerged. Today, a loosely organized group of academics and practitioners are joined in an effort to advance theoretical knowledge. The Public Administration Theory Network (http://www.PAT-Net.org) allows interested persons to share their ideas on political and social theory, philosophy and ethics, theory of institutions and organizations, and other related concepts, problems, and issues. The group publishes a quarterly journal, *Administrative Theory & Praxis* (ATP).

Specify Data-Gathering Method

The three primary ways to collect data with questionnaires are: (1) in-person or *face-to-face* interviews, (2) telephone interviews (also called *voice-to-voice* interviews), and (3) mailed survey instruments that are *self-administered*. Today data may also be gathered over computer networks. Self-administered questionnaires may be mailed to respondents, handed out in public locations such as shopping malls, or dropped off at homes or offices. Each of these approaches has its own advantages and disadvantages.

Face-to-Face Interviews

The primary advantage of conducting in-person interviews is that they usually make it possible to gather large amounts of information in a relatively short period of time. Also, people who might not otherwise participate in the survey can often be encouraged to do so by a persuasive interviewer or researcher. Another advantage is that the data gatherer can help respondents who might not understand a word or a question. In-person administration is particularly helpful when branching questions are used in the questionnaire. This involves asking people certain questions, based on their response to one or more screening questions. Other respondents are instructed to move to a different section or set of questions.

There are four major disadvantages associated with the use of in-person interviews:

1. They take longer to administer than any other method.
2. They tend to be the most costly method of collecting survey data.
3. The changing demographic makeup of the country means that fewer adults of working age will be at home during the day.
4. Interviewers are subjected to potential personal harm when interviewing takes place in some urban areas.

One way that researchers get around these problems is by conducting interviews in public places, such as shopping malls or recreational facilities. While this tends to eliminate the poor and older citizens from the sample, it does allow a large number of completed questionnaires to be gathered in a very short time.

Telephone Interviews

The major advantages of telephone surveys are (1) the relative speed with which the data can be gathered, (2) their lower cost, and (3) the opportunity for the researcher to ask questions that might not be answered in a face-to-face situation. To reach people at home, most interviews are conducted on weekday evenings or on Saturdays; this allows public administration researchers to use public agency or office telephones after the working day, further cutting the costs of data gathering. Today, telephone interviews are usually conducted from a central location, thus reducing researcher travel time and its related cost.

The major disadvantages of telephone interviewing are the inability to make eye contact with respondents and to know that people with the desired demographic profiles are answering the questions. Another disadvantage is the limited length of time that the respondent is willing to give to the interview. Also, many respondents are wary of providing personal information to strangers over the telephone. They may assume that the caller is a telemarketer rather than someone who is conducting legitimate research, or they fear that the caller has sinister motives. Finally, no one is as yet aware of the effect the wide use of cellular and car telephones will have on response rates for telephone interviewing. Researchers do know that it is becoming increasingly difficult to acquire the desired number of completed instruments in the time allowed for data gathering.

Mailed Questionnaires

Mailing questionnaires is often the least expensive of all data-gathering processes. On the other hand, this method often results in the lowest return rates of all data-gathering methods. Return rates are referred to as response rates when applied to face-to-face and voice-to-voice interviewing. They all mean the number of completed questionnaires received by the researcher. It is important to plan for return rates when planning the sample size. For example, it is not uncommon to achieve return rates of 10 percent or less in a mailed questionnaire, although the typical rate is closer to 25 to 40 percent. This means that for a sample of 100, the researcher may have to mail out from 400 to 1,000 survey instruments.

Determine Analysis Procedure

The way that the gathered data will be coded, tabulated, analyzed, and interpreted plays a big role in the way the questionnaire and individual questions are developed. Today, computers using readily available, easy-to-use statistical software tabulate almost all survey results. For this reason, most questionnaires are precoded (classification numbers appear beside each question and each possible response), making data entry simple and less prone to error. The increasing use of machine-readable answer forms further improves the data entry process.

Responses to open-ended questions are grouped into categories, which are then translated into numerical form for counting and additional statistical analysis.

Select Question Type and Structure

There are many different ways to classify types of questions. The most common way is by the type of measurements they produce: *nominal, ordinal, interval,* or *ratio* data. Another is by the character of the measurement values; that is, are the values *discrete* (as in "yes" or "no" answers) or are they *continuous* (such as incomes, weights, attitude scale data, etc.). A third classification system is based on the form of the responses; that is, are the answers *open-ended* or *closed-ended.*

A fourth way to classify question types is based on the *objective* of the generated response; that is, on the cognitive level of the information produced. Folz (1996) has identified these six broad categories of objective-based questions: *factual, knowledge, opinion, attitude, motive,* and *action* or *behavior* questions. Each question type is intended to deliver a different type of information and must be worded in such a way that this objective is achieved.

Table 9.1 displays the question types alongside respondents' level of cognitive activity addressed by each type. These three stages are (1) the *cognitive* (knowledge) stage, (2) the *affective* (attitudinal) stage, and (3) the *action* (or behavioral) stage. Examples of the information each type of question produces is also shown.

Select Best Wording for Each Question

Very great differences in responses can occur with small variations in the wording of a question. As a result, extreme care must be taken in developing questions. The key qualities to look for when writing questions are *clarity, brevity, simplicity, precision, freedom from bias,* and *appropriateness.*

Clarity

Questions must be worded so that everyone completing the questionnaire understands what is being asked. Each question should address a single topic.

Table 9.1

A Classification of Question Types by Content

Cognitive awareness stage	Type of question	Information acquired
Cognitive stage	Factual	The facts about people or things
	Knowledge	What people know about things
Affective stage	Opinion	What people say about things
	Attitude	What people believe about things
	Motive	Why people act the way they do
Action stage	Behavior	How people act, what they do; how they will react to certain stimuli

Trying to include too much in a question often results in what is called *a double-barreled* question, which combines two or more questions into one. They are confusing not only to the respondent, but also to the researcher, who cannot be sure what part of the question generated the response.

Brevity

Questions should always be as short and to the point as possible. Somewhat longer questions can be included with in-person interviews and mail surveys, but short questions—less than twenty words—should be used in telephone interviews (Folz 1996).

Also, be sure that the questionnaire itself is not too long. A rule of thumb to follow is that interviews should not take longer than an hour or so to complete. Phone surveys should be kept to less than twenty minutes. Mailed, self-administered instruments should be kept to four standard pages or less.

Simplicity

Never ask questions that are complex or difficult to answer. Make sure the question is one that subjects can answer knowledgeably. Use short words and simple sentences. This is not to say that respondents should be given the idea that they are being looked down upon. Rather, focus on words that are in common, everyday use.

Precision

The wording of every question must be as precise as possible (focus, focus, focus!). Never use ambiguous words in the body of the question. Examples of words with ambiguous meanings are "sometimes," "possibly," "maybe," and so on. And always make sure that each question asks just one thing.

Freedom from Bias

Avoid asking questions that arouse strong emotions, generate resistance, or result in a refusal to answer. If you must ask these questions, place them at or near the end of the questionnaire, so that they do not result in only partially completed instruments. Such questions will often cause respondents to simply stop answering all questions, resulting in an incomplete instrument.

Do not ask leading questions that direct or influence the response toward one point of view. These, too, will often cause subjects to not respond to the survey.

Large numbers of refusals to answer can greatly influence the results of a survey by introducing what is known as *nonresponse error* or *bias*. Often, subjects who do not complete the questionnaire would respond far differently from those who do respond.

Appropriateness

As has been said, be sure that each question is one that needs to be asked. Avoid fishing expeditions. Relate every question to the study objectives. This point is related to the bias issue, as well. Today, many persons have very strong opinions about what should and shouldn't be asked. Federal privacy laws also confound this issue. This is particularly true with classification or demographic questions. Gender, marital status, ethnicity, income, and the like are potential stumbling blocks in any questionnaire. Ask only such questions if they are critical to the study. It they are not absolutely needed, they are inappropriate and should be left out of the questionnaire.

Organize Questions into a Logical Order

The sequence of items in a questionnaire can also unintentionally influence or bias answers to questions that occur later in the instrument (an item is just another word for a question). Therefore, the researcher needs to carefully organize the questionnaire in such a way that subjects are encouraged to follow through with answers to all questions.

Questions are usually arranged in an order that begins with the broad, easy-to-answer questions placed before the more focused, in-depth questions. The latter often require a significant effort on the part of the subject to answer. If the task is too difficult, respondents will often skip the question. This format

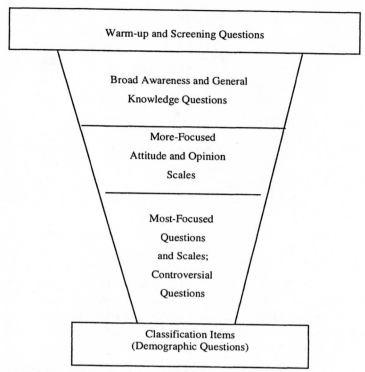

Figure 9.2 **The Funnel Approach to Questionnaire Structure**

is called the *funnel sequence* of questioning (Oskamp 1977; see Figure 9.2).

Every questionnaire is composed of five distinct parts: (1) the title and identification of the survey's sponsors, (2) instructions to respondents, (3) warm-up questions, (4) the body of the survey, and (5) classification questions.

Title, Purpose, and Sponsor Identification

Questionnaires should have a title; they should indicate the purpose of the survey, including how the information will be used. The public likes to know who is sponsoring the survey and to know that individual anonymity is guaranteed. These items should all be included at the top of the first page of the questionnaire, although in mail surveys it is also acceptable to include some of this information in a covering letter attached to the questionnaire.

Instructions

Instructions are particularly important for self-administered questionnaires. They should be clear and easy to follow. Care must be taken to clearly spell out what is expected of the respondent. It is also a good idea to introduce early in the questionnaire information about potential points of confusion that might appear later, such as who is expected to answer sections of questions after a screening or branching point in the questionnaire. These instructions should be repeated right before the branching occurs.

Warm-up Questions

These are simple, easy-to-answer questions that subjects can answer quickly and with a minimum of effort. They are often dichotomous or, at most, simple multiple-choice questions. These are usually questions designed to discern factual or knowledge information; they seldom dive right into gathering attitudinal data.

Items in this section of the questionnaire are often *screening* questions— that is, questions to determine whether the respondent qualifies as a primary target subject. Examples of screening questions are displayed in Figure 9.3.

The objective of this section is to ease respondents into the questionnaire and to bring them to a level of comfort with the questions and the question-answering process. Therefore, questions that are potentially contentious, controversial, or personal in nature should never be included early in the instrument. The best place for potentially controversial questions is right after the body of the questionnaire and just before the classification questions.

In the past, some researchers have used warm-up questions that have no connection whatsoever to the study, but that were asked only in an attempt to capture subjects' interest in the survey process. There have not been any convincing reports in the literature on the effectiveness of this ploy, however. Because of the already existing difficulty of gaining subjects' willingness to participate in yet another survey, it is probably a good idea not to waste a question this way. Researchers are encouraged to stick to the point and focus all their attention on gaining only meaningful data.

Body of the Questionnaire

This is where the most important questions should be placed. Again, the easiest of these questions should appear before the more difficult or complex questions. The questions should be placed in a logical order that does not require the respondent to leap from one idea to another. When changes in direction are necessary, a line or two of additional instructions or words calling the shift to the respondent's attention should be considered.

The first third of this section is sometimes used as a transition section between the introduction and ultimate core section of the questionnaire. Researchers use this section to ask questions to determine subjects' awareness of the survey issue. Other questions test their knowledge of component factors,

1. Do you consider yourself to be a Democratic or a Republican voter?	Democratic	☐
	Republican	☐
2. Do you drive your personal car to work more than three times a week?	Yes	☐
	No	☐
3. Do you own a bicycle?	Yes	☐
	No	☐

Figure 9.3 **Examples of Screening Questions**

indicators, and possible causal factors. These are usually broad questions that build an overall view of the study for the researcher.

In the second third of the instrument, researchers often employ more focused attitude, opinion, or other types of scales—*if* scales are included in the design. Because they often require the subject to *think* about the question before answering, this is often where nonresponse error creeps into the survey. Another type of question that is sometimes included in either the second or last third of the body of the instrument is for gathering what is called *lifestyle* information. These data are often grouped together into a category of information called *psychographics*. Lifestyle information is used to develop a more in-depth profile of the respondents, adding *attitude*, *opinion*, *value*, and *activity* information to the traditional demographic profile.

The final third of the body of the questionnaire is where the most focused questions should be placed, as should all potentially controversial or personally embarrassing questions. The reason for this placement is that while subjects might skip a threatening question because it appears near the end of the questionnaire, they will have already provided answers for the bulk of the instrument. Questionnaires that are *mostly* completed are almost as valuable as those that are completely answered.

Classification Items

Classification items are questions that enable the researcher to describe the sample in some detail and to compare the responses of one or more subgroups of subjects with responses of other subgroups. Classification information is sometimes referred to as demographic data because it usually consists of demographic statistics about the subjects themselves.

These data are, indeed, important to the research results, but not as critical as the information contained in the body of the questionnaire. This is because researchers are seldom interested in any one subject's responses, but instead want to know the mean (average) scores for the entire group. Thus, missing some classification data does not render the instrument completely useless.

Pretest and Revise the Questionnaire

Every questionnaire should be pretested on a group of subjects that as closely as possible reflects the same characteristics as the study sample. This is the critical debugging phase of questionnaire construction. No matter how many times the researcher or members of the research team go over the instrument, some problems are almost sure to surface in the pretest. Typographical errors and misspellings are the least of these potential problems.

People in a career path will often share a particular sense of meanings for words and phrases that are not likely to be shared by everyone else. Thus, subjects who share the experience and characteristics of the study sample, not the research team, must look at the wording of the questions. The best way to do this is to administer the questionnaire to a random sample of subjects from the population of interest. The results from questionnaire pretests should not be included with the findings of the final study sample.

Writing Questions

Responses to questions produce what is called *raw data*. Only when coded, tabulated, and interpreted does raw data become information. The way in which questions are formed influences the way they are coded, tabulated, and interpreted.

Questions may be written in many different ways; they may include a limited set of responses from which the respondent must choose (closed-ended), or they may allow respondents to provide answers freely and in their own words (open-ended).

Most survey questions used in descriptive research designs are closed-ended. While this results in survey instruments that tend to be more objective than those with open-ended questions, it can also work as a disadvantage. Closed-ended questions force subjects into using the same ideas, terms, and alternatives that the researcher uses—thus following the potential bias of the researcher (Oskamp 1977).

Open-ended questions are far more difficult to code and tabulate than are closed-ended questions. Therefore, open-ended questions are used most often in a small sample, exploratory research design, or as a component in an otherwise completely qualitative design.

Open-Ended Questions

Open-ended questions can also be divided into two broad types: *completely unstructured response* and *projective techniques*. Unstructured response questions are entirely the subject's own responses to a question. The researcher provides no clues or direction for the response, although subsequent questions may probe for more information. The subject may answer the question in any way desired, with a short or a long answer, and with or without qualifying statements. Projective techniques also allow subjects to respond to some stimulus in their own words. The stimulus can be words, pictures, or symbols. The questions are structured in such a way that the respondent unconsciously *projects* hidden feelings or attitudes into the response. It is believed that in this way projective questions can produce answers that might not otherwise surface.

Five different types of projective techniques are used in social and administrative science research. These are: (1) association, (2) construction, (3) completion, (4) ordering, and (5) expressive techniques. Each is discussed in more detail below.

Association Techniques

With association techniques, subjects are asked to react to a particular stimulus, such as a word, an inkblot, or other symbol, with the first thoughts or ideas that come to mind. The technique is believed to be a good way to discern the underlying values that certain words or symbols convey.

Construction Techniques

With construction techniques, subjects are asked to create a story, either about themselves or others, or to draw a self-portrait. The idea is that even if the story is not about them, their underlying values and attitudes will be reflected in the general sense of the story.

Completion Techniques

These techniques require the subject to finish an already started stimulus, such as a sentence or a picture. In the sentence completion version, subjects are asked to finish a sentence with any statement that they wish. The rationale for this approach is that the subjects' responses will not emerge from a vacuum; rather, the words chosen for the sentence completion will reflect the subjects' subconscious attitudes.

In the picture version of this process, the subjects view a photograph or a drawing of two characters. One of the characters is portrayed making a statement. Subjects are asked to put themselves in the other character's shoes and respond in the way that the second character would. Again, the belief is that without consciously doing so, the subjects will interject their own feelings or opinions into the created response.

Ordering Techniques

Also called classifying or choice techniques, these require the subject to arrange a group of stimuli into some order or to choose one or more items from a group of items. The item(s) selected are supposed to be most representative of the idea or thought involved. This method can also measure what is known as *salience*, which is another way of indicating the importance that a respondent places on each of the items.

Expressive Techniques

In these techniques, subjects are asked to creatively express themselves in some way, such as by drawing a picture, cartoon, or finger painting. The method is often used in conjunction with the construction technique. The two are considered to reinforce each other. The picture will reveal an underlying attitude, with the subject's description of the events or components of the picture often indicating salience.

It is important to recognize that projective techniques require skilled and empathetic interpretation that goes far beyond the abilities of most students of public administration. On the other hand, in the hands of a trained professional, they can and do provide valuable information that might not otherwise surface in a traditional, scale-driven attitudinal research study.

Closed-Ended Questions

Closed-ended questions can be organized into two broad classes: *structured answer* (dichotomous and multiple-choice), and *scales*. Structured answer questions are used for warm-up, introductory, and classification portions of the questionnaire, while scales are more commonly found in the body of the instrument.

Structured Answer Questions

Structured answer questions are the easiest type to write and easiest for respondents to answer. There are two types of structured answer questions: *dichotomous* and *multichotomous*. For both types, the data provided is *discrete* (also known as *categorical data*).

Dichotomous questions require respondents to select from just two alternative answers. Examples include gender (female/male), behavior (do/do not), intentions (will/will not), status (employed/unemployed), and any number of such two-alternative answer forms. Multichotomous questions allow for more than two possible answers (they are also called *multiple-choice* questions). Figure 9.4 shows examples of dichotomous and multichotomous questions

63.	Where do you work most of the time?	Field [₂]	Jail [₁]			
64.	Your gender:	Male [₂]	Female [₁]			
65.	Years with the department:	1-5 [₅]	6-10 [₄]	11-15 [₃]	16-20 [₂]	20+ [₁]
66.	Highest level of education you have attained:	Graduate work or degree [₆]	4-year college degree [₅]	2-year college degree [₄]	Some college [₃]	High school graduate [₂] Not a HS graduate [₁]
67.	Do you have supervisory responsibility?	Yes [₂]	No [₁]			

Figure 9.4 Examples of Dichotomous and Multichotomous Questions
Source: McNabb, Sepic, and Barnowe 1999.

that were taken from a public safety agency survey of organizational climate and culture.

Scales

The types of scales that are used most often in public administration research are: *attitude scales, ordinal* (ranked) *importance scales, comparative* and *noncomparative rating scales,* and *ratio scales.* Figure 9.5 displays example questions to illustrate some of these types of scales.

However, the types of scales used most often in public administration research are *attitude scales.* An attitude can be defined as a *relatively enduring, learned disposition that provides motivation to respond in a consistent way toward a given attitude object* (Oskamp 1977). Public administrators are interested in people's attitudes for any number of reasons:

- Voters' attitudes toward candidates and issues directly influence the outcome of elections.
- Citizens' attitudes influence the formation and adoption of public policies.
- People's attitudes influence their behavior and the consistency of that behavior.
- Attitudes determine group support for issues and programs.

Many different types of scales have been developed for measuring attitudes. The attitude scale methods that are used most often today are (1) Thurstone scales, (2) Likert scales, (3) semantic differential rating scales, and (4) a related semantic differential approach, the Stapel scale. Each is discussed below.

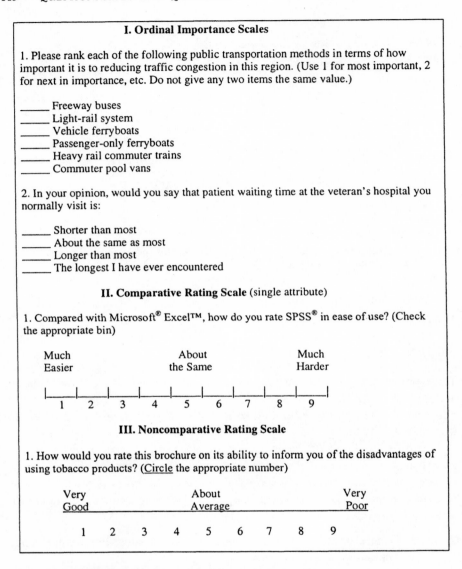

I. Ordinal Importance Scales

1. Please rank each of the following public transportation methods in terms of how important it is to reducing traffic congestion in this region. (Use 1 for most important, 2 for next in importance, etc. Do not give any two items the same value.)

_____ Freeway buses
_____ Light-rail system
_____ Vehicle ferryboats
_____ Passenger-only ferryboats
_____ Heavy rail commuter trains
_____ Commuter pool vans

2. In your opinion, would you say that patient waiting time at the veteran's hospital you normally visit is:

_____ Shorter than most
_____ About the same as most
_____ Longer than most
_____ The longest I have ever encountered

II. Comparative Rating Scale (single attribute)

1. Compared with Microsoft® Excel™, how do you rate SPSS® in ease of use? (Check the appropriate bin)

| Much Easier | | | | About the Same | | | Much Harder | |
| 1 | 2 | 3 | 4 | 5 | 6 | 7 | 8 | 9 |

III. Noncomparative Rating Scale

1. How would you rate this brochure on its ability to inform you of the disadvantages of using tobacco products? (Circle the appropriate number)

| Very Good | | | About Average | | | Very Poor | | |
| 1 | 2 | 3 | 4 | 5 | 6 | 7 | 8 | 9 |

Figure 9.5 **Additional Types of Attitude Scale Questions**

Thurstone Scales. The Thurstone scale is as much a method as it is a scale. More formally known as "Thurstone's Method of Equal-Appearing Intervals," it was developed in the late 1920s as a way of measuring the precise amount of difference between one subject's attitudes and another subject's.

With the Thurstone process, the researcher collects a hundred or more opinion statements about a subject. These should be positive, negative, and neutral. The next step is to have a large number of "informed judges" rate the degree to which each statement is favorable or unfavorable. Judges then sort the statements into eleven equally spaced categories based on this favorable/unfavorable continuum. When judges disagree widely about a statement, it is discarded.

The remaining statements are then assigned scale values based on the median favorable value assigned by the panel of judges. The statements with highest panel agreement are then included in a final attitude scale that is administered to the sample of interest.

While Thurstone's method does a good job of scale development, it is so time-consuming and tedious that it is seldom used outside of the laboratory or classroom.

Likert Scales. By far the most favored attitude-measuring tool in use today is the Likert scale, developed by Renis Likert in the early 1930s. Likert scales do not require a panel of judges to rate the scale items. The researcher prepares a pool of items that express an opinion—usually by agreeing or disagreeing with the statement—about a subject or one of its contributing aspects. Each item is an individual statement. While the resulting data are most appropriately considered to be *ordinal-level data*, some researchers treat them as *interval-level* and process Likert data with interval-scale statistics. O'Sullivan and Rassel (1995, 274) summarized the argument this way:

> The level of measurement of a Likert-type index is ordinal. The items do not really measure the quantity of a characteristic, but we can use the items to rank the cases. However, by adding together the numbers assigned to the response categories for each item, we are treating the measurement as if it were interval. This practice allows us to use more statistical techniques for analysis. Many analysts feel that treating Likert-type scales as if they were interval measures provides more advantages than disadvantages.

The objective of the Likert scale is to measure the extent of subjects' agreement with each item. The extent is measured on a five-point scale: *Strongly Agree, Agree, Undecided, Disagree,* and *Strongly Disagree.* The items are assigned values running from 1 through 5, respectively. Depending on how the statements are worded (positively or negatively, approving or disapproving), the researcher can use low mean scores to equate with either positive or negative attitudes, while using high mean scores to reflect the opposite attitude. Researchers are typically not concerned with subjects' responses to any one item on the scale. Rather, an attitude score is established by summing all ratings of items in that scale.

Reverse scoring must be used when items stated in positive and negative terms are used together in the same Likert scale. An example of a six-item, seven-point Likert-type scale designed to measure subjects' attitudes or opinions about one aspect of an organization's climate is displayed in Figure 9.6. Responses are coded in reverse order for the first two questions in that scale. Because low scores are assigned to negative attitudes, agreeing with the statement in question 18 is coded with low values. Question 19 is assumed to register a positive attitude toward the company. Positive attitudes are assigned with high values. Hence, agreeing with the statement is coded with high values.

Individual attitude statements to be used as statements or items in the Likert scale are often generated by an exploratory study that uses a series of in-depth interviews with key informants in the organization or sample.

Semantic Differential and Stapel Scales. Two additional scales are often used to measure attitudes and opinions. These are the *semantic differential* and its close relative, the *Stapel scale.* Semantic differential scales are pairs of opposing adjectives, with spaces between each for subjects to mark their opinion. A seven-point scale typically separates the adjectives. Subjects are asked to make a personal judgment about a characteristic or a complete concept. For example, the adjective pairs can be used to help researchers build a picture of how subjects rate the service they receive at a particular agency. Or, the adjective pairs could pertain to the agency as a whole.

For example, subjects could be asked to rate the overall effectiveness of a proposed public service announcement for an AIDS prevention campaign. Subjects are asked to read the brochure, then rate it on a five-point scale, checking the boxes that most closely match their perceptions of the document. Figure 9.7 shows the paired adjectives.

The Stapel scale is almost identical to the semantic differential, except that only *one* of the polar adjectives is used instead of both; the scale is *unipolar* rather than *bipolar.*

In practice, many researchers consider the points on both the semantic differential and Stapel scale to be equidistant, thus providing interval-level data. However, because the assigned differences are arbitrarily assigned, other researchers feel that these scales provide only ordinal data. This conflicting interpretation has resulted in a reduction in the use of the scales in social and administrative science research.

Summary

Researchers use two different approaches when gathering primary data in quantitative research studies; they may collect data by *observing* and counting overt acts of behavior, or they may use a *questionnaire* to generate responses to specific questions.

Questionnaires are the most popular way to gather primary data. They are particularly appropriate when the research problem calls for a *descriptive* design. Questionnaires have many advantages. The greatest of these is their *flexibility.* Questionnaires can be custom designed to meet the objectives of almost any type of research project.

	Very Definitely Describes ⇓						Does Not Describe ⇓
18. The philosophy of our management is that in the long run we get ahead fastest by playing it slow, safe, and sure.	[ ]₁	[ ]₂	[ ]₃	[ ]₄	[ ]₅	[ ]₆	[ ]₇
19. You get rewarded for taking risks in this organization.	[ ]₇	[ ]₆	[ ]₅	[ ]₄	[ ]₃	[ ]₂	[ ]₁
20. Decision making in this organization is too cautious for maximum effectiveness.	[ ]₁	[ ]₂	[ ]₃	[ ]₄	[ ]₅	[ ]₆	[ ]₇
21. You won't get ahead in this organization unless you stick your neck out and take a chance now and then.	[ ]₇	[ ]₆	[ ]₅	[ ]₄	[ ]₃	[ ]₂	[ ]₁
22. We do things by the book around here; taking risks is strongly discouraged.	[ ]₁	[ ]₂	[ ]₃	[ ]₄	[ ]₅	[ ]₆	[ ]₇
23. We have to take some pretty big risks occasionally to make sure the organization meets its objectives.	[ ]₇	[ ]₆	[ ]₅	[ ]₄	[ ]₃	[ ]₂	[ ]₁

Low values = negative attitudes; high values = positive attitudes. Positive statements are reverse scored.

Figure 9.6 Likert-Type Statements to Measure Attitudes Toward Risk in an Organization

Source: McNabb, Sepic, and Barnowe 1999.

Clear	[ ]	[ ]	[ ]	[ ]	[ ]	Confusing
Simple	[ ]	[ ]	[ ]	[ ]	[ ]	Difficult
Complete	[ ]	[ ]	[ ]	[ ]	[ ]	Incomplete
Realistic	[ ]	[ ]	[ ]	[ ]	[ ]	Phony
Valuable	[ ]	[ ]	[ ]	[ ]	[ ]	Worthless

Figure 9.7 An Example of a Semantic Differential Scale

Seven steps are followed in questionnaire construction: (1) establish what information is needed, (2) specify the data-gathering method, (3) specify procedures for analyzing the data, (4) select question type and structure, (5) select the best wording for each question, (6) organize the question in a logical order, and (7) pretest and revise the questionnaire, if necessary.

Questions may be written as a limited set of responses from which the respondent must choose (closed-ended), or they may allow respondents to provide answers in their own words (open-ended).

Open-ended questions can be divided into two broad types: *completely unstructured response* and *projective techniques.* Unstructured response questions are entirely the subject's own responses to a question. Projective techniques allow subjects to respond to some stimulus in their own words. The stimulus can be words, pictures, or symbols. The questions are structured in such a way that the respondent unconsciously *projects* hidden feelings or attitudes into the response. Five different types of projective techniques are used in public administration research: association, construction, completion, ordering, and expressive techniques.

There are two types of closed-ended questions: *structured answer* (dichotomous and multiple-choice) and *scales.* Structured answer questions are used for warm-up, introductory, and classification portions of the questionnaire; scales are usually found in the body of the questionnaire. The types of scales used most often in public administration research are importance scales, rating scales, and readiness-to-act scales and attitude scales.

Many different types of scales have been developed for measuring attitudes. The attitude scale methods that are used most often today are Thurstone scales, Likert scales, semantic differential rating scales, and their related approach, the Stapel scale.

Suggested Reading

Alreck, Pamela L., and Robert B. Settle. 1995. *The Survey Research Handbook.* 2d. ed. Boston: Irwin McGraw-Hill.

DeVellin, Robert F. 1991. *Scale Development: Theory and Applications.* Newbury Park, CA: Sage.

Folz, David H. 1996. *Survey Research for Public Administration.* Thousand Oaks, CA: Sage.

Oskamp, Stuart. 1977. *Attitudes and Opinions.* Englewood Cliffs, NJ: Prentice Hall, 1977.

O'Sullivan, Elizabethann, and Gary R. Rassel. 1995. *Research Methods for Public Administrators.* 2d ed. White Plains, NY: Longman.

Part 4

Quantitative Analysis Methods

10 Using Descriptive Statistics

Two types of statistics are used in quantitative research, *descriptive* statistics and *inferential* statistics. Some descriptive statistics are found in almost every type of research report. Descriptive statistics are used for two major purposes. First, they are used to *summarize* a data set. Second, they are used to *numerically describe* sample units, phenomena, and other variables of interest. Inferential statistics, on the other hand, are used when sample data are used to infer application for populations as well. Inferential statistics comprise a large body of powerful statistical tools that are used to make assumptions or inferences about populations from the measurements taken of sample units drawn from the population. This chapter focuses on the four major descriptive statistics used in social and administrative science research, and includes a brief introduction to the idea of data distributions. Chapters 13–15 will cover inferential statistics.

Neither researchers nor administrators can get much use from unprocessed, unorganized sets of raw numbers. Considered in bulk, unprocessed data are, at best, coarse measurements. The data must be brought into some sort of order before their meaning can be found. This occurs in a series of six phases (Figure 10.1). In the first phase, the researcher decides upon an appropriate measurement program. This entails preparing items and questions that produce the most powerful data possible commensurate with the objectives of the study. In the second phase, the data are gathered using questionnaires or schedules in personal interviews, by telephone, or by mailed surveys. Once the data are gathered, the third phase of computer coding and tabulating (counting) all responses begins. This key organization and structuring phase is followed by the first of two key statistical procedures: the fourth phase is the production of frequency counts and percentage distributions of all responses; the fifth phase is the produc-

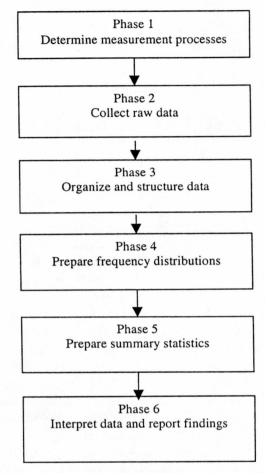

Figure 10.1 **A Model of the Phases of Descriptive Statistics Data Processing**

tion of the desired types of summary statistics. In the sixth and final phase, the researcher prepares a written report interpreting the statistical information produced by whatever statistical software is used.

Summary Statistics

Researchers use four different types of descriptive statistics to convey summary information (Lang and Heiss 1990).

- Measures of central tendency
- Measures of variability

- Measures of relative position
- Measures of correlation

These four types of measures described by Lang and Heiss make it possible to reduce a large data set down to a few meaningful numbers that everyone can understand. These summary numbers can then provide essential information about the internal structure of the raw data.

An example of how the first three of these summary measurements can be used in public and nonprofit organization applications is in the records of the performance characteristics of a sandbag-filling machine used by a state roadway maintenance crew. The quality-assurance processes employed by the department include measuring the performance of the filling equipment by the periodic weighing of samples of filled bags. Since it is unlikely that the weights of filled sandbags are always exactly identical, performance will typically fall within some *range* of values. Wet sand might partially clog the filling equipment one day, with dry sand flowing smoothly the next day. Spillage may occur, an operator might miss an equipment breakdown, or any other random factor may have an effect on the process.

The production manager will want to know the average weight of filled bags and whether the range of bag weights falls within what roadway engineers have established as the acceptable upper and lower weight limits. The manager might also want to know what value appears most often and how widely the filled sandbags vary within the range. These measurements are discussed in detail below.

Measures of Central Tendency

The main purpose of measurements of central tendency is to identify the value in the data set that is "most typical" of the full set. This "typical" value may then be used as a summary value. Several different numbers can be used as measures of location. These include the mean (either algebraic or geometric), the median, and the mode.

The easiest way to quickly summarize a set of measurements is to identify the most typical value in the set (sometimes called the "most representative score"). Five types of measurements are used to communicate central tendency:

- The arithmetic mean
- The median

- The mode
- The geometric mean
- The trimmed mean

Calculating the Mean

The term "central tendency" refers to a point in a data set that corresponds to a typical, representative, or central value. The measurement used most often for this is the *arithmetic mean*. Means are only valid for use with data that are ratio or equidistant interval (i.e., quantitative). Attitude scales used by marketing decision makers are a typical example of an application where a mean (or "average") score for the total sample conveys far more information than the response of any one subject in the sample. A mean score of 1.2 on a 5-point scale item, with low scores equating with negative attitudes and high scores with positive attitudes, clearly suggests an interpretation for the attitude held by members of this sample.

The Arithmetic Mean

Also known as the "average of all scores," the mean is the number arrived at by adding up all the values of a variable and then dividing by the number of items or cases in the set. It is used when the distribution of scores is fairly symmetrical about the center value. When plotted, a symmetrical distribution produces the typical bell-shaped curve.

Mean scores or values are generally not valid for use with categorical (i.e., nominal and ordinal) measurements, although most public administration researchers have accepted use of the mean with certain ordinal data. Say, for example, that a state natural resources agency conducts a series of meetings with outdoor sportsmen to establish preferences for a proposed salmon protection program. Citizens are asked to rank five different programs in their order of preference. The agency wants to know which of the programs has the best chance of being accepted across the state. Normally, a "mean rank" value would not be an appropriate statistic for these categorical data. However, establishing mean ranks is a requirement for certain nonparametric statistical tests. Thus, mean rank values are encountered on some statistical program printouts and are reported by some researchers. It is more scientifically accurate, however, to use the mode rather than a mean in such cases.

In an example with nominal data, subjects are asked to indicate their occupation from a list of eight or nine categories. The number of responses for each category is informative; the modal category is the one that was checked most often. Determining the "mean" occupational category is nonsense.

Frequencies and means are of interest for both populations and samples. Their computation is similar, but separate notation or symbols differentiate them:

N = the total number of cases in a population
n = the total number of cases in a sample
μ = the mean of a population (pronounced "mew")
$\bar{X}$ = the mean for a sample (pronounced "X-bar")

The Median

The *median* is the halfway point in a set of numbers. Half of the values are above the median value; half are below. The median is appropriate for all data types, but is particularly useful with ranking (ordinal) data or when the data set contains *outliers*—extreme values that could disproportionately influence the mean. Because the median deals with structure or order in the data set, it can be used with ordinal and interval/ratio data, but it is meaningless with nominal (categorical) data.

For a small-sample example of how the median is computed, assume that during the first half-hour of a fund-raising event, a public broadcast radio station received donations in the following amounts: $25, $18, $20, $22, and $100. The mean donation value is the total amount divided by the number of donations, or $185 divided by 5 ($185/5), or $37. It should be obvious that a mean of $37 is misleading, because the $100 donation (an *outlier*) unduly influences the result. A more meaningful measure of location in this case would be the median, which is $22. This is arrived at by rearranging the data in ascending order ($18, $20, $22, $25, and $100), followed by selecting the value that falls in the center. Two donations fall below $22, and two fall above $22. For larger data sets, the median can be computed by subtracting 1 from the total number of cases and then dividing by 2. The formula for computing the median is:

$$\text{Median} = (n + 1)/2.$$

The Mode

The *mode* is the value for a variable that appears most often. It is the value with the greatest frequency of occurrence. The mode can be used for a quick estimate of the typical or representative score.

The mode is the only measurement that makes sense when dealing with nominal-level variables. It is defined as the value that appears most often in a collection of all counts for a variable. For example, a focus-group study was conducted at college running tracks for a marketer of sports shoes. Subjects were asked which of four shoe styles they preferred. Individual styles were assigned identifying code numbers ranging from 1 to 4. The final tally of subjects' preferences was: 3, 2, 1, 1, 3, 4, 2, 3, 1, 2, 1, 1, 1. The category value "1" appears most often in the data set: six times. This gives the decision maker the maximum amount of information. Since the numbers represent specific styles and are not quantitative, both the mean and the median clearly would be inappropriate measures of location in this example.

Public facilities managers and designers are often interested in the modal distribution. They look at distribution of public-area usage in order to provide appropriate space for heavy- and light-use activities in building designs.

The Geometric Mean

The *geometric mean* is the root of the product of all items in the data set. It is particularly appropriate when computing an average of changes in percentages. For some reason, not all statistics texts include a discussion of the geometric mean. However, it has many uses in statistical research applications.

Few social and administrative science statistics texts today include a discussion of the geometric mean. This is a mistake. There are many instances where a geometric mean is far more appropriate than an arithmetic mean. An appropriate use of the geometric mean is when a program manager wants to know the average change in operating costs for a series of percentage changes. Say, for example, that an administrator has gathered the following figures for a four-year period and wants to know the overall average percentage change (Table 10.1). The arithmetic mean for the 1997–2000 period is 7 percent ($12 + 7 + 2/3 = 21/3 = 7$). Computing the geometric mean, however, arrives at a more appropriate measure. This mean is computed by multiplying each percentage change in sequence; note that each change is the new change plus the base 100 percent (which is the previous value), then determining the root for the cases included (in this case, the cube root):

$$G = \sqrt[3]{(X_1 \times X_2 \times X_3 ... \times X_n)}$$

Table 10.1

Costs in the Portland District, 1997–2000 (in thousands)

	Year			
	1997	1998	1999	2000
Costs ($)	4,000	4,800	4,940	4,890
Change (%)	—	12	7	2

Table 10.2

Excel Worksheet Setup for the Geometric Mean

	Year				
	1997	1998	1999	2000	Gmean
Costs ($)	4,000	4,800	4,940	4,890	
Change (%)	—	112	107	102	106.922

Note: 106.922 = 6.9%

$$G = \sqrt[3]{(112 \times 107 \times 102)}$$
$$G = \sqrt[3]{1,234,352}$$
$$G = 6.92\%$$

Thus, a more accurate average rate of cost increase over the period is 6.92 percent, not the 7 percent of the arithmetic mean.

Excel Example

Calculating the geometric mean is a quick and simple process with Microsoft Excel (Figure 10.2). The data are arranged in a column array; the GEOMEAN option is then selected from the Function Wizard. All computations are conducted in the Wizard, which computes a geometric mean to four decimal points. Follow these steps; the worksheet will look like the material in Table 10.2.

The Trimmed Mean

The *trimmed mean* is used when researchers are interested in the core set of values and feel that the upper and lower ends of the data set do more to confuse the issue than they add; it is considered to be more

- Insert all labels and values into a new worksheet. Cell A1 contains the label for column 1, "Variable."

- In cells B1 through E1, insert the years 1993 through 1996. Type the label "Gmean" in cell F1.

- Insert the labels and data. Percentage changes must be written as hundreds: e.g., a 7 percent increase must be inserted as "107."

- In cell F4, insert an equals sign (=).

- Select the Function Wizard (*fx*). Scroll down to GEOMEAN. "= GEOMEAN" will appear in the worksheet formula bar for that cell.

- Hit return to begin the calculation.

- The value for the geometric mean will appear in cell F4, alongside the last inserted percentage change value.

Figure 10.2 **Microsoft Excel Process for Computing the Geometic Mean**

resistant to the influence of extreme values than the arithmetic mean (Brase and Brase 1999). It is calculated by eliminating *both* the top 5 percent and the bottom 5 percent of the set of values. The trimmed mean is then calculated from the remaining values in the same way as the arithmetic mean is calculated.

Measures of Variability

Measurements of variability (sometimes referred to as measures of dispersion) tell us how the individual measurements vary within the set. They include the *range*, the *variance*, and the *standard deviation* of a set of measurements. Percentiles and the nature of the distribution of the data numbers are also used to indicate position and variation in a range. The last topic to be examined in this chapter, correlation, explores the relationships or associations between two or more variables.

Once the administrative decision maker has determined which is the appropriate measure of location, the next concern is to determine how the *distribution* of numbers in the data varies around the central value. The questions to answer here are: *How and to what extent are the scores or values different from one another? How can this variability be summarized?* The three most common ways to express variability are the *range*, the *variance*, and the *standard deviation*; these all provide information about the distribution of responses within the range.

The Range

The *range* is the easiest statistic to compute. It is determined by subtracting the lowest value from the highest value in a distribution. It can be misleading, however, and is not used very often by itself. Alone, the range does not take into consideration the actual variation of scores within a distribution; it is, therefore, only a crude approximation of variability. For example, consider the following two sets of data:

Data Set A: 65, 80, 81, 82, 83, 84, 98
Data Set B: 65, 69, 74, 78, 87, 89, 98

Both sets have the same range: 98 – 65 = 33. However, a closer look at the two sets reveals that Set B clearly has more internal variability than Set A. In Set A, five of the seven values are in the low 80s, whereas in Set B, the values are spread across the entire range.

Also limiting the usefulness of the range is the fact that it uses only two values in the set of measurements: the highest and lowest values. As a result, *percentiles* (also called *fractiles*) are often used with the range to give more meaning to this measurement. Percentiles are values below which some proportion of the total scores or observations fall. The most commonly used percentiles divide the data into *quartiles*. These divide the data into roughly 25 percent segments. A quarter of the values fall below the first (or 25 percent) quartile; half are below the second (or 50 percent) quartile; and three-fourths are below the third quartile. The second quartile value is the same value as the median.

The Variance

The *variance* is an index of how scores or values in a data set vary from their mean or average value. Because it is only an index of variation, interpreting the variance is more art than science. Statistically, the variance is defined as the average of the squared deviation of all values in the range, divided by the number of cases in the data set minus 1. The size of the value is used for subjective interpretation; larger variance values that indicate the data are more spread out, whereas smaller variances mean that the values are more concentrated around the mean.

Many comprehensive statistics texts distinguish between the variance of a set of scores for a sample and the variance of a set of values for a population. The formulas for computing each are slightly different: for a population, the divisor is N; for a sample, the divisor is $n-1$. Similar differences occur with the standard deviation of populations and samples. Because researchers and administrators most often deal with samples rather than total populations, the variance for a sample is the statistic used most of the time.

The Standard Deviation

Because the variance is only an index or rough indicator of variation and, thus, somewhat abstract, it is far more common to find variability stated in terms of the standard deviation rather than as the variance. The standard deviation is nothing more than the square root of the variance. Rather than a squared value, which suggests or implies variation, the standard deviation is a more exact measurement, stated in exactly the same units as the original data.

Because the standard deviation focuses on variation from the true mean, it is probably the most reliable of all the measures of variability and is the one used most often.

As with the variance, standard deviations for samples and for populations vary slightly in their computation formulas. The divisor for the standard deviation of a population is the total number of cases (N); for a sample, it is $n-1$.

Excel Instructions

Excel's procedures for obtaining both the variance and the standard deviation for samples and populations are included under the STATISTICS function on the main toolbar. The subcommand for the variance of a sample is VAR; for the variance of a population, it is VARP. To obtain the standard deviation for a sample, the function command is STDEV; for the standard deviation of a population, the command is STDEVP.

Measures of Relative Position

Measures of *relative position* are used to compare one score against any other score in the data set. Two types of measures can be used for this: *percentiles* and *standard scores*.

Percentiles

Percentiles are points or values used to indicate the percentage of subjects or of measurements with scores below that percentile point. Percentiles are very common in education statistics. Every secondary school student's scores on the SAT exams include an indication of how that set of scores compares with all other students' scores for that test set. Similar applications exist for the Law School Aptitude Test (LSAT), General Management Aptitude Test (GMAT), and the Graduate Record Examination (GRE).

Say, for example, a graduate business school applicant scores 580 on the GMAT. This might be reported as falling in the 85th percentile (P_{85}) of all scores for persons taking the test at that time. This means that 85 percent of all applicants had lower scores than the applicant's 580. If the applicant had scored 450, this might have fallen in the 65th percentile (P_{65}), and so on. The 50th percentile (P_{50}) is always the median value for that set of scores.

One important application of quartiles used in organizational research is the *interquartile range*. This includes all values above the first quartile and below the third quartile, which is the same as the range for the central 50 percent of all cases.

Excel Example

Microsoft Excel includes procedures for obtaining any-level percentiles as well as standard quartiles. These functions are incorporated into the STATISTICS toolbox of the Function Wizard (*fx*). When the Function Wizard is selected, two lists appear in the window. The left-hand list shows categories of functions, one of which is STATISTICS. Within the STATISTICS master-category function are a variety of specific functions. These appear in the right-hand window. Scroll bars must be used to display all the choices available.

The commands for Excel's percentile function are slightly different from most applications. In Excel, a single-digit value between 0 and 1 must be entered. For example, to arrive at the 90 percent percentile value, the user must enter 9. In most other applications, the values to be entered are a number between 0 and 99.

With the Excel Quartile function, the user may set the QUART value from 0 to 4. Setting it to 1, 2, or 3 will return the corresponding quartile values. Setting it to 0 or 4 will return either the minimum or maximum values in the data set range. Excel uses the median value for the second quartile.

- Arrange the raw data into a one-column array. Use the Arrange Wizard to arrange the data in ascending or descending order.

- Calculate the mean for the total sample using the Function Wizard.

- Calculate the standard deviation for the total sample using the Function Wizard.

- Using the STANDARDIZE option in the Function Wizard applications, insert the three appropriate values.

Figure 10.3 **Excel Process for Conducting Standardized Scores (Z-Scores)**

Standard Scores

Standard scores are the original, raw, scores of the data set that have been statistically transformed in order to establish a common measurement foundation for all scores. They are often used to compare one score against another.

When scores are all transformed in the same way, it becomes possible to compare any two or more scores against one another on an equal basis. The standard-score transformation used most often is the *Z-score*. Z-scores are raw scores that have been converted into standard deviation units. The Z-score indicates how many standard deviation units any one score is from the mean score for the total group.

Z-scores also make it possible to compare a single subject's scores on two different scales. For example, the SAT includes a section that tests communication skills and a section that tests mathematics skills. The mean score for each of these components serves as the common reference point for the test population; standard deviations are the common unit used to measure variability. By using the Z-scale to interpret the individual's scores, a clear picture of how they compare with the total group's scores is readily apparent.

Excel Example

Standardized scores (Z-values) are easy and quick to compute with Microsoft Excel. All that is required is to highlight the data set and then select the STANDARDIZE optional command from the Function Wizard.

The formula for standardization requires three numbers: (1) the value(s) to be standardized; (2) the mean for the sample; (3) the standard deviation

Table 10.3

Weights of Sample Sandbags, A.M. Shift

Hour	Sandbag weights (in pounds and tenths)					
	Sample 1	Sample 2	Sample 3	Sample 4	Sample 5	Sample 6
1	18.4	17.9	18.6	19.0	17.8	18.7
2	18.2	18.0	18.5	19.1	17.4	19.0
3	18.0	18.1	18.4	19.2	16.9	18.8
4	17.9	18.2	18.6	19.1	17.6	18.5

Table 10.4

Standardized Values for Weights of Sandbag Samples, A.M. Shift

Raw score	Sample mean	Sample SD	Standardized (Z-score)
18.4	18.3	0.582707	0.1216
18.2	18.3	0.582707	−0.2164
18.0	18.3	0.582707	−0.5694
17.9	18.3	0.582707	−0.7682
17.9	18.3	0.582707	−0.7365
18.0	18.3	0.582707	−0.5148
18.1	18.3	0.582707	−0.3432
18.2	18.3	0.582707	−0.1716
18.6	18.3	0.582707	0.5148
18.5	18.3	0.582707	0.3432
18.4	18.3	0.582707	0.1716
18.6	18.3	0.582707	0.5148
19.0	18.3	0.582707	1.2013
19.1	18.3	0.582707	1.3729
19.2	18.3	0.582707	1.5445
19.1	18.3	0.582707	1.3729
17.8	18.3	0.582707	−0.8581
17.4	18.3	0.582707	−1.5445
16.9	18.3	0.582707	−2.4026
17.6	18.3	0.582707	−1.2013
18.7	18.3	0.582707	0.6865
19.0	18.3	0.582707	1.2013
18.8	18.3	0.582707	0.8581
18.5	18.3	0.582707	0.3432

Table 10.5

Data Types and Their Appropriate Correlation Statistics

Data type	Measurement statistic
Nominal	Chi-square (X^2) [phi and Cramer's V]
Ordinal	Spearman's rho
Interval	Pearson's r (r or r^2)
Ratio	Pearson's r (r or r^2)

(SD) for the sample. To calculate Z-scores with Microsoft Excel, follow the simple steps in Figure 10.3. For example, data from the sandbag-filling example are displayed in Table 10.3. The results of an Excel standardization of the measurements from Table 10.3 are displayed in Table 10.4.

Measures of Correlation

Measures of *correlation* are used to reveal the relationships or associations between two or more variables or subjects. Measures of correlation are commonly included in social and administrative science research reports along with other descriptive statistics.

Data are grouped into two categories, depending upon the type of measurements they represent—*discrete* or *continuous*. Nominal and ordinal data are categorical and, therefore, represent *discrete numbers*. Interval and ratio data can vary within a set of ranges; they are considered to be *continuous*. Except for interval and ratio data, different correlation measures must be used with different data types, as indicated in Table 10.5.

It is important to remember that correlation should be considered as a summary measurement. Values ranging from 0.0 to 1.0 ($\pm$) should be considered as indicators of a relationship between the two variables, not as an indication of causality. In this way, they provide the researcher with suggestions for further research involving experiments and causal designs.

Understanding Distributions

It is important at this point for researchers to have some idea about the role of distributions. A distribution is a representation of the way all the measurements for a single variable would look if each were to be plotted on an x- and y-axis. A line that follows the top of the distributions provides a graphic view of how the responses are distributed.

Understanding the information contained in a given set of scores or values requires looking at the ways that frequency distributions of scores can be distributed around their mean value. We are most familiar with what are called normal distributions. Normal distributions result in the typical bell-shaped curves that enclose a group of individual scores or measurements. Students' test scores often follow this type of distribution. Normal distributions tend to be symmetric, with the mean and median falling near one another at the middle or high point on the curve. The modal value is often close to this point as well.

- Approximately 68 percent of all the items will be within one standard deviation of the mean.

- Approximately 95 percent of the items will be within two standard deviations of the mean.

- Almost all items will be within three standard deviations of the mean.

Figure 10.4 **Empirical Rules That Apply to Normal Distributions**

Step 1. Arrange the data in a spreadsheed data array.

Step 2. Highlight the data only (do not highlight the row or column labels.)

Step 3. Select the Tools option followed by the Data Analysis option.

Step 4. In the Data Analysis option, select Descriptive Statistics.

Figure 10.5 **Procedure for Producing Descriptive Statistics with Excel**

Most distributions encountered in public administration and social science research tend to be normal. That is, the bulk of the responses or scores cluster around the mean, with the rest trailing off toward both ends. When the distribution of scores does not cluster around the mean, the distribution cannot be described as normal. Nonnormal distributions may see the scores grouped at either end of the scale or in more than a single concentration.

Nonnormal distributions are known as *skewed* or *asymmetrical* distributions, and somewhat different distribution rules prevail. The information about normal distributions in Figure 10.4 has been found to be true so often that it is now accepted as a "rule."

In normal distributions, one standard deviation value above the mean will include close to 34 percent of all the cases in the data set. Similarly, one standard deviation below the mean will include another 34 percent of the sample, for a total of 68 percent falling within a range of plus or minus

Table 10.6

Descriptive Statistics, Total Sample, Produced by Microsoft Excel

Mean	18.32917
Standard error	9.118945
Median	18.4
Mode	18.4
Standard deviation	0.582707
Sample variance	0.339547
Kurtosis	0.061706
Skewness	−0.050748
Range	2.3
Minimum	16.9
Maximum	19.2
Sum	439.9
Count	24
Confidence level (95.0%)	0.246055

Table 10.7

Descriptive Statistics, Individual Samples, Produced by Microsoft Excel

	Sample			
	Hour 1	Hour 2	Hour 3	Hour 4
Mean	18.4	18.36667	18.23333	18.31667
Standard error	0.191485	0.261619	0.323179	0.2182
Median	18.5	18.35	18.25	18.35
Mode				
Standard deviation	0.469042	0.640833	0.791623	0.534478
Sample variance	0.22	0.410667	0.626667	0.285667
Kurtosis	−1.45702	−0.67794	1.130976	−0.43236
Skewness	−0.26166	−0.34933	−0.78347	0.132737
Range	1.2	1.7	2.3	1.5
Minimum	17.8	17.4	16.9	17.6
Maximum	19	19.1	19.2	19.1
Sum	110.4	110.2	109.4	109.9
Count	6	6	6	6
Confidence level (95.0%)	0.492228	0.672512	0.830756	0.560899

one standard deviation. Another 27 percent of the cases will be included if one more standard deviation above and below the mean is included. Thus, together some 95 percent of all cases will fall within two standard deviations above or below the mean. Finally, when three standard deviations are included, 99.7 percent of all cases will be included under the curve (this makes the normal distribution *six standard deviations wide*).

As might be expected, not all distributions are normal. Some have a majority of the values gathered at either the low or the high end of the scale. Other distributions have the great majority gathered at the center, whereas others may bunch up in two or more points or modes. The terms used to describe these nonnormal distributions are *positively skewed*, *negatively skewed*, and *bimodal distributions*.

Positively skewed distributions have their peak nearer the *left-hand* end of the graph, with the line stretched out toward the lower right-hand corner. Negatively skewed distributions have greater concentrations at the *right-hand* side, with the left line stretched toward the lower left-hand corner. Bimodal distributions have two concentrations of scores, with curves resembling a two-humped camel's back. Multimodal distributions have three or more concentrations or peaks.

Calculating Descriptive Statistics with Excel

The Microsoft Excel Data Analysis package contained in the Tools subprogram will produce a complete set of summary statistics with very little effort (Figure 10.5). Table 10.3 displays the data from the sandbag packaging process example introduced earlier. The results are displayed in Table 10.6.

To produce complete descriptive statistics for each hourly sample of six packages each, click on the box that indicates that the data are arranged in rows (each row is a sample of six packages). Table 10.7 displays the Excel-produced complete descriptive statistics for each of the four samples.

Summary

Descriptive statistics are used to summarize data and describe samples. Four categories of descriptive information can be used for these purposes: measures of central tendency, measures of variability, measures of relative position, and measures of correlation. All of these statistics can be quickly calculated with Microsoft Excel.

Five measures of central tendency can be used in descriptive statistics. They include the arithmetic mean (also called the average), the median, the mode, the geometric mean, and the trimmed mean. Three measures of variability are the range, the variance, and the standard deviation.

Two measures of relative position—percentiles and standard scores—make it possible to compare one score against any other in the data set. The most commonly used standard scores is the Z-statistic, which states variation in values of standard deviations from the mean. For most data sets, almost all scores fall within plus or minus (±) three standard deviations of the group mean.

Measures of correlation are used to numerically identify the level of relationships between variables. Care must be taken to avoid unsubstantiated cause-and-effect relationships from correlation values.

When plotted, a distribution of individual scores on a variable can take several different shapes. Distributions that take on the shape of a bell are considered to be "normal" distributions. This is an important fact since a required assumption of many statistical tests is that the data approximate a normal distribution. Most distributions will approximate a normal distribution, although some distributions will be positively or negatively skewed, while others will be bi- or multimodal distributions.

Suggested Reading

Berenson, Mark L., and David M. Levine. 1996. *Basic Business Statistics*. 6th ed. Upper Saddle River, NJ: Prentice Hall.

Brightman, Harvey J. 1999. *Data Analysis in Plain English, with Microsoft Excel*. Pacific Grove, CA: Duxbury Press.

Einspruch, Eric L. 1998. *An Introductory Guide to SPSS for Windows*. Thousand Oaks, CA: Sage.

Lang, Gerhard, and George D. Heiss. 1997. *A Practical Guide to Research Methods*. 6th ed. Lanham, MD: University Press of America.

Phillips, John L. 1996. *How to Think About Statistics*. 5th ed. New York: Freeman.

Sincich, Terry. 1996. *Business Statistics by Example*. 5th ed. Upper Saddle River, NJ: Prentice Hall.

11 Using Tables, Charts, and Graphs

A principal objective of statistics is to summarize the information contained in a data set. When first collected, data usually have little or no meaning for the researcher or decision maker. "Raw data" must be put into some kind of order or structure; then they are grouped together into sets that have logic and meaning. Numbers do not speak for themselves; they acquire meaning only when they are organized in terms of some mutually understood framework (Wasson 1965).

The nature of the data influences the way they are presented. For example, summary data are usually displayed in the form of a table or a graphic presentation of some kind. There are a number of different ways to present data in graphic form, including *scatter plots*, *histograms*, *bar charts*, *pie charts*, and *relative frequency polygons*. These graphic tools can be used to present summary statistics, frequency distributions, relative frequencies, and percentage distributions with greater impact than is possible with simple tables.

Graphic displays and other illustrations make reports more readable and more effective in meeting their communications objectives. In the process, they serve several important purposes. First, they make it easier for the researcher to capture the meaning of the data. Second, they allow the researcher to more clearly apply the data to the decisions or actions that are going to be taken based on the results of the study. Third, they make it easier for readers of the research report to see how the analyst arrived at the conclusions and interpretations presented in the decision-making report (Wasson 1965, 176).

This chapter describes how researchers structure and display raw data. It describes how graphic representations can be used to display the meaning of a study and to improve the quality of research reports. The chapter begins with a section on how to make sense of ungrouped or "raw" data and then discusses how to create and use tables, charts, and graphs.

Making Sense Out of Ungrouped or "Raw" Data

A collection of raw data by itself typically contains very little information; analyzing and applying order to the data set are required before research results make sense. Tables, charts, and graphs are used for this purpose.

Stem-and-Leaf Diagram

One of the first analysis steps the researcher takes to give meaning to raw data is to construct either a *stem-and-leaf diagram*, a *frequency distribution table*, or a *histogram*. Nearly all statistical-analysis reports include frequency distribution tables and/or histograms; stem-and-leaf diagrams are used far less often. However, stem-and-leaf diagrams can be more informative than simple frequency tables because none of the underlying data are lost in the analysis; all values are displayed. Histograms present summary data, but they do not display individual values for a class in the way that a stem-and-leaf diagram does.

The first step to take in preparing any graphic tool is to organize and enter the responses for each of the cases into a computer database. There are several different ways to do this, but today data are usually entered into a simple *spreadsheet data file*. In all spreadsheets, each variable is entered as a separate column, with "cases" entered in rows running across the page. The stem-and-leaf diagram is a visual representation of the data from a single variable —entered as one spreadsheet column. The following example presents the steps to take to create a stem-and-leaf diagram from columnar data.

Building the Stem-and-Leaf Diagram

In this example, the supervisor of a sandbag filling process is responsible for ensuring that the filling equipment loads eighteen pounds of sand in each bag. Statistics can be used to monitor this process. It would not be cost-effective to weigh every single sandbag; instead, the supervisor can accomplish the task by randomly selecting and weighing several samples of bags from the filling line.

Over a four-hour morning shift, six packages are pulled and weighed each hour, for a total sample of twenty-four bags. The weight of each bag is entered on a spreadsheet; a Microsoft Excel Data File is used for this purpose (Table 11.1). The supervisor can then create a *stem-and-leaf diagram* to prepare a summary of the measurements for the production manager.

In the spreadsheet, the column on the left contains the number assigned to each bag. The second column displays the number of the sample (1 through 4). The variable column contains the weights of all bags weighed for all samples.

Table 11.1

Spreadsheet Display of Sample Sandbag Weights

Bag no.	Sample no.	Bag weight
1	1	18.4
2	1	17.9
3	1	18.6
4	1	19.0
5	1	17.8
6	1	18.7
7	2	18.2
8	2	18.0
9	2	18.5
10	2	19.1
11	2	17.4
12	2	19.0
13	3	18.0
14	3	18.1
15	3	18.4
16	3	19.2
17	3	16.9
18	3	18.8
19	4	17.9
20	4	18.2
21	4	18.6
22	4	19.1
23	4	17.6
24	4	18.5

Normally, the researcher would be most concerned with the average weight of the six packages in each hourly sample (the mean weight for each sample), but for the stem-and-leaf diagram, the important information is the weight of each individual package. The stem-and-leaf diagram displays *variability in the sample* and is a good way to pictorially display the shape of the total distribution of package weights. A stem-and-leaf display is also a way to display at one glance all of the measurements for each major value; the "major values" in this example are the full pounds. These full numbers become the "stem" of the diagram: 16, 17, 18, and 19. The leaves are the partial-pound measurements (numbers after the decimal point). Examples include .0, .1, .2. and so on up to 9.

Excel Example

Excel does not include a special function or wizard for creating stem-and-leaf diagrams. However, it is possible to come up with a satisfactory diagram with several simple intermediate steps (Figure 11.1).

Step 1. Copy the Table 11.1 data as a spreadsheet data array with the data as a single column (as in Table 11.2, left column).

Step 2. Copy these data into an adjacent column.

Step 3. Convert to descending or ascending order (Table 11.2, right column).

Step 4. Form a stem-and-leaf diagram from the ordered data (Figure 11.2).

Figure 11.1 **Steps in Preparing a Stem-and Leaf Diagram Using Excel**

Table 11.2

Ordered Weights of Sample Sandbags

Raw data	Ascending order
18.4	16.9
18.2	17.4
18.0	17.6
17.9	17.8
19.9	17.9
18.0	18.0
18.1	18.0
18.2	18.1
18.6	18.2
18.5	18.2
18.4	18.4
18.6	18.4
19.0	18.5
19.1	18.5
19.2	18.6
19.1	18.6
17.8	18.7
17.4	18.8
16.9	19.0
17.6	19.0
18.7	19.1
19.0	19.1
18.8	19.2
18.5	19.9

15.												
16.	9											
17.	4,	6,	8,	9								
18.	0,	0,	1,	2,	2,	4,	4,	5,	5,	6,	6,	7,	8
19.	0,	0,	1,	1,	2,	9							
20.												

Figure 11.2 **Stem-and-Leaf Diagram of Sample Sandbag Weights**

The first step is to copy the bag weight from Table 11.1 onto a new two-column Excel worksheet; this is shown in Table 11.2. The first column should contain the raw data for all samples collectively. All the data must be entered in a single column. The second step is to copy these data into an adjacent column. The third step is to use the Sort Wizard to sort the copied data into ascending order (from the lowest value to the highest).

Then, to form the stem-and-leaf diagram, enter each stem value into an empty cell, beginning with the lowest value and ending with the highest value. Enter the tenths values for each stem value alongside the appropriate stem point. The completed stem-and-leaf diagram should look like the example displayed in Figure 11.2.

Presenting Data in Tables

The summary information displayed in the spreadsheet recording of the sample sandbag weights can also be presented as a *frequency distribution table*. An example of this form of display is presented in Table 11.3. However, the variability of the data shown in the stem-and-leaf diagram is lost when the data are shown in tabular form.

The first step in the analysis and interpretation of statistical data is to select a set of classes or categories among which the responses are to be distributed. Each category must be assigned its own specific code value. For example, the question, "What is your gender?" has two categories of responses, male and female. For computer processing of the data, a numerical value is assigned to each of these categories. "Female" may be assigned the value of 1 and "male" may be assigned the value 2.

In quantitative studies, the selection of categories and assigning of a value for each usually occurs in the questionnaire-preparation phase of the study. In qualitative studies, categories are selected after the data are gathered in a process known as *content analysis*. Closed-ended questions use established categories. The researcher subjectively selects categories for open-ended questions *after* the data are collected.

Table 11.3

Weights of Sample Sandbags, A.M. Shift (revised format)

	Sandbag weights (in pounds and tenths)			
Package no.	Sample 1	Sample 2	Sample 3	Sample 4
1	18.4	18.2	18.0	17.9
2	17.9	18.0	18.1	18.2
3	18.6	18.5	18.4	18.6
4	19.0	19.1	19.2	19.1
5	17.8	17.4	16.9	17.6
6	18.7	19.0	18.8	18.5

Note: Same data as Table 10.3.

Once categories and their individual values are established, the data can then be tabulated, with results presented in a table. Tables are sets of numbers and their identifying labels that have been organized in some logical way. These are called *frequency distribution tables*, or simply *frequencies* for short.

Frequency distribution tables are the most commonly used method of bringing order to raw data. Tables are used to reveal the underlying structure in a data set. Also, when data are arranged in tables, it is easier for anyone reading the report to spot trends, relationships, and/or differences in the data. Usually, however, the researcher will want more information than just the counts in a frequency distribution table. As a result, tables often also include the *percentage* of the total each class represents. Percentages are easily understood and typically convey more meaning than simple frequencies.

The following set of issues or concerns should be addressed when arranging data in a table:

- What is the total number of classes or categories to include?
- What are the upper and lower limits of each category?
- What title, captions, headings, and legends should be included?
- What additional explanatory numbers should be included (such as the relative percentage each number of occurrences represents, the percentage of each class when there is missing data, etc.)?

Establishing Categories or Classes

The total number of categories or classifications that cover all possibilities is called a *category set*. The number of classes or categories in the set depends on the purpose of the researcher. Simple decisions require less precision in the measurement than do more critical decisions. For example, decisions that involve spending large sums of public money, or that have the potential for loss of life if the wrong decision is made, will require far greater precision than decisions that deal with routine activities.

The number of categories or classes selected for tables is influenced by the nature of the data. For example, dichotomous data (male–female, yes–no, pass–fail, etc.) requires two and only two classes. With multichotomous data, more classes must be selected (*multichotomous* means more than two categories). Scales may require three, four, five, seven, nine, or even more classes of responses. There are no fixed rules for the numbers of classes to use in a scale. Despite the assumed "scientific" nature of statistics, researchers disagree on the number of classes, recommending anywhere from five to as many as ten or twenty.

Very large numbers of choices may create difficulties for respondents and for readers of the research report. When people are presented with numbers of classes beyond eight or so, some confusion or loss of continuity can occur. Because a key purpose for presenting data in tables in the first place is to communicate meaningful patterns in the data, it is best to limit the categories to a number that makes the most sense to the people reading the tables. This usually means using the *fewest* categories or classes possible. A good rule of thumb to follow is not to have more than eight categories in a table—and fewer if possible.

Working with Ordinal Data

When working with ordinal (ranked) data—such as people's preferences for programs or items, needs, priorities, and the like—the most commonly used number of classes range from around six to a maximum of twelve subjects. Experienced data analysts are convinced that most people experience difficulty when asked to rank more than six to eight items. People are usually able to quickly rank the top and lowest few, but distinctions blur when respondents must deal with a large number of unfamiliar items in the middle rankings.

Establishing Class or Category Widths for Tables

Table 11.4 displays partially grouped (raw) data that records the number of building permit applications processed by a county building department, Monday through Saturday, over a thirteen-week period. The data are shown organized into rows and columns. Each column is a different day's total (these values are known as the frequency of responses). Rows (across the page) are the numbers assigned to a sample. Sample units consist of all permits processed during the given week.

Table 11.4

Daily Permit Application Totals for Quarter 1

Week	Monday	Tuesday	Wednesday	Thursday	Friday	Saturday
1	110	83	95	112	110	72
2	99	121	115	105	112	59
3	120	80	92	103	111	61
4	121	95	87	125	103	63
5	73	113	78	92	93	64
6	91	83	122	107	93	71
7	107	130	85	111	112	56
8	99	69	74	104	106	57
9	123	105	111	101	117	66
10	85	105	109	88	109	55
11	108	99	117	106	109	61
12	102	75	74	128	116	54
13	64	124	91	118	85	63

The width or inclusiveness of each class is influenced by the nature of the data, the frequencies of occurrence, and the guidelines for the maximum number of classes to include. The range is determined by subtracting the lowest value from the highest value. A formula to establish class width follows:

$$\text{Class width} = \frac{\textit{Range of the data}}{\text{Preferred number of categories}}$$

By scanning through the data in Table 11.4, it is apparent that the highest number of permits processed (130) occurred on Tuesday of Week 7. The lowest number (54) occurred on Saturday of Week 12. Therefore, the range is 130 minus 54, or 76.

Suppose the researcher wants to present the data after it is grouped in six classes. To establish class widths, first substitute the range values in the formula to come up with a class width as follows:

$$W = \frac{76}{6} = 12.66$$

A class width of 12.66 is, at best, difficult to work with. However, since the nature of the data seems to lend itself to groupings of ten, the researcher could use a class width of 10 rather than the cumbersome 12.66. Or, if this resulted in too many classes, a width of 15 could be tried. Table 11.5 displays class ranges for 10-, 12-, and 15-wide classes for the data in Table 11.4.

Table 11.5

Class Widths and Range of Values for 10-, 12-, and 15-Wide Categories

Number of classes	10-wide classes range of values	12-wide classes range of values	15-wide classes range of values
1	50–59	48–59	45–59
2	60–69	60–71	60–74
3	70–79	72–83	75–89
4	80–89	84–95	90–104
5	90–99	96–107	105–119
6	100–109	108–119	120–134
7	110–119	120–131	
8	120–129	132–143	
9	130–139		
10			

Ten-wide ranges for each class should be 50–59, 60–69, and so on up to 130–193, rather than 50–60, 60–70, and so on up to 130–140. Nine classes would be needed to include all the data. Class ranges for 12-wide categories might begin with 48–59 and end with 132–143; eight classes would be needed for the data. With 15-wide classes, the lowest category range could be 45–59, with 120–134 the highest range; only six classes would be required. The important thing to remember is that all the classes *must* be the same size (equal in width) and that each measure can fall into one and *only* one class.

Additional guidelines for presenting data in tables begin with numbering each table and including a caption. Most often, it is easier to read the table when the data are arranged vertically, as opposed to having them spread across a page. Columns and rows must be identified, with qualifiers placed under the table in the form of footnotes. The caption and figure number of a table is always printed above the table; captions for graphs, charts, and other illustrations are presented below the figure.

Univariate and Multivariate Tables

Tables can be used for presenting any type of data and may be univariate, bivariate, or multivariate. Table 11.6 is a *univariate* table; it displays the counts of a single variable (gender only); Table 11.7 is *multivariate* (gender, height, and weight). Multivariate tables can be used to display the counts and other measurements of any number of variables. As such, they are an excellent way to display comparative information.

Table 11.6

Sample Univariate Table

	Number	Percent
Males	456	78.9
Females	122	21.1
Totals	578	100.0

Table 11.7

Sample Multivariate Table

Gender	n	Mean height (inches)	Mean weight (pounds)
Females	18	66.6	139
Males	12	71.3	177

Frequency Distribution Tables

A type of table often used in research reports is the frequency distribution table. Frequency distribution table measurements are grouped into classes. Then, the number of measurements or responses for each class is reported. The totals for each class are called the *frequency of responses* for that class. Frequency distribution tables present the frequencies or counts of the occurrence of each value (class or category) of a variable.

Frequency tables also display the *relative frequency* for each class. Relative frequency is the *proportion* of the total each group or value represents. Knowing the relative frequency of responses can be important for comparing the distribution of responses or measurements. It is conveniently communicated as a percentage. Table 11.8 is an example of a simple frequency distribution table showing responses to a multichotomous scale of exercise participation.

Some Rules for Frequency Tables

There are a few rules to follow when preparing frequency distribution tables. First, the table must be *internally consistent*. That is, groups or classes must be equal in size—except when dealing with outriders. In Table 11.9, except for the highest level, all classes consist of three-hour intervals. While the highest category appears to be open-ended, it is presented in this way for a purpose: It permits the analyst to deal with "outriders." Note that a category for "Missing" data has also been included in the table.

Table 11.8

Weekly Exercise Rates, Total Sample (Frequency)

Weekly hours of exercise	Frequency	Relative frequency	Cumulative percent
3 hours or less	5	0.156	15.6
4 to 6 hours	7	0.219	37.5
7 to 9 hours	10	0.312	68.7
10 to 12 hours	8	0.250	93.7
13 hours or more	2	0.063	100.0
Totals	32	1.00	

Table 11.9

Weekly Exercise Rates, Total Sample (Count)

Weekly hours of exercise	Count	Percent	Valid percent	Cumulative percent
3 hours or less	5	14.3	15.6	15.6
4 to 6 hours	7	20.0	21.9	37.5
7 to 9 hours	10	28.6	31.2	68.7
10 to 12 hours	8	22.8	25.0	93.7
13 hours or more	2	5.7	6.3	100.0
Missing	3	8.6	—	
Totals	35	100.0	100.0	

Outliers are "abnormal" values (either excessively high or low counts) that fall outside of the assumed normal distribution. Researchers should be careful not to lose all information about the case that ignoring it would entail. If the outrider is abnormally high, it should be grouped with the highest class. If it is abnormally low, it should be grouped with the lowest class.

An outlier example for the data in Table 11.9 would be if one member of the fitness program exercised more than three hours a day, six or seven days a week. This would require a "21 hours or more" class in the variable. However, the gap between thirteen and twenty-one hours creates the need for two *blank* classes. Including the outrider in the highest "normal" class eliminates the need for blank classes and reduces the outrider's influence on the group average.

Second, frequency distribution tables usually include the *relative frequency* and often, but not always, the *cumulative frequency*. Frequency tables prepared with the Excel Function Wizard do not display either of these percentage values. However, when the frequency tables are produced with the HISTOGRAM function in TOOLS: DATA ANALYSIS, it is possible to include a column of cumulative percents with the standard table.

Relative frequency can be stated as a decimal or as a percentage. In decimal form the total must always equal 1; in percentages, the total must equal 100 percent. In Table 11.8, the relative frequency of the lowest category is .156, or 15.6 percent.

The last column in Table 11.9 displays the cumulative relative frequency. This is nothing more than the sum of a class and all preceding classes. For example, the cumulative relative frequency for the second level, four to six hours, is its value (21.9 percent) plus the value of the three-hours-or-less class (15.6 percent), for a total of 37.5 percent.

Finally, some statistical software packages include provision for computing relative frequencies when the data contains missing values. A missing value occurs, for example, when a subject refuses to answer a particular question on a survey. When this occurs, the relative frequency distribution column will include the proportion of the total represented by the missing values.

A separate column labeled *Valid Percent* will appear in the table alongside the relative frequency column. Say, for example, the sample included thirty-five workers instead of thirty-two, and that three of them did not respond to the question of how many hours they exercised each week. The valid percent column would compute percentages only for the thirty-two respondents; the data for the three nonrespondents would not be included.

Communicating with Charts

Many research reports contain descriptive statistical data that are presented in graphs or charts, as well as in tables. Descriptive statistics particularly are often presented in some sort of graphic form. The type of chart or graph used often depends upon the preference of the researcher or administrator presenting the information. With today's increasingly powerful spreadsheet and statistical software programs, together with color printers, these pictorial or graphic tools are easy and quick to produce. Among the more commonly used types of charts are *bar charts* and *histograms*.

Bar Charts

Bar charts show how many measurements or observations fall into each class or category of each variable. Printers may use asterisks (stars) or shading to represent the extent of the relative frequencies. It is important to remember that the bars are not accurate measures; they are *symbolic* only. The bars in any one chart may not appear exactly to scale, but they do give a clear *visual impression* of the variation among the values in the class.

In bar charts and histograms, the horizontal line (the x-axis) displays the

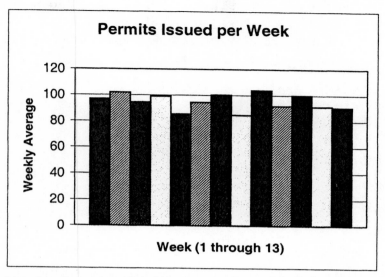

Figure 11.3 **Bar Chart of Weekly Six-Day Averages for Issued Permits**

measurement values of the data, while the vertical (y-axis) represents the frequencies or counts of how often the values occur.

An Excel Example

An example of a bar chart produced with Microsoft Excel is displayed in Figure 11.3. The raw data was the weekly mean or average number of permits issued during a 13-week study period (see Table 11.4 and Table 11.5).

Bar charts may be displayed either vertically or horizontally; the Excel Chart Wizard provides a number of different options for the researcher. Charts with many classes should typically use the horizontal form (page width limitations may otherwise force the chart into an overlap, confusing the viewer). When bar charts are used to show changes or trends over time, the horizontal line (y-axis) is always the time line, while the vertical line (x-axis) represents the data values.

Histograms

Another way to graphically display a frequency distribution is with a *histogram*. A histogram has a visual appearance much like a bar chart, except that in histograms the bars are usually displayed horizontally, while the bars of a bar chart are displayed vertically.

Table 11.10

10-Wide Classes of Permits Issued ("Bins") and Frequencies for Each Bin

Bin	Frequency
40	0
50	0
60	5
70	8
80	8
90	7
100	11
110	18
120	13
130	8
140	0
More	0

Before a histogram can be produced with Excel, the researcher must decide how to group the responses into distinct classes. Excel calls these classes of a variable "bins," and allows the researcher to create bins of any size. If desired, the researcher can let the program divide the data into any number of categories that seem appropriate.

When it is possible to use *either* a bar chart or a histogram, bar charts should be used when displaying *discrete* data—that is, data in distinct categories such as gender or occupations. Histograms can be used to display *both* discrete and continuous data. Examples of continuous data include incomes, height, weight, and other similar measures. As with frequency distribution tables, continuous data categories or classes used in histograms must exhibit internal consistency; all classes must be of the same width.

An Excel Example

Excel's TOOLS/DATA ANALYSIS/HISTOGRAM Wizard was used to construct the bin width for the frequency table shown in Table 11.10 and the histogram in Figure 11.4. Recall that a computed class width using the mathematical formula resulted in a value of 12.66, which is a cumbersome span. Bin widths of 10 or 15 measurements can be used with similar results. The histogram in Figure 11.4 was calculated using a bin width of 10 permit applications. Different bin (or class) widths would have resulted in different bar charts. Remember: There is no rule regarding the number of classes or bins that should be used in either tables or charts. Rather, a rule of thumb is to keep the number of classes around six to eight and never to exceed ten—if at all possible.

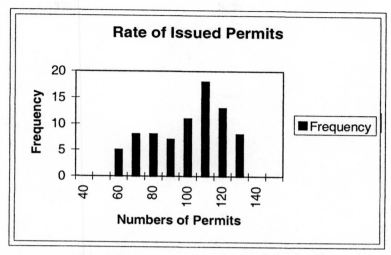

Figure 11.4 **Bar Chart of Permits Issued During the 13-Week Quarter**

Using Graphs

Graphs are another way to present a visual summary of data. The types seen most often in research report applications are line graphs, scatter plots, frequency polygons, and pie charts.

Line Graphs

Line graphs (also know as line charts) are used to show how values of a variable change over time. The time periods are always shown on the horizontal axis, while the vertical axis displays the values of the variables being examined. When plotting continuous data, the points at each time period represent the middle level of the class. Simple line graphs are used to display *trend lines* of single variables. Compound line charts displaying the component values of a larger sum are used to visually display comparisons over time. Figure 11.5 is an example of a line chart produced with Microsoft Excel's Chart Wizard. It displays a trend line that illustrates variation in the daily number of permits issued (using revised data).

Frequency and Area Polygons

Frequency polygons display data in much the same way as line charts; they show the total occurrences for each value of a variable. In appearance, the

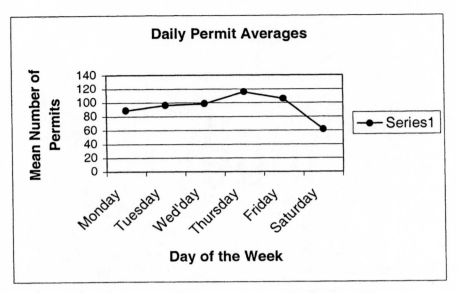

Figure 11.5 **A Line Chart That Displays Daily Means of Permits Issued**
(Revised Data)

only difference is that frequency polygons include a color block under the trend line; line graphs do not show this color block. For many years, when statistical computations were done by hand or, at best, with a hand calculator, frequency polygons were the most often used method to graphically display frequency distributions because they are extremely easy to construct. However, today they are not used nearly as often as bar charts and histograms.

With all frequency polygons, two axes are need. The vertical y-axis represents the frequencies; the horizontal x-axis displays the categories of the variable. With grouped data (such as age categories of ten years each), the midpoint of the interval is used. When plotting specific data such as individual scores, the actual score value is used. Lines connect all total frequency values. The lines of a polygon are often extended to one value above and one below the observed data so as to "close off" the polygon instead of leaving it hanging in midair.

Frequency polygons can also be used to plot and compare two or more sets of scores or values that are based on separate scales. In this case, use the *relative frequency distribution* in place of actual frequency distributions. Figure 11.6 is an area polygon constructed on the same data as the line graph in Figure 11.5.

Scatter Plots

Scatter plots are another way to visually present data. Scatter plots are used to display a series of points of two or more variables that are related in some

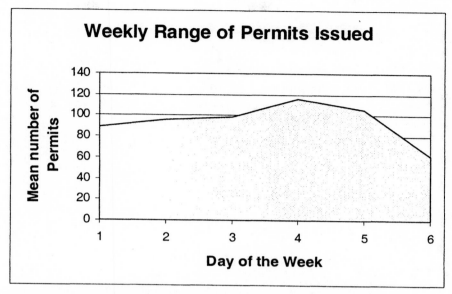

Figure 11.6 An Area Polygon That Displays Averages of Permits Issued (Revised Data)

way. When all measures are plotted, a visual picture of the relationship between variables can be seen. Scatter plots are visually similar to line charts, except that no lines connect the various points on the scatter plot. Figure 11.7 is a scatter plot of the daily permits displayed earlier. The vertical axis displays the number of permits issued; the horizontal axis represents the time period, the thirteen–week extent of the study. The plot was produced with the Excel Chart Wizard.

A modified scatter plot is presented in Figure 11.8. In Figure 11.7, the time period variable (thirteen weeks) was shown on the horizontal axis. In Figure 11.8, the time period is the half-hour intervals over which visitors were counted. This time variable has eighteen classes or categories. Each is one half-hour period during the day. Data for the variable "Number of Visitors" is plotted on the vertical axis. When scatter plots are used to display dependent-independent variables, the horizontal axis should always be the independent variable (Table 11.11).

Pie Charts

Pie charts (also called *pie graphs*) are another popular way to graphically display data. In a pie chart, the data are displayed as proportions of a 360-degree circular "pie." Each portion of the pie roughly represents the same

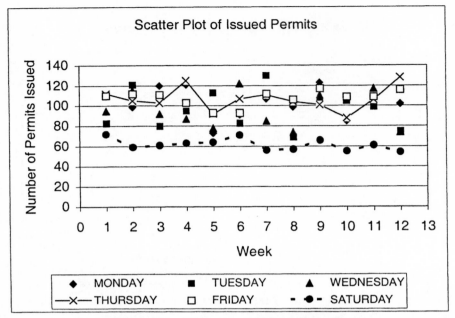

Figure 11.7 **Scatter Plot of Permits over a 13-Week Period, with Thursday and Saturday Trend Lines**

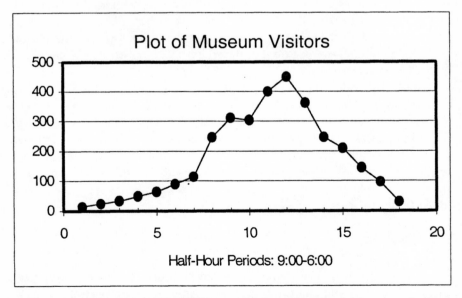

Figure 11.8 **A Trend Line Plot of Museum Visitors by Interval** (produced with Scatterplot)

Table 11.11

Number of Museum Visitors by Half-Hour Periods

Period	Time	Number of visitors
1	9:00–9:29	15
2	9:30–9:59	25
3	10:00–10:29	34
4	10:30–10:59	50
5	11:00–11:29	65
6	11:30–11:59	90
7	12:00–12:29	115
8	12:30–12:59	247
9	1:00–1:29	312
10	1:30–1:59	304
11	2:00–2:29	400
12	2:30–2:59	450
13	3:00–3:29	362
14	3:30–3:59	247
15	4:00–4:29	210
16	4:30–4:59	145
17	5:00–5:29	97
18	5:30–5:59	32

Table 11.12

Contribution by Region

Region	Percentage
Pacific Northwest	11
Mountain states	20
Southwest	15
Central	27
New England	13
Southeast	14
Total	100

portion of a total that each group or category of the variable represents. In the example shown in Figure 11.9, the categories are portions of the United States. The contribution to some total variable that each regional area contributes is shown both as a portion of the pie and a percentage of the total. These data are displayed in Table 11.12. The pie chart in Figure 11.9 was produced with the Excel Chart Wizard. The hatched filling in each section was chosen from a list of color and texture options. The Chart Wizard will make a default selection if the black-and-white pie chart is selected from the 'Custom' options menu that appears at the first selection of the Chart Wizard.

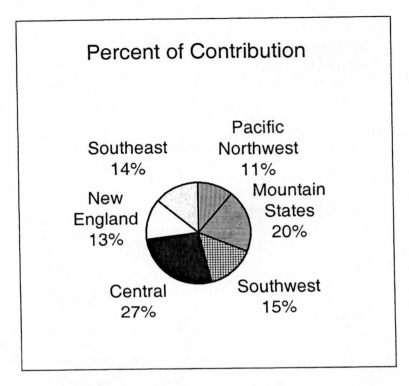

Figure 11.9 **An Example of a Pie Chart with Data from Table 11.2**

Summary

Before administrators can use research data, it must be ordered and classified into a structure that has meaning and is relevant to the decision problem. Often, the first step in making sense of raw data is the preparation of univariate, bivariate, or multivariate tables. These present the data in summary form. Stem-and-leaf diagrams are also used for this purpose.

Graphic displays of data are used to make it easier to communicate meaning to readers. Bar charts, histograms, line and area charts, frequency and area polygons, scatter plots, and pie charts are used to graphically display the structure found in data sets.

Statistical software programs like Microsoft Excel and SPSS can make preparing tables, charts, and graphs a simple and quick process. Both of these software programs require that the data be entered in a spreadsheet format. All tables and graphs in this chapter were produced using Microsoft Excel.

Suggested Reading

Berenson, Mark L., and David M. Levine. 1996. *Basic Business Statistics*. 6th ed. Upper Saddle River, NJ: Prentice Hall.

Brightman, Harvey J. 1999. *Data Analysis in Plain English, with Microsoft Excel*. Pacific Grove, CA: Duxbury Press.

Einspruch, Eric L. 1998. *An Introductory Guide to SPSS for Windows*. Thousand Oaks, CA: Sage.

Green, Samuel B., Neil J. Salkind, and Theresa M. Akey. 2000. *Using SPSS*. Upper Saddle River, NJ: Prentice Hall.

Neufeld, John L. 1997. *Learning Business Statistics with Microsoft Excel*. Upper Saddle River, NJ: Prentice Hall.

Witte, Robert S., and John S. Witte. 1997. *Statistics*. 5th ed. Fort Worth, TX: Harcourt Brace.

12 Research Hypotheses

Risk and uncertainty are present in all organization decisions; decision makers hardly ever know with absolute certainty the outcome of an organization situation. One important reason for this is that the outcomes will occur in the future. No one can predict the future; however, some attempt at doing so must take place. When decision makers do predict future outcomes, they use probabilities as indicators of their confidence in the likelihood of the outcome.

Because it is usually impossible to test or measure entire populations, decision makers use sample statistics to make inferences about population parameters. This chapter applies these basic concepts to a key initial step in all statistical analyses: forming and testing hypotheses.

A systematic series of steps must be followed in the application of all statistical analyses. First, someone must establish a purpose or goal for the activity. Second, data relating to the issue or question must be gathered. Third, one or more statistical tests must be conducted. Finally, the person directing the activity must decide whether the gathered and analyzed data satisfactorily meets the need spelled out in the purpose.

As this abbreviated procedure indicates, before any data are gathered, processed, or interpreted, someone must establish a foundation for the activity. In statistics, this foundation is called a *hypothesis* (the plural form of hypothesis is *hypotheses,* spelled with an "e" in the last syllable instead of an "i"). All subsequent statistical analysis follows from this foundation. A hypothesis is a *statement that explains or suggests a conclusion about some phenomena.*

In organizations, all data is, or should be, gathered for a purpose. Also, it should be gathered according to some design or method. Purpose is established by clearly defining the organization's problem or situation for which data are needed. Following a design means following a plan for collecting, analyzing, interpreting, and reporting the findings of the study. As we saw earlier, there are three broad classes of research designs: exploratory, descriptive, and causal. The same steps must be followed in each design. To restate the list, they are:

1. Define the organization's problem or the decision to be made.
2. Form hypotheses about the problem or decision.
3. Select a research design.
4. Select the appropriate statistical test or tests.
5. Select a sample.
6. Collect the data.
7. Analyze and interpret the data.
8. Report the findings or make the decision.

Defining the organization's problem is the first step in this process because it sets the stage for all subsequent steps in the process. Most often, the problem is associated with some action that a manager must take. Typically, the administrator becomes aware of the problem through observation of its symptoms. For example, a decline in citizen participation in a recycling program is likely to be a symptom of any one of many different problems, ranging from the poor quality of the collection procedures to lack of communication about the program.

After the researcher defines the research problem, he or she makes one or more *hypotheses* about the relationship between potential causes and the decline in participation and then sets out to test that hypothesis or hypotheses.

This chapter is about how decision makers write hypotheses about problems, decisions, or situations in their organizations and then test those hypotheses statistically. Hypothesis tests are made about one-sample characteristics, as well as about two or more samples. This chapter also addresses some of the fundamentals of hypothesis testing and some techniques for one-sample hypothesis tests. Additionally, this chapter provides a brief introduction to the rationale behind p-value decisions about hypotheses. Because hypothesis testing is founded in probability theory, most decisions about hypotheses are made on the basis of some level of probability concerning the acceptance region of a statistic; this is called the *p-value approach* to hypothesis testing.

Types of Hypotheses

Management decisions based on inferential statistics are made on the basis of what is *probably* true, not on what is actually true. Therefore, probabilities are the basis of all statistical inference. Usually decision makers do not have perfect information before them when they are required to make a decision. To gain information and reduce uncertainty, decision makers use the results of sample studies as approximations of what is actually true of a population. Sample studies may be conducted for production, marketing, human resource management, investments, and most other types of organization decisions.

One of the biggest limitations of sample studies is that a study based on another sample taken from the same population might produce entirely different results. One way to lower the risk of this happening is to increase the size of the sample. Larger samples lower the influence of extreme values— what we earlier identified as *outliers*—in a data set. But collecting data costs money and takes time, both of which are limited resources in organizations. Therefore, decision makers develop formal hypotheses about the problem or situation before actually seeking data. Hypotheses tell them what to look for and what to test.

There are many definitions of hypotheses, but most boil down to the fact that hypotheses are simply statements or *predictions* by someone that explain or suggest some conclusion, event, or thing. Hypotheses are only suggestions or beliefs about something; they are not "true" statements. The manager's degree of faith in the truth of the statement is called the level of *confidence*; confidence levels are typically stated as *probabilities*.

Hypotheses can be written to address *relationships* between variables or as *differences* between values. They can be stated as facts or as distributions. Traditionally, they are written as negative statements. Examples include "There is no association between the age of a machine and its production-error rate"; "There is no difference in a sample of runners' preferences for running shoe brands"; and "There is no disproportionate distribution in the frequencies of responses among different age groups to a question on political issues."

In formal terms, decision makers deal with three main types of hypotheses: predictive, comparative, and association.

Predictive Hypotheses

These are typically predictions about the future value of a measurement. Examples include predictions about client use over the next several quarters, predictions about the movements of labor costs, and the government's predictions of annual growth in the deficit, in productivity, and in unemployment.

Comparative Hypotheses

These make comparisons among groups of people, companies, countries, products, and the like. Such comparisons are often used in hypotheses about differences between scores of one group compared with another. Examples include differences in mean product preference scores between two samples of beer drinkers, and production-rate differences encountered after a change in environmental conditions (sometimes called a treatment).

Association Hypotheses

These deal with the levels of relationship or association between two or more variables. Examples include measuring whether new advertising, a change in price, or product modification influences sales levels or whether temperature variations during the production process influence failure rates in microchips.

The Null Hypothesis

As noted earlier, hypotheses are statements about events or things that decision makers or analysts believe are true. Statistical tests are carried out to verify the statement. In practice, hypotheses are employed in pairs. The first hypothesis is typically stated in negative terms: something is *not* true; variables are *not* related; mean scores of groups are *not* different. This is called the *null hypothesis*; it is represented by the symbol H_O. Null hypotheses are always stated as the status quo or as if there are no (statistically significant) differences in the values. Paired with the null hypothesis is an *alternate hypothesis*; it is represented by the symbol H_A. The alternate hypothesis is the obverse of the null hypothesis and stated in terms exactly opposite from the null hypothesis. Hypothesis tests are used to test for differences between statistic and parameter values that are known or unknown (inferred).

Researchers gather data to support the alternate hypothesis and to decide against the null hypothesis. The null hypothesis is what is being "tested" in a statistical test. Say, for example, you determine the mean value of a sample; you would conduct a one-sample hypothesis test to establish whether this statistic is "different" from the mean of the larger population. If it falls within an acceptable range of values, you determine that the statistic is not different; it falls within the sample distribution of the mean.

When a statistical test of the null hypothesis fails to support the belief statement, decision makers say that the null hypothesis must be rejected. They cannot say that the statement is "true." For example, say a statistical test is carried out for differences between two groups' mean scores on an attitude scale. The null hypothesis is that there is no (statistically significant) difference between the two means. The alternate hypothesis is that the two mean scores are not the same. If the difference is great and the probability that the difference did not occur by chance is lower than a preset confidence level, the null hypothesis must be rejected and the alternate hypothesis retained (or accepted).

Hypotheses can be stated as recognizing no difference or change ($H_O = H_A$); change in one direction (less than or greater than) only ($H_O < H_A$, or $H_O > H_A$); or change in any direction ($H_O \neq H_A$). A one-direction change (either greater or less) is called a *one-tailed test*. When the test involves difference in any direction, it is called a *two-tailed test*. Statistical programs such as SPSS for Windows print out test statistics for both one- and two-tailed tests for the same data. The *t*-test in Excel also computes a value for a one-tailed test, a two-tailed test, or both tests.

Making Inferences About Populations

Decision makers almost always use sample statistics as the basis for making inferences about populations. These inferences can be based on confidence levels or confidence intervals established by the manager or from the results of statistical tests. The latter method is referred to as significance tests. For most organization statistics, confidence levels are predetermined at one of three standard points: the 99 percent, 95 percent, or 90 percent confidence interval, which is another way of saying the .01, .05, or .10 level of confidence.

Confidence intervals are based on the proportion of sample means that can be expected to fall within a specified range of the estimated population mean. For samples with a normal distribution, 95 percent of all sample means can be expected to fall within ±1.96 standard errors from the population mean, whereas 5 percent will fall outside of these limits (Poister 1978).

Confidence limits can be established in two different ways: (1) statisticians use either the Z- or *t*-distribution to establish the probability of a mean falling within a specified number of standard errors of the population mean; (2) the probability levels computed with tests carried out with most statistical software packages are used for hypothesis acceptance or rejection decisions. For example, an analysis-of-variance (ANOVA) test for statistically significant differences will produce an F-statistic and a probability (significance) level. If the researcher has selected the .05 level of confidence, if computed significance value is .05 or less, the null hypothesis should be rejected and the alternate hypothesis retained.

By itself, the significance level of a sample statistic gives the manager very little information. It tells nothing about the size or magnitude of the relationship or difference between the variables. Therefore, it should be used only as an *indicator* and not as a final test. Rejecting the null hypothesis on the basis of the significance value suggests that a relationship or a difference exists, but nothing more. Information regarding the strength and/or direction of the connection is of more importance.

Analyzing Errors of Analysis

Regardless of what confidence level is selected or computed, several errors of analysis may confound the results of a study. There are two types of such errors associated with hypothesis tests: *Type I* and *Type II* errors (Figure 12.1).

Type I errors occur when a null hypothesis that is actually true is rejected. This is also called *falsely rejecting the null hypothesis*. Type I errors are related to the confidence level adopted for a decision. Thus, with a confidence level of .10, we can falsely reject the null hypothesis 10 percent of the time. Lowering the confidence level to .05 means we can expect to be wrong only 5 percent of the time. As can be seen, tightening confidence levels lowers the likelihood of Type I errors occurring.

As noted earlier, rejecting a null hypothesis does not mean that something is "true." Rather, it means we reject this hypothesis and retain or reject the alternate hypothesis. Type II errors occur when we do *not* reject the null hypothesis when it is, in fact, false. Type II errors occur less often than Type I errors; procedures for computing their possible occurrence are usually found in comprehensive mathematical statistics texts. In general, decision makers can reduce the likelihood of Type II errors occurring by increasing the size of the sample.

Hypothesis Testing in Action

Hypothesis tests have been developed for use with one sample and with two or more samples. This chapter will address one-sample hypothesis tests; the next chapter will look at comparisons of the means of two or more samples. Hypothesis tests can also be carried out on categorical (nominal) and ordered (ordinal) data; those tests will be discussed in a later chapter on nonparametric statistics. Hypothesis tests can be carried out in situations involving a single mean, for differences between two independent means, for differences between dependent or paired means, in situations involving single proportion, and for differences between proportions.

One-sample hypothesis tests are used to determine whether a sample statistic, usually the mean, falls within a set of upper and lower critical values. One-sample tests are also used with proportions and to establish the distribution of the statistic. These tests are important because two key assumptions in most interval and ratio data hypothesis tests are (1) randomness, and (2) a normal distribution.

	Reject the the null	*Accept (retain) the null*
Null is false	Correct decision	Type II error
Null is true	Type I error	Correct decision

Figure 12.1 **Type I and Type II Errors in Hypothesis Testing**

The hypotheses formed and statistical tests employed will naturally depend upon the specific decision facing the manager, the data-collection process to be followed, whether the variance is known, and whether the test is one-tailed or two-tailed. The decision to accept or reject a null hypothesis is based upon an acceptance value that is called a *confidence level*. The required degree of confidence the manager must have in the decision to be made will dictate the level of confidence to be used. Confidence levels are probabilities that the results of the test could not have occurred by chance. For example, a confidence level of .05 means that the mean values of the sample will fall within the same range as the population parameter 95 out of 100 times. In this way, significance tests are decision tools for all inferential statistics.

With normal distributions, roughly half of the possible values of the sample statistic could fall above the mean and half below. Values falling out of this range are those that would call for rejection of the null hypothesis. The entire set of possible values within this range is called the *confidence interval*. The confidence interval is the range of values within which we expect the "true" value of the population (mean) parameter to fall—with some researcher-selected level of probability. The values delineating the confidence range are known as the *upper* and *lower confidence limits*; together they form the bounds of the confidence interval. That is, with a 95 percent confidence value (and a normal distribution), we expect that only 2.5 percent of the values to be above the statistic value and 2.5 percent below.

Testing Hypotheses with Excel

Inferential statistics involves using measurements of a sample to draw conclusions about the characteristics of a population. We can never know with complete certainty that the statistics of the sample match the population parameters. We do know that drawing other random samples will most likely produce similar but different values for their statistics. The decision maker wants to know with what degree of probability the sample statistic (such as the mean, mode, or median) will fall within an acceptable range of possible values. This acceptable range is called the confidence interval. In other words, if all possible samples of the same size were taken, the decision maker wants to know what percentage of them would include the parameter for the population somewhere within the interval of their statistic values? Since the actual parameter value is seldom known, an estimate must be made. Microsoft Excel's CONFIDENCE function can quickly establish an estimate for the range of values above and below the hypothesized population mean. Three values are needed to complete the CONFIDENCE test:

1. *Alpha* (the manager-determined significance level to be used to compute the confidence level; a number greater than 0 and less than 1).
2. The standard deviation of the population (since this is seldom known, the SD for the sample is substituted).
3. *N* (the total of sample items involved).

The sandbag production line data in Table 12.1 can be used for an example with the CONFIDENCE test in the Microsoft Excel Function Wizard. The test determines the range of the confidence level for the mean of the population. Say that a machine fills sandbags by weight rather than volume. Some variation is expected to naturally occur within a range of weights. Each bag is labeled as weighing a total of 18 pounds. Every hour in each eight-hour shift, a sample of five bags is randomly selected and weighed. Table 12.1 displays the test results for a single shift.

The selected significance value, standard deviation, and number of cases in the sample must be inserted for the Excel Confidence text to produce a value that is exactly one-half of the confidence interval. The sample mean of 18.3125 pounds and standard deviation of 0.6941 and sample size of 40 produce a confidence value of .2151. Thus, any mean falling within the range of 0.2151 over and –0.2151 below eighteen pounds (18.2151 and 17.7849) results in a rejection of the null hypothesis and acceptance of the alternative hypothesis: The sample mean does fall within the normal range of the population mean. The decision maker may assume the filling process is in specifications. When a sample mean falls outside this range, a discrepancy is in effect, and an adjustment to the process is necessary.

A significance value of .05 is established at the decision value or cut-off point for accepting the null hypothesis. The mean for this sample of forty observations is 18.31 pounds; the standard deviation is 0.6941 pounds. The

Table 12.1

Sandbag Weights (in pounds) for **Shift One**

Hour	1	2	3	4	5	Mean	SD
1	17.36	18.61	18.17	17.37	17.39	17.7800	0.5783
2	17.45	18.62	18.39	17.19	19.03	18.1360	0.7848
3	17.66	17.38	18.31	17.90	19.19	18.0880	0.7042
4	18.18	17.88	17.90	18.09	18.61	18.1320	0.2958
5	18.33	19.10	17.75	18.18	18.53	18.3780	0.4950
6	18.54	18.77	17.28	18.31	18.88	18.3560	0.6403
7	18.66	18.90	19.15	19.54	19.89	19.2280	0.4929
8	19.90	18.11	18.01	18.00	17.99	18.4020	0.8388
40-observation totals						18.3125	0.6941
40-observation confidence interval							0.2151

production manager believes that the variances for the entire shift's production are the same as those of the samples. A null hypothesis that might be tested is: *There is no statistically significant difference in the mean weights of all samples.*

The means for hours 1 through 4 all fall within the acceptable confidence interval, so change to the process is unnecessary; the null hypothesis is retained. However, the means for hours 5 through 8 all fall outside of the upper limit of 18.2151 pounds (no statistic falls below the lower limit of 17.7849 pounds). Therefore, the null hypothesis is rejected for the samples for hours 5 through 8. Clearly, an adjustment to the filling equipment is called for.

Tests for a Normal Distribution

A key condition of many statistical tests is the requirement that the samples be drawn from a population with a normal distribution and normal variance. It is common for this to be stated as a hypothesis. Therefore, one of the first tests carried out on a sample data set is often a test for normality—that is, a test to see if the population parameter has a normal distribution. It is important to remember that this test should be done only with a probability sample— that is, one that meets requirements for random selection. Decision makers are often required to compute the area under a normal curve and/or to establish probabilities associated with the normal distribution.

Microsoft Excel's statistical analysis capabilities under the Function Wizard (f_x) include five functions that pertain to normal distributions. The first of these is the STANDARDIZE function, which computes standardized Z-values for given raw scores. The second function relation to the normal distribution is the NORMSDIST function. This function computes the area under the curve (probability) that is less than a given Z-value. The third function, NORMSINV, computes a Z-value that corresponds to a given total area under the normal curve. This function is the converse of the NORMSDIST function. The fourth Excel normal distribution function, NORMDIST, computes the area (probability) that is less than a given measurement value (X), such as a sample-bag weight in the earlier example. The last function in this family of tools is the NORMINV function. This function—the converse of the NORMDIST function—computes the measurement value (X) that corresponds to a given area under the normal curve.

In addition to these five specific normal distribution-related tests, Excel also includes the capability to conduct one-tailed and two-tailed, one-sample *t*-tests; a two-tailed (only) Z-test; and a confidence interval test. These will be discussed in later chapters.

Summary

Before any data are gathered, processed, or interpreted, someone must establish a foundation for the activity. In statistics, this foundation is called a *hypothesis* (the plural form of hypothesis is *hypotheses*). All subsequent statistical analysis follows from this foundation. A hypothesis is a statement that explains or suggests a conclusion about some phenomena.

This chapter discussed how public administration decision makers write hypotheses about problems, decisions, or situations in their organizations and how they then test those hypotheses statistically. Hypothesis tests are made about one-sample characteristics, as well as about two or more samples.

Hypotheses can be written to address *relationships* between variables or as *differences* between values. They can be stated as facts or as distributions. Traditionally, they are written as negative statements.

In formal terms, decision makers deal with three main types of hypotheses: (1) predictive hypotheses, (2) comparative hypotheses, and (3) association hypotheses. Predictive hypotheses are typically predictions about the future value of a measurement. Comparative hypotheses make comparisons between groups of people, companies, characteristics, responses, services, products, or scores of one group compared with another. Association hypotheses are used to test the levels of relationship or association between two or more variables.

Suggested Reading

Brightman, Harvey J. 1999. *Data Analysis in Plain English with Microsoft Excel.* Pacific Grove, CA: Duxbury Press.

Fleming, Michael C., and Joseph G. Nellis. 1991. *The Essence of Statistics for Business.* New York: Prentice Hall.

Levine, David M., Mark L. Berenson, and David Stephan. 1997. *Statistics for Managers Using Microsoft Excel.* Upper Saddle River, NJ: Prentice Hall.

Salkind, Neil J. 2000. *Statistics for People Who (Think They) Hate Statistics.* Thousand Oaks, CA: Sage.

13 Testing Hypotheses About Two or More Groups

The underlying concepts of one-sample hypothesis testing discussed in Chapter 12 also apply to a body of statistical techniques designed to test hypotheses about two or more samples. These tools permit managers to test whether the different values found in two or more samples are statistically significant or whether they could have occurred by chance. Another way to look at a hypothesis test is to consider it a *significance test*, the results of which help managers evaluate certain characteristics in measurements. *Differences* are one class of characteristics; *relationships* are another.

As we saw in the last chapter, a null hypothesis is what is tested in statistics. Null hypotheses are always stated as either the status quo or as no difference. This chapter will examine a number of the statistical tools used to test for significant differences between parametric statistics for two or more groups or subgroups. An example of subgroups is the males and females in a sample or population. The next chapter will look at relationships between variables. A later chapter will examine a number of difference and relationship tests used with nonparametric statistics.

Statistics for specific measurements vary from sample to sample. Measurements taken after a modification to a machine or a change in working conditions will be different from the measurements taken before the change (such a change is sometimes called a "treatment"). Managers need to know if the differences seen in such measurements are "real" or if they are simply chance-related variations that are seen every time a new measurement is made and that would fall within the range of a normal distribution of the statistic. They are looking for differences that are *statistically significant*. A difference that is statistically significant is one with a high probability it did not occur through chance alone. It is important to remember that the analyst never knows if the differences are, indeed, "real." Rather, within a predetermined acceptable *level of confidence*, such as 90, 95, or 99 percent, the procedure entails rejecting or accepting a hypothesis or hypotheses about a difference.

Collectively, these tests are often referred to as "difference tests," although some texts treat them all as "significance tests." A body of statistical techniques exists to test for differences with all types of data (levels of measurement). Managers will most likely find themselves using the several tests for comparing differences in means. However, the choice of a particular statistical test for differences between measures depends upon the nature of the measurements themselves. A scale based on categorical measurement (nominal data) two groups should *not* be measured with the same scale used for a continuous (nominal or ratio level data) variable, for example.

Managers are interested in significance tests and tests for differences in a wide variety of situations. One of the more basic uses is to determine whether the values of a randomly selected sample statistic are distributed in the same way they are in a population—the test of *normality* discussed in the previous chapter. A similar application is available for testing the distribution of responses for a categorical variable. Called a *goodness-of-fit test*, this looks at the data to determine whether the distribution of response frequencies is disproportionate, that is, whether the frequency distribution is the same as would be expected with a normal distribution. Difference tests also weigh disparities between two or more groups in their rankings or ratings of a set of items (ordinal- and interval-level data). Probably the most commonly encountered difference tests, the *t*-test and F-test for differences between the mean scores of two or more groups, fall into the interval- and ratio-data group of tests.

Statistical Significance

Hypothesis tests are sometimes called *differences tests* or *significance tests*. *Statistical significance* is the term used to describe the point or value beyond which researchers accept or reject a null hypothesis; decisions are made in accordance with preselected levels of confidence, typically either .01, .05, or .10. The .05 level of confidence is used most often.

In the past, the critical values of a statistic had to be read from a table of values found at the end of most statistics texts. These were then compared with a value that was found by following steps in a formula for calculating the statistical test. Today, the value at which the decision can be made appears with a *probability* value in the results of inferential statistical tests. This is called the *p-value approach*.

Remember: Just because the result of a statistical test is *statistically significant*, it does not automatically mean that it is socially, culturally, administratively, or even logically significant (Poister 1978). A result can be statistically significant and totally irrelevant or trivial at the same time. On the other hand, a small difference can have great practical significance. It is up to the researcher to make these determinations.

Interpreting Results with *p*-Values

Most public administration and social science researchers make hypothesis acceptance decisions at the .05 level of confidence. However, the nature of the study and required level of confidence in the results often requires that a level of .10 or of .01 be employed. In statistical notation, the lowercase Greek letter *alpha* (α) is used to represent the confidence value. When analysts use, say, the .05 level of confidence, they are in fact saying that they are 95 percent sure about a hypothesis decision. This 95 percent, known as the *confidence coefficient*, is the probability that a null hypothesis is retained when it should be retained.

It is important that significance levels are not confused with "importance." The two concepts are not related in any way. Importance refers to the weight or value the decision maker places on the information received from a statistical study. Statistical significance is a product of a selected confidence level.

Confidence levels are closely related to confidence intervals, discussed in the previous chapter. Before widespread acceptance of the *p*-value approach to hypothesis testing, managers were required to compute acceptance and rejection levels and to look up decision values in tables. Today, most statistical packages, such as SPSS and Excel, compute critical *p*-values along with *t*-test, z-test, and F-test values. The decision whether to retain or reject the null hypothesis can now be made by comparing the computed *p*-value with the confidence level or *alpha*; *p*-values of the same or greater value than the selected alpha (.01, .05, or .10) result in retaining (or accepting) the null hypothesis; *p*-values less than the significance value require that the null hypothesis be rejected.

Goodness-of-Fit Tests

The term *goodness-of-fit* refers to an evaluation of the frequency distribution of values for any type of measurement. Basically, the test compares the actual frequency results against a hypothetical distribution, referred to as an "expected" distribution, assuming a normal distribution. The most commonly used statistical test for goodness-of-fit tests is the chi-square (X^2) statistic, which is one of a series of nonparametric tests. Nonparametric statistics are considered to be "distribution free." While most nonparametric tests were developed for nominal- and ordinal-level data, the X^2 *goodness-of-fit* test can be used with nominal and ratio data as well, although other, more powerful tests provide more information.

Goodness-of-fit tests are just one of the uses for the chi-square statistic. Among other applications, it can be used as a test of independence between variables, as a test for normality (normal distribution), or as a one-sample relationship test. As a goodness-of-fit test, it compares two sets of data. One set is the actual collected data (called the *observed data*); the second is a hypothetical data set (called the *expected data*). The hypothetical data represent what the data would be if the null hypothesis of no difference were really true. They also show that there is no relationship between the variables. For a goodness-of-fit test, the null hypothesis might be "the distribution of responses found in the collected data are not different from the expected distribution." If the collected data differs significantly from the expected distribution, the null hypothesis must be rejected.

Statistical software packages calculate a chi-square and a *p*-value. Large chi-square values usually suggest that the null hypothesis must be retained. Small chi-square values usually mean that the null hypothesis must be rejected. A computed *p*-value is used to make the final decision; *p*-values of less than the selected significance value call for rejecting the null hypothesis. Finally, when carrying out a goodness-of-fit test, it is important that there be at least five responses in each category or cell; if not, the results of the test are considered to be *spurious*, that is, likely to have occurred by chance and, therefore, not reliable.

Two-Group Hypothesis Tests

As can be seen in Figure 13.1, an extensive body of statistical tools has been developed for testing hypotheses about statistics for two or more groups. Various tests exist for use with *parametric* and *nonparametric* statistics. Parametric statistical tests can only be used with data at the equidistant-interval or ratio level. When the data are either ordinal (ranked data) or nominal (categorical), a body of tests known as *nonparametric* statistics must be used. In addition, parametric statistics require that the data be from random samples and have a normal distribution. When these assumptions cannot be met, nonparametric tests must be used in place of parametric tests. Some parametric tests require that the samples be independent from one another, while other tests have been developed for use with dependent or paired samples. Separate-but-related statistical tests have been developed to meet either independence requirement.

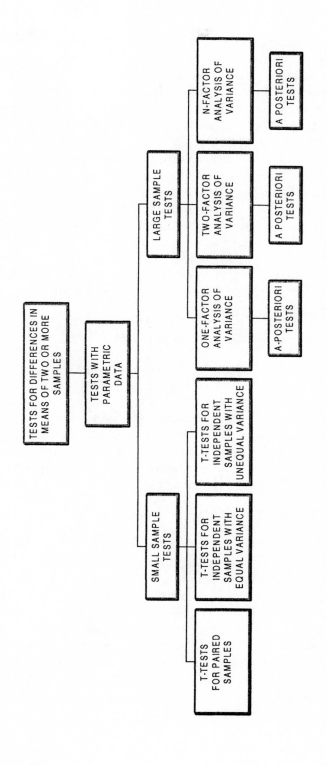

Figure 13.1 **A Schematic Display of Two-Sample Differences Tests**

Tests for differences in the mean values of two or more samples can be used for both interval and ratio data. Whether the samples are independent (as most are) or are dependent (or paired), some minor differences will be found in the computational formulas—and associated computer statistics package selection—for several of the tests, although their interpretation is identical.

Two of the statistical tests often used when comparing the mean values for independent samples are the *Student's t-test* for independent samples and the one-way, two-way, and *n*-way *analysis of variance* (F-ratio) tests (ANOVA). When the decision maker has any doubt about the independence of the samples, testing a null hypothesis for dependence with the *Levene test for independence* can be done before selecting either of the difference tests.

Once the decision maker is assured that the samples are independent, he or she must then decide whether the *t*-test or analysis of variance F-test is appropriate. The *t*-test has more limitations than the F-test, but is well suited for comparisons between the means of two, and only two, relatively small samples (typically around thirty cases) when each sample has the same number of observations or cases.

Testing for Differences with the *t*-Test

The *t*-test is used to compare the means of no more than two groups with approximately equal variances—for example, the test scores of two groups of employment applicants. Or scores from a group of trainees gathered prior to a training program might be compared with scores for the same group after completion of the training. The *t*-test might also be used to compare different sample means in production line situations, such as filling boxes or bottles. Many similar uses are possible. Minimum required assumptions for using the *t*-test are listed in Figure 13.2.

When to Use the t-Test

The *t*-tests in the Microsoft Excel program are to be used only when the manager has all the raw data (individual measurements) available. When this is not the case, when the manager has only the means at hand, it is possible to make a similar comparison using just summary data and the Excel mathematical formula capability. ANOVA, which compares variances between samples, also requires that the raw data be available.

As in one-sample hypothesis testing, the first step must be to prepare the null and alternate hypotheses. It is possible to perform both a one-tailed test and a two-tailed test with the pooled variance *t*-test in Excel. A typical two-tailed test hypothesis pair, to test for a statistically significance difference in population means, is the following:

1. The measurements are of at least interval-level data.

2. The samples are randomly selected.

3. The scores are randomly distributed.

Figure 13.2 **Minimum Requirements for Applying a *t*-Test**

$$H_O: \quad \mu_1 = \mu_2$$
$$H_A: \quad \mu_1 \neq \mu_2$$

If a one-tailed test is desired, either a greater or lesser hypothesis pair must be written as follows:

$$
\begin{array}{llll}
\mu_1 & > & \mu_2 & \quad \mu_1 < \mu_2 \\
H_O: & \mu_1 \geq \mu_2 & & \quad H_O: \quad \mu_1 \leq \mu_2 \\
H_A: & \mu_1 < \mu_2 & & \quad H_A: \quad \mu_1 > \mu_2
\end{array}
$$

The difference between *one-tailed* and *two-tailed* tests is that in one-tailed tests the researcher specifies the direction of the difference: it is either greater or lesser. The probabilities calculated with the *t*-test on a one-tailed test are half of the probabilities for a two-tailed test. It should be noted that selecting either the one- or two-tailed tests should not be done arbitrarily. If the manager has no specific reason to expect a difference in one direction, it follows that no prediction can be made in advance. The manager is obligated to use the two-tailed test.

Only two sets of means can be compared at any one time using the *t*-test. The DATA ANALYSIS tool in Excel contains three different types of *t*-tests:

- Paired two-sample for means
- Two-sample assuming equal variances
- Two-sample assuming unequal variances

Two factors influence the choice of approach. The first is the nature of the two samples for which measurements are available: *Are they paired or independent?* This question must be answered before selecting one of the several different *t*-test computational methods.

The second key characteristic of the data is what is known as *degrees of freedom*. Degrees of freedom refer to the limits to which a set of measurements may vary. The concept is rooted in physics, where an object that can move on a flat plane is said to have *two degrees of freedom*. If it can move in only a straight line, it has just one degree of freedom. In statistics, this idea is used to mean the *number of independent comparisons that can be taken between sets of data.*

With two observations, for example, analysis is limited to just one independent comparison. Two "observations" means two independent measurements, such as would be taken from a sample of just two individuals. If there are three observations, then two independent comparisons are possible, and so on. In statistical notation, this is written as "$n - 1$ degrees of freedom" (the n means the total number of observations).

Degrees of freedom are computed differently depending upon whether the data are collected from the same individuals, as in a pretest and a posttest situation, or from different sets of individuals (two independent samples). Data collected from the same individuals at different times are called *correlated data.* Data collected from separate samples are called *uncorrelated data.*

To determine the degrees of freedom for *correlated* data, 1 is subtracted from the total number of cases. To compute the degrees of freedom for *uncorrelated* data, 1 is subtracted from each sample. In statistical notations, this is shown as: $df = n_1 + n_2 - 2$. The various *t*-tests contained in Excel include these different values in their computations; all the manager needs to do is to select the correct option.

Excel's DATA ANALYSIS function includes three different *t*-test options: a test for paired samples and two tests for independent samples. The two independent sample tests differ in that one assumes the samples were taken from populations with equal variance, while the second test assumes two populations in which the variance is unequal. In practice, this means the manager should select the equal variance option when comparing the means of two samples, both of which were randomly selected from the same larger population. The unequal variance option is to be used when the populations are different. An example would be comparing the means of samples taken from two separate production lines or processing machines.

All two-sample *t*-tests compare sample (or group) means by computing a student's *t*-value and comparing the significance of whatever difference is found between the means. Considered to be only slightly less "robust" than the F-test statistic used in analysis of variance procedures, the *t*-test can be used to test the means for either different (independent) samples or paired samples. "Different samples" refers most often to different groups within a larger sample.

For example, the attitudes of nonsupervisory personnel might be compared with the attitudes of management; the responses of females in a sample might be compared with those of males. Paired sample testing refers to testing for differences between two separate variables. Examples include comparing the mean scores on a pretest given before a training activity (variable 1) with the

Table 13.1

Subject Scores Before and After Computer-Assisted Training

Pretest scores (variable 1)	Posttest scores (variable 2)
20.7	19.3
21.7	23.9
17.2	19.9
18.0	24.0
15.1	17.7
21.1	21.5
24.5	25.9
17.8	19.1
23.6	24.0
19.0	
19.5	

mean of a second test given after the training session (variable 2). Table 13.1 displays data from a paired-sample, pre- and posttest example.

Comparing Groups with ANOVA

Analysis of variance is a powerful tool for comparing the differences in means between any number of groups and for doing so at more than one level. With ANOVA, it is possible to test the role of each of several variables independently and then to determine whether two or more variables *interact* to influence any differences between groups' scores.

A classical example often cited is testing the influence of farm plot location (or any other variable, such as amount of water applied) and the amount of fertilizer on crop yields. Each variable can be tested by itself. Then the two are tested for interactive influence on the yield result. Analysis of variance is also regularly used in market research studies to compare mean attitude scores of potential customer groups.

In all applications, analysis of variance uses an F-statistic (actually, a ratio) in a comparison of the variances of mean scores. The test compares the variance of the mean to the overall variance found in the sample. Decisions about the null hypothesis are based on these comparisons.

To make its comparisons, analysis of variance compares the means of two samples or two groups within a sample. Furthermore, analysis of variance results include summary statistics for each sample or group, an F-ratio and a probability value. This makes interpretation simple: The means are "statistically different" if the p-value is less than the analyst-selected confidence level. Interpretation is not as easy when more than two groups or levels are compared. Another way to interpret the test is to refer to the "critical F" value produced along with the F-statistic and p-value (in the past, analysts had to look this value up in a table of t-values). The critical F-value is compared with the computed F-statistic (called the F-*ratio*); if the computed F is smaller than the critical value, the null hypothesis is rejected.

The p-value of the F-ratio will indicate whether the null hypothesis is to be rejected, but it will not indicate where the differences lie. Another test, called an *a posteriori* test or a *post hoc* test, is required. When one of these is selected, actual differences will be indicated. Thos differences that are statistically "the same" will be so marked. None of these "after the fact" tests are available in Microsoft Excel, but they are available in more powerful statistical packages such as SPSS.

Managers have three different versions of analysis of variance to choose from: a one-way version, a two-way version, and an "n-way" version. One-way analysis of variance is the basic procedure; it is used when two or more groups' means are being compared across a single factor. For example, a marketing manager might want to know if teenage and preteen customers respond differently to an advertisement for a breakfast cereal than do their parents. The response variable must be at least interval level; the grouping variable can be any level data. Each of the several different types of analysis of variance is discussed in greater detail below.

One-Way Analysis of Variance

One-way ANOVA compares the mean scores on a scale variable across two or more categories of a single categorical variable. The group of cases or subjects that make up each category are referred to as *subsamples* or *subgroups*, and the categorical variable itself is called a *grouping variable*. Grouping variables are often demographic characteristics, such as gender, marital status, ethnic group, education level, and occupation.

Three different ways of estimating variance are possible: (1) a total estimate of the variance of all cases, (2) a between-group estimate based on the variation of the subgroups' means around a "grand mean," which is nothing more than a mean of the means, and (3) a within-group estimate that is based on the variation of subgroup cases around their subgroup mean. ANOVA divides the between-group variance by the within-group variance to come up with a value that is called the F-ratio, or F-statistic. The total group variance is not used in ANOVA.

When using one-way ANOVA to compare group means, the null hypothesis should be that the means of the subgroups are the same (or equal). Another way to state the null hypothesis is that there is no statistically significant difference in the means of the two (or more) groups.

Degrees of Freedom

The number of degrees of freedom affects estimates of population variance in ANOVA tests. A different F-distribution has been calculated for nearly every combination of degrees of freedom; these values are included in the appendixes of almost all statistics textbooks. Until the advent of powerful desktop computers, researchers were forced to manually calculate the three different variances and an F-ratio. This F-ratio was then compared with the appropriate statistic in the F-tables. Tabular F-values were available for both the .05 and .10 levels of confidence. Null hypothesis decisions were based on these comparisons. Today, however, most statistical packages calculate an F-ratio and a significance value for every set of variables. Hence, it is no longer necessary to determine the number of degrees of freedom. Since they are identified for the researcher, it is still traditional to include the number of degrees of freedom in the results of ANOVA analysis.

Remember, if the significance value is less than .05 (the traditional decision point), the null is rejected; the subgroups' means are (statistically) different.

Interpreting One-Way ANOVA

Researchers should report the value of the F-statistic (F-ratio), the degrees of freedom involved in the test, and the associated probability or significance (sig.) value. The following example represents the method used for testing differences in the mean scores of two groups. A new manager was named at a government agency. Employee morale has declined dramatically, product quality and customer service was ranked very poor by the company's customers, and employee absenteeism was becoming a major problem. The manager wanted to determine if both managers and staff workers perceived the company climate in the same way. A seven-point composite organizational climate scale was administered to a random selection of twenty-five workers and twenty managers. Individual scores on the scale are shown in Table 13.2.

The manager's null hypothesis was "there is no difference in the way managers and staff employees rate the organization's climate." To test this hypothesis, a one-way analysis of variance procedure was used. The results of that procedure are presented in Figure 13.3.

To interpret these results, refer to the p-value of 0.0000 printed next to the F-ratio of 29.80722. The large F-value alone would indicate that the difference

Table 13.2

Organizational Climate Scales Scores, Staff and Management

	Scores							
Staff					Management			
3.0	5.0	3.0	4.0	5.0	2.0	2.0	3.0	4.0
5.0	6.0	5.0	5.0	3.0	4.0	3.0	4.0	2.0
3.0	3.0	4.0	6.0	3.0	4.0	2.0	2.0	1.0
7.0	4.0	5.0	6.0	2.0	1.0	1.0	3.0	2.0
3.0	5.0	6.0	4.0	5.0	3.0	2.0	3.0	1.0

Table 13.3

Daily Sales by Position and Day of Week

Position	Sales by Day of the Week ($)			
	Wednesday	Thursday	Friday	Saturday
1	933	979	1,240	1,610
1	1,004	1,112	1,299	1,020
1	933	1,003	1,353	1,003
1	979	980	1,222	1,900
2	1,217	1,172	1,175	1,945
2	1,171	1,034	1,371	1,837
2	1,178	1,011	1,421	1,958
2	1,230	1,021	1,314	1,851
3	1,021	1,871	1,889	1,835
3	1,015	1,735	1,948	1,631
3	1,041	1,642	1,872	1,500
3	995	1,675	1,919	1,720

in the two groups' means is statistically significant. This is supported by the very small p-value. In this case, the null hypothesis is rejected.

Two-Way Anova

Two-way analysis of variance designs are the simplest example of a class of statistical tests developed for what are called "factorial experiments" or "factorial designs." In all such cases, the goal of ANOVA is to test the means of two or more groups on two or more variables or factors at the same time. In addition, the procedure tests the *interaction* effect—whether two or more of the variables working together may have had an impact on the differences.

Here is an example of a two-factor analysis of variance procedure. An advertising manager for a restaurant wants to establish which is the best day to advertise in the local paper and in which section of the paper the ad should

Anova: Single Factor				
SUMMARY				
Groups	Count	Sum	Average	Variance
Staff	25	110	4.4	1.666667
Management	20	49	2.45	1.102632

ANOVA					
Source of Variation	SS	df	MS	F	P-value	F crit
Between Groups	42.25	1	42.25	29.80722	0.0000	4.067047
Within Groups	60.95	43	1.417442			
Total	103.2	44				

Figure 13.3 **Results of Excel Single Factor ANOVA Test**

appear. The two factors are *day* and *position*. Four days are tested: Wednesday, Thursday, Friday, and Saturday. Three positions are tested: general news (the first two sections of the paper), the sports section, and the family section (which includes the entertainment pages). Responses to be compared are daily sales totals. In setting up the experiment, *position* is to be the manager's grouping variable. Table 13.3 displays the two factors and sales totals; Figure 13.4 is the results of an Excel two-factor analysis of variance procedure.

The two factors being tested are *position* and *day* of the week. Four levels of the *position* variable are included in order to match the four levels of the *days*, making it necessary to record forty-eight total observations. Analysis of variance will compare the mean of the four levels of each of the three positions with each of the four days in each position.

This analysis of variance procedure will compute an F-table with *p*-values and critical F values for each of the three positions, the four Day variables (labeled as "columns" in the ANOVA summary table), and a measurement of the effect of any interaction between *position* and *day*.

There are three results to interpret in the ANOVA results produced in this Excel application of this test: The first null hypothesis was that there is no difference in the *position* factor. These are the groups in the table; each includes four iterations of sales results. The second null hypothesis is that there is no difference in the days of the week on which the advertisement is placed. The final null hypothesis is that there is no interaction between the two factors as they relate to the differences, if any. We can interpret these results in two ways. First is the traditional *p*-value approach. Since these are less than the .05 level of confidence, we reject all three of the null hypotheses.

Another way is to compare the F-statistic with the critical value of F. In the

Anova: Two-Factor with Replication

SUMMARY	WEDNESDAY	THURSDAY	FRIDAY	SATURDAY	Total
GENERAL NEWS (1)					
Count	4	4	4	4	16
Sum	3849	4074	5114	5533	18570
Average	962.25	1018.5	1278.5	1383.25	1160.625
Variance	1244.916667	4008.333333	3548.333333	198328.9167	74228.38333
SPORTS (2)					
Count	4	4	4	4	16
Sum	4796	4238	5281	7591	21906
Average	1199	1059.5	1320.25	1897.75	1369.125
Variance	836.6666667	5713.666667	11287.58333	3912.916667	112788.3833
FAMILY (3)					
Count	4	4	4	4	16
Sum	4072	6923	7628	6686	25309
Average	1018	1730.75	1907	1671.5	1581.8125
Variance	358.6666667	10224.25	1124.666667	20045.66667	127379.3625
Total					
Count	12	12	12	12	
Sum	12717	15235	18023	19810	
Average	1059.75	1269.583333	1501.916667	1650.833333	
Variance	11807.29545	121749.9015	94174.81061	108985.9697	

ANOVA

Source of Variation	SS	df	MS	F	P-value	F crit
Sample	1419238.042	2	709619.0208	32.67190463	0.000000008	3.25944427
Columns	2431282.229	3	810427.4097	37.31327129	0.000000000	2.866265447
Interaction	1502755.958	6	250459.3264	11.53151619	0.000000360	2.363748308
Within	781903.75	36	21719.54861			
Total	6135179.979	47				

Figure 13.4 **Two-Factor ANOVA Results for Sales/Advertising Media/Day of Advertisement**

past, analysts had to look this value up in a table of values for various degrees of freedom and values for the .05 and .01 levels of confidence. This is no longer necessary. The critical value for the data and degrees of freedom are presented alongside the *p*-value. If the F-statistic is smaller than the critical value from the F-table, the null hypothesis is retained. In this example, the F-statistic is larger than the critical F for all three hypotheses. Hence, all three null hypotheses must be rejected. The samples (newspaper locations) are statistically different from one another.

Three-Way ANOVA and More

This design is very much like two-way ANOVA. The principle effects of each factor are examined to see if it makes a difference between groups. This is followed by tests for interactions among the variables. However, now these interactions are expanded; two-way interactions, three-way interactions, and more are evaluated. The results are interpreted in the same way as one- and two-way analyses.

Designs have been developed to test the impact on differences for more than two sets of groups at the same time. These tests compare all factors against each grouping variable at a time, then test for interaction, and then test for combinations of groups. These tests are known as *multivariate analysis of variance* (MANOVA). Finally, a technique has been designed that combines regression analysis with ANOVA. Known as ANCOVA, it makes analyzing a data set a complex experience. Information about MANOVA and ANCOVA is available in most advanced statistical methods textbooks.

Summary

This chapter has looked at a number of the ways researchers test for differences in data sets. With regression and correlation analyses, difference tests are probably the inferential statistical tools used most often by researchers and managers in public administration and nonprofit organizations.

Two broad classes of tests were discussed. First, the various two-sample *t*-tests were examined. Minor variations in portions of the computation formulas are necessary for paired or independent samples. The Microsoft Excel analysis programs Function Wizard and Data Analysis Tools both take these differences into consideration, allowing the researcher to specify which computation procedure to follow. *t*-tests can be used to compare the means of only two groups at a time. Typically, *t*-tests are used with small sample sizes (around a total of thirty cases), and with groups that are equal in size. To summarize *t*-test applications, the paired-sample *t*-tests in Microsoft Excel will compare the means for the two variables (pretest and posttest), report the difference in the means, and calculate a *p*-value for the *t*-statistic. The samples may be paired or independent. Independent samples may be from one population with equal variance or from different samples with unequal variance.

Second, analysis of variance (with the F-test) is used for samples of any size and with any number of groups or subgroups. Three different levels of analysis of variance (ANOVA) tests were discussed.

Suggested Reading

Berenson, Mark L., and David M. Levine.1996. *Basic Business Statistics*. 6th ed. Upper Saddle River, NJ: Prentice Hall.

Brightman, Harvey J. 1999. *Data Analysis in Plain English with Microsoft Excel*. Pacific Grove, CA: Duxbury Press.

Levine, David M., Mark L. Berenson, and David Stephan. 1997. *Statistics for Managers Using Microsoft Excel*. Upper Saddle River, NJ: Prentice Hall.

14 Looking for Relationships

Measurements of two or more variables often appear to be related to each another. Measuring the strength of such relationships is, in fact, one of the basic tasks of data analysis in public and nonprofit organizations. For example, suppose that public use of recycling service provided by a municipal government agency has declined each of the past three years.

The agency director might suspect that the public's use of the service is directly related to the price charged for that service—the decline began right after a 30 percent increase in the fee. Although the city has been growing rapidly, new residents have not been signing up for the service. Citizens' complaints about the rude behavior and slovenly appearance of the collection staff have increased in number. A group of university students conducted a study of 100 residents to determine the attitudes of citizens toward the service. The findings included a high level of concern that the town's largest employer is considering closing its local factory because of the high cost of dealing with wastes generated by the operations of the plant.

The department director called a meeting of department heads and first-line supervisors. The following conclusions came out of that discussion session:

- Public awareness of environmental issues is related to perceived issue importance.
- Jobs are more important to local citizens than protecting the local environment.
- Maintaining consistent quality of the service is a product of employee satisfaction.
- The level of service provided to citizens by a government agency's staff is related to staff workload.
- Individual employee productivity is related to the amount or type of training received.

A group of administrators looked at the study information and came to these conclusions:

- Public awareness of environmental issues is related to the amount and type of information they receive.
- Program quality is affected by the commitment of staff providers to the program mission.
- Government employees' job satisfaction is related to the announcement of a deferred pay increase.
- Employee productivity varies with changes in the weather (e.g., spring fever).

It is not possible for the director to look at any of these conclusions and determine that a cause-and-effect relationship exists. Without conducting some sort of experiment, all that the director can deduce from the information at hand is that two or more variables might be related in some way.

At first glance there might seem to be intuitively obvious relationships or associations between two or more variables. However, the relationship is not always what it might appear to be. Variables appear to be associated, but there may be another, "confounding" factor affecting the issue.

Obviously, it would be completely irresponsible for the director to make major decisions based on his or her "feelings" about such relationships. Instead, it is safer to assume that associations do not exist until "proven" statistically—that is, until they are shown to be *statistically significant*. The phrase "statistically significant" is a way of stating the researcher's conclusion that the relationship did not occur because of chance alone—some other factor is involved.

Before making an important decision, the department director must look for additional evidence and then weigh how strong that evidence is. Fortunately, an extensive body of easy-to-use statistical tools exists to help decision makers identify and weigh relationship evidence.

The term used to describe relationships between any two or more variables is *correlation*, although words like *relationship* and *association* are also used interchangeably; they are assumed to have the same meaning.

Correlation can be measured in many ways, depending upon the nature of the measurement data. However, the logic behind correlation tests is similar to that found in hypothesis testing. A null hypothesis states that the variables are independent; they are not related. We use relationship tests for testing these kinds of hypotheses. Public agency administrators want to know, first, whether the variables are related; second, in what way they are related; and third, how strong the relationship is.

Understanding the Meaning of Correlation

Association between variables is a product of the way they *covary* (the way and the amount that they vary *together*). Covariance means that there is some connection between the variables, as seen by the way they change together. We cannot conclude that one variable is causing another variable to change with it; relationship is not causation. However, covariance does mean that the two variables are related in some way that results in the two of them moving together.

Analysts are interested in three key measurements associated with correlations. First, they want to know the strength of the relationship. Strength is indicated by the size of the *correlation coefficient*, which, except for nominal data, can run from −1.0 to +1.0.

The numerical values in correlation analysis serve as a mathematical *summary* measure of the degree of correlation between the X and Y variables. The summary number is called the *correlation coefficient*. It is expressed in statistical notation as the lowercase Arabic letter, r.

With nominal data, the range of values only runs from 0.0 to 1.0, with no way to determine the direction of the relationship. Plus or minus 1.0 is considered to be a "perfect," or a 100 percent, relationship. When the correlation coefficient is squared, it loses its sign, but can then be used as a way of explaining the difference in percentage points. For example, an r^2 of 0.56 means that variable A (the independent variable) explains 56 percent of the change in variable B (the dependent variable).

Second, researchers want to know the direction of the relationship. That is, is it a positive or negative relationship? Is a positive (or upward) change in one variable reflected by a positive or upward change in the second variable? Or is the relationship the obverse, with a positive change in one variable reflected in a negative or downward change in the other variable?

The third thing that people want to know about a relationship is its *statistical significance*. Statistical significance relates only to interval/ratio data (scale data in SPSS); it is of interest only when dealing with inferential or parametric statistics. Statistical significance is a test of the likelihood that the sample results reflect the total population of interest. It is often described as a *confidence test only*. Statistical significance tells the analyst the likelihood of the sample relationship representing a similar relationship in a larger population. If the relationship is not significant, there is always a greater chance that the relationship does not exist in the larger population and that it occurred only by chance in the sample data.

How do researchers know for certain that the relationship is "real"? Of course, they can never be 100 percent certain, but can put lots of trust in the computation of significance values by modern statistical software. Significance is identified for all correlation coefficients when it is significant either at the .05 or the .01 level of confidence, or at both. The indication appears as a single or a double asterisk.

What Does Correlation Tell Us?

Although correlation tests are also used for prediction, most of the time the test is used as an *explanatory* tool. One or more tables of bivariate (two variables at a time), linear relationship can be found in nearly all quantitative study reports. The correlation table should be looked upon as a summary table. Researchers develop descriptive, explanatory statements about the relationships printed in the summary table, highlighting the highest and, often, the lowest bivariate correlation values and their significant level, if available. Some researchers also use the table results to suggest—make inferences about—causality for higher-level coefficients, although this is not an appropriate use for correlation.

Finally, reporting the tables in the research report when a large number of scale values are compared at once can be extremely confusing. As a result, analysts often make some arbitrary cut in what they report and what they leave out. A typical example is to include all correlation coefficients that exceed ± 0.40 or 0.50, or, if a great many still exist, raise the cutoff to 0.60.

Testing for Relationships

Relationship tests have two broad applications in hypothesis testing: (1) they can be used to examine the way in which variables vary together (*covariation*), and (2) they can be used to suggest whether a *causal* relationship exists.

An example of a *covariational* relationship is the statement "Wisdom increases with age." The hypothesis is that as people get older, they also get smarter; the two phenomena change together. An example of a *causal* relationship is a prediction that if expenditures on communication are increased, awareness of the service provided by an agency will also increase. The hypothesis in this instance is that communication "causes" public awareness. Researchers and administrators are always on the lookout for these *cause-and-effect* relationships. Because covariational relationships are seldom studied in public administration organizational applications, only causal relationships will be discussed here.

All causal relationships have three key characteristics in common. First, the variables always vary together (either positively or negatively). Second, a time factor is always involved. One variable must change in order to "cause" a commensurate change in the other. The *independent variable* always changes first, followed by the *dependent variable*.

Finally, the relationship is statistically significant; it did not appear through chance alone. In other words, it is not a "fake" or "spurious" relationship. An example of a fake relationship occurred some fifty years ago when scientists reported an increase in the number of people being diagnosed with cancer. It was also reported elsewhere that more families were cooking with pots and pans made of aluminum. Reporters assumed that a cause-and-effect relationship existed between these two independent social factors. Knowledgeable scientists quickly debunked this spurious relationship. People still cook with aluminum pots and pans, and the incidence of most cancer-causing deaths is down.

The Link Between Regression and Correlation

The analytical techniques used to test relationships fall into two families of tests: *regression analysis* and *correlation analysis*. Correlation and regression analyses should be used only with interval- and ratio-level measurements. When dealing with categorical or ranked data, other, somewhat less powerful relationship tests are available.

Regression analysis provides a way of estimating the value of one variable from the value of another, or of determining the way in which two or more variables are associated. Correlation analysis, on the other hand, measures the degree to which the two variables are related; this is called the "strength" of the relationship. Correlation analysis measures the strength of the relationship and, with data above nominal level, indicates the direction of that association—positive or negative. Correlation analysis should be used instead of regression analysis when the only question the decision maker has is: "How strongly are the two variables related?"

The concept of correlation analysis is closely linked to that of regression analysis. That is, if all the paired points of X and Y lie on a straight line, then the correlation between the variables is said to be "perfect"; the correlation value is 1.0. The value 0.0 is used when there is no association whatsoever between the variables.

The value 1.0 represents a perfect *positive* correlation; −1.0 is the value for a perfect *negative* correlation. A negative correlation means that as the values on the x-axis *increase*, y-axis values *decrease*; oppositely, as x-axis values decrease, y-axis values increase.

For *nominal*-level measurements, the value of any r falls between 0.0 and 1.0 (negative relationships are not noted). For all other measurements (*ordinal*, *interval*, and *ratio* data), the value falls between −1.0 and +1.0 (negative relationships are noted).

Some writers use the term *agreement* to refer to the relationship between variables. For example, when applicants to graduate management education programs take an evaluative test such as the General Management Aptitude Test (GMAT), separate scores are reported for mathematics and language abilities. If an applicant receives perfect scores in both parts of the examination, the scores are said to be *in perfect agreement*. If, on the other hand, the applicant receives a perfect score on one part and a very low score on the other part of the examination, the scores are said to be in *perfect disagreement*. This is an example of the *covariational* application of correlation discussed at the beginning of this chapter.

The Coefficient of Determination (r^2)

The coefficient of determination (r^2) is the square of the correlation coefficient value (r); it is probably the most useful measurement in correlation analysis. It provides a clear, easy-to-understand measurement of the *explanatory power* of a correlation coefficient. In addition, r^2 can show how closely the computed r describes relationship between two variables.

For example, say that a correlation coefficient of 0.667 is found to exist between the variables *awareness* and *communications*. Squaring this value gives an r^2 of 0.44. Thus, the coefficient of determination can be used for an interpretation that everyone can understand. It would be interpreted as follows: Forty-four percent of the variation in the variable *awareness* is 'explained' by variation in spending on *communications*, while 56 percent is 'unexplained.' That is, it may be due to other, unidentified factors.

An important caveat to keep in mind when making such interpretations of the results of correlation analysis is that it is never possible to say for certain that a dependent variable or variables actually *causes* a change in the independent variable (that "X causes Y"). Instead, the researcher can report only the existence and strength of a statistical relationship.

Calculating and Interpreting Correlation Values

It takes only three quick steps to provide most of the information a researcher needs to have about the potential relationship between a set of values. If Microsoft Excel is used, these steps are:

- The XY SCATTER PLOT in the Chart Wizard
- The CORREL command in the Function Wizard
- The RSQ calculations, also in the Function Wizard

Table 14.1

Interpretation Guidelines for Correlation Values

0.00–0.19	Little or no relationship
0.20–0.39	Some slight relationship
0.40–0.59	Substantial relationship
0.60–0.79	Strong useful relationship
0.80–0.99	High relationship
± 1.00	Perfect relationship

Source: Adapted from Miller 1991.

A set of categories has been established for describing correlations (relationships) in terms that have meaning for everyone; the categories range from 0 to 1, in units of twenty percentage points for each level. The categories, their labels, and their respective values are displayed in Table 14.3. It is important to remember that these are only intuitive interpretations; others use different but similar labels for the correlation values.

Table 14.1 displays another suggested plan for interpreting correlation coefficients. This interpretation scheme is presented in Delbert Miller's *Handbook of Research Design and Social Measurement* (1991). Miller includes the following additional interpretation guidelines: (1) the usefulness of a correlation is determined by its size, (2) the sign of the coefficient has no bearing on the strength of the relationship; it determines only the direction of the relationship: positive or negative.

Interpretations of the correlation coefficient (r) and the coefficient of determination (r^2) are slightly different. For example, for two-test scores data, an r-value of –0.99 could be interpreted as follows: "The correlation coefficient of –.99 suggests that the relationship between the two test scores is very strong; the two variables have a nearly perfect negative relationship."

The r^2 of this coefficient (the coefficient of determination) is 0.95; it could be interpreted in the following way: "The r^2 of 0.95 suggests that 95 percent of the movement in the Y variable is explained by movement in the X variable."

Regression Analysis

Regression analysis is a statistical procedure developed to determine whether two or more interval- or ratio-level variables are related and whether the change in one variable is "caused" by movement in the other or others. To put it another way, regression analysis allows the decision maker to determine how different values of one variable (called the *dependent variable*) might or might not *explain* variation in another variable (the *independent variable*).

This is the methodology underlying experiments, which are often specifically designed to determine whether changes in one variable will influence changes in another variable. The test marketing of a new product is an example of an experiment. In such an experiment, a marketer might take the product to three or more similar markets. In each, one or several variables will be changed, with all other variables kept as constant as possible. For example, different prices might be set for the product in each test market, while advertising and distribution remain unchanged. At the end of the test period, sales results in each test market will be compared to see if price had any impact on demand. In this way, marketers often establish the final market price for new products.

In addition to measuring the way in which variables are related, regression analysis also enables managers to predict responses or reactions to changes in independent variables. Such predictions are often needed before making expenditure decisions. In the above example, a marketer will be able to predict with some level of certainty the number of consumers' purchases of the product at different price levels. This, in turn, will enable the production manager to predict how many machines and how much raw material will be needed. The finance staff will be able to predict how much money to borrow to build the factories needed to make the product. Sales managers can predict how large a sales staff they will need. And the distribution manager can predict how many trucks and drivers will be needed to get the product to market. Prediction is one of the most important (if not *the* most important) uses of regression analysis results.

The Regression Procedure

The regression analysis procedure begins with collecting a data set that includes pairs of observed values or measurements. One set of measurements is needed for each variable to be included in the analysis. The idea of *pairs of measurements* may be somewhat misleading. It does not mean regression analysis is restricted to analyzing just two variables at a time. With multiple regression analysis, many variables can be included. The term *pairs* refers instead to measurements for a *dependent* and one or more *independent* variables.

The next step in the procedure is to produce a scatter plot of all measurements. Value pairs should be plotted as points on a *scatter diagram*. A scatter diagram has two axes: a vertical line called the *y-axis* and a horizontal line called the *x-axis*. The vertical line represents values of the dependent (or changed) variable. In the test market example above, the dependent variable (Y) is purchases in each market (sales). The horizontal axis would be marked off in increments of the independent variable (*price*).

Regression analysis evaluates all recorded data points and computes a regression equation. A *function*, or numerical value, is produced which, when multiplied with independent variable values, lets the decision maker *predict* the value of the independent (*Y*) variable given a value of the *X* variable or variables. The final step in the regression analysis procedure is interpretation of the findings.

The Regression Equation

As noted earlier, interpretation of the findings of a regression analysis statistical procedure begins with fitting the sample data to a "best-fit" line. The regression analysis procedure does this through a process called the *method of least squares*. This process measures the amount each point varies from a proposed line, squares each deviation, and then sums the squares.

After computing these values, the minimum squared value of all differences establishes the slope of the regression line. At the same time, the regression process determines the point at which the y-axis (the vertical line in the scatter diagram) and the computed regression line would meet. This point is called the *intercept*.

Once this point is known, the regression equation is used to predict additional points along the line, given a value for the x-axis. In statistical notation, the regression equation is expressed thus:

$$Y = a + bX$$

where

Y = the value of Y calculated from the estimated regression equation
a = the point on Y where the regression line intercepts on Y
b = the amount of change in X required for a corresponding change in Y
which, when plotted, represents the slope of the line

X = a measured value for X

(Note: In some statistics texts, the statistical symbol for the Y intercept point is given as b_0, and the symbol for the regression slope value as b_1.)

The Linear Regression Equation

The regression equation for straight-line regression (linear) is depicted as:

$$Y_i = b_0 + b_1 X_i$$

where

Y_i = the predicted value of Y for measurement i
X_i = the value of X for measurement I

In general terms, the analyst would interpret the $Y = a + bX$ equation in this way: "As X changes, Y also changes by b times the change in X."

Once the regression equation has been obtained, predictions or estimates of the dependent variable can be made. For example, say that we have computed the following regression equation:

$$Y = 4.0199 + .00896 * X$$

This could be interpreted to mean that the regression line begins at the point on the vertical axis that coincides with the value of 4.0199. Then, any subsequent increase in a value on the x-axis, multiplied by 0.00876, will equal a corresponding change in Y. By moving along the x-axis and periodically plotting the increases to both X and Y, connecting each point, it is possible to get a graphic impression of the regression line.

The Shape of the Regression Line

The shape of the regression line is an indication of how much of the change in the independent variable is explained by the dependent variable. The regression equation indicates how steep the line must be and whether it slopes to the right or left or is curvilinear. Decision makers look for a *linear* relationship, one that shows a definite relationship between the variables. When very little or no relationship exists, the scatter plot will show the data points distributed haphazardly around the space with no connection visible.

Not all relationships will be linear. Some are curvilinear; some are more or less flat, showing no relationship whatsoever; some are U-shaped; and others take on S-like patterns. Techniques are available for dealing with nonlinear relationships, but are not part of most introductory management statistics texts and are not discussed here.

A Simple Regression Example

The Department of Motor Vehicles currently has 148 outlets servicing citizens and businesses across the state. Licensing management is interested in knowing what the relationship, if any, is between the number of customers and gross sales. The data will be used to help outlet managers establish their staffing requirement for the coming fiscal year. The agency administrator draws a random sample of 20 outlets and collects from each the number of

Table 14.2

Customers and Gross Sales at 20 Vehicle-License Offices, July 7–14

License outlet	Weekly customers	Sales ($)
1	853	8,000
2	916	9,534
3	259	4,420
4	372	4,798
5	345	4,740
6	444	5,098
7	431	4,765
8	255	3,623
9	365	3,652
10	320	5,210
11	575	6,132
12	425	4,610
13	358	5,003
14	507	5,876
15	476	6,100
16	380	4,775
17	710	8,733
18	438	5,244
19	972	9,989
20	452	6,340

customers served per week and the gross sales volume. The data are shown in Table 14.2.

A regression analysis is then conducted on the data. In this simple example, decision makers may use three Microsoft Excel Wizard applications. First, the Excel Chart Wizard XY SCATTER PLOT program may be used to graphically display the type of relationship that exists between the two variables. If the scatter diagram reveals a linear relationship, the next step is to call up the CORREL (correlations) program under the Function Wizard. The value produced is the correlation coefficient (also referred to as the *Pearson Product Moment Correlation Coefficient* after the statistician who first reported its application).

The third step is to interpret the relationship findings. Using the RSQ (*R*-square) capability in the Function Wizard makes it much easier to make an interpretation. The r^2 value produced is the *coefficient of determination*; it is used to express the relationship as a *percentage*.

The final step in this process is to compute the slope of the regression line and its intercept with the y-axis. These are two separate steps in Excel: INTERCEPT and SLOPE. The results of these tests are shown in Table 14.3.

Table 14.3

Results of Excel CORREL and Related Regression Analysis Tests

Test results	
CORREL	0.950299
R²	0.903069
INTCEPT	$1,725
SLOPE	8.336909

Two Approaches to Regression

When carrying out a regression analysis procedure, two approaches are possible. They differ only in the number of variables used in the regression equation. The first is called "simple regression" and includes just one independent variable to explain one dependent variable.

The second approach is known as "multiple regression analysis" and, as its name implies, involves more than one independent variable in the regression equation. The test statistic in both simple and multiple regression analysis is *Pearson's r*, which ranges in value from −1.0 (a perfect negative relationship) to +1.0 (a perfect positive relationship). The square of Pearson's r (r^2) is the *coefficient of determination*. This value represents the *proportion* of the variation in Y that can be explained by linear regression on X. This makes interpreting the results easy. The researcher simply states the obvious: "An r^2 of .37 means that 37 percent of the variation (or change) in Y can be explained by changes in the combination of variables in X."

The Standard Error of the Estimate

One of the key concepts of statistics discussed early in this section on quantitative analysis had to do with measures of variability. These included the range, variance, and standard deviation. The point made was that seldom, if ever, do measurements fit neatly into values that decision makers would like them to be. Instead, they vary, positively *and* negatively, around some central point. In our discussion of descriptive statistics, this central point was the mean score. A similar variability applies in regression analysis, although now the central point is the computed best line of regression. Because the observed data points do not all fall on the regression line, the regression equation is not a perfect indicator of association; rather, it is an estimate. How close it comes to estimating can be judged by computing one additional value, the *standard error of the estimate*.

In statistical notation, the standard error of the estimate is indicated by the symbol S_{yx}. When calculated, the standard error of the estimate provides a measure of the variation around the fitted line of regression. It is measured in the same units as the dependent variable (Y) in much the same way that the standard deviation measures variability around the mean.

In application, the standard error of the estimate is used to make inferences about the predicted value of Y. For example, a small standard error suggests that the data points cluster relatively closely to the plotted regression line. In a word, the data are *homogeneous*. A large standard error suggests that data points are widely dispersed on either side of the regression line and that a high degree of variability exists.

A second inference statistic is produced with the standard error of the estimate: a p-value. The p-value can be used to make decisions about the statistical significance of the relationship between the two variables.

Summary

Several different relationship concepts were discussed in this chapter. The two key concepts are *regression analysis* and *correlation analysis*. Regression tells the decision maker if and how two or more variables are related. Correlation analysis provides information about the strength and direction of the relationship. Typically, regression and correlation tests are done for one of two purposes. First, a decision maker may be interested in seeing how two or more variables vary together; this use is not encountered as often as the second application, which is predicting the change in one variable by the movement in two or more other variables—measuring "cause and effect." Using regression analysis as a prediction tool is the most common application in public administration, nonprofit organization, and business research.

Two types of regression analysis are used: *simple regression analysis* and *multiple regression analysis*. Simple regression tests the correlation between just two variables, whereas multiple regression analysis computes a regression equation that incorporates the influence of any number of variables on how the first variable moves. Microsoft Excel includes programs in its Function Wizard for simple regression and correlation analysis and the capability to compute multiple regression analysis in its Data Analysis Tools.

Suggested Reading

Brightman, Harvey J. 1999. *Data Analysis in Plain English with Microsoft Excel.* Pacific Grove, CA: Duxbury Press.

Jendrek, Margaret P. 1988. *Through the Maze: Statistics with Computer Applications.* Belmont, CA: Wadsworth.

Neufeld, John L. 1997. *Learning Business Statistics with Microsoft Excel.* Upper Saddle River, NJ: Prentice Hall.

15 Experiments and Experimental Design

Decision makers at all levels of government and nonprofit organizations are often faced with the need to determine which of several options is the best course of action to select. One way for the researcher to make this decision is to design and conduct an *experiment* first. In an experiment, the research takes an active rather than a passive role in the data-gathering process. Rather than simply collecting data from other sources, in an experiment the researcher purposefully manipulates one or more variables. *Manipulation* simply means changing the variable in some way. The purpose of making these changes is to measure what effect, if any, they will have on some other variable. The manipulated or changed variable is called the *independent variable.* The variable that an independent variable may have an impact upon is called the *dependent variable* or *response variable.* Both variables are sometimes referred to as *factors*.

Experimental research is often called *causal research* because researchers are checking if the manipulated variable "causes" a change of any direction in the other variable. The purpose of the experiment is to establish whether the independent variable causes a *predictable* level of change in the dependent variable. When this happens, the administrator can initiate or make changes in a public service while having a strong idea of the public's reaction to the change.

In public administration, the dependent variable is often some measure of the public's acceptance of a proposed program or satisfaction with some level of service; the manipulation could be adding or deleting components of the proposed program before measuring acceptance or satisfaction. In experimentation, these manipulations are known as *treatments*. Examples of dependent variables include the following:

- Different prices for services
- Different ways of doing things, such as methods of training workers
- Different types of something, such as different methods of public transportation
- Different amounts of a product or service, such as several different amounts of fertilizer applied to municipal parks and golf courses

An example of a public administration experiment is testing the effectiveness of different communications methods to inform and educate a sample of high school students about ways to prevent contracting AIDS. One instructional method is distributing brochures in the classroom; another method is requiring attendance at an illustrated lecture given by a health-care professional; and a third is showing a film in a health education class. In this experiment, the researcher would randomly assign students to groups using each of the three methods. The different groups' scores on a quiz administered after the three education events would be compared to weigh the relative effectiveness of the methods.

Experiments also play an important role in public agency operations and systems design, management tools that are receiving much attention in today's public administration research. Montgomery (1991) added quality control procedures to the list of possible uses for experiments. He described an experiment as "a test in which some purposeful changes are made to the [independent] variables of a process or system." The changes are made to allow the researcher to observe and record possible reasons for changes in the dependent variable. Thus, experimental methods play an important role in the design and development of organizational processes, as well as in continuous process improvement.

Key Considerations in Experimental Design

The term *experimental design* is used to refer to a variety of different-but-related approaches to conducting an experiment. The term design is used to indicate that the experimental method selected is the researcher's decision. The design selected depends first upon what information the administrator needs and second on the resources available to do the research to acquire that information.

There are six key issues to consider when making decisions about what design to follow in an experiment:

1. What *independent* variable or variables should be used in the experiment?

2. What *manipulations* (changes) in the independent variable are most appropriate?
3. Which variable is the most appropriate *dependent* variable?
4. How should changes in the dependent variable be *measured*?
5. What subjects or elements should be chosen as the *test units*?
6. Which *external variables* should be controlled in the experiment?

Selecting the Independent Variable(s)

An *independent variable* is a variable whose values can be changed or manipulated by the researcher. Using different instructional methods, applying different levels of disinfectant chemicals, selecting different prices for a service, using different formats for reports, and trying different performance measurement methods are all independent variables. The researcher can select any variable that can be changed or altered in some way.

Independent variables are variables that the researcher *suspects* influence changes in the dependent or variable of interest. The researcher describes this suspected influence in a *hypothesis*. The object of the experiment, then, is to test if and in what way, if any, the suspected influence occurs.

In simple experiments, only two different values of the same independent variable and one dependent variable are tested. For example, in order to identify more effective delivery of prenatal care to indigent females in a farming community, a researcher designs an experiment to determine which of two prenatal service-delivery approaches results in healthier newborn infants. The researcher randomly assigns subjects seeking care to one of two groups. One group will receive prenatal care at a central hospital emergency facility; the second group will receive care in a storefront clinic near where most patients live. Care is taken to ensure that the same level and type of patient care are provided at both locations.

The researcher uses the two-category care-location variable as the independent variable. The dependent variable in the study is the measure of birth complications recorded for each independent group. The group receiving prenatal care at the hospital emergency facility, which is the traditional delivery location for care to the indigent, is called the *control group*. A control group is the body of subjects whose treatment is not changed; conditions are said to *remain constant*. The experiment is designed to test the program administrator's idea that a storefront delivery system will encourage more of the target population to take advantage of the service. Therefore, the group receiving care at the storefront facility is the *test group*.

Changing the Independent Variable

Values of independent variables can be any of the four classes of measurement: *nominal*, *ordinal*, *interval*, or *ratio* data. In public administration research, however, independent variables are usually nominal or ordinal. This makes them *categorical* in nature.

In the prenatal care delivery example above, the changes are the different locations of the service. In a slightly more complex design, three or more methods could be included with very little additional effort required for processing the results of the experiment. Additional independent variables could also be included in the design.

For example, suppose the researcher wants to determine whether women living in rural areas respond differently than do women in either suburban or urban locations. Such a design is a "three-by-two" design—three residence locations and two care delivery locations. The researcher would now have the results of six different groups to compare.

The researcher might also want to know if first-time mothers respond differently than patients giving birth for the second or more time. In this case, the researcher would have a "three-by-two-by-two" design, involving twelve groups instead of six.

Adding too many levels or independent variables to the study can cause problems by increasing the complexity of the design and the number of groups to compare. In addition, to make sure that each group is large enough to provide meaningful data, the total sample size must be increased. To avoid such complexity and the added cost of a bigger sample size, most public administration experimental research is done with simple, one-variable, random designs.

Selecting the Dependent Variable

Selecting the right variable to test in an experimental study begins with the first statement of the study problem and its relevant component parts. Other terms to identify these parts of a study problem are *constructs*, *concepts*, and *component factors*. Next, the researcher must decide what the most important *measurable* indicators of each basic construct are. For example, in a study designed to measure program performance, indicators might be absenteeism, turnover, or employee morale. Each of these can be measured, and each can be a dependent variable in an experiment.

The next step is to develop a hypothesis for each of the indicators and the variables that the researcher believes can impact upon the indicator —that is, "cause" a change in the dependent variable. Variables that can conceivably "cause" increases or decreases in these indicators are what will be tested in the experiment; they are the independent variables.

To learn as much as possible about the problem and its component factors, a researcher often begins with an exploratory study. A primary activity in exploratory studies is conducting a series of interviews with "key informants." Key informants are persons who are assumed to have a greater than normal familiarity with the problem, its symptoms, and its probable causes. Key informants are typically excellent sources of information about the main components of a problem.

Measuring Changes in the Dependent Variable

To identify appropriate units of measurement for a dependent variable in an experiment, the researcher begins by listing everything that can be considered an indicator of one or more facets of the study problem. As noted, "indicators" are variables that, first, can be identified and measured and, second, can be influenced by another variable in some way. Examples of measurable indicators for a program are the following:

- Citizens' ability to recall what a program does
- The number of citizens using the program
- How well people can describe activities of the program
- How much people like the program
- How much people are willing to invest in the effort to participate
- People's ability to describe the benefits of participating

There is obviously more than one way to measure each of these indicators. The unit selected will depend for the most part on the objectives of the study. Possible units of measurement for indicators include the following:

- A numerical scale of client satisfaction
- Growth in the number of clients served
- The amount clients are willing to pay for the service
- The total number of client complaints received
- The percentage of the target population enrolled in the program
- The number of positive statements in subjects' descriptions of the program
- Numerical values assigned to a quantity of acceptable cost (including social cost)
- Number of subjects who can name program benefits

Selecting Test Units

Test units are the clients, citizens, staff members, cities, towns, counties, or any other entity whose responses to manipulations of the independent variable are to be measured. Individual units should be selected randomly from a list of all population units, where every unit has an equal chance of being selected for the study and of being assigned to any of the groups to be tested. Random samples are also known as *probability samples*. A list of potential study subjects is called a *sampling frame*.

Researchers try to achieve sample groupings with *matching units* wherever possible. When this is a concern, it means that the sample selection process is not entirely random. Rather, this process involves what are called *stratified samples*. Selection of a stratified sample is still a random process, but the units are selected from portions of the population that are more or less the same on the characteristic of interest. The point is for the samples to match as closely as possible the characteristic-distribution of the population.

Controlling External Variables

External variables (also known as *confounding* or *extraneous variables*) are variables that may also affect the dependent variable, but that the researcher feels do not directly cause changes in the outcome variable. They can *influence*, but not *cause*, change. Therefore, the researcher takes special steps in the design of the experiment to control or eliminate the effects of these variables. McDaniel and Gates (1993) identified four approaches that are used to control for the effects of extraneous variables:

1. Randomly assigning subjects to treatment groups
2. Physically controlling factors that might influence the results, such as matching subjects on selected characteristics
3. Controlling the design to ensure that only relevant causal variables are manipulated
4. Using statistical control procedures that can make adjustments for the effects of extraneous variables. Analysis of covariance (ANCOVA), for example, does this by making statistical adjustments in the dependent variable value for each treatment

In addition to controlling for the effects of external variables that might confound the determination of causation, researchers must also control for a variety of other potential experimental design errors (Zikmund 1994). The two main types of error that the research must consider are random sampling

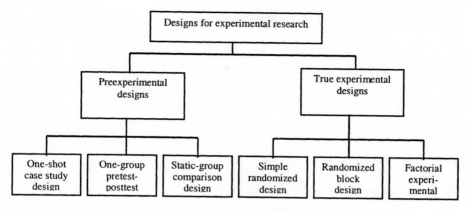

Figure 15.1 **A Classification of Experimental Designs**

error and constant or systematic error. Another word often used to describe constant error is *bias.*

Adhering to random sample selection procedures can control sampling error. Constant or systematic error occurs when external variables, such as testing conditions, are allowed to creep into the experiment. Constant error will distort the results of an experiment in a particular direction.

Types of Experimental Designs

There are many different types of experimental designs. These can be grouped into two basic types: *preexperimental designs* and *true experimental designs.* The basic difference is the amount of independent variable manipulation that is possible. Figure 15.1 is a graphic classification of the main preexperimental and true experimental designs.

Preexperimental Designs

Preexperimental designs are conducted with the same goal as true experimental designs. This is the determination of the ability of an independent variable (or variables) to influence changes in a dependent variable. However, in preexperimental designs the researcher has little if any control over external factors. These designs are appropriately used in exploratory research for identifying potential hypotheses; they should not be considered as strong tests of existing hypotheses. Their major advantage is that they are simple and inexpensive to conduct. There are three main types of preexperimental designs: one-shot case studies, one-group pretest and posttest studies, and static-group comparisons (McDaniel and Gates 1993).

One-Shot Case Study Designs

One-shot case study designs involve exposing a single group of subjects to a single treatment, then measuring the effect on the dependent variable. Only one treatment is used, no control group is involved, and only an "after" measurement is taken. This makes it impossible to determine whether a "caused" change in the dependent variable has taken place. The design does not control for the effects of external variables. The only reason to use this design is to identify possible causal hypotheses.

One-Group Pretest–Posttest Designs

This is a very popular design. It allows the researcher to measure change in the dependent variable. Its major drawback is that it does not include a control group, which puts severe limitations on the researcher's ability to control for extraneous variables. Another weaknesses of the design is that it does not control for any learning or historical effect that might have taken place between the pretest and the posttest. Subjects can often become "test savvy," learning to provide answers that they believe the researcher desires.

Static-Group Comparison Designs

This design is closest to true experimental designs. It involves two samples, a test group and control group. The groups are subjected to different treatments, but no pretesting takes place. Nor are subjects randomly assigned to the different groups.

This design is popular in education research. The test and control groups are different classes; each class receives a different treatment. Instead of individual students being randomly assigned to a group, different classes in the school are assigned as either a test or control group. This is done to minimize disruption of normal classroom routine. One instructional method is used with one class, with a different method used in the second class. At the end of the experiment, both groups are tested. Differences in achievement scores are often used as dependent variable measurements.

True Experimental Designs

The three types of true experimental designs used most often in social and administrative science research are simple randomized designs, randomized block designs, and factorial designs. A number of variations are possible within each of these categories. Several are discussed below. Before proceeding with that discussion, however, a brief caveat about the results of experiments is in order. It is important for researchers to remember that experimental results will almost always differ from subject to subject, and the effect, if any, of external variables will have greater or lesser impact on individual subjects as well. Therefore, when researchers concern themselves with experimental results for groups, the results should be considered only an estimate of the "true" effect. The only way the "true" effect could ever be determined is if all members of the population were to be included in what is otherwise a perfectly controlled experiment. This never happens in the real world.

A good experimental design will address this issue by controlling error so that the estimate is as good as possible. An experimental design that achieves this will have the following chief characteristics:

- The design ensures that the observed changes in the dependent variable are unbiased by controlling for randomness error.
- The observed changes (called *treatment effects*) in the dependent variable can be reliably measured, thus controlling for systematic error.
- The effects can be measured with the desired degree of precision (as indicated by the computed confidence level).
- The design will permit an objective test of the null hypothesis; it is an efficient design, one that satisfies all requirements at the "best" cost.

Simple Randomized Designs

Sometimes called *one-factor* designs, simple randomized experiments test for a causal relationship between just one independent and one dependent variable. In a simple randomized design, each treatment is independently administered to a different group (*not applying* or *changing* a treatment is the same thing as a changed treatment). All sample units are randomly chosen from the parent population and assigned to groups without bias.

The simple randomized design is also known as a *one-way classification* design. This is because only one independent variable is used at a time. However, that variable can have any number of different levels. For example, if the treatment variable in an employee training experiment is training methods, the researcher is not limited to just two different methods; any number of different methods can be included in the same design. As in all true experiments, sample units must be randomly assigned to test and control groups. Graphic representations of simple randomized two-level and four-level designs are displayed in Tables 15.1 and 15.2.

Table 15.1

A Simple Randomized Two-Group Design

Group	Method of unit selection	Treatment variable	Dependent variable
A. Experimental	Random	X_1	O_1
B. Control	Random	X_2	O_2

Where X_1 = Treatment 1;
O_1 = Dependent variable change 1;
O_2 = Dependent variable change 2.

Table 15.2

A Simple Randomized Four-Treatment Design

Group	Method of unit selection	Treatment variable	Dependent variable
A. Experimental$_1$	Random	X_1	O_1
B. Experimental$_2$	Random	X_2	O_2
C. Experimental$_3$	Random	X_3	O_3
D. Control	Random	X_4	O_4

While the two-group example in Table 15.1 does not indicate whether a pretest occurred, the design does not preclude that possibility. Conducting a pretest would make it easier to measure effects in the dependent variable and would make it possible to be more precise in the final interpretation of the test.

Table 15.2 depicts a simple randomized design with three different treatments and a control group (the control group makes up the fourth treatment group). Test subjects are, again, randomly assigned to each of the four groups.

Randomized Block Designs

In a randomized block design experiment, test units are placed into groups according to selected characteristics of an *external* (extraneous) variable. The purpose of the block design is to make sure the test groups are matched as closely as possible on the characteristics of the external variable. This is a method of controlling for any variation "caused" by the extraneous variable.

In the following example, the director of a student club wanted to determine the best way to inform high school students about after-school programs at the club. With the support of school officials and teachers, she designed an experiment that began by randomly assigning students into three different groups. One group was to learn about the club through a brochure distributed in a classroom. A second group would be shown a short video that

Table 15.3

A Two Level Randomized Block Design

	Treatments		
Block	Treatment A (brochure)	Treatment B (video)	Treatment C (lecture/discussion)
X (urban)	A_X	B_X	C_X
Y (rural)	A_Y	B_Y	C_Y

described the club's activities, while a third group would be informed about the club in a classroom presentation given by a club counselor serving as a guest lecturer.

The club director believed that an external factor that could limit club participation was the location of students' residences. Students living in town could travel to and from the club using public transportation. Students residing in rural areas were unable to use city transportation; therefore, she decided to use *residence location* as a blocking variable. This meant that the design now required samples for both urban and rural students. This design is displayed in Table 15.3.

Factorial Designs

Experimental designs that test two or more independent variables at the same time are called "factorial experiments" or "factorial designs" (independent variables are also known as *factors*). In addition to testing for statistically significant differences among individual factors, the procedure also tests whether two or more of the variables *working together* have an impact on the differences. The term used to describe this combination effect is *interaction effect*.

In the following example of a two-factor analysis of variance procedure, a food service manager wanted to determine the best day to publicize menu specials in the department's weekly newspaper. She also wanted to know in which section of the paper the notice should appear. The two factors for this design are *day* and *position*. The design called for notices to run on four different days: Tuesday, Wednesday, Thursday, and Friday. Three locations in the paper were to be tested: general news about the government (the first section of the paper), department news, and the news about employees and their families. Comparisons were to be based on daily sales volume. Table 15.4 displays the design for this experiment. Three levels of the *position* variable were included for each of the four levels of the *day* variable, making it necessary to test a total of twelve groups.

Table 15.4

A Two-Factor Factorial Design

Factor I (position)	Factor II (day)			
	Tues	Wed	Thur	Fri
Position A	A-1	A-2	A-3	A-4
Position B	B-1	B-2	B-3	B-4
Position C	C-1	C-2	C-3	C-4

Interpreting Experimental Results

Various versions of the analysis of variance (ANOVA) statistical procedure are used to interpret the results of experiments. ANOVA compares the differences between any number of groups and does so for two or more levels. With ANOVA, it is possible to test the role of each of several variables independently and then to determine whether two or more of the variables interact to influence any differences in the dependent variable. ANOVA allows the researcher to test the influence of each factor or variable independently. Then, two or more variables can be tested together to determine if they are interactive in any way in their influence on the result.

The ANOVA Procedure

To make its comparisons, the ANOVA procedure compares two or more samples or groups within a sample. ANOVA procedures were introduced as *hypothesis tests* in Chapter 13. Although the test and its interpretation are the same, the difference in primary focus requires that some of that material also be briefly discussed here.

Analysis of variance uses the F-statistic to calculate variances in mean scores. It then compares the variance of the mean for each subgroup to the overall variance found for the sample. Researchers' decisions about the null hypothesis are made based on these comparisons.

ANOVA statistical software provides three key pieces of information for the researcher: (1) summary statistics for each sample or group, (2) an F-ratio, and (3) a probability value. This makes interpretation simple: The means are interpreted as being statistically different if the p-value is less than the analyst-selected confidence level. Traditionally, confidence levels used in public administration are .01, .05, or .10, with the .05 level used most often.

If the computed p-value is less than the researcher-selected .05 level of confidence, the null hypothesis is rejected. Say, for example, that the researcher selected the .05 level of confidence and the ANOVA program calculated a computed p-value of 0.0467. The researcher could then state a conclusion this way: "With 95 percent reliability, there is no statistically significant difference in the mean scores of these two groups. The null hypothesis is, therefore, rejected, and the alternate hypothesis accepted."

Analysis of Experimental Design Data

Managers have three different versions of statistical tests to choose from when analyzing the results of an experiment: a one-factor version, a two-factor version, and a version that examines the results of three or more factors (n-way version); the analysis of variance procedures discussed in Chapter 13 are used in all three. The one-factor design is the basic procedure; it should be used when the means of two or more groups are being compared across a single factor.

Analysis Procedures for a One-Factor Experiment

The method for testing differences in the one-factor scores of two groups was discussed in detail in Chapter 13. A new manager was hired at a public agency. Employee morale had declined dramatically, and the agency's clients had rated program quality and client service as poor. Legislators were demanding that the agency director find the problem and fix it. Before making any internal changes, the manager wanted to know if both supervisors and staff perceived the company climate in the same way. A seven-point scale to measure composite organizational climate was administered to a random sample of twenty-five staff members and twenty supervisors.

The manager's null hypothesis was "There is no difference in the way managers and staff employees rate the organization's climate." To test this hypothesis, the manager used a one-way analysis of variance procedure.

Analyzing Factorial Designs

The two-way analysis of variance statistical test is used for what are called factorial experiments or factorial designs. In all such cases, the goal of the test is to compare the results of two or more groups on two or more variables or factors at the same time. In addition, the statistical procedure determines if two or more of the variables working together may have had an impact on the differences—the *interaction effect*.

ANOVA computes an F-table with p-values and critical F-values for each level of all variables, and for interaction. There are three statistics to interpret in the ANOVA results produced in this Excel application. The first tests the null hypothesis that there is no difference in the first factor. The second tests the null hypothesis that there is no difference in the second factor. The third tests the null hypothesis that there is no *interaction* between the two factors as they relate to any differences. These three test results can be interpreted using the *p-value approach*.

Three-Factor and More Designs

The three-factor design is evaluated in a manner very much like the two-factor test. The principal effects of each factor are examined to see if the factor makes a difference between groups. This is followed by tests for interactions among the variables. However, now there are more of these interactions to interpret. Regardless of the number of factors and interactions, the results are interpreted in the same way as in the two-way analysis procedure.

Testing More Than One Variable at a Time

Thus far, we have been examining analysis of variance tests for only one dependent variable at a time. Designs have also been developed to test for more than two dependent variables at the same time. These tests first compare all factors against each grouping variable at a time; they then test for interaction; finally, they repeat the tests for combinations of groups.

This statistical process is known as *multivariate analysis of variance*, (MANOVA). In addition, a technique has also been designed that combines regression analysis with ANOVA. Known as ANCOVA, it corrects for internal variation while comparing mean variances. Students are encouraged to seek more information about these powerful tests in standard statistical texts or SPSS documentation. Because they are used so seldom in public administration research, neither MANOVA nor ANCOVA is described in any greater detail here.

Summary

Public administrators and researchers in public administration must often design and carry out laboratory and field experiments. Experiments are used to test hypotheses about the effects of changes in a dependent variable that have been influenced or "caused" by manipulations in an independent variable. Experimental design is the term used to describe a variety of different approaches to experimentation. These can be grouped into two broad categories of experiments, *preexperimental* designs and *true experimental* designs.

Analysis of variance (ANOVA) procedures are used in experimental designs to test for statistically significant differences in the results of two or more groups. These tests use the F-statistic to compare variances between samples or groups. Analysis of variance procedures do not limit the number of groups being compared. Three, four, or more levels or group scores can be compared at the same time. Equally, analysis of variance can test for differences with more than one factor at a time.

One-way analysis of variance tests a single factor for differences. Two-way analysis of variance tests two factors individually and then tests whether the two factors interact in some way to influence the differences. More than two-factor analysis of variance procedures, together with tests that permit testing a number of factors with more than one grouping variable (MANOVA), have been developed. Finally, a procedure that combines analysis of variance with regression analysis, ANCOVA, makes it possible to do all these tests at one time.

Suggested Reading

Berenson, Mark L., and David M. Levine. 1996. *Basic Business Statistics: Concepts and Applications*. 6th ed. Upper Saddle River, NJ: Prentice Hall.

Einspruch, Eric L. 1998. *An Introductory Guide to SPSS for Windows*. Thousand Oaks, CA: Sage.

Montgomery, D. C. 1991. *Design and Analysis of Experiments*. 3d ed. New York: John Wiley.

Rosenthal, Robert, and Ralph L. Rosnow. 1991. *Essentials of Behavioral Research*. 2d ed. New York: McGraw-Hill.

16 Using SPSS to Process Statistical Data

SPSS (Statistical Package for the Social Sciences) is a powerful software package that performs statistical analyses of quantitative data. The program enables users to create, modify, and analyze very large sets of data. It can also produce such graphic displays as tables, charts, and graphs.

Data entry is facilitated by the use of a standard spreadsheet format; cases are in rows, and variables are in columns. A *case* is the responses or measurements of a single subject or study element. A *variable* is something that the researcher is able to measure or count in some way.

How to Start Using SPSS

SPSS is loaded on many but not all of the personal computers (PCs) in college and university computer labs. When it is available, it is an easy and powerful way of processing large-sample databases; it is essentially unlimited in the number of either subjects or variables it can process at any one time.

The process of launching SPSS software is the same as any other frequently used software. At the initial window, double-click on the SPSS icon. The Data Editor window will appear on the screen. (If the SPSS shortcut icon does not appear on the main Windows screen, click on Start, then Programs, then select SPSS. The opening SPSS screen should appear.) Superimposed on this opening screen may be a dialogue window that asks "What would you like to do?" Available options include:

- Run the tutorial
- Type in data
- Run an existing query

- Create a new file using the Database Capture Wizard
- Open an existing file

If you have a database loaded on the hard drive or on an inserted floppy disk, you may call up that file for immediate activity. Or you may select Cancel, which opens the Data Editor for data entry. You *must* have entered data in the Data Editor before SPSS can perform any operations. Data can be entered directly or imported from an existing file, such as an Excel spreadsheet or a word-processing program.

The SPSS Opening Screen

The SPSS opening screen will show two toolbars at the top of the screen and a full-screen spreadsheet (with grid lines). Along the left side of the screen are row numbers. At the top of the spreadsheet is a row for you to indicate the names of the variables in your study.

Above the spreadsheet is the Main Menu Bar (for all versions lower than Version 10, this is the SPSS Data Editor Toolbar). Menus are named; tools are displayed as icons.

Main Menu Bar

Look at the top line on the SPSS screen. Running across the screen are the names for ten file menus. These menus allow you to access every process, tool, and feature contained in SPSS. Beginning at the left and running across the screen, these file menus are:

- *File* menu: This allows you to open, close, save, and otherwise work with all types of SPSS files.
- *Edit* menu: This allows you to cut and paste, move files, and find elements in a file or record (a *record* is all the data for a single case).
- *View* menu: This allows you to turn on or off visible features, change fonts, and show grid lines.
- *Data* menu: A key option, this allows you to define variables, indicate the type of measurements used, and assign labels to variables and values.
- *Transform* menu: This feature allows you to convert or change variable values, count responses, recode values, and so on.
- *Analyze* menu: Along with the Data menu, this is the option you will use most often; it can be considered the *heart* of SPSS. It allows you to name any type of analysis you want to carry out.

- *Graphs* menu: This feature allows you to select from fifteen different ways to graphically display data, including tables, graphs, and charts.
- *Utilities* menu: This allows you to call up information about your variables and your data file.
- *Windows* menu: This allows you to switch from one window to another, and back.
- *Help* menu: the standard online help feature that explains all features and tools needed by the analyst.

Entering Variable Labels: SPSS Version 10 and Above

Version 10 of SPSS employs a slightly modified procedure for identifying variable labels in a data set. Rather than simply clicking on the first cell under the column indicator, you must now go to a separate file. When you are in this file, it is possible to define all variables in a data set at one time. This should be done before any data are entered.

How to Define Variables and Assign Value Labels

Look at the bottom left-hand corner of the SPSS Data Editor dialogue box. You should see two file tabs: One says Data View, and the other says Variable View. Click on the Variable View tab. You are now ready to define your variables and their values. In this file, all information about each variable is entered in *row* format, going across the page (this is an important distinction because data for each variable will later be entered in *column* format). The first row will hold all the information for your first variable; row two will hold all information about your second variable, and so on. SPSS will *automatically* move this information into the appropriate column for the variable.

You will have ten decisions to make about each variable in your data set, although several will be made for you (in what is called the *default* mode). These choices are in ten columns. To enter defining information, click on the cell in the appropriate column, as follows.

> **Column 1.** This is where you enter the name of the variable. Names can be no longer than eight characters in length and must start with a letter of the alphabet. On the screen, variable names appear in lowercase type.

Column 2. This permits you to change the form of the variable data. The default is "numeric," which is the form you will use almost always. Make sure that is what appears in the cell.

Column 3. This establishes the width of the cell. The default is eight spaces. You can widen or narrow it, or leave the default width of eight spaces. The defining characteristic is the number of characters you use for the variable name *or* the number of characters in a value for that variable. For example, a variable name that is six characters wide (such as *Gender*) might have values that are only one character wide (such as the number 1 for "female" and 2 for "male"); the cell will require a column width of six characters—the length of the *variable* name. If, however, the name of the variable is only three characters wide (such as *inc* for *income*) but the values might require five characters for an income amount (such as 45000), then the column width for this variable will be based on the number of characters required for the *largest value*, *not* on the three-character-wide variable name.

Column 4. This changes the number of decimals you want to use for each variable. The *default* is two decimal points. It can be raised or lowered or left as it is. For categorical data, it is usually best to make this number zero (0).

Column 5. This is where you may enter a longer label for the short (eight characters or less) variable name you entered in column 1. The longer variable label will then appear along with the shorter variable name in all printouts, making it easier for you to later remember what the statistical results apply to; this is very important with databases with many variables. Variable labels can be up to forty characters in length, including spaces and symbols.

Column 6. This opens the box for providing definitions to the *values* of a variable. Value labels can be up to twenty characters in length, including spaces and symbols. Follow this five-step procedure to input these value labels into your data dictionary:

Step 1. Click on the blank cell in this column. Then click on the small three-dot box that will appear at the right-hand side of the cell. This will bring up the Values dialogue box.

Step 2. Enter a number you have assigned for the value in the Values window.

Step 3. Enter a label (less than twenty characters in length) for the value in the *Value Labels* window.

Step 4. Click on the Add button. This is a critical step; you must do this after entering each value and value label!

Step 5. Repeat the process for each value of the variable. Click on OK.

Column 7. This is where you assign a value for any data missing for this variable. Follow this procedure:

Step 1. Click on the three-dot button.

Step 2. Click on the Discrete missing values button.

Step 3. Enter the number you want to use to signify missing data for this variable.

Step 4. Click OK. You can use any number or numbers that are not actual values that you have assigned for categories of the variable. For most variables, the value 9 is used. This is an important step. If you leave a cell blank, it will still be counted and used as part of the divisor when calculating statistics.

TIP: *Never* leave a cell blank; *never* leave a row blank! (You will know if it is blank because a faint period (dot) will show up in the cell when you are in the Data View file).

Column 8. This column allows you to specify how wide the variable name will be. The *default* is the exact width of the name as it appears. If you want to change the default, change the width to match the number of characters taken by the name, but no more than eight. Most of the time you will not need to change this value.

Column 9. This allows you to specify the alignment you want for the data in each cell—flush right, flush left, or centered.

Column 10. In this column you must tell the computer the type of measurement for the variable—scale, ordinal, or nominal.

Check Your Progress

When you have identified all variables, values, and data types, click on the Data View tab at the lower left-hand corner of the screen. All the information you entered for each variable will be inserted in its proper location, with each variable and value now defined. Remember: you can always go back and change anything by clicking on the Variable View tab and moving your cursor to the proper cell.

You are now ready to enter data. Remember: all data for any one case *must* be entered in rows and inserted in the correct columns for that variable. And remember to regularly save the data on a data disk.

SPSS Data Editor Toolbar: Version 9 and Lower

For Version 9 and lower, the Data Editor Toolbar allows quick access to commands dealing with data and datafiles. A string of sixteen different icons is displayed on the toolbar, running across the screen just under the Main Menu bar. These icons are shortcuts to a variety of SPSS commands, most of which are also embedded within the main menus. Using the icons just makes it easier and quicker to do your analyses. Beginning at the left of the toolbar, the icons represent the following actions:

- *Open* a file.
- *Save* the file you are working on.
- *Print* a file or output from a statistical process.
- *Recall* the last dialogue box you used.
- *Undo* (i.e., reverse) the last process.
- *Go to* a named chart in the file.
- *Go to* a named case in the file.
- Access information about *variables*.
- *Find* a record in a file.
- *Insert* a case (record) into a file (cases are *rows*).
- *Insert* a variable into a file (variables are *columns*).
- *Split* a file on some dimension of a variable.
- *Weight* (i.e., assign weights to) variables.
- *Selects* cases according to a user-selected dimension or measurement.
- *Turn value labels* on or off in the visual display.
- *Create* a set of variables to use as an index, etc.

You should now be ready to define and enter your data.

Entering SPSS Data

SPSS has few limitations in what it accepts as "data." While it is possible to enter data in other forms, the easiest way to deal with these limits is to treat all information that is going to be processed in an SPSS analysis as *numeric data*. Other than names developed for *variables* and measured or assigned *values* of those variables, only numbers should be entered for processing. Thus, SPSS data are numbers used to signify a set of measurements or labels for a specific set of cases.

The term *case* is used to mean a single entity in a data set. Examples include one person among a group of people studied (i.e., in a *sample*), one city in an investigation of a group of cities, or one household in a group of political precincts examined for voting results. Whatever the element included in the study, the collective group of cases is usually referred to as a *sample*.

Cases are always listed in *rows* in an SPSS data file. Each case in the sample is assigned its own identifying number (1, 2, 3. . .). Each case contains a set of features that are identified and recorded as numbers. These features are the values assigned to each of the *variables*. Examples of variables include the *gender* of a subject (*subject* is another word for a case), the number of school-aged children in a community, or the number of citizens in a precinct who voted in the last election. A more formal definition of a variable is this: Any feature or concept that can be measured or assigned a value on any one of the four measurement scales (nominal, ordinal, interval, and ratio) can be considered as a *variable*.

Variables are always listed in *columns* in an SPSS data file. The measurements or values for each variable must always be placed in the data file in the same reference order. For example, if the values assigned to the variable *gender* follow the values assigned to the variable *age* in the first case entries, they must always be entered in this same order. In an SPSS data file a complete row for an individual case is called a *record*.

It is possible to enter data in an SPSS data file in two different ways. The one used most often is called the *fixed format*; the other is *Free Format*. In a fixed format file, every value for every variable is always entered in exactly the same column in the data file. Thus, every line of the data file will have the same number of columns, with the data for a variable always in the same place in the file. This is the format used by most researchers because it allows for easier editing and proofreading of a file; it is the only format to be discussed here.

If desired, empty spaces may be left between each variable, as in the fixed format example in Table 16.1. If empty spaces are not used, each row of the file would look like this: 01119121501, 02218111482, and so on.

In this data file, 1 and 2 were used as database values for the two possible genders, female and male. Education is indicated by the number of years of school completed; "MS" refers to number of parents at home. "State" refers to place, with each state assigned a numerical value. "UrbSub" stands for the location of the subjects' residence—the value 1 is used for an urban location; 2 is used for a suburban residence.

Data (the numerical values you collect and/or assign to your collected

Table 16.1

A Sample SPSS Database with Variable Labels

SNO	Gender	Age	Educa	MS	State	UrbSub
01	1	19	12	1	50	1
02	2	18	11	1	48	2
03	2	17	11	1	32	1
04	1	16	11	2	32	2
05	1	19	12	1	50	1
06	2	18	11	1	48	2
07	1	17	12	2	46	1
08	1	19	12	1	50	1
09	2	18	11	1	47	1
10	1	20	13	2	47	2

information) is entered into a file using the SPSS *data editor capability*. This can be done in several different ways. The most common way is to manually type the data directly into the appropriate columns in the Data Editor window. However, to do it this way, you must first define your variables and assign labels to all possible values of each variable.

Variables and Values in SPSS

As we have seen, a variable is a characteristic, a concept, or a descriptive property that can take on different values or categories. Another way to say this is that a variable is something that can vary. Research deals with four broad classes of variables:

1. An *independent variable* is the characteristic that is supposed to be responsible for bringing about some change in another variable. It is sometimes called a "cause" variable.
2. A *dependent variable* is the characteristic that is altered or otherwise affected by the changes in an independent variable. It is sometimes called an "outcome" variable.
3. An *extraneous variable* is a characteristic or factor that is not part of the independent/dependent variable relationship. It may increase or decrease the strength of the relationship between two variables, but has no part in whatever "causation" might be present.
4. An *intervening variable*, sometimes called a "confounding variable," serves as a link between the independent and dependent variables. Often, the relationship between the independent and dependent variable cannot occur without the presence of an intervening variable; that is, the "cause" variable will work only in the presence of an intervening variable.

Variable Names [Version 9 or Lower]

When you first open SPSS, the Data Entry Window automatically appears on the computer screen. The first cell in the upper left-hand corner of the spreadsheet will have a dark line around it. This signifies the location of the cursor. You must now click on the Data selection on the menu bar. This should bring up a gray box in the middle of the spreadsheet. This is the Define Variables dialogue box. Now, type in the name of the first variable in the open box just to the right of the Variable Name prompt on this dialogue box. Here are some tips to help you with defining your variables.

- Variable names must be no longer than eight characters; they can be less than eight; spaces cannot be used.
- Variable names must always *start* with a letter of the alphabet, but can include some numbers and symbols among the eight characters. For example, you can name variables *var1* and *var2*, but not *1var* and *2var*.
- Every variable must have its own distinct name; never repeat a variable name.
- Use names for variables that have some meaning to you and that are easy to remember. For example, instead of *plofbrth* for the variable *place of birth*, you might want to instead use the full word *state*, or *birth*, or *place*. It is always your choice!
- Some words cannot be used as variable names. These are words used in computational syntax, such as "AND," "OR," "BUT," "LESS," and "MORE."
- All variables will be entered in *lowercase* type, so forget about using capital letters. For example, you might type in *gender* or *GENDER* for a variable name, but it will always be displayed as 'gender' on the screen and in all statistical output.
- Always remember to also enter longer variable labels when there is a possibility of confusion or misunderstanding. These labels can be as long as forty characters (including spaces). They will always be printed along with the shorter variable names in statistical output.

Variable Labels

It is typical to have a longer, more meaningful statement or label for the variable name spelled out in all SPSS statistical output. This is particularly important if the name assigned to a variable is an abbreviation of two or more words or an acronym. SPSS makes this possible by allowing you to add a longer name once during the Define Variables phase of the data entry. You can then continue to use the shorter variable name in your processing commands. The variable label can be as long as forty characters. For example, you might select the three-character name DOB for a variable referring to subjects' date of birth. You could then add the longer variable label Subjects' date of birth. to avoid confusion later. Follow this brief procedure to add longer labels into your program file:

1. Click on the Data box in the dialogue line. The Define Variables dialogue box should appear.
2. If you have not done it previously, type in the variable name *DOB* in the appropriate location.
3. Now, look at the area in the center of the dialogue box that is titled Change **Settings.** There should be four different choices under this heading: Type, Missing Values, Labels, and Column Format.
4. Click on the Labels box. This should bring up a new dialogue box that permits you to enter the longer name for the variable—*and* to assign labels for each of the values you must assign to variables.
5. If you do not wish to add labels for the different values possible for each variable, click on the OK box. You have now added a longer label for the variable name.
6. Repeat this process for each variable in your data set. Remember: Variable names must be *eight characters or less in length*; variable labels can be up to forty characters long (including spaces and/or symbols).

Value Labels

Most of the time, adding a longer name for each variable is not enough. You will also want a name printed out for each value of your variables. For example, if the variable is gender, you will have two possible values, one for female and one for male (and possibly a third value for a category where subjects did not respond to this question). If you only enter the numeric values, you will get results for each numeric value when the data are processed, but your reader will not know that you meant 1 to signify females and 2 to signify males. If you add labels for each value, they will always appear with the results of any statistical analysis carried out with that variable.

Entering value labels is as easy as entering labels for variables. (It is also possible to go back later and add, change, or remove values and their labels.) To add labels in a new data set, follow this simple procedure:

1. Click on the Data box in the dialogue line. The Define Variables dialogue box should appear.
2. If you have not done it previously, type in the variable name *DOB* in the appropriate location. Do the same for adding longer variable labels.
3. In the dialogue box titled Change Settings, select the Labels option. This should bring up a new dialogue box that permits you to enter the longer name for the variable—*and* to assign labels for each of the values you must assign to variables.
4. In the Value Label section of this dialogue box, enter the number for the first value for this variable. To return to the *gender* example, enter the number 1.
5. Now click on the Value Label box beneath this value and enter the label you wish to use. Value labels can be twenty characters or less in length.
6. Click on the Add box. The value and label assigned should appear in the larger white area alongside the Add button.
7. Click on the Value Label box again to add the next value and its label. Be sure to click on the Add button after entering every value and its label.
8. When you have entered all values and their labels for a variable, click on the Continue button; this brings you back to the Define Variables dialogue box. If you are finished, click on the OK button. However, you may also wish to add values for missing values. That procedure is discussed in the next section.
9. Repeat this process for each value of each variable in your data set.
10. Remember: Variable names must be eight characters or less in length; variable labels can be up to forty characters long (including spaces and/or symbols); and value labels can be up to twenty characters in length.
11. To change or remove values and/or their labels, as would be necessary if you were to combine two or more values into one, click on the Change or Remove buttons in the Define Labels dialogue box and follow instructions. Length limitations still apply.

Missing Values

SPSS considers every cell in a data set to have some numeric value entered—even if it is left blank. Typically, a blank cell is read as a 0. Therefore, when entering data it is a good idea not to leave any cells blank. However, you do not always have data for every cell; often subjects will intentionally or accidentally omit a response to a variable. When this happens, researchers using SPSS usually enter a value to indicate that the data are missing. These values are counted separately and not included in analysis requiring a mean (average) of the data. An example of a missing value is the number 9 entered when subjects fail to indicate their gender on a self-administered questionnaire. If there is any possibility that some data cannot be collected or is otherwise unavailable, missing-value codes must be assigned for the affected variables. SPSS requires the analyst to assign a missing-value code for each variable in the data set. Any code number that has not already been assigned to a value of the variable may be used. It is also possible to use the same missing-value code for more than one variable. Assigning missing value codes is not necessary if all the data is available and is valid. The values 9 and 0 are usually used.

Whatever value is assigned to represent missing data, that same number must not be used for another response in the same question. For example, if subjects are asked to indicate their rank order preference for a set of 9 or 10 items, neither 9 nor 10 can be used to signify "missing data" in the datafile. To add labels in a new data set, follow this simple procedure:

1. Click on the Data button in the dialogue line. The Define Variables dialogue box should appear. Choose the Change Settings option.
2. In the dialogue box titled Change Settings, select the Missing Values option.
3. This should bring up a new dialogue box, Missing Values. Two buttons appear at the top of the box. One is titled No Missing Values; if you have not already assigned a value, this button will show a black dot inside. The second option is for Discrete Missing Values. Click on this second button.
4. Enter the number you wish to use to signify missing data in the first of the three small boxes below the Discrete Missing Values button.
5. When you have entered the missing value for a variable, click on the Continue button; this brings you back to the Define Variables dialogue box.
6. You may now select the Value Labels option to add a label for a number you want to use to signify a missing value. This is done in the same way as adding all value labels. First enter the value, and then enter the label Missing Values, or No Response, or any label you want to use. Remember to click on the Add button when you have entered the value and its label.
7. If you are finished, click on the OK button. Repeat this process for each missing value of each variable in your data set.

Data in SPSS

The final option in the Define Variables dialogue box is a box labeled Measurement. This box has three options: Scale, Ordinal, and Nominal. These tell the statistical analysis processor what type of data it has for each variable. Different types of data (or measurements) require different types of statistical analyses. When you indicate to the data file editor the type of data represented by each variable, it will automatically select the correct analysis technique for each test you ask it to do.

Types of Data

Scale data consists of measurements that are considered to be at least *equidistant interval* (usually simply identified as *interval*). Statistical analyses conducted on these types of data usually provide the researcher with the greatest amount of information possible. Examples are comparative rating scales, attitude scales, awareness scales, and similar types of questions. The key to understanding this type of measurement is that the intervals between the various points on the scale are (or are considered to be) exactly the same size; they are equidistant from one another. They are the closest things to a "ruler" that we have available in the social sciences.

A second variety of scale data encountered in statistical texts is called *ratio* data. In these measurements, an equal difference remains between points on the scale, but the *ratio scale* has a "fixed" or absolute zero point. The same statistical analyses are used for both variations of scale data.

Another way of defining scale measurements is that the data produced are considered to be *continuous* rather than *discrete*. Continuous data (or data from continuous variables) are data that can be any value on the scale. For example, an "average" or mean score on a five-point attitude scale can be 2.0, 3.4, 1.7, or 4.3. The second option in this question about the type of measurement data gathered for a question is what is called *ordinal scale data*. The easiest way to differentiate ordinal data from scale or nominal measurements is that these measurements are *ranked* or *ordered* on some set of characteristics, but that the differences between rankings are not known or considered to be equidistant. All rank order *preference scales* are ordinal measurements.

Discrete data are data taken from *nominal scale* measurements. An example of discrete data is the values assigned to a dichotomous question such as "What is your gender?" The answer could only be female or male (i.e., 1 or 2). No mean can be calculated. Another example is a list of eight different types of occupations from which subjects select the one that applies to them.

Table 16.2

SPSS Data Types and Their Applicable Rules

Data type	Applicable rules for differentiation
Nominal	Different numbers always refer to different things.
Ordinal	The numbers can be ranked or ordered on some dimension.
Scale	The different points on the scale are equidistant (i.e., equal), and the scale must have a fixed or absolute zero.

Frequency distributions of all responses for a sample would result in a distribution of responses across the eight options; no mean can be calculated. The set of rules in Table 16.2 differentiates between the different types of measurements; prior rules also apply to higher-level data.

Entering Data

Once you have indicated the type of measurement data used for that variable in the small circle alongside the data type, click on the OK button on the Define Variables dialogue box. You are now ready to begin entering data into your data file. This is a very simple process, much like all other spreadsheet programs. Data are usually entered across the page in rows that correspond to an individual case or subject. You can move from cell to cell using either the tab or arrow keys. :

Figure 16.1 is a classification of some of the main layers of statistical analysis seen in public administration research reports, together with the statistical analysis tools in SPSS and the commands for conducting those analyses.

When all the variables and values are defined and all the data have been entered into your data file, it is time to save this information into an SPSS Save file.

Putting SPSS to Work

Assuming that you have successfully entered data to a data file, defined all the variables in that file, and established labels for variables and values of those variables, you have competed the setup phase of SPSS. Now you can begin to use this powerful software to manipulate and analyze the data set. The remainder of this chapter will focus on four analytic processes: (1) developing descriptive statistics for the data set, (2) designing and preparing graphic displays of the data, (3) transforming and recoding the raw data for refined analysis, and (4) performing some simple inferential statistical analysis on the data.

Analysis Level	Analysis Process	Data Type	Available Statistics	SPSS Commands
Level 1-A (Descriptive)	Univariate frequency distributions	Any data	Counts, percentages, chi-square	**Frequencies, Explore, Descriptives**
Level 1-B	Bivariate frequency distributions	Any data	Counts, percentages, chi-square, phi, Cramer's V	**Crosstabs, Multiple Response**
Level 2-A	Bivariate relationship tests	Nonparametric (nominal and ordinal data)	Phi and Cramer's V Spearman's rho	**Crosstabs**
Level 2-B	Bivariate relationship tests	Parametric (interval and ratio data)	Pearson's r	**Correlation, Simple Regression**
Level 3-A	Bivariate differences tests	Nonparametric (nominal and ordinal data)	Chi-square Mann-Whitney U or Wald-Wolfowitz runs test	**Nonparametric Statistics: Chi-square, M-W-U, W-W runs**
Level 3-B	Bivariate differences tests	Parametric	T-test F-test (ANOVA)	**Compare Means: T-Test** **One-way ANOVA**
Level 4-A (Relationships)	Multivariate association tests	Parametric (and nonparametric with data transformations)	Multiple regression analysis, multiple discriminant analysis, time series	**General Linear Model: Multivariate** **Classify: Discriminant** **Time Series**
Level 4-B (Differences)	Multivariate differences tests	Parametric (and nonparametric with data	Multiple analysis of variance	**Compare Means: Means**
Level 5 (Data Reductions)	Multivariate statistics	Parametric	Cluster analysis, factor analysis	**Classify: Hierarchical Cluster Analysis** **Data Reduction: Factor**

Figure 16.1 **A Classification of Some Key Statistical Analysis Procedures in SPSS**

Developing Descriptive Statistics

SPSS calculates descriptive statistics for three types of measurements: Scale, ordinal, and nominal. *Scale* is the label SPSS uses to identify both interval and ratio data. Measurement data are often described in at least two additional ways. First, data may be *discrete* or *continuous.* Second, data may be described as *qualitative* or *quantitative.*

Discrete data consist of numbers used to identify specific groups or categories, such as female and male, or undergraduate and graduate student. They are sometimes described as *categorical* data. Researchers are concerned with how many subjects fall into each category; this information can be presented either as a simple count or as a percentage of the total. Nominal data are always discrete (or categorical). Because of this nature of the data, they are also considered to be *qualitative.*

Continuous data, on the other hand, are considered to be *quantitative* because they can consist of any value within a specified or possible continuum. Values are not restricted to whole numbers. While the number of children in a family is *discrete* data because the count must be a whole number, the annual income of a sample of families is *continuous* because it can be any amount. Another example of a continuous variable is the amount of electrical energy consumed each year by households in Shelton, Washington. SPSS considers all data from *scales* (such as questions about attitudes or beliefs) as continuous data. Ordinal data is categorical data, but in social science usage, it is often treated as continuous data.

Univariate Descriptive Statistics for Categorical Measurements

Qualitative measurements are numbers that are applied to categorical variables. The values assigned to categorical variables refer to mutually exclusive groups, categories, or classes within a variable and have no quantitative reference. Examples include the categories used to differentiate subjects by gender, by race, by political party affiliation, and by voting behavior (did vote vs. did not vote). Researchers want to know how many cases fit into each category. The statistics used for these measurements are called *nonparametric.*

The SPSS procedure used to develop descriptive statistics for categorical variables is called Frequencies. This procedure counts the number of cases in each designated category, and identifies the *mode* for the variable (the mode is the category with the most cases). The mode is one type of "average" (or *measure of central tendency*); it is the only average to use with this kind of data.

SPSS Frequencies produces its results in the form of a table—sometimes referred to as a *frequency distribution* table. Within each Frequencies table are five columns of information; moving from left to right, these are:

1. User-assigned Value Labels (such as female, male, yes, no, etc.)
2. The Frequency (i.e., the count) with which this category occurs.
3. The Percent of the total that each row represents. If any data are missing, a row will indicate what percentage of the total the missing cases represent.
4. A Valid Percent column, in which is displayed the percentages of the total *minus* any missing cases that are accounted for by the counts for each category. If there are no missing cases, this column will be a repetition of the third (Percent) column.
5. Finally, a Cumulative Percent column, which totals the percentages of each row *plus* all rows preceding this row. For example, if the percent of responses for the first category on a five-point rating scale is 13, and the percent of the second category is 12, the cumulative percent for the first category is 13 and the cumulative percent for the second category is 25. If the percent for the third category is 10, the cumulative percent for this third row is 35. The cumulative percent column has no statistical relevance to qualitative variables, however, and should be ignored when processing this kind of data.

Using the Frequencies Dialogue Box

To carry out the SPSS Frequencies procedure on data entered into a data file, first click on the Analyze option on the main tool bar. Then click on the second option from the list that appears: Descriptives. You will then have four options from which to choose: (1) Frequencies, (2) Descriptives, (3) Explore, or (4) Crosstabs. Click on the Frequencies button.

The Frequencies dialogue box contains two large windows and several different command options. All variables in the data file will appear in the large window at the left side of the box. Highlight the variable you wish to analyze by clicking on it in the list. Then click on the small arrow between the two large windows. The selected variable will now appear in the right window. To remove it, simply reverse the process. It is possible to highlight as many variables as you want to at the same time. One click on the center arrow will move all variables you select to the Analyze window.

Now click on the small window that reads Display Frequency Tables—it appears just beneath the main variable list. A check mark showing in the small window means that a table will be produced.

Now go to the Statistics button located near the bottom of the gray dialogue box. This will bring up the Frequencies: Statistics dialogue box. You may request percentile information, measures of dispersion (such as the standard deviation), measures of central tendency, or measures of distribution. Go to the Central Tendency section and click on the small window alongside the Mode.

All you need to do to have SPSS process your request is to click on Continue in this dialogue box and then click on OK in the Frequencies dialogue box that will then reappear.

Univariate Descriptive Statistics for Quantitative (Continuous) Measurements

Statistical analysis of *quantitative (numerical)* measurements can be said to take place on two fundamental levels: *descriptive* statistics and *inferential* statistics. (There are, of course, statistical tools that do not fall into either of these categories; learning about them is best left to a course in quantitative methods.) The statistics used with these types of measurements are called *parametric*.

Descriptive statistics are used to summarize the numerical information in a data set, to numerically describe the cases in a data set, and to provide some sort of structure to the data. *Univariate* descriptive statistics do this one variable at a time. However, it is also possible to develop descriptive statistics for two variables at the same time; this is called *bivariate* statistical analysis. It is also possible to analyze more than two variables at once in what is called *multivariate* statistical analysis, but these processes are not discussed here.

Three SPSS processes can be used to produce univariate statistics for quantitative variables (i.e., variables with ordinal, interval, or ratio data). These procedures are (1) Frequencies, (2) Explore, and (3) Descriptives.

How to Use the Frequencies Command

The use of Frequencies with quantitative—nominal—data is the same as it is for qualitative data, except for the selection of the appropriate measure of central tendency. For quantitative variables, the *mean* and *median* are also calculated. The mean is the *arithmetical average*; the median is the midpoint in the range of possible values. Also important for quantitative measurements are *measures of variation* and of *dispersion*. To employ the Frequencies procedure, follow this set of steps:

1. Select Analyze ⇒ Descriptive Statistics ⇒ Frequencies

2. Select the variable or variables desired; move them into the Variables window.
3. Click on the Display Frequency Tables button
4. Select Statistics ⇒ Central Tendency ⇒ Mean, Median, and Mode
5. Next, in the Dispersion box of the Statistics dialogue box, select Standard Deviation, Range, Minimum, and Maximum.
6. Select Continue.
7. Select OK.

How to Use the Explore Command

To calculate descriptive statistics for a variable using the SPSS Explore process, begin by clicking on the Analyze command on the Main Menu bar. From the list of available statistical processes, select Descriptive Statistics. Then select Explore. This will bring up the Explore dialogue box. This box has four windows. The largest box displays the names of all the variables in your data set. Highlight the variable you want to analyze. Then click on the small arrow alongside this box; the variables will be moved to the window labeled Dependent List.

When you want complete analysis for one variable at a time, ignore the other two windows (i.e., Factor list, and Label Cases By). Click on OK and complete descriptive statistics will be produced for each variable named.

The Explore process can also be used to develop descriptive statistics for different levels of a variable. The phrase "different levels" means the different categories represented in the variable. For example, the variable *gender* has two levels (also referred to as *categories* or *groups*): female and male. The variable *political party* might have three levels: Democrat, Republican, and Independent. The variable *class standing* might have five levels: freshman, sophomore, junior, senior, and graduate. The Explore command will quickly and easily produce descriptive statistics for each subgroup in the variable.

1. Select Analyze ⇒ Descriptive Statistics ⇒ Explore.
2. Select the variable or variables desired; move them into the Dependent Variables window.
3. Select the grouping variable for which you want the statistical breakdown and move it into the Factor List window.
4. Click on the Display Frequency Tables button.
5. Click on the Statistics button.
6. Select Continue.
7. Select OK.

How to Use the Descriptives Command

Descriptives is the third way to produce descriptive statistics for numeric data with SPSS; it provides a quick list of each variable, the number of valid responses for each variable, and selected descriptive statistics. To access the program, follow these steps:

1. Select Analyze ⟹ Descriptive Statistics ⟹ Descriptives.
2. Select the variable or variables desired; move them into the **Variables** window (remember to *not* include qualitative variables).
3. Select **Options**. For quantitative data, click on Mean, Standard Deviation, and if desired, Minimum and Maximum.
4. You can choose to have the data presented in any one of four different ways:
   - By the way the variables appear in your variable list
   - In alphabetic order
   - By ascending value of their means
   - By descending order of their means

Both frequencies and descriptive processes produce the same information.

Bivariate Descriptive Statistics

Known as two-way frequency distribution tables, the results of a Crosstabulations table present the distribution of responses, with percentages, of two or more variables at the same time. In addition, a wide variety of statistical analyses are included in the Crosstabs procedure. All types of data can be analyzed in a Crosstabs table.

The SPSS Crosstabs procedure is a tool for displaying the data from one variable against the data of another variable or variables. The *rows* of a crosstabulation table (called a Crosstab by SPSS) represent the different values or levels of one variable, while the *columns* of the table represent the values of a second variable. A simple 2 x 2 Crosstab will look something like Table 16.3. Convention requires that each box in a table (except for those with labels) be called a *cell*. This, in the Table 16.3, the data for females who answered yes will fall in cell 1, data for females/no in cell 2, males/yes in cell 3, and males/no in cell 4.

Crosstab tables can have as many rows and columns as required. However, a table with more than five or six rows or columns can become cumbersome to read and difficult to interpret. Crosstabs produces statistical tests for use with interval, ordinal, and nominal (i.e., categorical) data.

SPSS permits up to four bits of information to be displayed in each cell.

Table 16.3

A Typical 2 x 2 Cross-tabulation Table with Cells Numbered

	Response	
Gender	Yes	No
Female	(Cell 1)	(Cell 2)
Male	(Cell 3)	(Cell 4)

These include: (1) the count of occurrences, (2) the percentage of the row total represented by the count in a cell, (3) the percentage of the column total in the cell, and (4) the percentage of the total number of counts for the variable. Row and column total counts and percentages are displayed in the table margins.

Crosstabs tables are most appropriately used when both variables are categorical (i.e., nominal data). However, sometimes a researcher wishes to display the distribution of ordinal- or interval-level responses across the entire range of cells. In such cases, the categorical variable is often referred to as a *grouping variable*, and its values are placed as rows. The scale data is displayed in columns. The example in Table 16.4 uses party affiliation data as its row variable and the responses of a sample of subjects to a five-point rating scale. Rating scale values in columns are *Strongly Agree, Agree, Neither Agree nor Disagree, Disagree*, and *Strongly Disagree*.

From the information in Table 16.4, it is obvious that this is a relatively cumbersome way to present data; the table is complex and "busy." Possibly a more meaningful way to present and analyze the information in the table would be a simple 3 x 1 table, with the means scores on the scale shown for each of the three categories of party affiliation. A one-way analysis of variance test could then be conducted to test for statistically significant different attitudes among the three party affiliation groups.

How to Use Crosstabs

The Crosstabs procedure is bundled into the same Summarize statistics package as Frequencies, Explore, and Descriptives. In addition to this summary table, another key feature of Crosstabs is its ability to produce both association and differences test statistics for nominal, ordinal, and scale data.

Tests for Independence

The *chi-square test of independence* can be used with all data types. Its purpose is to test whether the row subgroups are independent of each other. The

Table 16.4

An Example of a 3x6 Cross-Tabulation Table with Counts and Totals

Political party affiliation	Response					
	Strongly agree	Agree	Neither agree nor disagree	Disagree	Strongly disagree	Totals
Democrat	38	27	15	9	7	96
Republican	7	10	12	22	30	81
Independent	10	11	7	8	10	46
Totals	55	48	34	39	47	223

chi-square test is interpreted by examining the probability value produced with the Chi-square value. When using a 95 percent confidence level, if this *p*-value is .05 or less, the null can be rejected and the alternative hypothesis is retained (that is, if the p-value is .05 or less, the responses of the groups can be assumed to be statistically different).

Measures of Association

Statistics for Nominal Data. There are four categories of statistical tests from which to select for nominal data: the contingency coefficient, phi and Cramer's *V*, lambda, and the uncertainty coefficient. Of these, the two easiest statistical tests to use for testing for association are the phi statistic and Cramer's *V*. Both the phi and Cramer's *V* statistic measure association in one direction; the values produced can range from 0.0 to 1.0. Therefore, while they indicate the strength of an association, they do not indicate the direction of that association (i.e., positive or negative). The phi statistic should be consulted for 2 x 2 tables only; Cramer's *V* is applicable for all rectangular tables. These are accessed through the same selection in the Nominal Data section of the Crosstabs⇒Statistics dialogue base.

Statistics for Ordinal Data. SPSS Crosstabs statistics provide a variety of optional association tests for use with ordinal data. The first of these, and the one that is often considered to be most appropriate, is the Spearman correlation coefficient, called *Spearman's rho.* This test is accessed through the Correlations button on the Crosstabs⇒Statistics dialogue box. The program produces both a Pearson's *r* correlation coefficient for use when the column variable is interval or ratio level, and the Spearman's rho when the column data are ordinal. Care must be taken in selecting the correct statistic, since the values appear in the same output box.

Both *r* and rho are interpreted in the same way—as indicators of the relative strength of an association. They should not be interpreted as measures of causation. Their values can range from -0.1 to $+0.1$.

Other ordinal-level statistical tests available in Crosstabs include gamma, Somers's *d*, Kendall's tau-b, and Kendall's tau-c. To determine what they do and when to use them, consult Marija J. Norusis's *SPSS for Windows Base System User's Guide* (2000).

Statistics for Interval Data. A test for association is also possible when one of the variables in a Crosstab is interval (or ratio) level and the other variable is nominal level. This is the *eta coefficient.* A table similar to that displayed in Figure 16.2 is an example. Eta is interpreted in the same way as Pearson's correlation coefficient. Eta does not assume that a linear relationship exists between the two variables. When squared, the value of eta can also be interpreted as a measure of the proportion of the total variability in the interval-level variable that can be known when the values of the nominal-level variable (gender, for example) are known.

Summary

SPSS and other spreadsheet-based statistical software packages have revolutionized the use of statistics in all branches of the social sciences, including public administration and political science. Statistics is no longer the exclusive territory of a small cadre of mathematically trained specialists. Rather, the new statistical software packages such as SPSS have made the task of learning how to use and interpret statistical tests accessible to everyone with a desktop or notebook computer.

SPSS allows researchers to quickly define the variables and the values assigned to different levels of each variable. Through this process of data definition, the researcher must make these definitions just once, at the beginning of the analysis process. All subsequent tests and their results will automatically display the researcher's assigned definitions and labels.

In addition, SPSS also allows the researcher to quickly and easily compute new variables from combinations of old variables, edit a data set, and recode or transform mathematical measurements with mathematical operations and functions. The researcher can save all calculations and operations in various output files on either a hard drive or a portable disk at any time during a data processing session. And, perhaps most importantly, SPSS statistical test results can be exported directly into reports prepared in most word processing programs.

The basic SPSS software package will allow the researcher to calculate and display all commonly used descriptive statistics. The package also makes it possible to display descriptive statistics in a variety of tables, charts, and graphs. Finally, SPSS has the capability to carry out an extensive array of one- and two-variable hypothesis tests, association (correlation) tests, and single and multiple regression analyses. Finally, the basic package contains provisions for data reduction with factor analysis and classification process with cluster and discriminant analyses, as well as provisions to conduct many nonparametric statistical tests.

Suggested Reading

Einspruch, Eric L. 1998. *An Introductory Guide to SPSS for Windows*. Thousand Oaks, CA: Sage.

Green, Samuel B., Neil J. Salkind, and Theresa M. Akey. 2000. *Using SPSS For Windows: Analyzing and Understanding Data*. Upper Saddle River, NJ: Prentice Hall.

Norusis, Marija J. 1998. *SPSS for Windows Base System User's Guide* (Version 9.0). Chicago: SPSS Inc.

———— 2000. *SPSS for Windows Base System User's Guide* (Version 10.0). Chicago: SPSS.

Part 5

Qualitative Research Strategies

17 Introduction to Qualitative Research

The term *qualitative research* describes a set of nonstatistical inquiry techniques and processes used to gather data about social phenomena. *Qualitative data* refers to some collection of words, symbols, pictures, or other nonnumeric records, materials, or artifacts that are collected by a researcher and that have relevance to the social group under study. The uses for these data go beyond simple description of events and phenomena; rather, they are used for creating understanding, for subjective interpretation, and for critical analysis as well.

Qualitative research differs from quantitative research in several fundamental ways. For example, qualitative research studies typically involve what has been described as "inductive, theory-generating, subjective, and nonpositivist processes." In contrast, quantitative research involves "deductive, theory-testing, objective, and positivist processes" (Lee 1999, 10).

Creswell (1994) identified five differences between these two approaches, based upon these five philosophical foundations: *ontology* (researchers' perceptions of reality); *epistemology* (the role or roles taken by researchers); *axiological assumptions* (researchers' values); *rhetorical traditions* (the style of language used by researchers); and *methodological approaches* (approaches taken by researchers). The differences identified by Creswell are displayed in Figure 17.1.

A key difference lies in the epistemology of the two approaches. In qualitative research designs, researchers must often interact with individuals in the groups they are studying. Researchers record not only what they see, but also their interpretations of the meaning inherent in the interactions that take place in the groups. Quantitative researchers, on the other hand, maintain a deliberate distance and objectivity from the study group. They are careful to avoid making judgments about attitudes, perceptions, values, interactions, or predispositions.

	Research Strategies	
Philosophical Foundations	*Qualitative Research Designs*	*Quantitative Research Designs*
Ontology *(Perceptions of reality)*	Researchers assume that multiple, subjectively derived realities can coexist.	Researchers assume that a single, objective world exists.
EPISTEMOLOGY *(Roles for the researcher)*	Researchers commonly assume that they must interact with their studied phenomena.	Researchers assume that they are independent of the variables under study.
AXIOLOGY *(Researchers' values)*	Researchers overtly act in a value-laden and biased fashion.	Researchers overtly act in a value-free and unbiased manner.
RHETORIC *(Language styles)*	Researchers often use personalized, informal, and context-laden language.	Researchers most often use impersonal, formal, and rule-based text.
METHODOLOGY *(Approaches to research)*	Researchers tend to apply induction, multivariate, and multiprocess interactions, following context-laden methods.	Researchers tend to apply deduction, and limited cause-and-effect relationships, with context-free methods.

Figure 17.1 **Five Differences Between Qualitative Research and Quantitative Research**

Another way to describe the differences between qualitative and quantitative research methods has been proposed by Cassell and Symon (1997). The most fundamental of these differences is a bias against using numbers for qualitative research, whereas quantitative research is biased heavily toward numeric measurements and statistical analysis—the *positivist* approach to scientific analysis (White 1999). The objective of this positive approach to research is to control events through a process of *prediction* that is based on explanation; it employs inferential statistical methods (White and Adams 1994).

The second difference is what is referred to as the *subjective-objective dichotomy*. Qualitative researchers "explicitly and overtly apply" (Lee 1999, 7) their own subjective interpretations of what they see and hear—often, they are active participants in the phenomenon under study. On the other hand, a foundation stone of the quantitative, positivist research approach is researcher *objectivity*. The researcher is expected to function as an unbiased, unobtrusive observer, reporting only what happens or what can be measured.

These two approaches also differ in a third way: qualitative researchers tend to approach the research process with a willingness to be flexible, to follow where the data lead them. Qualitative researchers try to approach a topic with few or no preconceived assumptions; conclusions are expected to appear out of the data as it is collected and studied. Quantitative research, on the other hand, tends to be guided by a strict set of rules and formal processes. Typically, specific hypotheses are established prior to the data gathering and are tested during the analysis. Variables are identified and explicitly defined beforehand. Searching for cause-and-effect relationships between defined variables that can be measured is a hallmark of quantitative research studies.

A fourth way that the two approaches differ has to do with the aim of the study. Qualitative researchers seek understanding of social interactions and processes in organizations, whereas quantitative studies are more often concerned with predicting future events and behaviors. To make these predictions, they often apply inferential statistical analyses to measurements taken from representative samples drawn from a population of interest.

A fifth difference is associated with the context of the study. Qualitative research is usually concerned with a situation or event that takes place within a single organizational context. A major goal of much quantitative research is to apply the study results to other situations; thus, quantitative research is what Lee terms "more generalizable" (1999).

A sixth way that these two approaches to research differ is the emphasis that qualitative researchers assign to the research process. The way that subjects interact with, and react to the researcher during the qualitative study is of as much interest as the original phenomenon of interest. Quantitative researchers tend to take great pains to avoid introducing extraneous influences into the study, seeking to isolate subjects from the process as much as possible by controlling for process effects.

Classes of Qualitative Research Strategies

Qualitative research strategies can be grouped into three broad strategic classes: (1) *explanatory research studies*, (2) *interpretive research studies*, and (3) *critical research studies*. These strategies and the four key approaches that are followed in most public administration research are displayed in Figure 17.2. These roughly correspond to the exploratory-descriptive-causal categories of quantitative research designs.

Explanatory Research

In his dictionary of terms and concepts encountered in qualitative research, Schwandt (1997) defined explanatory research as studies that are conducted

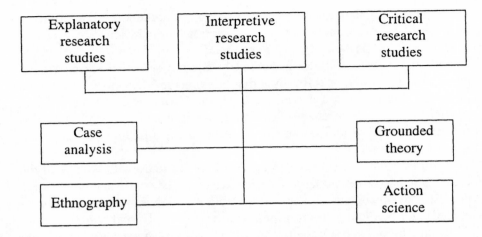

Figure 17.2 **Qualitative Strategies and Approaches in Public Administration Research**

to develop a causal explanation of some social phenomenon. The researcher identifies a specific social event or circumstance (a *consequence*)—such as crime in the inner city—that he or she wants to investigate. The researcher then seeks to identify the social, economic, climate, practice, or other such characteristic (variable) in the social environment that can be explained as a *cause* of the consequence of interest.

One of the major objectives of explanatory research is to build *theories* that researchers can then use to explain a phenomenon and then to predict future behavior or events in similar circumstances. The ability to predict responses allows investigators a measure of control over events. Therefore, the ultimate goal of all explanatory research is the control of natural and social events (White 1999). Explanatory research is the easiest approach to understand and apply, and is often used simply for this reason.

Explanatory research is also seen by many as the fastest way to produce a cumulative stream of knowledge in a field or discipline. Possibly because of this trait and the aspect of control, studies that are designed to explain a phenomenon are the most common in public administration research.

Explanatory strategies fulfill much the same role in qualitative research that exploratory research does in quantitative research; they are used as a means of gathering fundamental information about the topic, its contributing factors, and the influences a phenomenon might have on various outcomes. This process can be described as *gaining insights and ideas* about a study problem. These studies are seldom complete in themselves; they are conducted as preliminaries to additional, follow-on research.

Interpretive Research

Not all research theorists agree that human events or actions can be defined by the causal explanations of explanatory research. Instead, these critics argue that human action can never be explained this way. It can be understood only by studies that follow the second approach in the triad of qualitative approaches, which is interpretation. The researcher arrives at an interpretation of a phenomenon by developing (subjective) meanings of social events or actions.

According to White (1999), interpretive research helps us understand people's actions in social circumstances and situations. He cites as an example the way an interpretive researcher goes beyond describing why a job-enrichment program is not working, using established hypotheses of motivation and job design. Instead, the interpretive researcher might circulate among employees in their job setting, asking them what they think about the program, what meaning it has for them, and how it conflicts or reinforces their existing attitudes, opinions, and behaviors. In this way, the researcher seeks to "discover the meaning of the program; how it fits with [the workers'] prior norms, rules, values, and social practice" (45).

Schwandt (1997, 73) has offered this description of interpretation: "A classification, explication, or explanation of the meaning of some phenomenon." Thus, interpretive studies require the researcher to go beyond simply describing or explaining what a phenomenon is to also "interpret" the phenomenon for the reader. This entails providing an interpretation of what it *means*, as well as what it *is*. Schwandt concluded that the term *interpretation* is used as a synonym for *hermeneutics* or *Verstehen* (the later term defines an approach to the social sciences that is committed to providing *understanding* of human actions).

Research can be classified as interpretive when it is built on the assumption that humans learn about reality from the meanings they assign to social phenomena such as language, consciousness, shared experiences, publications, tools, and other artifacts. The task is made difficult because a fundamental tenet of interpretive theory is that social phenomena are constantly changing, so the meanings that people assign are in constant flux. At the same time, interpretive research is always *context-laden*. Thus, interpretation is like shooting at a constantly moving target.

A primary goal of the interpretive research approach is to provide many-layered descriptions and interpretations of human experiences (Meacham 1998). To achieve this goal, interpretive research looks at the way humans make sense out of events in their lives—as the events happen, not as they are planned. Therefore, to thoroughly understand an event or an organization, the researcher must also understand its historical context.

Interpretive research is important for the study of government organizations and agencies (White 1999, 45). The fundamental objective for interpretive research makes this approach particularly relevant in applications such as these:

> The basic aim of the interpretive model is to develop a more complete understanding of social relationships and to discover human possibilities. Recent studies of organizational culture demonstrate the importance of interpretive methods for properly understanding norms, values, and belief systems in organizations.

Seven Principles of Interpretive Research

Klein and Meyers (1999) developed a set of seven fundamental principles to help researchers conduct and evaluate interpretive research studies. The first and most fundamental of these principles is the *hermeneutic circle*, derived from document and literary analysis. The hermeneutic circle was devised to illustrate a phenomenon of the learning/understanding process. People develop understanding about complex concepts from the meanings they bring to its parts, such as words, and the way that these parts relate to one another. Interpretations of the larger whole move from a preliminary understanding of the parts, to understanding the whole, and then back again to a better understanding of the parts, and on and on. The process of understanding thus moves continuously in an expanding circle of greater and greater understanding.

The second principle of interpretive research, mentioned earlier, is the importance of the *contextual nature* of the studied phenomenon or organization. The researcher's "meaning" is derived out of the particular social and historical context in which the phenomenon is imbedded; at the same time, all patterns that can be discovered within this embedded context are constantly changing. The organization that is interpreted is thus time- and situation-specific.

The third of the seven principles of interpretive research is *interaction between researchers and the subjects* they study. Information is not something inherent in the phenomenon; rather, it is developed as a result of the social interrelations of both subjects and researcher. Gummesson (1987) likened this relationship to the interaction that often results in the researcher metamorphosing into an "internal consultant" during case study research. The researcher, by interacting with participants, becomes one with the members of the group under study.

Abstraction and generalization together make up the fourth principle of interpretive research. Such research deals with abstractions as it attempts to bring order to disunited parts by categorizing them into generalizations and concepts with wider application. The inferences that are based on the researcher's subjective interpretation of the single case must be seen as theoretical generalizations.

The fifth principle of interpretive research is *dialogical reasoning*. In this intellectual process, the researcher explicitly weighs all preconceptions and/or biases brought to the planned research activity against the information that emerges from the actual research process. This principle forces the researcher to begin by defining the underlying assumptions that guide the research and the research paradigm upon which the study is based. By a process of dialogue with participant actors, the researcher defines and redefines the assumptions and research questions in light of the data that emerges.

The *principle of multiple interpretations* demands that researchers aggressively compare their historical and contextual interpretation of the phenomenon against all other available interpretations and the reasons offered for them. Thus, the researcher subjects his or her own preconceptions and biases to comparison against competing interpretations, including those of the participants in the organization under study. Even if no conflicting interpretations are found during the study, the researcher is expected to probe for them and to document the fruitless process. In this way, the researcher strengthens the conclusions and interpretations derived from the analysis.

The final principle of interpretive research is *suspicion*. This requires the researcher not to accept an interpretation at face value. To avoid making false interpretations, the researcher must examine every personal preconception, conclusion, definition, and derived meaning with a healthy dose of skepticism.

Critical Research

Critical qualitative research is a third approach to investigations of social phenomena adopted by public administration researchers. Critical research in public administration has evolved from the traditions of Marxian *critical sociology* and Freudian *psychotherapy* (Argyris, Putnam, and Smith 1985). According to Klein and Meyers (1999), a study can be considered *critical* in nature if it is a social critique that exposes harmful or alienating social conditions. Furthermore, the purpose of the critique should be to emancipate members of the society from the harmful conditions, thus eliminating the causes of the alienation. Members of the society are not told how to change their conditions, but are instead helped to identify on their own alternative ways of defining their society and of achieving human potential.

The primary objective of critical research is to help people *change* their beliefs and actions as part of a process of helping them become aware of the often unconscious bases for their actions or beliefs. By becoming aware of *why* they live and think the way they do, critical research "points out inconsistencies between what is true and false, good and bad; it compels [people] to act in accordance with truth and goodness" (White 1999, 46).

Critical public administration research begins with the assumption that a crisis exists in some aspect of society. The researcher approaches the study of this crisis from a deeply personal and involved commitment to help the people involved. Recognition of a crisis, then, is one of the key concepts of the approach.

Schwandt (1997, 24–25) identified a number of structural themes that characterize critical research. The two that seem to appear most regularly in the literature of critical research methodology are distortion in the perceptions held by members of a group and rejection of the idea of the disinterested scientist. With the first theme, the goal of critical research is to integrate social theory and application or practice in such a way that the members of social groups become cognizant of distortions and other problems in their society or their value systems. Then, the group members are encouraged to propose ways to change their social and value systems in order to improve their quality of life.

The second key theme in critical research is the refusal to accept the traditional role of the social scientist as objective or disinterested, replacing this with the concept of the active, change-oriented researcher whose emphasis is on motivating change processes in social groups and individuals.

Blyler (1998, 33) addressed the issue of adopting a critical perspective in "professional communication" in general, defining the technique thus:

> The critical perspective aims at empowerment and emancipation. It reinterprets the relationship between researcher and participants as one of collaboration, where participants define research questions that matter to them and where social action is the desired goal.

Which Strategy Is Best?

The choice of which strategy to adopt when designing a qualitative study will depend upon what objectives the researcher has identified for the study. These must be clearly stated prior to going into the field to embark on the collection of data.

Possibly because it is often considered the easiest of the three strategies to carry out, by far most public administration research studies follow an *explanatory* design. However, according to White (1999) and others, there is a strong movement among researchers in all the social and administrative sciences to go beyond a simple descriptive explanation of a phenomenon to also explore whatever meaning underlies the behavior, event, or circumstance.

Professionals, administrators, sponsoring agencies, and the public at large are asking researchers to explain what things *mean*, rather than simply describing them as they appear.

A smaller number of researchers are extending the range of research even further by designing studies that begin with a critique of a social phenomenon and end with the design and introduction of subject-sponsored new ways of addressing old problems (Robinson 1994). The critical approach in public administration is still in its infancy, however (White 1999). The critical approach has been employed often enough, however, to result in a reputation for making it difficult to transform research results into meaningful program applications. The method requires subjects to form alternative concepts or courses of action; the role of the researcher is to assist the group first to identify and then to resolve their social problems themselves. Despite this difficulty, the critical approach is seen as an important way of addressing single-case studies.

The Changing Paradigm

One important consequence of this push to extend the scope of research has been a widespread increase in the use of subjective qualitative methods to augment, if not replace, the once prevalent emphasis on objective, positivist research principles. Lan and Anders (2000) have described this change in emphasis as a major paradigm shift. Building their argument on the seminal work of Thomas S. Kuhn (*The Structure of Scientific Revolutions*, 1970), Lan and Anders concluded that more than one approach to research is not only possible, it is desirable. If science does progress by shifts in paradigms, as their interpretation of Kuhn's work suggests, and if it is indeed true that more than one paradigm can exist within a single discipline, then the question of which research approach to take is moot. Researchers are not required to follow the same set of rules. White and Adams (1994, 19–20) have summarized this point in reaching this conclusion:

> We are persuaded by the weight of historical and epistemological evidence that no single approach—even if accorded the highly positive label *science*—is adequate for the conduct of research in public administration. If research is to be guided by reason, a diversity of approaches, honoring both practical and theoretical reasons, seems necessary.

Research Without Limits

There are no limits to what may be researched or how researchers go about conducting their research activities. Nor are researchers limited to one or even a few different approaches to their scientific investigations; many different types of qualitative research strategies can be followed.

Just as there are no restrictions on research topics, there is no set rule that limits any of the six following types to any one-application focus, although case studies or ethnography may be more appropriate for research with an exploratory focus. Grounded theory and hermeneutics, on the other hand, are approaches that are typically employed in interpretive research strategies; phenomenology, hermeneutics, and action science are most applicable for research that follows the critical model. Clearly, these approaches and applications often overlap, just as different observers may see different approaches taken in any individual research study.

Approaches to Qualitative Research

Many different types of research approaches are employed for conducting qualitative research in public administration. The four research approaches most often followed in public administration are case studies, grounded theory, ethnography, and action science. These are not the only approaches seen in research in the administrative and social sciences, however. Others include phenomenology, hermeneutics, ethnomethodology, atmospherics, systems theory, chaos theory, nonlinear dynamics, grounded theory, symbolic interactionism, ecological psychology, cognitive anthropology, human ethnology, and holistic ethnography (Patton 1990; Denzin and Lincoln 1994; Morse 1994; Marshall and Rossman 1999).

Figure 17.3 displays six popular research approaches, their disciplinary traditions, some common ways data are gathered, and a suggestion of some of the types of research questions addressed. The disciplinary approaches compared include (1) *ethnography*, (2) *phenomenology*, (3) *the case study approach*, (4) *hermeneutics*, (5) *grounded theory*, and (6) *action science*.

Ethnography

Anthropologists developed the approach to research known as ethnography as a method for studying different cultures and how members of different societies develop and employ coping mechanisms for social phenomena. A differentiating characteristic of this approach is its emphasis on specific ways to prepare field notes and on rules for writing about cultural events.

The primary data-gathering technique used in ethnography is *participant observation*. Ethnographers often live, work, and play with the members of the group under study for long periods of time. Their aim is to be absorbed into the group, with the underlying objective of becoming accepted as a nonthreatening or nonintrusive member of the groups so that events and interrelation-

Qualitative Research Approach	Disciplinary Traditions	Typical Data-Gathering Methods	Types of Research Questions
Ethnography	Anthropology	Participant observation, unstructured interviews, analysis of cultural artifacts	"Culture" questions: What are the values of this group? What is accepted behavior? What is not acceptable?
Phenomenology	Philosophy	Personal experience narratives, video or audiotaped discussions, in-depth interviews	"Meaning" questions: What is the meaning of a person's experience? How do group members cope with various phenomena?
Case studies	Psychology, public administration	Observation, personal interviews, organizational studies	"Explanatory" questions: What is distinct about this group?
Hermeneutics	Biblical studies, literary (text) analysis	Content analysis, narrative and discourse analysis	"Interpretation" questions: What meaning does this text hold?
Grounded theory	Sociology, social psychology	Personal interviews, diaries, participant observation	'Process' questions: What theory is embedded in the relationships between variables? Is there a theory of change?
Action science	Social psychology, education	Discourse analysis, intervention studies	"Critique" questions: How can we emancipate group members? What inhibits change?

Figure 17.3 **Various Approaches to Qualitative Research, Their Foundations Methods, and Typical Focus**

ships unfold as they would naturally, as if the observer were not in attendance.

Ethnography methods are used in the administrative sciences to analyze and diagnose organizational cultures (Wilson 1989; Schein 1992). However, the rules for conducting fieldwork and preparing field notes tend to be less rigorously applied than in anthropology research.

Phenomenology

The phenomenological approach to qualitative research has its roots in such traditions of philosophy as existentialism and the study of the meaning of language and other symbolic behaviors. In public administration research, it is used to establish "meanings" that social actors apply to events, works, symbols, and the like. Phenomenology researchers use participant observation, in-depth interviewing, and passive recording of life histories as data-gathering methods.

The underlying concept of interest is the *life history* of individual persons. Researchers often employ taped discussions and other narrative recording tools to study the everyday personal, often socially aberrant behavior. Examples include the narrative personal histories of gang members and of participants in the drug culture. The goal of the researcher is for the subject to define the meaning of the behavior.

The Case Study Approach

The case study approach to research in the social and administrative sciences focuses on the agency, organization, person, or group under study, rather than dealing with variables (Schwandt 1997). The objective of the case study is to serve as a defining description of the organization. In this way, the case description serves as an example of similar groups.

Today, case studies are used extensively in education, although their disciplinary roots are centered in psychology. The case study is one of the most often used approaches to conducting research in public administration. The following examples are articles taken from a single issue of the public administration journal *Public Productivity & Management Review* (March 2000):

- "The Dual Potentialities of Performance Measurement: The Case of the Social Security Administration."
- "Organizational Change Issues in Performance Government: The Case of Contracting."

- "Comprehensive Management and Budgeting Reform in Local Government: The Case of Milwaukee."
- "Implementing Performance Accountability in Florida: What Changed, What Mattered, and What Resulted."

Each of these articles described in some detail the organization and its experiences with some aspect of administration. They were designed to serve as examples for other administrators or agencies to follow.

Hermeneutics

Hermeneutics is an approach to qualitative research that focuses on the *interpretation* of such social phenomena as tools, works of art, texts, statements of people, and particularly, the actions of humans in social environments. Developed at the end of the eighteenth century, it was originally concerned with interpreting classical, legal, and biblical texts. Today, however, it is often used as an approach in investigating social phenomena, such as statements and behaviors in public administration groups and agency settings.

Researchers in many different disciplines have discovered that they use a number of similar hermeneutic methods and principles in arriving at their interpretations. This type of interpretation can be applied to the study of social action because of an "assumption that social situations display some of the features of a text and that the methodology for interpreting social action develops some of the same procedures of text interpretation" (White 1999, 130).

The principal analysis technique in these studies involves what is called *the hermeneutic circle*. This describes the method of relating parts of the text or conversation to the whole, then back again to the parts. Analysis proceeds in this circular way until the entire text is interpreted. Furthermore, every interpretation is connected to earlier interpretations and understandings; nothing exists outside of interpretation.

The following four laws guide all hermeneutic interpretation processes (White 1999, 143–145): (1) social actors and their beliefs and actions must be understood on their own terms and not be imposed by the investigator; (2) the interactions of all actors in the social setting must be understood within their own context; (3) the researcher must have some preexisting experience with the group members—some common experience must bind them together, and (4) the interpretation arrived at by the investigator must conform to the intentions of the actors.

Grounded Theory

The *grounded theory* approach to research in the administrative and social sciences has its roots in sociology and social psychology. According to Strauss and Corbin (1998), this approach to research has as its primary objective the development of theory out of the information gathered, rather than the testing of predetermined theories through a process of experimentation. Grounded theory researchers approach their study organization by gathering all possible facts pertaining to the problem through personal interviews, analyses of participants' diaries, and participant observation. Once the data are collected, they are analyzed and interpreted by the investigator, who finally develops a theory from that analysis and interpretation.

As developed by Strauss, grounded theory employs a detailed list of rigorous steps and processes for developing theory out of social situations. Insights and ideas are generated only after in-depth analysis of the data, during which the analyst searches for commonalities and differences in the data. These are compared and contrasted as the analyst weighs possible theories against opposing interpretations. Ultimately, a theory that is grounded in the data emerges.

The Action Science Approach

The action science approach has been defined as a way of changing social systems by studying the way they function. It has also been described as "an informal, qualitative, formative, subjective, interpretive, reflective, and experimental model of inquiry in which all individuals involved in the study are knowing and contributing participants" (Gabel 1995, 1).

Chris Argyris and others developed this approach from the earlier contributions of John Dewey—who proposed separating science and practice—and Kurt Lewin in field group dynamics, an area of study in social psychology. Dewey's contribution led to Lewin's separation of the idea of *diagnosis* of an organization or other social group from the idea of *intervention*, which is working to bring about change (Argyris, Putnam, and Smith 1985; Schein 1996). As White (1999, 142) has noted: "The evaluation of social situations is the point of any action theory, which strives to help actors understand their situations in a different light and to make value judgments about whether or not their situations should be changed." Although Lewin never explicitly defined the action science method as such, his early work in developing approaches to interventions and change in social organizations led Argyris to give him credit for developing of most of the techniques involved in the approach (Argyris, Putman, and Smith 1985; Schein 1996).

Five Themes in Action Research

The following five themes in action research were developed by Lewin and used by Argyris in developing the approach as it is used today. First, the approach entails applying change experiments to real problems in existing social systems, with the goal of helping the organization or system resolve the problem. Second, the research method involves a cyclical process of problem identification, planning, acting, and evaluating—over and over again. Third, a major component of the proposed change is reeducation to change the way group members think and act. The fourth theme is an emphasis on participation and free choice in the resolution of the problem—a reflection of Lewin's emphasis on democratic values. Finally, there is a dual purpose or goal in action research: research results should contribute to basic social science knowledge, while also improving everyday life in social groups (Argyris, Putman, and Smith 1985, 8–9).

Action research can be used to test two kinds of statements: *dispositional attributions* and *theories of causal responsibility*. The first of these is an assertion by an actor in the social group about the perceived mental outlook, tendency, or characteristic of another actor in the group. Examples of a dispositional attribution are the statements "John is insensitive (to my feelings)" and "Mary is a thoughtful, caring supervisor." An example of a theory of causal responsibility is "Our supervisor's insensitivity to minorities is causing discomfort and dissatisfaction in our work group."

Two additional important points about action research are (1) what Argyris terms the *domain of action research*, and (2) the *data of action research*. "Domain" is another way of describing the appropriate area of application for the approach, whereas "data" refers to the type or form of information gathered. Action science should be used when the researcher is concerned with *actions* and *interpretive understandings*. Argyris, Putnam, and Smith (1985, 54–57) explained that the data of action research are *actions* that are taken by members of the social group under study. The most important of these actions is *talk*.

> The first point to note is that talk *is* action . . . talk is meaningful . . . when people talk they are performing such actions as promising, justifying, ordering, conceding, and so forth. Using talk as data for the empirical testing of theory forces us to deal with the issues raised by interpretation.

In practice, action research activities should follow this circular process (Gabel 1995):

1. Reconnaissance: An understanding of the problem in the organization is developed through a study of its whole.

2. General plan: Plans are developed for an intervention to resolve the problem.
3. Monitoring the intervention: Observations of the process are collected.
4. Reflection and revision: New intervention strategies are implemented, if necessary, with the cycle beginning anew. It is continued until a satisfactory understanding or change is reached.

Collecting, Analyzing, and Interpreting Qualitative Data

All qualitative research strategies and approaches involve three basic components: (1) collection of data, (2) analysis and interpretation of that data, and (3) communicating research findings in one or more communications media, such as producing a written report (Strauss and Corbin 1998).

Collecting Qualitative Data

The major methods used to collect qualitative data include: (1) participation in the group setting or activity, (2) personal and group interviewing, (3) observation, and (4) document and cultural artifact analysis. There are also many secondary methods of collecting information (Marshall and Rossman 1999), including historical analysis, recording and analysis of live histories and narratives, films, videos and photographs, kinesics, proxemics, unobtrusive measures, surveys, and projective techniques. Kinesics is the study of motion; proxemics is the study of special relationships.

Some researchers collect qualitative data by actually participating in a social situation and writing down what they see, while others unobtrusively observe social interrelationships and behaviors. Researchers also gather qualitative data for analysis by video- or audiotape recordings of narrative accounts of life histories, events, perceptions, or personal values; they question subjects using structured or unstructured, personal or group interviews. Still others collect qualitative data by examining collections of printed documents, past and present artifacts, or cultural or artistic creations, including the media. And some use a combination of these and other methods.

Analyzing Qualitative Data

The analysis and interpretation of qualitative data begins with bringing the raw data into some level of order. First, the researcher identifies and selects a set of relevant *categories* or *classes* in which to sort the data. Comparing the data across categories—a step that is typically used in the testing of hypotheses—often follows the initial comparing phase of the analysis. Strauss and Corbin (1998) call this a process of *conceptualizing*.

Conceptualizing means reducing the often bulky amounts of raw data into workable, ordered bits of information that the researcher can manage with confidence. Kvale (1996) described this act of data categorization as a key qualitative research activity, one that most distinguishes qualitative strategies from quantitative research.

Another procedure sometimes used for this purpose is what is known as *power* or *influence analysis*. In this process, the researcher first collects data by observing the way people interact or by questioning them on their perceptions of such factors as power and influence in the organization. The researcher can then draw a diagram or chart to illustrate the interactions and responses to others within the group. Examples of graphic displays of this type include context charts, linkage patterns and knowledge flowcharts, and role and power charts (Miles and Huberman 1984).

Interpreting Qualitative Data

The next step in analysis of qualitative data is interpreting the patterns and connections that are revealed or hidden by bringing the data into order. Interpretation occurs when the researcher draws conclusions from whatever structure is revealed in the data. If graphic diagrams are used, the researcher must examine and describe the personal connections, misconnections, interfaces, relationships, and interplay of behaviors. These descriptions become the gist of a cogent and meaningful report, the production of which is the third step in the process.

These three steps must be followed in all studies, regardless of which discipline underlies the study, which approach the researcher follows, or which technique is used to gather and analyze the data.

Summary

Qualitative research describes a set of nonstatistical inquiry techniques for gathering data about social phenomena. *Qualitative data* are words, symbols, pictures, or other nonnumeric records, materials, or artifacts collected by a researcher. The uses for these data go beyond simple description of events and phenomena; they are used for creating understanding, for subjective interpretation, and for critical analysis as well.

Qualitative research differs from quantitative research in several fundamental ways. Qualitative research studies employ inductive, theory-generating, subjective, and nonpositivist processes, while quantitative research uses deductive, theory-testing, objective, and positivist processes.

Creswell (1994) identified five ways these two approaches differ, based upon these five philosophical foundations: *ontology, epistemology, axiological assumptions, rhetorical traditions,* and *methodological approaches.*

Qualitative research strategies can be grouped into three broad classes: (1) *explanatory research studies,* (2) *interpretive research studies,* and (3) *critical research studies.* These roughly correspond to the exploratory-descriptive-causal categories of quantitative research designs. The choice of which strategy to adopt when designing a qualitative study will depend upon what objectives the researcher has identified for the study. These must be clearly stated prior to going into the field to embark on the collection of data.

Many different types of research approaches are employed for conducting qualitative research in public administration. Among the disciplinary approaches often followed in public administration are *ethnography, phenomenology, case studies, hermeneutics, grounded theory,* and *action science.*

All qualitative research strategies and approaches involve three basic components: (1) collection of data, (2) analysis and interpretation of that data, and (3) communicating research findings in one or more communications media, such as producing a written report.

The major methods used to collect qualitative data include: (1) participation in the group setting or activity, (2) personal and/or group interviewing, (3) observation, and (4) document and cultural artifact analysis. There are also many secondary methods of collecting information, including historical analysis, live histories and narratives, films, videos and photographs, kinesics, proxemics, unobtrusive measures, surveys, and projective techniques.

Suggested Reading

Cassell, Catherine, and Gillian Symon, eds. 1994. *Qualitative Methods in Organizational Research.* Thousand Oaks, CA: Sage.

Creswell, J.W. 1994. *Research Design.* Thousand Oaks, CA: Sage.

Denzin, Norman K., and Yvonna S. Lincoln, eds. 1994. *Handbook of Qualitative Research.* Thousand Oaks, CA: Sage.

Lee, Thomas W. 1999. *Using Qualitative Methods in Organizational Research.* Thousand Oaks, CA: Sage.

Marshall, Catherine, and Gretchen B. Rossman. 1999. *Designing Qualitative Research.* 3d ed. Thousand Oaks, CA: Sage.

Miles, Matthew B., and A. Michael Huberman. 1984. *Qualitative Data Analysis: A Sourcebook of New Methods.* Beverly Hills, CA: Sage.

Strauss, Anselm, and Juliet Corbin. 1998. *Basics of Qualitative Research: Techniques and Procedures for Developing Grounded Theory.* 2d ed. Thousand Oaks, CA: Sage.

18 The Case Study in Public Administration Research

The case method has long been one of the most popular approaches in public administration research. Whelan (1989) traced the approach as far back as 1948, when a planning committee was formed at Harvard University to develop guidelines for applying the method to research in public administration. Under the leadership of Harold Stein, the original committee became the *Inter-University Case Program* (IUCP) in 1951. The IUCP published a text with twenty-six cases just a year later. In the introduction to that casebook, Stein (1952, xxvii) defined the public administration case as "a narrative of the events that constitute or lead to a decision or group of related decisions by a public administrator or group of public administrators."

A number of now classic case studies were published beginning about the same time as the method was evolving at Harvard. Philip Selznick's *TVA and the Grass Roots* appeared in 1949; Herbert Kaufman's study of the forest service, *The Forest Ranger*, was published in 1960. A third classic case study, Michael Lipsky's (1980) study of city bureaucracies, *Street-Level Bureaucracy*, helped the case approach to achieve recognition as a valid and important research methodology.

These larger case studies were mirrored in miniature by acceptance of the approach in the discipline's professional literature. In his detailed overview of the state of public administration research methods, Yeager (1989) found that one or more case studies appeared in every issue of *Public Administration Review* (*PAR*) for more than forty years. If their continuing appearance in *PAR*—the discipline's leading publication—and other public administration journals is any indication, case studies are just as popular today as they were when Yeager examined the field in the late 1980s.

The popularity of the case study approach lies in its great flexibility. Case studies can be written to serve as examples of what a public administrator ought not to do, as well as what should be done. However, their primary purpose is to instruct public administrators in what other administrators are doing, to inform administrators about what is going on in their field. Today, this means that administrators are able to learn about managerial and administrative experiences from agencies, locations, and levels of government around the globe.

Defining the Case Study Approach

Many different definitions for case studies have been proposed. Yeager traced most of them to Harold Stein who, in an article published in 1952, was one of the first to promote the method as a way to do public administration research.

Another definition of the case study referred to by Yeager (1989, 685) was that proposed by the marketing scholar T.V. Bonoma in a 1985 *Journal of Marketing Research* article. Bonoma's definition had a general management focus:

> A case is a description of a management situation based on interview, archives, naturalistic observation, and other data, constructed to be sensitive to the context in which management behavior takes place and to its temporal restraints. These are characteristics shared by all cases.

In the first edition of Robert K. Yin's important book on the case method (1984), he wrote: "As a research strategy, the distinguishing characteristic of the case is that it attempts to examine (a) a contemporary phenomenon in its real-life context, especially when (b) the boundaries between phenomenon and context are not clearly evident."

Case studies are often intensive studies of one or a few exemplary individuals, families, events, time periods, decisions or set of decisions, processes, programs, institutions, organizations, groups, or even entire communities (Lang and Heiss 1997).

Discussing the case method as one of three qualitative approaches for research in organizational communications, Arneson (1993, 164) saw it as an appropriate research method when a case involves some noteworthy success or failure, adding, "Qualitative case studies most appropriately address programs directed toward *individualized* outcomes."

The subject selected as a case example typically is chosen for study because it points out some underlying problem or because it represents a successful solution to a problem. The researcher hopes that publishing the successful experience can provide a model for others to emulate.

Because public administration researchers have used the case study for so long and in so many different ways, it is not surprising that many different purposes for the method have surfaced. However, most authors agree with Lang and Heiss (1990, 86) that underlying all case studies is this one fundamental principle:

> The basic rationale for a case study is that there are processes and interactions . . . , which cannot be studied effectively except as they interact and function within the entity itself. Thus, if we learn how these processes interact in one person or organization, we will know more about how the processes as factors in themselves and perhaps apply these [what we have learned] to other similar type persons or organizations.

Categories of Case Studies

Stake (1994) grouped cases studies into three categories: (1) intrinsic case studies, (2) instrumental studies, and (3) collective studies.

Intrinsic case studies are done when the researcher wants to provide a better understanding of the subject case itself. This type of case is not selected because it is representative of a larger genre or because it serves as an illustrative example of something. Nor is it selected because the researcher plans to build a theory upon what is found in the analysis of the case. Rather, the case is studied simply because the researcher is interested in it for some reason.

Instrumental case studies, on the other hand, are used when the public administration researcher wants to gain greater insight into a specific issue. In these situations, the subject case is expected to contribute to a greater understanding of a topic of interest, such as performance measurement. The subject case itself is of secondary interest; examining the case improves understanding of the phenomenon, not the case.

The third type of case study is what Stake called the *collective case*. This is a multiple-case design. A group of individual cases are studied together because they contribute to greater understanding of a phenomenon, a population, or some general organizational condition. Another name for this type of case is *multisite qualitative research* (Yeager 1989).

Others have proposed a number of different scenarios for when the case study method is a particularly appropriate design. Van Evera (1997), for example, identified these five purposes for case studies: (1) to establish a theory or theories, (2) to test theories that already exist, (3) to identify a previous condition or conditions that lead or contribute to a phenomenon (what Van Evera called *antecedents*), (4) to establish the relative importance of such contributing conditions, and (5) to establish the fundamental importance of the case with regard to other potential examples.

Establishing a theory upon which to base predictions of future events is an important reason for much of the published research in the administrative sciences. In his review of works that used the case study method to examine city planning and planners, Fischler (2000) noted that case studies are uniquely suited for exploring the interaction of personal behavior and collective institutions, and the interplay of agency and structure. Fischler saw the planning case as contributing to the development of a theory of government planning practices.

Fischler called cases "the most essential tools" in theory development. Developing theory from case studies occurs through a four-phase process: (1) formulation of research questions and hypotheses, (2) selection of the case and definition of units of analysis, (3) data gathering and presentation, and (4) analysis and theory building. Finally, he concluded that case studies should remain an important study approach: "Case studies that explore the behavior and experience of innovative practitioners and innovative organizations, be they public, private, or not-for-profit, should therefore be placed high on our agenda" (194).

Bailey (1994) also identified a variety of purposes for the case study in public administration. They can be descriptive, interpretive, or critical; they can be used for solving administrative problems or for forming a theory. They can have a purely practioner-oriented focus, or they can be "esoteric scholarly studies." For maximum value, however, Bailey concluded that the ideal case study was one that had value for *both* practitioners and academics.

Developing Case Studies

Case studies can be single-case or multicase designs. Designs that compare one case against another are called either multicase or cross-case designs. For both the single and multicase approaches, the purpose of the study is never to furnish a representative picture of "the world," but rather simply to represent the specific case or cases (Stake 1994). While this is certainly true, it is also true that good case studies do include features of the case that are uniform and generalizable, as well as those that appear to be unique to the case under study (Bailey 1994, 192).

Single-Case Studies

Most case studies that are conducted in the behavioral and administrative sciences are single-case studies; they are found in all the social and administrative sciences, making them what Miles and Huberman (1998, 193) called the *traditional mode of qualitative analysis.*

An early example of the single-case study is the 1951 analysis of the Glacier Metal Company in London by a team of researchers led by Elliott Jacques. Jacques explained the report as a case study of developments in the social life of one industrial community; as a case study, the report was not intended as a statement of precise and definite conclusions. Rather, it was written to show how managers and employees in one company deal with change.

An example of a public administration single-case study is Soni's (2000) study of a regional office of the U.S. Environmental Protection Agency. The study focused on workplace diversity and the attitudes of agency personnel toward mandated awareness initiatives. Soni first determined how employees valued workplace diversity and then looked at whether the staff supported the agency management-development program. That program was designed to enhance worker acceptance of racial, age, and gender diversity in the organization. This included requirements for diversity-management initiatives in five-year strategic plans and diversity goals at the local or agency group level.

Analysis of this single case led Soni to conclude that workers accept and support diversity to a far lesser extent than the ideal published in the literature. In addition, diversity-management programs appeared to have only minimal effects in changing workers' sensitivity to differences, increasing their acceptance and valuing of diversity, reducing stereotyping and prejudice, or any of the other goals established for the program.

Case studies such as that carried out by Soni should not be used to infer similar behaviors or conditions in other or related organizations. The results of a case study are applicable only to the organization or group examined. No inferences can nor should be made from the results. Soni reflected this possible limitation of the method by adding the following caveat at the conclusion of the paper: "The racial and gender effects found in this case study may be a consequence of the many specific organizational characteristics and cannot be assumed to be representative of other organizations" (407).

In another example of a single-case study in the public administration literature, Poister and Harris (2000) examined a "mature" total quality management program in the Pennsylvania Department of Transportation. The program began in 1982 with the introduction of quality circles and evolved into a major strategic force in the department, with quality concepts incorporated into all levels of the culture of the organization. Poister and Harris (175) pointed to the experience of this department as an example for other agencies to emulate—one of the key purposes of the case study. They concluded their study with the statement that the department "has indeed transformed itself over the past 15 years around core values of quality and customer service. Hopefully, its experience along these lines will be helpful to other public agencies that have embarked on this journey more recently."

Multicase Studies

Ammons, Coe, and Lombardo (2001) used a multicase approach to compare the performance of three public sector benchmarking projects. Two of the projects were national in scope, while the third was a single-state program.

The first project was a 1991 program sponsored by the Innovation Groups to collect performance measurement information from cities and counties across the country. This information was eventually incorporated into a national performance-benchmarking information network, eventually named the PBCenter. Participants were charged a $750 fee to join the project. Although the effort started aggressively by measuring forty-three programs, ultimately both participation and enthusiasm among potential users of the information were disappointing.

The second case in this multicase study, the Center for Performance Measurement, was a national program sponsored by the International City/County Management Association (ICMA). This program was established in 1994 by a consortium of thirty-four cities and counties with populations over 200,000. Performance measurements were collected and shared in these four core service areas: police services, fire services, neighborhood services, and support services. Neighborhood services included code enforcement, housing, libraries, parks and recreation, road maintenance, garbage collection, and street lighting.

The third case examined in the study was a state project that began in 1994 in North Carolina; its purpose was to provide performance statistics to the state's city managers. By 1995, it had evolved into the North Carolina Local Government Performance Management Project, run by the Institute of Government at the University of North Carolina at Chapel Hill. By 1997, thirty-five cities and counties were participating. The Ammons, Coe, and Lombardo study concluded that all three programs had failed to deliver results that even approached the expectations of their participants, many of whom felt that program costs exceeded any benefits.

On the basis of this comparative analysis of the three cases, the authors recommended that administrators of similar projects in the future should make sure that participants have realistic expectations for benchmarking before they buy into their programs.

In another multicase design, Fernandez and Fabricant (2000) examined two cases from Florida's experience with privatization of child support programs in an effort to compare the effectiveness of public and private service providers. Their analysis concluded with recommendations on ways to avoid problems encountered in the evaluation process.

The primary objective of this study was to determine whether or not the research methodology used by the state of Florida to compare the relative efficiency of private versus state agency providers was accurate. The topic was collection of delinquent child support payments from an absent parent. The initial report issued by the state indicated that, in one case, the state agency produced a collection rate that was 307 percent greater than that of the private or contracted group. The authors revealed that Florida's study design was fatally flawed. The agency success report was based on a sample that represented the total population of cases, whereas the sample worked on by the private firm represented only those cases that had been delinquent for longer than six months and that the state agency had been working on unsuccessfully for the six-month period. The authors suggest that a negative correlation probably existed for the period of time a case is delinquent and the probability of collecting owed child support. Had the state of Florida used similar samples for both the public and the private agencies, it could have avoided the results produced by its faulty design.

Steps in the Case Study Method

The model presented in Figure 18.1 illustrates various steps in the selection and preparation of a case study. The model can be considered a *flowchart*; case study activities should begin at the top and proceed downward. The concepts included in the model owe much to Robert Stake's 1994 synopsis of the case method. Additional contributions to the model came from the five components of a case study design identified by Yin (1994, 20): (1) the study question, (2) its propositions (others call these *hypotheses*), if any, (3) the unit or units of analysis, (4) the logic that links the collected information to the propositions, and (5) the criteria selected by the researcher for interpreting the case.

Step 1: Frame the Case

The first step in researching a case study is to establish a *frame* for the research. Framing goes beyond identifying the basic research problem. Instead, when framing the case, the researcher must answer three questions: First, why should the case study method be used in preference to any other research method in this situation? Second, why should this particular case be studied? Are there more representative cases available for study? And, third, why choose these specific behaviors or phenomena to study?

Step 2: Operationalize Key Constructs

Operationalizing relevant themes, issues, research questions, and variables is the second step in the process. "Operationalizing" describes the process of

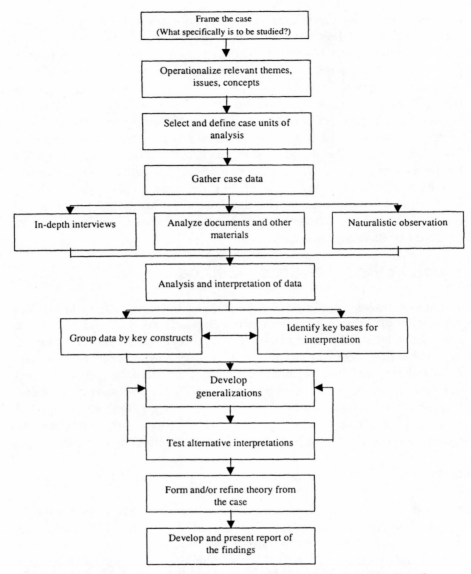

Figure 18.1 **Steps in Planning, Analysis, and Presentation of Case Studies**

defining or *conceptualizing* the key constructs or themes that form and shape the research. Operationalizing also requires the researcher to identify any limitations and assumptions for the research. The purpose is to impose *order and structure* on the data in order to ensure that the needed data will be collected during case interviews and observations. Finally, when a researcher operationalizes the salient themes or constructs for a case study, it is much easier to organize the data as it is collected.

Defining the categories also involves providing some amount of descriptive information in any number of ways. Strauss and Corbin (1998) defined defining the categories as the process of applying order to collected data by placing them in discrete categories, adding that researchers are almost certain to include descriptive material along with the code descriptions and category definitions.

Gathered information must be coded and assigned to its proper category. Coding is based on a researcher-selected set of general properties, characteristics, or dimensions. In their discussion on coding of qualitative data, Strauss and Corbin added that conceptualizing is also the first step in theory building. A concept is the researcher's description of a significant event, object, or action-interaction. The researched must be named in order to be organized into logical groupings, classifications, or categories that share some common characteristic or meaning. Thus, "a labeled thing" is something that can be located, placed in a class of similar objects, and *classified* in some way (103).

Step 3: Define Units of Analysis

The third step in case study analysis is defining the *units of analysis*. This critical step hinges upon how the researcher has defined the problem to be studied. As noted earlier, case studies can focus on many different types of phenomena; they can be either single-case or multicase studies. While most case studies focus on individuals, pairs (dyads), small or large groups, processes, or organizations (Marshall and Rossman 1999), they can also be about decisions made by administrators, supervisors, or work teams. They can focus on programs, agencies, small subunits of agencies, or groups of agencies that address a similar problem or service. They can even be about entire communities.

These are all what is meant by the term *unit of analysis*. Deciding on the unit of analysis is what Yin (1994) called a *narrowing of the relevant data*. Narrowing the data allows the researcher to focus the study on topics identified in the research objectives.

Taking the unit-of-analysis decision to the next level depends first on the way the researcher has defined the study question. For example, a study designed to bring to light the effects of a reduction in the number of beds available at a state mental health hospital could be addressed from several points of view. First, the study could chronicle the effects that inability to access treatment might have on one or a category-group of patients. Another study might focus on the impact the closures will have on community-based treatment centers. An even more focused study could limit the investigation to locally funded charitable organizations treating the client base. A broader view might look at the economic impact that funding the services locally will have on other community-based programs competing for shares of the same funding pool. Clearly, defining the unit of analysis is a critical first step that must take place before moving to the next step, collecting information.

Finally, operationalization requires that the researcher identify each of the procedures that will be followed, both in data collection and analysis; identify the coding plans and methods that will be used; and prepare a preliminary list of categories for the analysis.

Step 4: Collect the Data

The fourth step, *data collection*, can take place in a variety of ways. The techniques used most often in public administration research include (1) interviews, (2) simple (also called *naturalistic*) observation, and (3) analysis of internal and external documents. One of the hallmarks of a good case study is the selection of two or more of these methods (Arneson (1993). As well as providing a means for *triangulation* (studying a phenomenon in two or more ways to substantiate the validity of the study findings), the use of more than one approach ensures that relevant data is not missed.

Interviews

Gathering data by interview may take one of several different forms. The method used most often in public administration research is the in-depth personal interview. Individual interviews occur as conversations between a researcher and a subject or respondent. To keep the conversation focused, the research uses a conversation guide in which are listed the key points that are to be covered in the interview. The respondent is free to provide any answer that comes to mind. Another type of interview is more structured, requiring respondents to reply to specific open-ended questions. An approach that is becoming increasingly important in public administration research is the *focus group interview*. A focus group consists of eight to twelve subjects who meet as a group to discuss a topic or issue. The discussion is free and open, with the researcher providing only minimal direction.

Observation

Naturalistic or simple observation is another way data are gathered for case studies. Marshall and Rossman (1999, 107) described this method as "the systematic noting and recording of events, behaviors, and artifacts in the social setting chosen for study." The researcher records events and behaviors as they happen, collecting the written records into compilations of impressions that are similar if not identical to the field notes that characterize data collection in ethnographic studies. In this type of observation, however, the researcher does not seek to be accepted as a member of the group, staying, instead, an outsider.

It is a toss-up which is more important in the case study approach to research: personal interviewing or simple observation. Each has its advantages and disadvantages. Interviews, for example, allow researchers to delve deeply into a subject, encouraging respondents to provide the reasons for their behavior or opinions. Interviews are time-consuming, however, and require interviewers with special questioning and listening skills.

Observation has long been an important data-gathering technique used in social science research. Although it is called "simple observation," it is not an easy process to employ. According to Marshall and Rossman (1999, 107):

> Observation is a fundamental and highly important method in all qualitative inquiry: it is used to discover complex interactions in natural social settings. . . . It is, however, a method that requires a great deal of the researcher. Discomfort, uncomfortable ethical dilemmas and even danger, the difficulty of managing a relatively unobtrusive role, and the challenge of identifying the "big picture" while finely observing huge amounts of fast-moving and complex behavior are just a few of the challenges.

One way that researchers try to get around the time and skills limitations of in-depth interviewing is by the use of group interviewing, what marketing and advertising researchers call *focus groups*. A focus group is a group of six to a dozen individuals with similar interests or characteristics who are interviewed together in the same room. The researcher functions as a moderator, keeping any one participant from monopolizing the conversation or intimidating other members of the group. As each participant is called upon to contribute, group interaction often occurs, providing a richer, more meaningful discussion of the topic.

Document Analysis

The study of documents and archival data is usually undertaken to supplement the information the case study researcher acquires by interview or by observing in a situation. These may be official government records, internal organizational reports or memos, or external reports or articles about a case subject. The technique that is usually used in document analysis is content analysis, which may be either qualitative or quantitative, or both. One of the key advantages of document analysis is that it does not interfere with or disturb the case setting in any way. According to Marshall and Rossman (1999), the fact that document and archival analysis is unobtrusive and nonreactive is probably the greatest strength of this research activity.

Step 5: Analyze the Data

The *analysis* of all qualitative data takes place in a progression of six separate phases. Figure 18.2 displays a version of the progression of analysis steps.

An important requirement inherent in all data analysis is that the data be reduced in volume at each stage. Unless this occurs, the researcher may be inundated with reams of unrelated information that make logical interpretation impossible. Organizing the data into sets of mutually exclusive categories is one way to reduce the volume of data.

Raw data in the case study method can be any or all of the collected information. The primary responsibility of the analyst is to remain focused on information that sheds light on the study question. This may mean ignoring or leaving to a later review highly interesting but extraneous data. Analysis of case data involves looking at and weighing the collected data from a number of different viewpoints before writing the final case narrative.

In Figure 18.1, these analysis steps are broken down into five separate steps: (1) grouping the data according to key constructs, (2) identifying bases for interpretation, (3) developing generalizations from the data, (4) testing alternative interpretations, and (5) forming and/or refining generalizable theory from the case study.

Data analysis does not always take place in the logical sequence illustrated in Figure 18.2. Rather, two or more of the activities may occur at the same time. In addition, data analysis does not simply end with the first set of conclusions; it is a *circular* process. Parts of the analysis may be moved forward to the next step, while other parts, even whole sections, may butt up against conclusions with dead ends. When this happens, the researcher must search for alternative explanations, test these against the themes that evolved in the operationalization phase, and then either reach new and different conclusions or adjust the themes and categories to reflect the reality of the data.

Step 6: Prepare and Present a Report of the Findings

The final step in the process is producing a comprehensive narrative of the case, in which the connections between key concepts and study objectives are addressed. The *narrative* is a descriptive account of the program, person, organization, office, or agency under study. All the information necessary to understand the case must be included in the narrative. It typically revolves

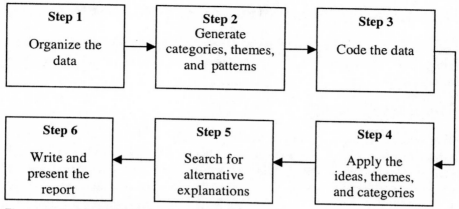

Figure 18.2 **A Procedure for Data Analysis**

around the researcher's *interpretation* of the behaviors and events observed in the case during the study period.

Patton (1980, 304) referred to the final case narrative as "the descriptive, analytic, interpretive, and evaluative treatment of the more comprehensive descriptive data" collected by the researcher. He saw the report-writing phase taking place in a series of three distinct steps:

1. Collecting and categorizing the raw case data. This is all the information that was gathered by interviews, by observing, and by reviewing any relevant documents and/or literature.
2. Constructing a preliminary record of the case. A case record is the researcher's coded and subsequent distillation of the mass of raw case data. It involves establishing categories and assigning the data to them in a logical order. A draft of the report eventually emerges from completion of this and the first step.
3. Producing a case study narrative. This is the final written narrative (or other presentation form) that communicates in a readable, informative, and evaluative way how the case meets the original objectives for the research. It includes all the information that readers need to fully understand the subject. It can be presented as a chronological record of events or according to a set of themes—or both.

The case study report must clearly explain what the researcher perceived to be the "facts." In addition, it must discuss relevant alternative interpretations and explain why the researcher chose not to accept those alternatives. Finally, the case study's conclusion should be soundly based in the interpretation adopted by the researcher (Yeager 1989).

Required Characteristics in Case Studies

A number of guidelines have been offered for preparing case study reports. Yin (1994) identified five key characteristics of the best, most informative case studies:

The Case Study Must Be Significant

"Significant" cases stand out as superior examples of the best in their class. They illustrate a particular point in a better or more succinct way than others that could have been chosen. The researcher thus not only indicates that the selection of the case or cases was appropriate, but that the study adds to the body of knowledge about the topic or issue; the study makes a significant contribution. Research problems that are trivial do not make good case studies. Yin (1994, 147) concluded that the best case studies are those in which:

- The single case or sets of cases are unusual and not "mundane."
- The case or cases are interesting to the public.
- The fundamental issues brought to light in the case have wide appeal—they are "nationally important" either as theory, as policy, or in practical application.

The Case Study Must Be Complete

Case studies that are "complete" leave the reader with the feeling that all relevant evidence has been collected, evaluated, interpreted, and either accepted or rejected. The operative word here, of course, is relevant. According to Yin (1994), a case study in not complete unless it is so on three distinct dimensions. First, in a complete case the phenomenon of interest is explicitly addressed. Second, all the relevant information is collected; no information that relates to a dimension should be left ungathered or, if collected, left uninterpreted and discussed in the final narrative. Third, the researcher must not impose any artificial conditions during the analysis or evaluation of the collected data. This means, for example, that the researcher must not stop collecting relevant information because he or she ran out of money or time, or for any other nonresearch constraint.

The Case Study Must Consider Alternative Perspectives

It is important that the researcher not limit the analysis of case data to a single point of view. Alternative explanations for a social phenomenon *always* exist

(Marshall and Rossman 1999). Throughout the analysis of the case data, the researcher is obligated to identify alternative explanations or interpretations of the raw data and to show why these are rejected in favor of the adopted explanation. Evidence that supports the selected interpretation must also be presented.

The Case Study Must Display Sufficient Evidence

Data reduction solely for the sake of brevity in a case analysis is not desirable. All the relevant evidence must appear in the final narrative. Certainly, the researcher must condense, distill, and combine data at each step of the analysis; otherwise, the final report would be little more than a hodgepodge of unrelated, disjointed, raw data. However, the researcher should probably err on the side of including *too much* material rather than finding out later that he or she has omitted important evidence from the final case report.

The Case Study Must Be Composed in an Engaging Manner

While this does not apply directly to the concept of completeness in a case report, it is relevant because it has a great influence on whether the case will ultimately be read, understood, and, where appropriate, used in policy development. It is a question of *style*. According to Yin (1994), a complaint often heard about case studies is that they are too long, cumbersome to read and interpret, and simply boring. He suggested that the writer of case studies should strive to engage readers' intelligence, entice their interest by hinting at exciting information to come, and seduce readers into accepting the underlying premise.

Summary

The case method has long been one of the most popular approaches in public administration research. Its popularity lies in its great flexibility. Case studies can be written to serve as examples of what a public administrator ought not to do, as well as what should be done. However, their primary purpose is to instruct public administrators in what other administrators are doing.

Case studies are often intensive studies of one or a few exemplary individuals, families, events, time periods, decisions or sets of decisions, processes, programs, institutions, organizations, groups, or even entire communities. Discussing the case method as one of three qualitative approaches for research in organizational communications, Arneson (1993) described it as an appropriate research method when a case involves some noteworthy success or failure.

There are three types of case studies: (1) intrinsic case studies, (2) instrumental studies, and (3) collective studies. *Intrinsic* case studies are done when the researcher wants to provide a better understanding of the subject case itself. *Instrumental* case studies are used when the public administration researcher wants to gain greater insight into a specific issue. The *collective case* is a multiple-case design; a group of individual cases are studied together because they contribute to greater understanding of a phenomenon, a population, or some general organizational condition. Another name for this type of case is *multisite qualitative research*.

Five purposes for case studies have been identified: (1) to establish a theory or theories, (2) to test theories that already exist; (3) to identify a previous condition or conditions that lead or contribute to a phenomenon, (4) to establish the relative importance of such contributing conditions, and (5) to establish the fundamental importance of the case with regard to other potential examples.

Case studies can be single-case or multicase designs. Most case studies that are conducted in the behavioral and administrative sciences are single-case studies. Multicase designs can be used to compare two or more cases or to gather extended evidence across a group of like cases.

The researcher designs and prepares a case study through a series of interlocking steps. In step 1, the case must be *framed*, which means that the researcher must determine what should be studied in what case, and why. In step 2, key constructs, variables, terms, and so on are operationalized so that no confusion occurs later in the analysis process. In step 3, the researcher selects and defines the unit(s) of analysis—individuals, groups, neighborhoods, or other entities. The researcher collects data in step 4, by conducting in-depth interviews, performing naturalistic or simple observation, and examining any relevant documentation. The data are analyzed in step 5, and a final case report is produced during step 6.

Suggested Reading

Denzin, Norman K., and Yvonna S. Lincoln. 1998. *Collecting and Interpreting Qualitative Materials*. Thousand Oaks, CA: Sage.

Marshall, Catherine, and Gretchen B. Rossman. 1999. *Designing Qualitative Research*. 3d ed. Thousand Oaks, CA: Sage.

Rubin, Jack, W., Barkley Hudreth, and Gerald J. Miller, eds. 1989. *Handbook of Public Administration Research*. New York: Marcel Dekker.

Stake, Robert E. 1994. "Case Studies." In *Handbook of Qualitative Research*, N.K. Denzin and Y.S. Lincoln, eds., 236–247. Thousand Oaks, CA: Sage.

Van Evera, Stephen. 1997. *Guide to Methods for Students of Political Science*. Ithaca, NY: Cornell University Press.

Yin, Robert K. 1994. *Case Study Research: Design and Methods*. 2d ed. Thousand Oaks, CA: Sage.

19 Grounded Theory in Public Administration Research

Since its introduction in the late 1960s, the *grounded theory* approach to research has captured the methodological interest and imagination of researchers in all the social and administrative sciences. One of its principal inventors, Barney G. Glaser (1999) described it as a methodology for getting from the systematic collection of data to production of a multivariate conceptual theory.

The grounded theory method has been used successfully in many different circumstances, disciplines, and cultures. The fact that it is easily generalizable to many different disciplines and research topics has contributed to its increasing acceptance worldwide. As Glaser (1999, 842) has noted:

> Grounded theory is a general method. It can be used on any data or combination of data. It was developed partially by me with quantitative data [which] is expensive and somewhat hard to obtain. . . . Qualitative data are inexpensive to collect, very rich in meaning and observation, and rewarding to collect and analyze. So, by default to ease and growing use, grounded theory is being linked to qualitative data and is seen as a qualitative method, using symbolic interaction, by many. Qualitative grounded theory accounts for the global spread of its use.

The grounded theory method evolved from roots in the *symbolic interactionism* theoretical research of social psychologist George H. Mead at the University of Chicago, his onetime student Herbert Blumer, and others (Robrecht 1995). Mead believed that people define themselves through the social roles, expectations, and perspectives they acquire from society and through the processes of socialization and social interactions. Blumer added three concepts to Mead's thesis: (1) the meanings that things have for people will determine people's behavior toward things, (2) these meanings come from people's social interactions, and (3) to deal with these meanings, people undergo a process of constant interpretation (Annells 1996). Grounded theory was "invented" by Glaser and Anselm Strauss (1967) as a way to develop explanatory and predictive *theory* about the social life, roles, and expected behaviors of people.

From its early roots in sociology and social psychology, the method has evolved and grown in importance to become what Brian Haig (1995) has described as "currently the most comprehensive qualitative research methodology available." Also noting this increased acceptance, Denzin and Lincoln (1994, 204) called it "the most widely used interpretive strategy in the social sciences today." Recently, this method has also become an increasingly important research approach in public administration. "Grounded theory has gone global, seriously global among the disciplines of nursing, business, and education and less so among other social-psychological-oriented disciplines such as social welfare, psychology, sociology, and art," according to Glaser (1999). Miller and Fredericks (1996, 538) have also commented on this growth:

> It is increasingly apparent that the grounded theory approach has become a paradigm of choice in much of the qualitatively oriented research in nursing, education, and other disciplines. Grounded theory has become a type of central organizing concept that serves to both direct the research process as well as provide a heuristic for data analysis and interpretation.

Grounded theory was first proposed as a reaction against the restrictions that its inventors saw in positivist research methodology. Chief among these perceived restrictions was the requirement to conduct research for the purpose of testing preconceived theoretical hypotheses. Today, the primary objective of all grounded theory research is to *develop* theory out of the information gathered, rather than to test predetermined theories through a process of experimentation.

The process begins with the researcher focusing on some area of study, which could be any phenomenon, circumstance, trend, or behavior, in any of the social or administrative sciences. Using such observation, interviewing, and other tools, the researcher gathers relevant data from as many different sources as are available. Analysis of the data begins with grouping it into categories and assigning codes. By continually comparing data in various categories, the researcher may generate theory.

Grounded theory requires the researcher to organize and apply *structure* to the data according to an eclectic set of researcher-determined groupings or *categories*. As the researcher forms categories, new data are compared across the formed categories. Linkages between categories and characteristics are also identified. The data and their linkages are assigned discrete codes that enable the researcher to identify them with their specific groupings. Similar

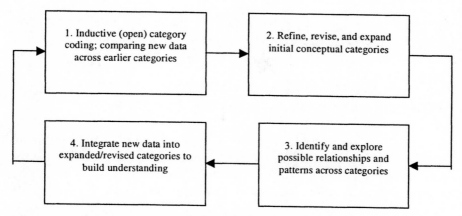

Figure 19.1 **Constant Comparative Method of Data Analysis**
Source: Maykut and Morehouse 1994, 135.

codes are in turn assigned to other data that fit into a broader category or categories. As the process continues, categories are constantly reevaluated and changed when necessary. Only when no additional revisions are intuitively possible does the analyst form a *theory* from the collected and analyzed data. Figure 19.1 illustrates the constant comparative method of data analysis.

Importance of Grouping and Coding

Rather than functioning only as a convenience for later reference, the actual assigning of data to their formed groupings is a critical early step in the analysis process. Strauss and Corbin (1998, 3) defined the coding process as the "analytical process through which data are fractured, conceptualized, and integrated to form theory." It is the key activity in the *microanalysis* stage of the data; it includes both the first and the second stages of coding.

The researcher applies a rigorous analytical process in order to develop theory out of the investigated social situation(s) *after* several runs through the raw data and coded categories. Thus, a key concept in grounded theory is the *continual analysis* of the data while and after they are collected.

Insights and ideas are also generated after in-depth analysis of the data. The analyst searches for commonalities and differences in the data. New data are fitted into the constructs or categories that are seen as pivotal in the data. Commonalities are compared and contrasted as the analyst weighs possible theories against other possible interpretations. Ultimately, a theory that is "grounded" in the data will emerge from the analysis.

Grounded theory researchers conduct their studies by gathering all possible facts that pertain to a problem through personal interviews, analyses of participants' diaries, and by participant observation. The data are analyzed and given an initial interpretation as they are collected by the researcher (Strauss and Corbin 1998). This initial interpretation is called *open* or *substantive* coding.

Two Approaches to Grounded Theory

The analysis process identified by Glaser and Strauss in 1967 has been modified over time, so today there are (at least) two approaches to grounded theory. Locke (1996) identified the two approaches as the *Straussian*—after Anselm Strauss—and the *Glaserian*—after Barney Glaser. Strauss and Corbin (1998), reporting that they observed their graduate students had great difficulty in organizing, coding, and analyzing their data, proposed that an additional step be added to the process. Glaser responded in 1992, taking issue with Strauss and Corbin for straying from the original emphasis on developing theory and adopting instead a process that he believed emphasized conceptual description over theory generation.

Both approaches are fundamentally similar, however; the controversy focuses on the addition of a third level of coding proposed by Strauss and Corbin. Glaser (1992) advocated sticking to the two steps in the coding process introduced in the original work. Both approaches emphasize the importance of coding as a key concept in the analysis.

Glaser's two coding processes are *open* (substantive) and *theoretical*. During the first phase, coding can be relatively freewheeling, open to continuous revision, compression, and merging. During the final, theoretical phase of the analysis, the researcher is advised to rework the groupings as required to bring substance to any emerging theoretical conclusions.

Strauss and Corbin (1998) reported that the grounded theory process as originally proposed in 1967 made it difficult for beginning researchers to produce clear and cogent theory from the data. Retaining the open and substantive coding levels, they proposed adding a third, intermediate step in the coding/analysis process. They called this intermediate step *axial coding* (Glaser 1992; Kendall 1999). This step—proposed as a way to "demystify" the grounded theory process—requires the researcher to place all the initially "open-coded" data into six categories specified by Strauss and Corbin. The six predetermined categories are (1) *causal conditions*, (2) *phenomena*, (3) *context*, (4) *intervening conditions*, (5) *actions/strategies*, and (6) *consequences* (Figure 19.2).

A number of authors have objected to what they see as an artificial restriction that axial coding forces upon the researcher. Hall and Callery (2001), for example, concluded that the intermediary six steps resulted in a "mechanical

Figure 19.2 **The Strauss and Corbin Paradigm Model for Axial Coding of Data**
Source: Adapted from Glaser and Strauss 1967.

approach" to data analysis that limited theory building. Kendall (1999) saw that axial coding could be advantageous for beginning researchers, but added that it forced her from her original research question when she used it in her dissertation. After several years of working with her data, she found herself spending so much time trying to fit the data to the Strauss and Corbin "paradigm model" that she stopped thinking about what the data was communicating about the original study question. She felt that using predetermined categories directed her analysis artificially by limiting her thinking only to the six categories.

The important thing to remember about the two different approaches is not that the two creators of the grounded theory method disagree on how many steps there should be in the coding process, but rather that they agree on almost all other aspects of the process. Data should be continually compared with new data, coded, and placed in categories for interpretation. The researcher selects both the code and category in the first and the last steps in the analysis.

Steps in the Grounded Theory Process

Lee (1999) proposed an eight-step process, shown in Figure 19.3, for conducting a grounded theory study. Lee emphasized the importance of continuous comparisons of categories in his eight-step process, but did not include the Strauss and Corbin axial coding step. Lee's model is therefore very similar to the original Glaser and Strauss proposal.

In contrast to Lee's eight-step process, Figure 19.4 is a model of a seven-stage process in a grounded theory research; it was developed to illustrate the sequential nature of the method. The seven key steps explained in the following pages were described in detail in Glaser and Strauss's 1967 narrative of how the method was developed and reiterated elsewhere (e.g., Glaser 1992; Strauss and Corbin 1998).

Step 1. The researcher comes up with ideas, questions, or concepts about some area of interest. These ideas can come from the researcher's own experience in the field, from a few key interviews, or from an analysis of the published literature.

Step 2. By creatively looking at the ideas, questions, or concepts, the researcher proposes possible underlying concepts for the phenomenon and their relationships (linkages).

Step 3. The researcher tests these initial linkages by comparing them with real-world data.

Step 4. By continually comparing the concepts to objective world phenomena, the researcher takes the first steps in testing a theory.

Step 5. By continually analyzing the data and testing new data against the concepts, the researcher integrates, simplifies, and reduces the concepts, seeking to establish core concepts.

Step 6. The researcher prepares "theoretical memos" (preliminary attempts to spell out possible connections and/or theoretical explanations). This ongoing process requires the researcher to continually test and revise possible theory.

Step 7. The researcher continues to collect data and to code data by categories and/or characteristics, while also producing theoretical interpretations of the material; this often requires the researcher to go back and repeat earlier steps in the process.

Step 8. The researcher prepares a final research report. In grounded theory research, this is not simply a "detached, mechanical process"; it is instead a key part of the research process.

Figure 19.3 **An Eight-Step Model for Conducting Grounded Theory Research**
Source: Adapted from Lee 1999.

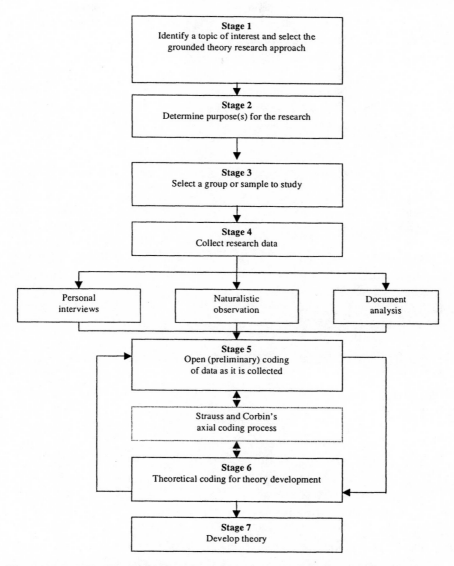

Figure 19.4 **A Model of the Grounded Theory Data Collection and Coding Processes**

Stage 1: Select a Topic of Interest

In public administration, theories explain and predict human behavior among public employees, the citizenry, or organizations that are in some way acted upon or that influence public decisions. "Theory is a strategy for handling data in research, providing modes of conceptualization for describing and explaining" (Glaser and Strauss 1967, 3).

Research topics—areas of interest to study—are not hard to find. They are everywhere in the researcher's field of interest, career field, and the practice of administrating for the public good. The key thing to avoid in grounded theory is approaching a study area with a preconceived hypothesis. The hypothesis *must* come from the data. Glaser (1992, 23), warning budding researchers to avoid the advice of others, cautioned:

> When a research problem is elusive or hard to come by a lot of people tend to give advice . . . the researcher's search for the preconceived problem is subject to the whims and wisdoms of advisors with much experience and of colleagues. He should be careful as he may just end up studying his advisor's pet problem with no yield for him and data for the advisor. And he will likely miss the relevance in the data.

It is important to remember that the identification of a research question is not a statement that clearly and succinctly identifies the topic that is going to be studied (Glaser 1992). Rather, the problem emerges from the data as it is collected. Open coding, selective (theoretical) sampling, and constant analysis of this information—these form a focus for the research study.

Stage 2: Determine a Purpose for the Research

Glaser and Strauss (1967) identified five main purposes or uses for grounded theory:

1. To evaluate the accuracy of earlier evidence
2. To establish generalizations based on experience
3. To identify a concept
4. To verify an existing theory
5. To generate a theory

Evaluating Evidence

Data from additional groups are collected to compare with data that have already been collected for the purpose of evaluating whether the first evidence was correct. This often serves as a test for replicability and can be applied for validating both internal evidence (from within the study group) and external evidence (data from sources other than the study group). This can be a powerful and important use for grounded theory because a study's categories and properties are generated from collected evidence.

Collected and compared evidence is used as a defining illustration of the conceptual category. Glaser and Strauss (1967, 23) considered these categories the fundamental building block of theory: "In generating theory, it is not the fact upon which we stand but the conceptual category that was generated from it."

Establishing Generalizations from the Data

If a theory is to emerge from the collected "facts," they must be generalizable to other situations; otherwise they remain isolated bits of data—interesting but irrelevant. If they are applicable only to a single case, group, circumstance, or situation, they remain descriptors of only that specific phenomenon. In searching for generalizations, or universals, the researcher establishes boundaries of applicability while at the same time, attempting to broaden the theory.

Specifying a Concept

This is the first step in a design requiring specific identification of a study sample or population for a one-case study. Grounded theory's comparative evaluations are used to clearly identify the key *concept* that makes the study group distinctive. Identified concepts tell your readers why you chose to study one group and not another. It involves comparing the unit of analysis (individuals or groups) selected for the study with other units that are not selected. This comparison often brings to light the distinctive properties of the selected unit.

For example, a study of homeless women—such as Alice Waterston's (1999) *Love, Sorrow, and Rage: Destitute Women in a Manhattan Residence*—has many different categories of subjects from which to select for a subject sample. Waterston chose to study a group of HIV-positive or possibly HIV-positive homeless women residing at a shelter in a metropolitan area. Her data analysis began with a comparison of the characteristics of this study group with those of other, similar groups of at-risk women. By revealing the specific characteristics of the study group that were of interest, she distinguished it from other groups that were not included.

Verifying a Theory

When conducting a grounded theory research study for the purpose of verifying an existing theory, the researcher focuses on finding information that corroborates the existing concept. In the process, the researcher generates new theories only for the purpose of adjusting or modifying the original theory. No new theories are sought. Neither Glaser nor Strauss says much about this potential use for the grounded theory method, emphasizing instead its role in generating new theory.

Generating Theory

This is the primary purpose of grounded theory research; the researcher's main goal is the systematic generation of new theories from the data collected. There are two broad types of theory that can be generated through this process: substantive theory and formal theory.

Substantive theory addresses specific empirical or applied tasks in public administration, such as police and fire department community relations, management development programs and employee training, solid waste disposal, water purity, road construction, and city planning.

Formal theory, on the other hand, deals with broader, often philosophical issues, such as public participation in the democratic process, authority and power in management situations, and reward systems.

Both of these applications are what Glaser and Strauss (1967, 32–33) identified as "middle-range," meaning they fall somewhere between practical working hypotheses in the everyday conduct of an administrator's job and all-inclusive "grand theories," such as global warming. It is important to note that both of these types of theories must be grounded in data if they are to be accepted as relevant.

Stage 3: Select a Group to Study

According to Strauss and Corbin (1998), determining where to go to get the data needed for a research study remains one of the major issues that confront grounded theory researchers. Researchers need to know who can provide the information that illustrates the central or core concept in the study. Strauss and Corbin call this the *theoretical sampling* problem, defining it as the process of picking the sources that can provide the most information about the research topic. The aim of theoretical sampling is "to maximize opportunities to compare events, incidents, or happenings to determine how a category varies in terms of its properties and dimensions" (202). This suggests that the researcher must be more concerned with ensuring the *representativeness* of the sample than in the concept of randomness. Researchers are encouraged to carefully select the subjects from whom information will be acquired. This becomes even more important as the study progresses. Sampling becomes more specific with time because the theory that is emerging must eventually control the sample selection. Once some categories are established, all further sampling must be focused on developing, solidifying, and enriching the formed categories. Glaser and Strauss (1967, 47) stated it this way in their description of their invention of the technique:

> The basic question in theoretical sampling is: what groups or subgroups does one turn to next in data collections. And for what theoretical purpose? In short, how

does the [researcher] select multiple comparison groups? The possibilities of multiple comparisons are infinite, and so groups must be chosen according to theoretical criteria.

Stage 4: Collect Research Data

There are no restrictions on how data are collected in a grounded theory design. However, most researchers use personal interviews, simple or naturalistic observation, narratives, and document or artifact analysis. One of the distinctive characteristics of the grounded theory method is that the data collection, coding, and interpretation stages of the research are carried out in concert, not as individual activities. One leads to the other, then on to the next, and back again. These steps "should blur and intertwine continually, from the beginning of an investigation to its end" (Glaser and Strauss 1967, 43).

Grounded theory methodology can be used for arriving at theories from data that are collected in any type of social research—quantitative and qualitative. All theories are developed for one or both of two fundamental purposes: to explain or to predict.

Stage 5: Open Coding of Data

Coding is the process of applying some conceptually meaningful set of identifiers to the concepts, categories, and characteristics. The key things to remember about open coding are that it is always the initial step in data analysis and that its purpose is to establish (or discover) categories and their properties.

Open coding is the free assignment of data to what the researcher sees as the naturally appearing groupings of ideas in the data (Lee 1999). The researcher creates as many categories as needed. These can be looked upon as the fundamental, explanatory factors that identify the central research concept. Each category contains as many bits of data as are found to fit in that category. Data bits are more or less indivisible, and the researcher intuitively fits each one into just one category.

The open coding process continues until one or more "core categories" are established (Strauss 1992). Then the coding process turns either to Strauss and Corbin's axial coding, using preconceived categories, or proceeds directly to the theoretical coding identified by Glaser and Strauss (1997); see also Glaser (1992). Axial coding is the process of assigning categories into more-inclusive groupings. Strauss and Corbin urged the researcher to use the six second-level classifications they proposed. Lee (1999), on the other hand, following the original Glaser and Strauss (1967) model, called for the researcher to propose the axial categories.

Table 19.1

Tactics for Generating Meaning in Conceptual Categories

1. Counting	7. Particular to general
2. Noting patterns, themes	8. Factoring
3. Seeing plausibility	9. Relationships
4. Clustering	10. Finding intervening variables
5. Making metaphors	11. Chain of evidence
6. Splitting variables	12. Theoretical coherence

Source: Adapted from Miles and Huberman 1984, 215.

The researcher first comes up with several categories that seem to bridge all the open-coded categories. Second, the researcher examines all the open categories to see which fit within the selected second-level category. The remaining data is then compared across the second researcher-selected broader category; those categories that belong are assigned. The process continues until all the data have been compared against all the second-level categories and classified. Additional axial categories might have to be added to encompass all the data. The term "axial categories" refers to the several major themes or constructs that the researcher selects during the data analysis.

How to Determine Categories from Data

There are no hard and fast rules for grounded theory research (Lee 1999). Even the inventors of the method disagree about how to go about coding and categorizing collected data. There are also many different ways to discover or establish meaningful categorical distinctions in data. Miles and Huberman (1984), for example, discuss twelve different ways to go about developing codes for raw data (Table 19.1).

An example of a code set developed for an educational site study can be found in Miles and Huberman (1984, 58–59). These five broad constructs (categories) and their codes were proposed in the preliminary coding: Innovation Properties (IP), External Context (EC), Internal Context (IC), Adoption Process (AP), Site Dynamics and Transformations (TR). These five constructs are the "core categories" of this study. A different number of characteristics or dimensions was identified for each of the categories. Five of the characteristics that were determined to contribute to the Innovation Properties category were Objectives, Organization, Implied Changes–Classroom, Implied Changes–Organization, and User Salience.

A complete set of definitions was developed for each of the categories and the specific characteristic associated with the category. For example, in the Site Dynamics and Transformations (TR) category, the code TR-START was assigned to data that fell into the Initial User Experience category and characteristic. The definition for this code was: "Emotions, events, problems or concerns, assessments, made by teachers and administrators during the first six months of implementation" (62). Similar definitions are produced for every category/characteristic in the study.

Glaser was adamant that open coding and category building *not* be forced into any preconceived second-level (axial) groupings. Strauss and Corbin, on the other hand, give the researcher more leeway in this decision. As a result, both approaches to grounded theory coding are found in the research literature. There is no disagreement regarding the third (and final) coding process: selective (or *theoretical*) coding.

Stage 6: Theoretical (or Selective) Coding of Data

Theoretical or selective coding is the name given to the process of imposing a final structure on the data and establishing rank-order importance of the conceptual categories (Lee 1999). Just as in the second-level coding process, the researcher proposes a small number of overarching categories. Next, these categories are ordered according to how the researcher sees their potential to contain or explain the collected data. In the third step, the researcher estimates which is the most powerful or important category; all of the data are then judged for their fit in that theoretical category. The researcher then repeats the process, picking a second most important category and all remaining data that fit in this category. The process continues until all data are categorized. The researcher is then ready to develop theory about the phenomenon.

The underlying purpose of all theory is to explain and/or predict. Theories are built in a process that moves from the *specific* (individual examples, incidences, or cases, for example) to the general. In this way, the researcher develops a *theory* that is applicable (explains and/or predicts) to more than the individual example, incidence, or case. The process occurs in the following six stages (after Miller and Fredericks 1996):

1. Preliminary (open) categories are formed from the first data collected.
2. More general or broad categories that include preliminary groupings are formed from this and new data as they are added to the analysis.
3. Categories are further refined and defined.
4. A set of *core* categories is finally accepted.
5. As data are analyzed, they are assigned as characteristics or dimensions of these core categories.
6. Continual comparison may produce a revised coding scheme, which, in turn, may require revisions to the characteristics/dimensions of the codes.

The purpose of the theoretical coding stage is to identify the relationships between categories and their properties as the associations are found in the data.

Stage 7: Develop a Theory

This is the culmination of all preceding activities in the process: forming a theory that is grounded in the data. Although it is last in this process model, theory development is not "saved for last." Rather, at each stage in the process of grounded theory the researcher prepares *theoretical memos* in which to record ideas, conclusions, propositions, and theoretical explanations of the phenomena under study. These memos summarize the researcher's conclusions—recorded as they are being formed—and are the gist from which a *theory* or set of hypotheses is developed.

To qualify as a *grounded theory*, it must exhibit these key characteristics (Locke 1996):

- The theory must closely fit the topic and disciplinary area studied.
- The theory must be understandable to and useful to the actors in the studied situation.
- Finally, the theory must be complex enough to account for a large portion if not most of the variation in the area studied.

Often, grounded theory researchers neglect to address the issue of theory in the presentation of their findings. This does not take anything away from the process, however, because in the description of what was discovered from the research and in the specific recommendations, some derived theory *must* underlie the conclusions. It is just a matter of putting it into words. The researcher would not have the confidence necessary to make recommendations regarding the findings unless he or she was sufficiently confident in the theoretical conclusions derived from the data.

A Warning About Grounded Theory

One of the reasons that Strauss and Corbin proposed their six preconceived categories for the second-level or axial coding step was that their graduate students were having great difficulty in conceptualizing the necessary categories for collected data. Lee (1999, 50) also commented on the difficulty of the method:

> Grounded theory is a long-term, labor intensive, and time-consuming process. It requires multiple waves of data collection, with each wave of data based on theoretical sampling. In addition, the iterative process should continue until a theoretical saturation is achieved. Given all this, researchers should avoid grounded theory approaches unless they can commit substantial resources to a study.

Grounded Theory Research in Practice

Example 1: Participation in Public Administration Policy Making

King, Feltey, and Susel (1998) used grounded theory methodology in their study of the underlying causes of public antipathy in the political process and ways to improve participation in public administration policy-making decisions. Using personal interviews and focus group discussions, they gathered data from private citizens and public administrators from several communities in Ohio. Focus-group members were asked to respond freely to four broad questions: (1) how more effective public participation can be achieved, (2) what public participation means to the participant, (3) what the barriers to participation are, and (4) what advice focus-group members had for people trying to bring about more, and more diverse, participation.

The analysis occurred in two stages. First, in the open stage of coding, the transcribed interviews were coded by each researcher working independently and using a qualitative form of content analysis. Second, the researchers synthesized the individually coded responses to come up with a set of categories and themes. These were discussed in detail in the final report. Specific quotations from respondents were woven throughout the narrative, thus providing insightful reinforcement of the thematic concepts that the researchers drew from the data.

King, Feltey, and Susel identified three categories of barriers to effective public participation: contemporary lifestyles, existing administrative practices, and current techniques for participation. The pressures and complexity of daily life, together with certain demographic factors such as class, income, education, and family size, and a breakdown in traditional neighborhood ties, were identified as probable causes for the lack of public participation in the communities studied. Existing administrative practices, such as abbreviating the time allowed for public contribution and waiting too long to call for public input in the policy development process, and some administrators' perception of participation as a threat, also hindered the amount and quality of participation. Finally, there was widespread agreement that current techniques used to gain public participation—such as the public meeting—were inadequate and, often, entirely ineffective.

The theory generated from this research included a three-part proposal for dealing with the three sets of barriers to participation. First, citizens within the community must be "empowered" and, at the same time, educated in ways to organize and to research issues and policies. Second, public administrators must be reeducated; their traditional role of "expert manager" must be replaced with one of "cooperative participant," or "partner." Administrators must also develop their interpersonal skills, including listening, team building, and the like. Finally, the structures and processes of administration must be changed to make it easier for the public to become involved and to contribute to the policy formation process.

Example 2: Recruitment of Employees

Strauss and Corbin have edited a volume of research studies—*Grounded Theory in Practice* (1997)—that illustrates a variety of applications of the grounded theory approach to research in the fields of health, sociology, business and public administration, and social psychology. Polish sociologist Krysztof Konecki's study of the recruiting process was done while he was enrolled in Anselm Strauss's grounded theory seminar at the University of California. Konecki conducted a series of twenty intensive interviews with employment recruiters, one with an employment candidate, and one with a company that used executive search firms. He also included previously published case study descriptions of the search process.

The Konecki study is noteworthy primarily for its clear, detailed description of his application of the Strauss and Corbin third-level, axial coding of the collected data. He compared the data from different types and sizes of search firms and wrote a number of theoretical memos to himself about the collected material. He then developed a conceptual matrix, subjecting the open-coded ideas to Strauss and Corbin's six established conditional categories of causal conditions, phenomena, context, intervening conditions, actions/ strategies, and consequences.

Konecki theorized that the effectiveness of an employment search process is affected by five conditions: work conditions, organizational factors, and interactional, market, and cultural conditions. He concluded that grounded theory methodology is "a very useful tool for the reconstruction of conditions and combinations of the conditions of a category" (Konecki 1997).

Other papers in the Strauss and Corbin book of example applications include studies on identity, physicians' interpretations of patient pain, abused women's self-definition, scientific knowledge about cancer, reproductive science, the evolution of medical technology, tuberculosis, and collective identity.

Example 3: Small Business and Public Policy

Cook and Barry (1995) used the grounded theory method to research the public policy interactions of managers and owners of small businesses. They chose the grounded theory method because of what they termed the "paucity of work" in the area and because of a desire to build a rich description of the business owners' ideas and beliefs about public policy and their ability to help shape it. Over the two-year study, Cook and Barry conducted thirty-one in-depth interviews with the owners of twenty-seven firms and with four government administrators. In addition to these in-depth interviews, Cook and Barry also attended a series of meetings scheduled by trade associations with a government-relations focus; more than fifty additional executives participated in the meetings. Concluding their data-gathering process, the researchers examined more than 150 public documents, papers, memos, and newspaper stories.

Acknowledging what is clearly one of the major disadvantages of the method—an overabundance of raw data—Cook and Barry reported that their initial transcripts produced more than 700 pages of data. Before they could code and analyze the data, they were forced to produce detailed abstracts of each transcript, thus eliminating some 60 percent of the original data.

Two levels of coding were then used on the remaining data: "received" coding and "emergent" coding. The first level was derived from the researchers' review of the literature in the field, their prior learning and biases, and categories that the interviewees themselves used. These were primarily descriptive and definitional in nature. These codes were then merged into broader codes—called *overarching dimensions*—that related to issues, issue characteristics, and the influence process.

In the sense of *theory*, Cook and Barry found it "evident" that interactions between owners of small firms and policy makers helped to create a system for interpreting and making sense of the process. These interactions determined (1) whether a small business executive would commit to working on a policy issue, and (2) how he or she would carry out that work. Executives tended to agree to work on issues that they believed they had some possibility of influencing and to ignore policy questions that they felt were beyond their reach.

Case Examples

Example 1

As a student in your university's Master's Degree in Public Administration program, you are asked to work with a team of three other students to design and conduct a research study dealing with a consortium of eleven public schools that intend to introduce global education into their curricula. According to the National Council for the Social Studies, the purpose of global education is to help students develop the knowledge, skills, and attitudes needed to live in a world of limited natural resources and wide ethnic diversity, cultural pluralism, and growing interdependence among nations and people (Lessor 2000).

The university's School of Public Administration has received a grant to fund a project involving graduate students working with and studying elementary and secondary school teachers. The overall objective of the grant is to improve education by widening the vision of teachers and students through instruction in global education. The objective of your study is to *develop theory* on the factors that influence the spread of global perspectives and actions in educational institutions. In order to facilitate infusion of global thinking and acting, your team needs to understand how successful teachers go about adopting global thinking, introducing global educational materials and methods, and, in the broadest sense, functioning as change agents in their schools.

Example 2

You have been assigned the task of designing and carrying out a research study to establish how life situations and extraneous events influence the onset of drug use and drug-using behaviors among an inner-city population of adult women (Roberts 1999). You are convinced that the personal and private nature of the issue, together with the lack of formal structure or cohesiveness in the sample, justifies your adopting a grounded theory approach to conducting the research.

Before beginning your study, you sought and were granted approval from the university's ethics committee for human subjects research. You then concluded that the best way to capture the subtleties of people's reactions to the study topic was to tape-record a series of personal, in-depth interviews with a cross-section of participants who fit the defined sample profile. You select subjects from a list of women receiving subsidized medical care at the university's medical school. To ensure that participants show up for their interviews, you have received permission to pay subjects $15 for each one-hour interview in which they participate. To guarantee anonymity, you will ask all subjects to use fictitious names.

Although the grounded theory method calls for interviews to be unstructured with *no* preconceived topics to cover, you believe that this study demands that you develop and follow a loosely structured schedule of topics in order to ensure that the research team will focus the interviews on the events that surround the phenomena of interest illicit drug use and the social conditions affecting its onset. You begin open coding of the information during and after the first interview and continue until all interviews are completed.

Summary

Grounded theory is a general qualitative research method that can be used on any data or combination of data. It was developed initially for use with both quantitative and qualitative data. However, quantitative data often are expensive and difficult to obtain. On the other hand, qualitative data are inexpensive to collect, they can be very rich in meaning and observation, and they are often rewarding to collect and analyze. So, by default and because of its growing use, grounded theory research today is linked to *qualitative* data; it is classified as a qualitative method that uses symbolic interaction (Glaser 1992).

The grounded theory research process begins with the researcher focusing on some area of study—a phenomenon, circumstance, trend, or behavior in any of the social or administrative sciences. Using observation, interviewing, and other methods, the researcher gathers relevant data from as many different sources as are available. Analysis begins with the researcher grouping the data into categories and assigning codes. Through a process of continually comparing data among categories, theory may be generated.

Grounded theory is a long-term, laborious, and time-consuming process. Before starting a grounded theory project, the researcher should have a substantial grounding in the area of interest and the ability to formulate broad, meaningful concepts about the topic. This does not mean that a "study problem" must be identified in advance but rather that the researcher must be conversant enough with a phenomenon to justify an open research project in the area. Furthermore, grounded theory research requires multiple levels of data collection, each based on theoretical sampling and continual comparisons, and the continuation of the coding and classifying process until a theoretical saturation is achieved. Researchers are advised to avoid grounded theory approaches unless they can commit substantial resources to a study.

Suggested Reading

Glaser, Barney G. 1992. *Emergence vs. Forcing: Basics of Grounded Theory Analysis.* Mill Valley, CA: Sociology Press.

Glaser, Barney, and Anselm Strauss. 1967. *The Discovery of Grounded Theory: Strategies for Qualitative Research.* Chicago: Aldine.

Lee, Thomas W. 1999. *Using Qualitative Methods in Organizational Research.* Thousand Oaks, CA: Sage.

Miles, Mathew B., and A. Michael Huberman. 1984. *Qualitative Data Analysis: A Sourcebook of New Methods.* Beverly Hills, CA: Sage.

Strauss, Anselm, and Juliet Corbin. 1998. *Basics of Qualitative Research: Techniques and Procedures for Developing Grounded Theory.* 2d ed. Thousand Oaks, CA: Sage.

———, eds. 1997. *Grounded Theory in Practice.* Thousand Oaks, CA: Sage.

20 Ethnography in Public Administration Research

Ethnographic methods are not employed as often in public administration research as is the case study approach, but when they are they can provide great quantities of important information. These study designs typically require more time to conduct than public administrators are able to devote to their research projects. In the parent disciplines of anthropology and sociology, ethnographic studies make take six months to a year or more to complete. When they can be used in public administration research, however, they have the power to produce powerful narratives that provide deep insight into the needs of society.

A hallmark of all ethnographic research is the practice of producing ethnographic reports with *thick description*, which refers to research notes that exhibit great depth and detailed complexity. An example cited by Neuman (2000) is the description of a social event that lasts only three minutes, but takes up many pages of descriptive narrative. This use of detailed description means that ethnographic methods can be an excellent design choice when the study objective is to provide deep background information for the formation of long-term, strategic public policy. On the other hand, ethnographic methods are generally not appropriate when a management decision must be made immediately on the basis of the findings of the research.

The Historical Background of Ethnography

Despite their drawbacks, ethnographic methods have a long and important history in research in the social and human sciences. They can be traced at least as far back as the Industrial Revolution, if not longer (Neuman 2000, 346).

Industrialization and the Social Sciences

A by-product of the industrialization of Western society was the belief of some observers that factory labor was dehumanizing society; unskilled workers were often seen as just another easily replaceable component in the production process. Beginning in the nineteenth century, however, concern over the deteriorating human condition in tenements and factories resulted in calls for changes in the way society treated its citizens. An increasingly educated public, the clergy, and a few in the governing elite came to recognize that the deterioration in social conditions needed to be stopped and, if possible, reversed. These early critics looked to *science* for solutions to the problems of the new industrialized society.

This faith in the power of science to produce answers to social problems encouraged adoption of a scientific approach to the study of the social problems and needed changes. If advances in the natural sciences and technology could be *profitably* applied to problems in industrial invention and innovation, these critics reasoned, why couldn't these advances also be applied to solving social problems? If science could be used to improve production, why couldn't it also be used to improve everyone's quality of life?

The new *social*, or *human* sciences that emerged out of the intellectual vitality that characterized the nineteenth century included sociology, psychology, and anthropology. Sociology emerged from early studies of the social ills that were identified as unwanted by-products of the industrialization process. At about the same time, early attempts at establishing a systematic way of explaining human behavior and mental aberrations resulted in the modern science of psychology. The tradition born in early travel stories ultimately forged a scientific way of studying indigenous cultures; this social science was called anthropology.

In each of these new scientific disciplines, curiosity about what was happening to society resulted in research that had the objective of understanding (1) why social problems occurred, and (2) what could (or *ought* to) be done to change society in order to improve the lot of the aged, children, the working poor, and the otherwise disenfranchised.

Early Field Research

The early missionaries and adventurers who traveled with European traders and explorers on voyages to new lands encountered new and, to them, strange cultures. Early reports of these encounters became extremely popular. Often, however, these reports were little more than lurid or bizarre tales of fancy, with little basis in reality. Despite their limited basis in fact—or possibly because of it—the tales often gained widespread distribution in books and the popular press of the time. Before long, these new social scientists were permitted to join the many voyages of discovery that were taking place. Some of these scientific expeditions were carried out specifically to study primitive cultures before they disappeared, were eradicated by disease, or were subsumed into the Western economic tradition.

These early researchers wanted to understand how the different primitive societies developed and how each one developed its own unique ways of coping with social phenomena. The result was a body of descriptive literature.

As these reports circulated in Europe and the Americas, a few of the early social scientists saw a need to apply what they called "scientific rigor" to the research that was being done. They turned to the research methodologies similar to those that had been emerging in the natural sciences, adopting the positivist model with its quantitative emphasis and causal focus. However, interpreting the coping behaviors, attitudes, and other cultural phenomena of primitive peoples was difficult, if not impossible, with the traditional positivist methodology that was applied. The researchers therefore modified the positivist approach by adding more verbal description and explanation to their investigations and reports. This new way of doing science became what we now call fieldwork, and the scientific disciplines that followed became the social sciences of anthropology and sociology.

Anthropology Research

Today, anthropology is divided into three main types: *cultural anthropology*, *physical anthropology*, and *archaeology*. Of the three, only cultural anthropology found a place in the research conducted in public administration.

Cultural Anthropology

What was traditional anthropology has become what is now called *cultural anthropology*. The *culturalists* concentrate on describing existing social cultures, no matter how small, distant, or foreign. The research method they use most often is called *ethnography*. Ethnographers often live with the groups they study for long periods of time.

Cultural anthropology, originally devoted almost exclusively to the study of distant, often primitive, cultures, was soon found to be an appropriate way of studying less complex but still modern world societies that had remained in relative isolation from the emerging industrialized world (Alasuutari 1995). From that expanded application it was not long before anthropology and its research tool, ethnography, were seen to have a place in the study of modern cultures and subcultures.

Physical Anthropology

The physical anthropologists followed Darwin's lead in studying the evolution of humankind. Physical anthropologists are concerned with determining the earliest primate ancestors of humans, the physical characteristics of ethnic groups, and so on. Physical anthropologists are sometimes called in to assist forensic scientists in the identification of crime and accident victims and to aid in the design of living and work spaces, including furniture and tools.

Archaeology

Archaeologists were at one time included under the cultural anthropology umbrella, but found their own niche by focusing on studies of ancient and unknown material cultures. Today, however, modern archaepologists can be found analyzing relatively recently deposited cultural artifacts. An example is the archaeological study of garbage dumps in order to analyze trends in fashion, invention, and other cultural phenomena.

Sociology Research

The traditional focus of sociology—another discipline that uses ethnographic methods in research—has also changed. Initially, the purpose of sociological research was to identify cause-and-effect relationships between the perceived ills and abuses of the new industrial society and the lives of adults and children forced to live and work in crowded, dangerous, and often unsanitary conditions. Sociologists worked closely with the earliest social workers to discover how modern industrial society functioned and how to resolve social ills. However, as Alasuutari (1995, 24) has noted, "many of the post-war [i.e., World War II], 'post-industrial' developments have evaded the conceptual net provided by established academic sociology, which in many countries became a tool for social engineering and social statistics." As a result, the rationale behind traditional sociological research is no longer the only purpose behind such research.

Because of the continually evolving nature of the focus of study for the social sciences, a new direction for ethnographic research emerged. Today, ethnographic studies are carried out in the inner cities of modern societies, in suburban and rural settings, in cross-cultural communities, and in large and small organizations; the purpose is to investigate the many ways that the social forces of culture and subculture impact people. More important today, however, is the emphasis on *interpreting* social behavior that has replaced the earlier model of simply *describing* a society. The role of the ethnographer has taken on the important task of contributing to the formation of public policy.

There is a fine line dividing sociological and anthropological ethnographic studies. Probably the easiest way to distinguish the two is to remember that sociologists are concerned with the impact of social circumstances and situations on people, whereas anthropologists pay greater attention to the role of culture and/or subculture on the behaviors of people. There is a place for both emphases in public administration research.

Through an eclectic process of trial and error, anthropologists and sociologists developed a way of conducting research that allowed them to meet their study objectives in all kinds of social and cultural settings. The name given to this method was *ethnography*. Researchers in public administration have also adopted this method of research. Ethnography is one of several important approaches for the study of *culture* and the act of governance, the formation of public policy, and the administration of diverse agencies and functions of government. The research conducted in these disciplines has often had a great influence on public policy.

Ethnographic Research

The practice of anthropology—and its principal research method, ethnography—evolved and expanded its focus over the last several centuries. Traditional positivist methods used to study primitive cultures and societies were found inappropriate for developing understandings of modern cultures and behaviors. Anthropologists in Europe and the United States eventually supplemented traditional research methods with a new approach to the study of primitive cultures and societies that was designed to improve the study of humans in social settings. A key element of this new approach was its emphasis on specific ways to prepare field notes and rules for writing about cultural events. The name of this new research approach was *ethnography*—which means graphically describing a society or social group. The new data-gathering process was called *fieldwork*.

The model presented in Figure 20.1 illustrates how anthropology, sociology, and psychology, with their different but related research focuses, have each contributed to the development of ethnographic research in public administration.

Ethnography, Ethology, or Ethnology?

Several different terms are used in reports of ethnographic research. Among these are "ethnography," "ethnology," and "ethology." *Ethnography* means

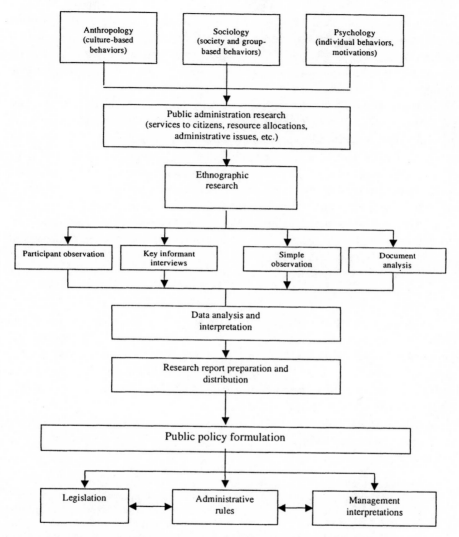

Figure 20.1 **A Model of the Relationships Between Social Sciences, Ethnography, Public Administration Research, and Public Policy**

the descriptive study of living cultures, while *ethnology* refers to the activity of *using* the information gathered by ethnography (Columbia On-line Encyclopedia 2000). Thus, a public administrator might use an ethnological report in the process of framing public policy. *Ethology* is simply a somewhat different approach to the research process; it refers to the less intense practice of simple observation (Jones 1996). The science of ethology is most commonly encountered in the context of the study of animal behavior, although a branch seeks to apply ethological principles to human behavior as well. Ethnography involves actively observing, recording, and explaining why a culture is described in the way it is by the ethnographer; it is sometimes used as a synonym for "participant observation." Ethology is used as a synonym for "simple" or unobtrusive observation.

For the ethologist, however, the process is not participatory. Rather, the researcher simply observes and records what is taking place, often conducting controlled behavioral experiments with animals and human beings. As a nonparticipating observer, the researcher is always an outsider, on hand simply to record what is seen, and never becoming a member of the group under study. The reports of ethologists tend to be primarily descriptive or explanatory and do not involve interpretation of the observed social setting.

Jones suggested a way to differentiate between ethnological and ethological research involving human behavior. The key differentiating characteristic is whether the research is conducted to develop a theory or to provide background information needed to make a management decision. Figure 20.2 illustrates that, despite the different steps involved, the two approaches are very similar.

All ethnographers immerse themselves in the day-to-day activities of the group they are studying in order to (1) describe the setting in as much detail as possible (a process called *thick description*), and (2) to come up with some theoretical ideas that allow them to interpret and explain what they have seen and heard. The goal is to learn as much as they can about the behaviors and social processes taking place in the culture.

Terry Williams (1996, 31–32), writing about his ethnographic study of the cocaine subculture in New York after-hours clubs during the 1970s and 1980s, defined ethnography as:

> a science of cultural description; more than that, it is a methodology. It is a way of looking at people, a way of looking at a culture. It is recording how people perceive, construct and interact in their own private world. It embraces the subjective realm of the individuals it seeks to understand. It defines the group the way the group defines itself.

Ethnographers live, work, and play with their study populations for long periods of time. Their aim is to be absorbed into the group. Their underlying objective is to be accepted as a nonthreatening, nonintrusive member of the group. Then, events and interrelationships will unfold as they would naturally, as if the observer were not in attendance. This process, which is called "gaining entry," is the key to a successful research project. Without acceptance, without entry into the inner workings of the group, the researcher remains an outsider, perceived as a threat and subsequently either shunned or lied to, at best.

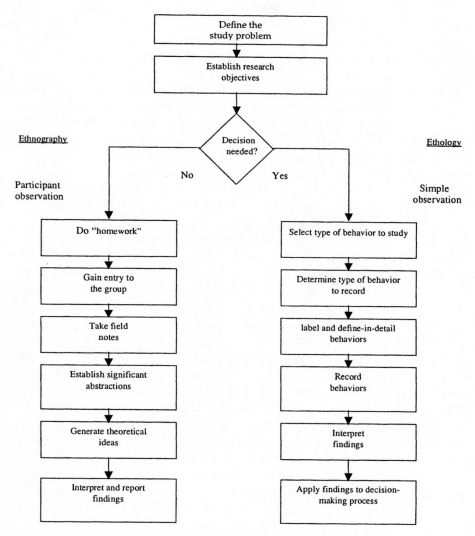

Figure 20.2 Fieldwork Processes for Ethnography and Ethology
Source: Adapted from Jones 1996, chapter 3.

The process of living with a social group (*doing fieldwork*) involves observing and recording individuals' behaviors. The ethnographer summarizes these field notes into a larger descriptive generalization that purports to describe the behavior of the larger society. The researcher must then develop *subjective descriptions* that are based on a large number of *generalizations*. In making these generalizations, the ethnographer moves from the *specific* to the *general*. That is, the behaviors of one person or a small group are used to infer that those behaviors are also those of the larger groups in similar circumstances. The ethnographer also develops *interpretations* of the observed behaviors; the question "why" should be answered to the best of the ethnographer's ability.

According to Jones (1996), one of the major attractions of ethnography for field researchers is that it permits them to develop meaningful, coherent pictures of the social group and setting. Researchers get to see the phenomenon as a whole, in all of its complexity, and not just bits and pieces.

For most of the early history of ethnography, study results were often little more than simple descriptions; interpretation of the event, setting, or behavior was left to the reader. This often resulted in readers' doubts about the *validity* of ethnographic generalizations. The following statement illustrates the older paradigm: "Ethnographic generalizations are by themselves only best fit statements about the incidence or frequency of occurrences in the society. By themselves they say little or nothing about what goes with what" (Cohen 1973, 37–38). Cohen's solution to this problem was to call for more correlational or *causal* research into ethnography. This, he believed, would improve validity by improving interpretation.

In its earliest applications, "doing ethnography" meant studying isolated, primitive cultures to develop a descriptive profile or summary of the social practices of the group of people (Naroll and Cohen 1973). Today, however, ethnographers are not required to seek out isolated, primitive groups for their research; rather, there are no limits to how and where ethnographic field research can be applied. Ethnography, like its parent discipline anthropology, is not restricted to the study of distant or nonliterate cultures. One reason for this is that there are few if any societies left untouched anywhere in the world. Most have been studied and restudied to the point that little new about their "primitiveness" can be learned. The world has become smaller, and distant, diverse societies no longer live in "glorious isolation." As Alasuutari (1995, 24) has noted, "the 'Other' have moved next door, and 'western' artifacts, television programmes, and economic networks have invaded practically the entire globe."

What Do Ethnographers Do?

According to Whiting and Whiting (1973) ethnographers collect samples of types of behavior in order to understand the cognitive and social-structure *regularities* in a society. Ethnographers study personality, the roles people adopt, economic systems, political systems, religious systems, and many other aspects of all types of social organizations and systems.

Duveen (2000) has described the work that ethnographers do as the production of thick description, a two-part process. First, the researcher writes down everything that he or she sees. Duveen referred to this "thick description" of events, settings, and behaviors as capturing the sense of the social actors, groups, and institutions being described. Second, the researcher's own interpretations of what is recorded influences the final description. The two-part process of observation-interpretation moves from one activity to the other, then backward to repeat itself again and again.

Figure 20.3 is a chart illustrating the key processes involved in conducting and presenting the results of an ethnographic study. It illustrates the several different layers of observation-interpretation that characterize good ethnographic fieldwork, field notes, and final report preparation.

Ethnographic methods are employed in a number of different forms. Examples of these variations are *ethnomethodology, community-based ethnography*, and *ethological methodology*. Each of these research approaches has its own advocates and detractors, but all are considered to fall under the larger category of *field research*.

Ethnomethodology

Ethnomethodology has been defined by Neuman (2000, 348) as "the study of commonsense knowledge." Combining themes from sociology and philosophy, it is usually seen as an application of *phenomenology* (Adler and Adler 1998). Researchers who follow this approach focus their concern on how people go about living their everyday lives. Ethnomethodologists study mundane, everyday behaviors in exceptionally close detail. They often use mechanical and electronic methods of recording the behavior of people. They then analyze in minute detail these audio- and videotapes, films, and other records, using what Adler and Adler (1998, 99) have described as "an intricate notational system that allows [them] to view the conversational overlaps, pauses, and intonations to within one-tenth of a second . . . they have directed a particular emphasis toward conversation analysis."

Community-Based Ethnography

Community-based ethnography, also called community-based research (CBR), is closely associated with the critical approach known as *action research* (Stringer 1997) and has been used primarily in research in education. Stringer described the purpose of community-based research as a way of providing workers in professional and community groups with knowledge that is normally available only to academic researchers. As with all action research, CBR is designed to help people expand their knowledge and understanding

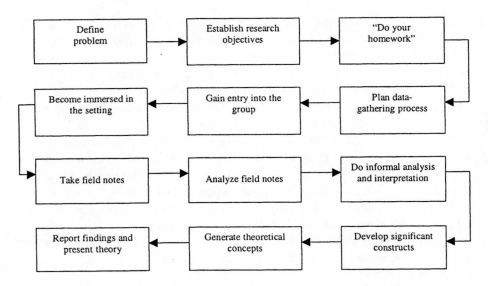

Figure 20.3 Ethnographic Fieldwork, Analysis, and Presentation Processes
Source: Adapted from Jones 1996.

of a situation so they can come up with effective solutions to the problems they face on their own. Everyone—researcher and researched—is involved in the process. Stringer described CBR as

> intrinsically participatory; its products are not outsider accounts, portrayals, or re-ports, but collaborative accounts written from the emic—or insider—perspective of the group. Such accounts, grounded in hermeneutic, meaning-making processes of dialogue, negotiation, and consensus, provide the basis for group, community, or organization action. People can review their activities, develop plans, and resolve problems, initiate projects, or restructure an organization. (17–18)

Ethological Methodology

Ethological research addresses many of the same issues addressed by traditional ethnography. Initially, the method focused primarily on animal behavior—Charles Darwin, for example, is considered one of the pioneers in this field of research. Today, however, this approach is often used in organizational research, where it is employed for identifying and describing behavior in social settings.

The approach taken in an ethology study involves *simple observation*, which can be either visible or hidden (unobtrusive). Organ and Bateman (1991), discussing ethological observation in the context of organizational behavior research, referred to the method as *naturalistic observation.* They identified a number of appealing characteristics, as well as some of the shortcomings, of this approach.

Possibly the most important advantage is what Organ and Bateman called the *contextual richness* that is possible with observation (36). This includes more than the thick description that characterizes ethnographic field notes. It also refers to the fact that this type of research has enjoyed wide acceptance over the years, with results published in many articles, books, autobiographies, newspaper stories, conversations, and speeches. In addition to this extensive body of available literature, the natural experience that researchers gain from working in and dealing with organizations of all types, sizes, and purposes is also an advantage. This is what is referred to as the *richness in personal insight* of naturalistic observation in organizational research. Summarizing their critique of the method, Organ and Bateman concluded:

> [Simple] observation is an attractive method of research because it confronts its subject head-on. It deals with raw, real-world behavior. Because the data are rich with the drama of human existence, it is easy to relate to accounts of these studies (37).

The main disadvantage of observation is that it often results in a report bias that is traceable to people's natural tendency to exercise *selective perception* and *selective retention.* Selective perception means that from all the myriad stimuli that people encounter, they see what they want to see, what they are interested in, what they think is important. Whether they do so consciously or unconsciously, people ignore much of what else goes on.

This idea has been suggested by a number of different investigators. John Dewey, for example, noted that human perception is never "neutral." Rather, human intelligence and knowledge, what we think of as *past experience,* always influence perception. Furthermore, judgment is involved in all perception. Otherwise, the perception is nothing more than a form of what Dewey called *sensory excitation* (cited in Phillips 1987, 9).

According to Hanson (1958), the theories, hypotheses, frameworks, and background knowledge held by researchers have the power to unconsciously influence everything that is observed. Therefore, observation cannot have a neutral foundation.

Selective retention means that people usually remember what they think was said, what they wanted to hear, what they believe occurred, or what fits within their personal framing of the issue. Hence, what is remembered is inherently subjective; it can never be considered the "truth."

Because observation is recorded as the field notes of one or more researchers, it will always contain what the researcher *feels* is important. Field notes will often omit what the researcher believes to be trivial or unimportant. We are all drawn to the dramatic or exciting in situations—it makes for interesting reading, even when it has little or no bearing on the central issue. Both field notes and the material that is eventually included in a report pass through a filter formed from the perceptions and memory of events held by the researcher.

Therefore, researchers must always struggle with the answerable question: Would another observer have drawn the same conclusion from these events? Researchers use thick description in an attempt to provide an answer.

Doing Fieldwork

All variations of ethnography involve fieldwork. *Ethnographic fieldwork* includes such activities as (1) engaging in participant observation, (2) collecting genealogies, (3) recording conversations, (4) writing field notes, (5) interpreting the findings, and (6) writing up the field notes and interpretations as reports. Field notes describe events, incidents that catch the researcher's eye, in addition to anything and everything that is deemed relevant to the study at hand at the moment it occurs.

According to Fetterman (1989), fieldwork is the key activity in all ethnographic research designs. The basic concepts of anthropology, the methods and techniques of collecting data, and analysis of the data are the fundamental elements of "doing ethnography." The selection of methods and equipment to use—including tape recorders, videotaping, and actual interviewing—is a major decision in fieldwork. "This process becomes product through analysis at various stages in ethnographic work—in field notes, memoranda, and interim reports, but most dramatically in the published report, article, or book" (12).

Anthropologists and sociologists who study cultures firsthand have determined that the best way to do their fieldwork is with a process called *participant observation*. The early ethnographic researchers chose participant observation as their preferred way to function in the field for many reasons. One was the great distances they often had to travel to reach the study society. They were therefore forced to spend long periods with the groups under study simply to justify the cost of the trip and the physical hardship they endured. Living for long periods of time in the primitive community, sometimes in the same huts or shelters as the members of the society under study, these early researchers were forced into being participants in order to survive—let alone understand what they were observing.

According to Bernard (1995), participant observation requires researchers to get close to people, making them comfortable enough to permit the researcher to observe and record observations about their lives. Establishing rapport with people in the new community means learning how to act in such a way that the people go about their day-to-day business when the researcher appears. Possibly most important, it means being able to retreat from the group-member role to think about what has been learned and write about it convincingly.

A reason for the evolution of ethnography from its former exclusive application to primitive cultures to now include research in today's settings was simply the long period of time needed to manually collect ethnographic information. Ethnographies are built on a combination of observations and extensive interviewing (Whiting and Whiting 1973), and these take time. Observation, regardless of the society or culture upon which it is focused, can be directed toward many different topics of investigation.

Whiting and Whiting have identified six subjects of potential focus for research: (1) an activity of some kind, (2) a larger category of acts, such as gang behavior, (3) an object or person that is the center of attention for a larger group of persons, (4) a person who functions as a representative of a status category, (5) a pair of individuals (a *dyad*), or (6) a setting for a social event.

Ethnography in Public Administration Research

When public administration evolved into an academic discipline in its own light during the early decades of the twentieth century, its own journals, professional associations, conferences, and academic departments soon followed. Bits and pieces from all the social and behavioral sciences were incorporated into its structure—and its research methodology. It is important to remember that *all* the tools and methods used in public administration research were invented for other purposes. Sociology, anthropology, archaeology, philosophy, economics, and business administration: all these and more have contributed to the lexicon of public administration research method.

Ethnography has become one of the most widely applied qualitative research methods in public administration (PA). It has been shown to be a valuable tool for gathering information about behaviors embedded in, and specific to, *cultures* and *subcultures*. It is often used to identify administrative options for making decisions on matters of public policy. Fetterman (1989, 11) defined the method and its focus this way:

> Ethnography is the art and science of describing a group or culture. The description may be of a small tribal group in some exotic land or a classroom in middle-class suburbia. [The] ethnographer writes about the routine, daily lives of people. The more predictable patterns of human thought and behavior are the focus of inquiry.

Ethnography methods are used in public administration to analyze and diagnose the *culture* and *operating climate* of organizations (Wilson 1989; Schein 1992). In this application, the purpose of the research is to improve the *practice* of administration in the public sector, while the ethnographic research itself is a way of acquiring the information that makes such improvement possible.

Yeager (1989, 726) described participant observation as an "old and widely used research method both in public administration and in other fields of study." In public administration use today, it incorporates many different techniques, including simple, group, and unobtrusive observations, depth-interviewing key informants, ethnography, and controlled observation techniques.

> Participant observation includes material that the observer gains directly from personally seeing or hearing an event occur. Often the participant observer establishes personal relationships with subjects and maintains those relationships over a period of time. . . . Rapport and trust are established with subjects to a far greater extent than in other methods. Typically, more exhaustive data are gathered on fewer subjects using participant observation that with other methods.

In public administration, the once traditional activity of spending long periods in the field is neither possible nor desirable because it is not considered to be worth the cost. Rather, the most important part of fieldwork is simply "being there" to observe, ask questions, and write down what is heard and seen (Fetterman 1989). Participant observation, like ethnography, has changed from its original concept of total immersion in a society under study to include new and different topics and locations of study, in addition to a wide variety of data-gathering tools and techniques.

Ethnographic field research requires the most intense connection between the researcher and the subjects of the study (Kornblum 1996); it is not unusual for ethnographers who have lived and worked within a group for many years to take on a self-identity that emphasizes loyalty and connection to the study group rather than to the researcher's prior connection.

While similar in method and analysis, ethnography as it is applied today is far different from the ethnography that evolved with the social sciences more than a century ago. "Ethnography is no longer a method used only to study foreign cultures; it has also become a method to study what is foreign or strange in our society and how social subcultures or subworlds are constructed—the adventure that begins just around the corner" (Flick 1999a, 641).

As ethnography moved beyond its original focus of describing small, distant, and primitive societies or examining the social disruption rooted in communities undergoing industrialization, it was used to study groups in locations that its founders would never have considered. One of these is the modern city.

All facets of urban life are now considered legitimate targets of ethnographic research for the purpose of contributing to the establishment of public policy. Studies have covered the public behaviors of homosexuals, ghetto dwellers, drug users, the urban poor and homeless, school children, and many other subjects. There is apparently no limit to what studies can or should be carried out using an ethnographic approach.

According to Fox (1977, 9), urban anthropologists take several different directions: the anthropology of *urbanism*, the anthropology of *poverty in urban settings*, and the anthropology of *urbanization*. Despite their differences, they all appear to have the following principles in common: First, there is near unanimous agreement among urban anthropologists that cities are important locations for research. Second, urban anthropologists are convinced that anthropology can make "important methodological and theoretical contributions to the study of urban place."

Urbanism Studies

Studies in the ethnology of *urbanism* are concerned with how movement from rural to urban locations has affected individuals, families, and larger groups. These major social movements are seldom seen in the industrialized West; researchers studying the rural-urban phenomenon today are likely to focus their attention on such locations as some poorer areas in Europe, India, Southeast Asia, South and Central America, and other third world regions.

An example of this type of modern ethnographic study is Narotzky's (2000) research with a small population in the rural Vega Baja del Segura district of Valencia in Spain. Narotzky conducted intensive fieldwork in a town of about 5,000 residents. The region is an irrigated plain with a mix of agricultural and industrial economic activities, with the greater contribution now coming from the shoe-making industry. Large shoe factories were established in the region during the 1960s and 1970s. During this period, many single men and women and young families migrated from small farms to the towns where the factories were located. Other families did piecework in their homes. Other people work in small sweatshops that produce shoe parts and components for larger jobbers and finish factories.

Today, a mix of large factories, small family farms, unregulated workshops, jobbers, home-based workers, and migrant farm workers characterizes the economy of the region. Narotzky was interested in how the local population has come to grips with a local, specialized industrial economy that is suffering shocks due to increased global competition. She described the region as one in which production processes are structured in diverse ways and where people tend to shift between different labor relations that vary greatly in their stability. Some people have stable work opportunities, while others do not. A major social problem that arises from this discontinuous character of the workforce is that many workers are unable to gain access to unemployment benefits and other worker welfare programs.

Urban Poverty Studies

Urban poverty is a global phenomenon; organizations as disparate as the United Nations, private foundations, universities, governments, and the World Bank either fund or participate in studies of its causes and effects. Ethnographers study social groups and highly concentrated ethnic subcultures in urban settings such as the ghetto and barrio. They also focus their attention on the homeless, alcoholics and other substance abusers, Native American populations, at-risk youth, and others whom Fox (1977) identified as social groups "whose lifestyles are described as being at the furthest cultural remove from the mainstream world."

Carol Stack (1996) is an example of an ethnographer conducting modern urban poverty studies. Over a three-year period she carried out participant observation in one of the poorest sections of a minority community in a large city in the American Midwest. Most of the residents of the area were unemployed; those with jobs worked in low-paying service jobs that left them little better off than those eligible for welfare. One of the key findings of her study was that families developed large kinship-based exchange networks that included many nonrelated individuals and family units. These networks provided extensive support for their members, helping the residents of the area to adapt to a life of poverty, unemployment or underemployment, and welfare dependency.

Another recent example of ethnographic research in the realm of urban poverty is the 1999 work of urban anthropologist Alisse Waterston: *Love, Sorrow, and Rage: Destitute Women in a Manhattan Residence*. Waterston spent two years studying the residents of a shelter for at-risk women in New York City. She employed what she described as an "interactive approach to data gathering," a practice that is common among qualitative researchers. Her primary method was participant observation, although she also used informal chats and formal tape-recorded, open-ended interviews with both the staff and the residents of the shelter.

Waterston developed the data for her study and final report from themes that emerged from her observation and extensive interviews. Among the themes she included in her study were poverty, homelessness, work, substance abuse, sexual violence, mental illness, AIDS, family and interpersonal relationships, sexuality, race, gender, and food. She found food and preparing meals to be a unifying concept around which many of the other themes were discussed.

Research on Urbanization Issues

Ethnographic research in the anthropology of *urbanization*, while similar to that of urbanism, focuses instead on the larger, evolutional *process* of urbanization that characterizes most modern industrial societies. How societies deal with health and safety concerns, waste management, work, play, and all the many other difficult social issues associated with urban living is the study topic addressed by these social scientists. The nature of the urban locale, cultural roles in society, demography, class organization, and government are all part of the greater area of interest. Fox (1977) further identified the field this way: "[The] interest centers on a process—urbanization—and its consequences for human social existence, rather than involvement with a form—urbanism—and its relations to human society and culture."

Lynne Nakano's 2000 study of volunteerism in modern Japan is an example of an ethnographic study of urbanization's effect on a society. Her study focused on the way some modern Japanese are achieving their self-identity by volunteering to help in the operations of government, nonprofit organizations, schools, corporations, community groups, and other social groupings. This type of study can have great impact upon public policy making, as well as providing significant direction for managers of nonprofit organizations in a community.

In the past, Japanese society held two distinct views. The more recent view was that people must develop themselves through self-expression, while the older, traditional view was that individuals must connect themselves to a social group, such as a firm or school, and define themselves through their commitment to that group. Since the 1990s, however, proponents of a third view—volunteerism—have proposed that *both* camps can be satisfied because volunteerism straddles the divide; it develops the self and contributes to society at the same time.

Nakano analyzed volunteering in a densely populated middle- to lower-middle-class residential neighborhood on the outskirts of Yokohama. The community contained a variety of housing types that reflected a mix of socio-economic lifestyles. On one end of the scale was a 1,040-household public housing project for low-income citizens. Other types ranged from rental apartments and privately owned condominium apartments to single-family detached homes at the top of the scale.

The practice of using volunteer activity for self-identity flourished in the area for several reasons. First, the neighborhood was aging, a trend led by the aged residing in the large public housing project, where one in four residents was sixty-five years old or older—nearly twice the average in Japan today. These older residents were both potential volunteers and the recipients of voluntary services. Second, identifying oneself as a volunteer served as "symbolic leverage" for neighborhood newcomers. "Newcomers" was defined in the largest sense of the word; barely one percent of the population of the region were descendants of the original landowning and farming families. Yet they remained as leaders of many social groupings in the region. Some "newcomers" had lived in the community for more than twenty years. Third, volunteerism was seen as a socially recognized activity that was particularly acceptable for middle-aged women and retired former "salary men," although volunteering was more of a social risk for men than for women. Becoming a volunteer, in fact, often resulted in a promotion in status for female homemakers who became quasi-public figures in their volunteer roles.

An earlier example of an urban ethnographic study is the research carried out by Ulf Hannerz in 1969 among urban blacks on Winston Street in Washington, DC, and described by Fox in his 1977 monograph on urban anthropology. Hannerz's study objective was to identify and describe ways in which ghetto lifestyles and social behavior differed from those in what he called "mainstream America." Hannerz identified four prototypical ghetto residents: mainstreamers, swingers, street families, and street corner men.

An example of a sociological ethnographic study is Alasuutari's (1995) report of his research involving long hours over a period of several months socializing with drinkers in a bar in Finland. He described the role that drinking and darts playing had for regular patrons of the bar. Alasuutari's study constituted a social commentary about a pattern of behavior that was thought to contribute heavily to illness, accidents, and suicide among Finnish men. He included some historical explanation of why Finnish men spent time in bars, tracing the practice to the erosion of traditional rural society and the immigration of farmworkers to urban centers. These were explained as significant contributors to the role that alcohol consumption plays in certain segments of Finnish society.

Researching the Culture of Public Organizations

Every organization, whether in the public or private sector, has its own distinctive culture and operating climate. The study of organizational culture owes much of its method and underlying principles to ideas produced through ethnographic research. Change-agent consultants working on organizational development projects are very likely to use either ethnography or ethology methods for their data gathering.

Organizational culture has been defined in many different ways, but most definitions are similar to that offered by Schein in 1985 (229): "Organizational culture is the shared, and implicit assumptions held by a group, and that determines how members of the group perceive, think about, and react to its various environments." Other definitions include those of Margulies and Wallace (1973), who defined organizational culture as the learned beliefs, values, and patterns of behavior that characterize an organization, and Peters and Waterman (1982) who saw culture as the shared system of values that manifests itself through different cultural artifacts.

In addition to its culture, an organization can also be said to have a distinct *operating climate* that results from the interaction of employees, administrators, and managers functioning within that culture. The operating climate reflects the content and strength of the salient values, attitudes, behaviors, and feelings of the people working in an organization (Schein 1996). Lewicki et al. (1988) saw operating climate as the level and form of organizational support, openness, style of supervision, conflict and conflict resolution, autonomy, and the existing quality of relationships that exist within the organization. Dastmalchian, Blyton and Adamson (1991) were more succinct, terming operating climate as simply the atmosphere prevailing in an organization.

According to Dyer (1991), the study of culture in organizations is approached from two broad perspectives: (1) studies that follow a traditional, positivist approach, and (2) studies that adopt a postpositivist approach. Researchers who study organizational cultures from a positivist viewpoint hold the opinion that there are clear, easily identified dimensions of culture that can be measured (usually with a questionnaire). McNabb and Sepic (1995), for example, developed a scale for diagnosing the organizational culture of an agency of the federal government. They measured employees' attitudes and opinions on nine dimensions of culture and climate: (1) organizational structure, (2) responsibility, (3) risk and challenge, (4) rewards, (5) warmth and support, (6) conflict, (7) organizational identity, (8) ethics, and (9) approved practices. The descriptive profiles developed with such studies of an organization can then be compared with the cultures of other groups. Organizational culture is something that can be reinforced or *changed*—the fundamental goal of an organizational development initiative.

The second school of thought follows an interpretist view. For these investigators, it is impossible to measure the culture of an organization because it changes form with each attempt to pin it down; each observer comes away with a different interpretation, based upon his or her personal values and experiences. Culture is, therefore, extremely difficult to manage; efforts to initiate a desired change may be fruitless—a mindless task with no hope of a concrete, lasting result.

One of the principal investigators in the field of organizational studies is Edgar H. Schein, who helped to establish the field of organizational studies at Massachusetts Institute of Technology. Building on earlier work by such pioneers in social psychology as Kurt Lewin and Ennis Likert, Schein believed that the innate culture of an organization often serves as a barrier to planned change. Schein (1996) noted that when organizations try to alter and improve their operations, they often run into resistance that is based in the culture and/ or subcultures that exist within all groups. This culture exists whether it is recognized or not. Members of the group are often not even aware of the culture of their group until they are faced with replacing it with something new and different.

Schein is critical of the positivist approach to the study of organizational culture. Traditional research has often resulted in a dependence upon abstractions about organizations and human behaviors in groups that are developed exclusively from a limited number of answers to questionnaires. These questionnaire-developed abstractions have created an artificial fabrication of reality. This has resulted in what Schein calls fuzzy theory—research findings that depend upon "massaging the data" statistically to establish significant results. His solution to this problem involved taking an interdisciplinary approach that includes ethnographic involvement in the research process: "Concepts for understanding culture in organizations have value only when they derive from observation of real behavior in organizations, when they are definable enough to generate further study" (229).

Case Examples

As you read the following examples (based on reports of actual studies), ask yourself why the researchers felt that an ethnographic research design was appropriate in each situation. Would you have used a different design?

Example 1: Trouble in the Projects

For many reasons, funding for welfare programs at both the national and state levels has declined greatly. Whether you feel the change is just or unjust, you and your agency have no alternative but to act within the policy mandates and regulations handed down by the governor, the legislature, and the director of your agency.

One of the most controversial proposals that has been circulating among state legislators is a plan to do away with all programs to ease the plight of indigent patients in the AIDS wards of public hospitals. Also to be eliminated are programs to aid homeless drug addicts; in the future, no state Medicaid funds are to be used for these patients. As part of a multiagency effort, the director of the Department of Social and Health Services has appointed a research team to gather information about current and potential recipients of public assistance. This information will be used by the legislative committee charged with developing a new program that will set public policy for the next ten years.

The team will begin its research in the section of the state's largest city known as The Portland Street Shipyard Projects. The Projects is a community of mixed ethnic background; the housing units were hastily constructed during World War II to house families of a since-closed naval shipyard. The units are small and often in need of extensive repairs. Today, the fastest growing ethnic groups in the community are newly arrived immigrants from Latin America, Ukraine, and Southeast Asia. Many of the residents of the Projects are unemployed, and most of those who are employed have low-paying service jobs that leave them not much better off than those who are eligible for welfare benefits.

Example 2: Ethnic Problems in the West

Over the past several decades, the economy of a Western state has undergone a series of severe shocks, the most telling of which has been the closing of sawmills and the resulting elimination of most of its employment base. The population of the region includes members of almost every major ethnic and racial group that has settled in the American West over the last century—Northern Europeans, Eastern and Southern Europeans, Latinos, Asians—but few African Americans. Only a small number of Native Americans remain in the area.

In the past, the region evidenced strong worker solidarity, with widespread trade union activity and one-party political loyalty. Few cultural antagonisms between the different groups have been encountered—until recently. With an increasing rate of migration of Latinos and Asians into the region has come an increase in the rate and severity of hate crimes.

As the strong labor union activity of the past has faded with the decline in the number of operating mills left in the region, new social organizations have filled the void. Many of these groups have white supremacist foundations. Others have strong ties to fundamentalist religion sects. Most have an "America First" clause in their platform, and most reject the idea of diversity. Clearly, there is strong potential for severe damage to the social and economic climate of the region.

The governor of the state has formed a blue-ribbon panel of university people, members of the clergy, local elected officials, business leaders, and state agency people to conduct research in the region before developing a broad policy statement for dealing with the many issues facing the region. The panel has contracted with the research group you have formed to conduct that research.

Example 3: Problems Recruiting Law Enforcement Officers

The newly appointed director of a local law enforcement agency is concerned over the apparent low morale and lack of commitment among the rank-and-file officers and staff. Not only are officers with high seniority leaving the force, the director is finding it increasingly difficult to recruit the educated, personnel dedicated to public service that he is convinced are necessary for the agency to maintain its high professional standards.

The agency is divided into five major administrative sections, each with its own chief officer and promotion structure: (1) county law enforcement, (2) contract law enforcement, with personnel more or less permanently serving as law enforcement officers of the several municipalities that contract for these services, (3) corrections officers, who run the county jail, (4) service bureau staff, who provide law enforcement services such as forensics to all law enforcement agencies in the county, and (5) administrative staff personnel. Several different unions represent the various sections in contract negotiations and grievance resolution. Each section operates semi-independently; there is considerable infighting for resources and recognition; and the entire department is rife with bickering, charges of sexual harassment, and favoritism.

Two recent events have brought the unrest in the department to the boiling point. A female patrol officer involved in a high-speed chase collided with a family minivan, resulting in the death of one child and crippling injuries to other family members. In a second incident, an officer on patrol in an area of high crime and drug activity shot and killed a popular minority teenage athlete who, it turned out later, was not engaging in any criminal activity, but simply jogging home from a high school graduation party.

Both events received extensive regional press coverage. Community leaders were highly vocal in their demands for retribution against the two officers, both of whom had been placed on paid administrative leave. However, union leaders of the police officers' union were demanding that the department not punish the officers and threatened to call a district-wide strike if both officers were not immediately reinstated. The department was in the middle of labor negotiations with the staff of the local corrections facility; their union was demanding pay and benefits equal to those of serving patrol officers. They threatened a strike if their demands were not met. The director of the agency resigned his office.

The new director of the agency wondered if an organizational development program, including team building and staff cross-training and employee empowerment, might ease tensions, renew employee commitment, and retain staff. Before he could begin such a program, however, he needed a better picture of the culture and operating climate of the organization. He has contracted with the research team you have formed to conduct the study.

Summary

The new social scientists who emerged in the eighteenth and nineteenth centuries were curious about primitive societies and the effects of industrialization on children, families, and the working poor. Their curiosity resulted in research efforts to understand why social problems occurred and what could (or *ought* to) be done to change society in order to improve the lot of the poor and disenfranchised. Adding to this curiosity was news about many strange and unknown societies and cultures.

Sociology evolved as a way to conduct systematic investigations into the newly emerging industrial society and the litany of social ills that was seen as an unwanted by-product of the industrialization process. Early attempts at establishing a systematic way of explaining human behavior and mental aberrations resulted in the creation of the science of psychology. Building on a tradition born of early travel stories and a scientific way of looking at indigenous cultures, another group of scholars forged the new social science of anthropology.

Through an eclectic process of trial and error, anthropologists and sociologists developed a way of conducting research that allowed them to meet their study objectives in all kinds of social and cultural settings. The name given to this method was *ethnography.* Researchers in public administration have also adopted this method of research.

Ethnographers often live, work, and play with the members of the group under study for long periods of time. Their aim is to be absorbed into the group, with the underlying objective of becoming accepted as a nonthreatening, nonintrusive member of the group so that events and interrelationships unfold as they would naturally, as if the observer were not in attendance. This process, called "gaining entry," is the key to a successful research project.

The process of living with a social group during fieldwork involves observing and recording individuals' behaviors. The ethnographer summarizes these field notes into a larger descriptive generalization that purports to describe the behavior of the larger society. The researcher must then develop *subjective descriptions* that are based on a large number of *generalizations*. In making these generalizations, the ethnographer moves from the *specific* to the *general*. That is, the behaviors of one or a small group are used to infer that those behaviors are also those of the larger group in similar circumstances. The ethnographer also develops *interpretations* of the observed behaviors; the question "why" should be answered to the best of the ethnographer's ability.

Suggested Reading

Alasuutari, Pertti. 1995. *Researching Culture: Qualitative Method and Cultural Studies*. London: Sage.

Bernard, H. Russell. 1995. *Research Methods in Anthropology*. 2d ed. Walnut Creek, CA: Alta Mira Press.

Fetterman, David M. 1989. *Ethnography: Step by Step*. Newbury Park, CA: Sage.

Fox, Richard G. 1977. *Urban Anthropology: Cities in Their Cultural Settings*. Englewood Cliffs, NJ: Prentice Hall.

Naroll, Raoul, and Ronald Cohen. 1973. *Handbook of Method in Cultural Anthropology*. New York: Columbia University Press.

Neuman, W. Lawrence. 2000. *Social Research Methods*. 4th ed. Boston: Allyn and Bacon.

21 Action Research in Public Administration

Action research is a way of initiating *change* in social systems—societies, communities, organizations, or groups—by involving members of the group in the research process. The researcher first examines the way the group functions and the problem affecting the group, and then helps members of the group bring about the needed change that they perceive is right for them.

The Contributions of Lewin and Dewey

The label "action research" was first used in 1948 by Kurt Lewin to describe an approach to solving practical problems in social groups. He described action research as taking place over four distinct steps: planning, executing, reconnaissance, and evaluating (Kuhne and Quigley 1997; Lewin 1948). His approach was characterized by a combination of research and theory building (Cunningham 1995). Lewin's perception of the change process included collaborative research between the social science researcher and the client. Lewin saw the method as *empirical research*—that is, an *applied* approach to social research, as opposed to a pure science or purely theoretical approach.

Lewin and his team of researchers at the University of Iowa and later at the Massachusetts Institute of Technology maintained a practical, participatory democracy focus in their research by studying citizens' participation in solving community problems. For example, early in the United States' participation in World War II, anthropologist Margaret Mead invited Lewin to do research with her for the Committee on Food Habits of the National Research Council. Lewin and his team began a series of studies to determine (1) the food consumption habits of Americans at the time, and (2) the best way to get people to change their eating habits in order to improve nutrition and to make up for widespread food shortages. Working under Lewin's direction, researchers at Iowa had recently completed a set of behavioral studies in autocratic and democratic situations, mostly through a series of experiments with preteenage boys. Applying that methodology to the food studies, Lewin took the early steps in what he was to call *action research*—the experimental application of social science to advancing democratic processes (Marrow 1977).

One of the most important conclusions to emerge from this research was that groups of people can do a thing better when they themselves decide to do it and when they also decide how they themselves will reduce the gap between their attitudes and actions (Marrow 1977, 130–131).

This emphasis on encouraging citizen participation is one of the reasons that action research is interesting to public administrators. Despite this interest, very little pure action research is conducted directly by or for public administrators. However, the action research approach has become widely accepted among social psychologists, sociologists, social workers, and educators, many of whom plan and conduct research on topics of interest to public administrators and managers of nonprofit organizations.

To summarize, action research is a form of inductive, practical research that focuses on increasing understanding of a social problem and on achieving a real change or improvement in the way people function in groups through a collaborative effort (Kuhne and Quigley 1997).

John Dewey was another early contributor to the development of action research, but rather than focusing on social organizations, Dewey was primarily concerned with the role of education in the process of becoming socialized. Born in 1859 and both a high school and university teacher, Dewey wanted to improve educational processes as a tool for teaching democracy and participation in democratic living. Lewin drew upon Dewey's philosophical writings in coming up with the action research approach that is now used for research in education, psychology, sociology, and other related disciplines.

Dewey was interest in developing theory, but theory that guided the *practice* of education and learning. Dewey also believed that by participating in democratic activities in classrooms, the large numbers of children of immigrant families flooding public schools in the early 1900s could learn concepts, ideas, and skills needed for cooperative living (Schmuck 1997). The work of Dewey sparked an interest in action research among educators in the 1950s. That interest quickly waned, however, and did not reemerge until publication in 1967 of Robert Schefer's book *The School as a Center of Inquiry*, in which Schefer recommended the use of action-oriented collaborative research by teachers (Quigley 1997). Today, because of its focus on early intervention and process improvement, action research has become one of the most popular qualitative research methods used in education. According to

Quigley, "[T]he movement has . . . grown to form a growing counterhegemony to traditional teacher preparation programs in public education and, more important . . . to traditional scientific positivism and the academic control of knowledge" (10).

Action research in education is conducted in the same way that it is in other fields of study. For example, in their *Guide to Research for Educators*, Merriam and Simpson (1984) identified a six-step process for conducting action research projects: analyzing the situation, getting the facts, identifying the problem, planning an intervention process, taking action on the problem, then repeating the cycle as new concepts and information emerge from the process.

Five Models of Action Research

Today, at least five different models of action research are in use by researchers in the human and administrative sciences (Small 1995). Small described four of the models in some detail: (1) traditional action research, (2) participatory action research, (3) empowerment research, and (4) feminist research. Although not discussed by Small, *action science* is a fifth school of action-based research. Each of these models is discussed below. These models and their relationships are displayed in Figure 21.1.

Traditional Action Research

The *action research* model, which developed from the work of Lewin and others beginning in the 1940s, is the most widely used. A victim of Nazi discrimination that ended his opportunity to participate fully in an academic career in Germany, Lewin immigrated to the United States in 1933. Reflecting on his experiences in Europe, he designed a field of research that looked at how democracy can disappear under the influence of a powerful, charismatic leader. He was convinced that social science could strengthen democracy, and searching for ways to make that happen became his life's work.

In the traditional action research approach established by Lewin and his followers, the researcher's primary objective is to help change dysfunctional social institutions, such as communities, while also contributing to the general fund of theory and knowledge. Lewin was convinced that researchers should be concerned with two kinds of knowing: (1) general laws of human and organizational behavior, and (2) specific information about the institution or system that is the focus of the change effort.

Gabel (1995, 1), building upon Lewin, Dewey, and other early contributors who formed the approach, described traditional action research as "an informal, qualitative, formative, subjective, interpretive, reflective, and ex-

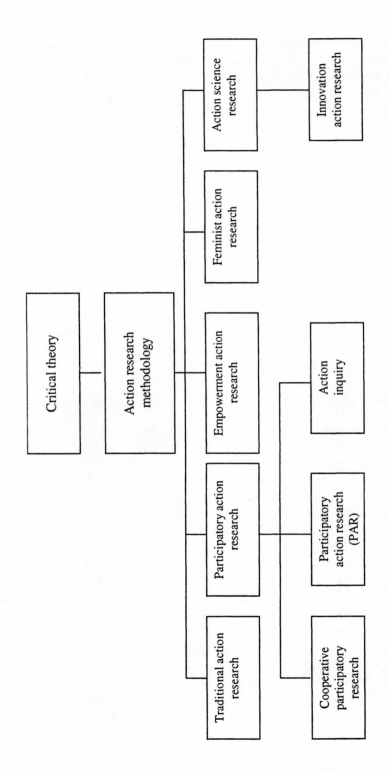

Figure 21.1 A Schematic Display of Five Models of Action Research

perimental model of inquiry in which all individuals involved in the study are knowing and contributing participants." He saw subject involvement in the process as a key characteristic of the research approach. Although it is usually considered to fall into a postpositivist tradition, no specific methodology is associated with action research; both quantitative and qualitative data are relevant for action research. However, the approach may be characterized by the following traditional practices.

First, data gathered in an action research study may be of any type and can be gathered by such different methods as structured survey questionnaires, simple observation, or unstructured personal or focus group interviews. Second, because of its interventionist nature, action research is always conducted in the location or setting of the social problem and usually involves the entire group (a universe) rather than a sample. Third, it usually focuses on a single case or organizational unit. Fourth, the researcher collaborates with subjects who are members of the group under study. The researcher brings scientific and theoretical knowledge and skills to the project, while group members add important practical knowledge and experience with the situations that frame the study. Both types of knowledge are deemed essential for the action research process to work.

Participatory Action Research

Participatory action research is the second model described by Small (1995). Researchers employing this approach are typically concerned with three activities: research, education, and action. It owes much to the emergence of critical theory, in that a primary goal of participatory research is to effect a fundamental, emancipating change in a society. Participatory research developed from social movements among oppressed societies in the third world, including Africa, Asia, and Latin America.

Participatory research has also gained a strong foothold in North America. For example, a four-year participatory research study with residents of the town of North Bonneville in Washington was conducted in the early 1970s (Comstock and Fox 1993). Groups of students and faculty from The Evergreen State College in Olympia, Washington, worked with some 450 residents of a town that was scheduled for demolition to make room for a new dam spillway and power plant.

During initial meetings with town residents, the U.S. Corps of Engineers refused to consider moving the town, as its residents desired, and instead offered payments for residents to move to other areas. Comstock and Fox described how residents overcame a critical hurdle in their path to achieving success in their dealings with the engineers:

> Very early in the struggle, the residents discovered the contradiction between the Corps's meaning of community and their own. To the Corps the community was individuals and physical structures. This ignored the reality of community values, attachments to the land, and social networks. Through a careful description of their community, the residents gained a more articulate description of their community and vitality as a community. (121)

Once residents learned how the corps perceived the community and its residents and how corps agents were using the agency's control of information as a wedge to divide citizen opinion, they moved to acquire technical information on their own. They then provided that technical information to everyone in a way that could be understood, thus breaking down the corps's monopoly of ideas. Town members eventually won their fight to survive; the Corps of Engineers built a new town in the location wanted by residents of the old town. The new city of North Bonneville was officially dedicated in July 1976.

Researchers using the participatory action model believe that if, through education, members of a society become aware of better ways to function, they will bring about the change themselves. Thus, a key part of the research process is helping community members become active participants in the study and its action aftermath. Participants are expected to take primary responsibility for the study, including its overall design, data gathering and analysis, and eventual distribution of the findings.

Small (1995, 943) made the following special note of the part that political activity plays in the participatory action approach:

> Participatory researchers are openly and explicitly political. Their ideology emphasizes large-scale structural forces, conflicts of interest, and the need to overcome oppression and inequality through transforming the existing social order. The lack of access to useful and valued forms of knowledge by oppressed or disenfranchised peoples is viewed as a major problem that can be overcome through the research process.

Comstock and Fox (1993, 123) also noted the political nature of the participatory action approach in their conclusions about how the people of North Bonneville were changed by the experience:

> Perhaps the most striking result of the North Bonneville experience has been the degree to which a self-sustaining political process was initiated . . . The growth of self-direction continued as residents, no longer content with their original demand that a new town be planned and built for them, demanded (and got) control over the design of their own community.

Finally, a key distinguishing characteristic of this approach is an emphasis upon empowering the people within the group or community, making it possible for them to take control of their study. In time, the researchers are expected to back away in order to follow the lead of the participants, rather than the reverse.

Empowerment Research

The third model of action research is what Small described as *empowerment research*. Small (1995) defined *empowerment* as being concerned with individuals and groups who are excluded by the majority on the basis of their demographic characteristics or their physical or emotional difficulties. The rationale for exclusion may have been experienced in the past or may be taking place in the present.

Empowerment research may be particularly relevant for use in public administration. Supporting this impression is the selective focus of most empowerment research that has been published thus far. Empowerment research typically addresses issues of mental health, citizen involvement, and community programs.

The empowerment research approach begins with the researcher identifying or creating situations in which a group has been silent and/or isolated— the "outsiders" of a society, an organization, or a community. As the researcher helps these outsiders understand the underlying issues, they gain a voice in and power over the decisions that affect them. In a word, it is a process designed to *empower* people. It is collaborative in nature: Researchers work with members of the group to identify group strengths and resources that may not have been recognized. As they become empowered, group members achieve a mastery over the internal and external forces that affect them.

Finally, the process focuses on bringing out the natural abilities and skills of the members of the group under study. Rather than focusing on group members' weaknesses, empowerment research aims to bring their strengths to the fore, providing guidance in the task of putting those strengths to work for the members' benefit.

Feminist Research

Feminist research is the last model of action research described by Small. He defined the focus of feminist research as promoting the feminist agenda by challenging male dominance and advocating social, political, and economic equality between women and men. As with all other models of action research, feminist research seeks to bring about social change, emancipate participants (i.e., women), and enhance the lives of the participants.

Feminist researchers are likely to adopt a postpositivist approach to their work, although there are no rules that make it the required epistemology.

While some have advocated that a distinctive set of feminist methods should exist, others are less convinced that a purely feminist methodology is possible. And, according to Small, a third group argues that although, indeed, no special feminist methodology currently exists, one is slowly being formed as more feminist research appears. Summarizing the feminist model, Small (1995, 947) concluded with the following statement:

> Feminist researchers share the values of overcoming oppression, empowering women, and transforming society so that equality between men and women can be achieved. The purpose of knowledge is to change or transform what is considered the patriarchal nature of society.

Action Science

Action science is the model of action research seen often in public administration and other organizational settings. Although it was not discussed in Small's overview, this approach clearly deserves an equal place alongside all other action research models. Chris Argyris and others developed the action science approach from the same contributions of John Dewey—who proposed separating science and practice—and Kurt Lewin, who contributed greatly to the field of group dynamics (an area of study in social psychology). Dewey's contributions and Lewin's separation of *diagnosis* of an organization from practitioner *intervention* became the concept of using research to bring about change (Argyris, Putnam and Smith 1985; Schein 1996). In this model, diagnosis of a problem by research is always followed by participant-led intervention (change).

Action science has been described specifically as an *intervention method* based on the idea that people can improve their interpersonal and organizational effectiveness by examining the underlying beliefs that guide their actions (Raelin 1997). As White (1999, 142) and others noted, this phase may also take the form of *evaluation*: "The evaluation of social situations is the point of any action theory, which strives to help actors understand their situations in a different light and to make value judgments about whether or not their situations should be changed" (142).

Lewin never explicitly defined action science method as such—he retained instead the label *action research*. However, his early work in developing approaches to interventions and change in social organizations led Argyris to give him credit for development of most of the techniques involved in the approach (Argyris 1985; Schein 1995). Argyris proposed the action science concept because: (1) then-current applications of action research were ignoring the theory-building element of the original approach, and (2) he believed that the practice of following traditional, positivist approaches to research was self-limiting and harmful to the growth of knowledge. Today, the two terms are usually used synonymously, together with other closely related variations such as "action learning" (Raelin 1997), "action inquiry" (Reason 1998), and "innovation action research" (Kaplan 1998), to name just a few.

Action Research and Critical Theory

Philosophically, action research is closely related to the *critical theory* approach to research; both seek intervention in social organizations for the purpose of helping people (clients) find better ways of living, socializing, and functioning in groups. Argyris, Putnam, and Smith (1985, 234) even go so far as to consider this approach a kind of critical theory. However, despite their similar purposes, they are not the same. Critical theory and research evolved from the emancipatory tradition of Marx and Freud, ultimately refined in the 1920s by Habermas and others of the Frankfurt School. Action research, on the other hand, has its roots in Kurt Lewin's work in participatory democracy and the education systems research of John Dewey.

The *Frankfurt School* is the name given to a group of philosophers who expressed their dissatisfaction with traditional epistemology and its positivist theory by constructing a new philosophy of social science. Today, that new philosophy of science is called *postpositivism*. The name given to the new type of theory associated with the postpositivist realm is *critical theory*. According to the Frankfurt School, critical theory has three fundamental characteristics that distinguish it from traditional positivist theory (Geuss 1981, 1–2):

1. Critical theories guide human action in two ways:
    a. They enlighten the people who have them, enabling these agents to determine for themselves what their true interests are; and
    b. They are inherently emancipatory; they free people from coercion, which may be partially self-imposed and based in ignorance of better ways to exist.
2. Critical theories are forms of knowledge. Hence, *education* must precede emancipation.
3. Critical theories have a different epistemological basis from the theories that exist in the natural sciences: critical theories are "reflective," whereas theories in the natural sciences are "objective."

To summarize, a critical theory is a reflective theory that gives people ("agents") a knowledge that is inherently enlightening and emancipating. Critical researchers help humans in social systems discover their own ways to change their world—that is, to become e*mancipated*—whereas action researchers *partici-pate* with groups to bring about improvement in the way the groups function. What brings the two approaches near to one another is their focus on bringing about *social change.*

Despite their differences, the two concepts are often combined into a single research design. DePoy and Hartman (1999, 560), for example, developed what they called a "model for social work knowing founded on the tenets of critical theory synthesized with principles and practices from action research." They applied the model to a case analysis of the Maine Adolescent Transition (MAT) project. The objective of the MAT was to provide at-risk adolescents access to vital health care services. The model identifies a twelve-step process, as follows:

1. Identify a social problem.
2. Convene a steering committee with representation from all stake-holder groups.
3. Identify (delimit) the scope of the research.
4. Select a specific set of research questions to guide the conduct of the study.
5. Determine specific change objectives for the study group.
6. Select a collaborative research team (including lay and professional researcher membership).
7. Train lay researchers in designing, conducting, and using inquiry.
8. Design the inquiry, with specific research questions, and analysis strategy.
9. Conduct inquiry and analysis.
10. Report findings in accessible formats to all stakeholder groups.
11. Submit findings.
12. Identify further areas for inquiry.

The Glanz Action Research Primer

Jeffrey Glanz (1999) prepared a small but informative "primer" on action research for school administrators, in which he identified just four steps for the process. The first step is to select a focus for the study by knowing what to investigate, developing questions to ask, and establishing a plan to acquire answers to the questions. The second step is to collect data, but only after narrowing the focus to a specific area of concern; data may be collected using either quantitative or qualitative approaches, or both. A key part of this step is to organize the data so they can be shared with other readers after the study is completed. The third step is to analyze and interpret the data in order to arrive at some decision. Making a decision is preliminary to the fourth and final step, initiating some action. The project is not complete until this action occurs; *corrective action* is fundamental to the idea of action research.

Key Themes in Action Research

In their important work on the philosophical underpinnings of action science, Argyris, Putnam, and Smith (1985, 8–9) identified five key themes of the process from the writings of Kurt Lewin and others. While these themes were applied specifically to the action science model, they are clearly applicable to the other action research models as well. The five themes are as follows:

1. Collaboration in the resolution of the problem.
    Action science (research) deals with processes and efforts to bring about *change* in real social systems. It targets a specific problem and then provides assistance to the client organization in resolving the problem.
2. Problem identification, planning, and acting.
    Action research proceeds through repetitive cycles of problem identification, planning, acting, and evaluation.
3. Educating and reeducating.
    Change in the social group or organization involves a process of *educating* and/or *reeducating* group members. This means changing the way people in the group think and act. Thus, the process works at reforming organizational culture. For reeducation to work, all actors in the organization must participate in the diagnosis and fact-finding stage of the process and contribute to identification of new ways of acting.
4. Democratic participation and action.
    Action research maintains a strong commitment to the idea of *democratic* action in improving group behavior and effectiveness. Thus, the method involves questioning the status quo from the perspective of democratic values.
5. Theory-building and practical application.
    Two key objectives of all action research are to contribute to basic knowledge in social science by developing theory and to improve action in social organizations.

Seven Phases of Planned Change

Ronald Lippitt, a student of Lewin and collaborator on much of his research, published *The Dynamics of Planned Change* in 1958, six years after Lewin's death. In that work Lippitt and colleagues identified a number of phases for planned change. Schmuck (1997) built upon the work of Lippitt et al. to suggest seven phases of planned change (Figure 21.2).

In *Phase 1*, someone associated with the social group recognizes that a problem of some type exists. This could be anything from an external threat to the organization's existence to a functional barrier that hinders effectiveness and fosters frustration. An example is the diagnostic action research study for a federal supply service office conducted by McNabb and Sepic in 1995. The unit had been required to reorganize for implementation of a total quality management program. Five very different functions, with different organizational cultures and traditions, were to merge into one functioning department. Unit leaders and long-term employees were balking at making the change. Refusing to accept the stalemate, the leader of one unit called the researchers in to help the group find a common ground for problem resolution.

In *Phase 2*, data about the situation are collected. In the federal supply office example, this phase began with a series of meetings, with representatives from all five units present at all sessions. This group became an ad hoc research advisory team, with membership remaining constant throughout the length of the project.

These sessions were tape-recorded, with transcripts circulated to all members for their concurrence and approval before the team moved on to other problem areas. The group then agreed upon a set of nine problem areas that were common to the majority of the units and that needed to be addressed. These problem areas served as constructs for the collaborative development of a comprehensive survey instrument. Unit leaders then administered the instrument to their own staffs.

In *Phase 3*, a diagnosis of the situation is made from the collected data. In this example, the research team conducted a preliminary analysis of the combined group discussion and questionnaire data. This was shared with members of the ad hoc advisory committee, with their interpretations solicited. With all data collected and both the research team and group participants in general agreement, a composite diagnostic report was prepared. Copies were distributed downward through the organization and upward to the organization's management personnel.

In *Phase 4*, both the researchers and participants collaborate on a plan-of-action step to be taken to resolve organizational issues and remove barriers to change. This step is considered the "heart" of the action research effort. Only action steps that address problems specifically identified in the diagnostic phase should be included in the plan. Once a set of proposed steps is agreed upon, everyone collaborates in setting priorities.

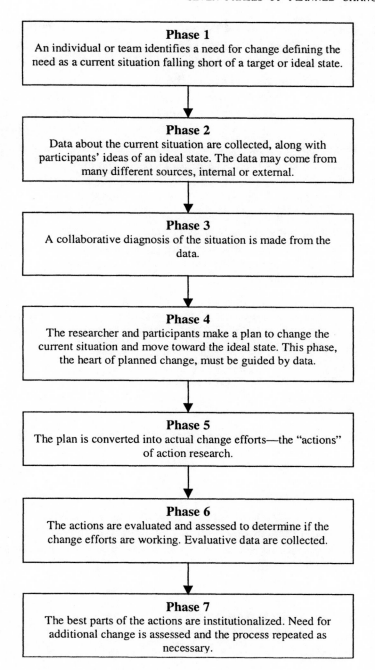

Figure 21.2 **Seven Phases of Planned Change**
Source: Adapted from R.A. Schmuck 1997, 143.

Phase 5 is the action phase in the action research process. Plans must be converted into actual change actions. In this example, the agency's dismal record in two broad areas of organizational climate was conceived as an absolute barrier to improving the employees' commitment to the organization and willingness to accept a mandated change for which they had not been consulted. These areas were the Rewards and Recognition and the Warmth and Support constructs. It is important to remember that neither the researchers nor the agency's senior management should be the ones to suggest specific changes. Rather, in order for the plan to succeed, the changes had to come from the entire organization staff. The researcher's role from this phase on is to function only as a catalyst for internally generated change.

Phase 6 is the evaluation stage; it begins with implementation of the change initiatives and continues through their complete acceptance or rejection by the organization. This phase often requires conducting additional research. Suchman (1967, 31) identified the following six ingredients as essential for an evaluation to be successful:

1. Clear identification of the change goals that are being evaluated
2. Analysis of the organizational or societal problem with which the activity was designed to cope
3. Thorough description and definition of the change activities
4. Measurement of the degree of change that took place
5. Determination of whether the observed change is due to the activity or to some other cause
6. Some indication of the durability of the effects

In *Phase 7*, the most successful parts of the change actions, those that meet with majority acceptance and approval and are made part of the continuing operating climate of the group, can be expected to eventually become part of the longer-term culture of the organization, accepted as "part of the way we do things around here" and passed on to the new members of the group. Where actions result in only superficial or cosmetic change, the members of the group must devise new change initiatives in a dynamic process of continuous evolution.

Goals of Action Research

The primary goal of all action research in public administration is to come up with the information that is needed for government action. This information is often called "practical" or "everyday" knowledge. Action research has particular value in the following four public administration applications:

1. Action research is well suited as a method of *identifying citizens' needs* in a community, with the added benefit of producing potential solutions for attaining the resources necessary to meet those needs.
2. Through its ability to generate knowledge, it is an excellent way of gaining the guidance necessary to *design the most effective programs* to meet citizens' needs.
3. Action research, because of its interventionist nature, is a highly appropriate means of carrying out *organizational development* activities and programs.
4. Finally, following in the tradition of early emancipatory theory, action research can play a very important role in *community development and redevelopment efforts.*

Achieving the Action Research Goal

To achieve their goal, action researchers gather data in many different ways. Among the most commonly used tools are group discussions, role-playing, unstructured interviews, and case discussions. A list of data-gathering methods identified by Argyris, Putnam, and Smith (1985) included the following tools:

- Observations accompanied by audiotaping
- Interviews
- Action experiments
- Participant-written cases

Argyris, Putnam, and Smith noted that, most often, action researchers rely on all four methods, but may have different purposes in mind when they select one over another. Common to all of these and other data-gathering methods used in action research are the following three critical characteristics:

- The data must be generated in a way that makes participants feel causally responsible for them.
- Each method is structured to elicit data about how participants actually act and what they are thinking and feeling at the time.
- Action experiments (such as role-playing) should be used to "unfreeze" people's reasoning and reactions. (239–241)

In all of the ways that data are gathered in an action research or action science project, the key to gathering the needed data is to *engage participants in free and open narrative discussions.* When people are discussing the problems of their organization, they are engaging in a cathartic activity. In this sense, "talk *is* action" (Argyris, Putnam, and Smith 1985, 57).

Applying Action Research

Action research takes place in a series of six steps that can be grouped into three distinct phases. The first phase, *planning*, includes three steps: identify and understand the problem, define the problem and the proposed intervention, and develop measurements. Phase two, *action*, is the critical step in the process; it includes only the fourth step, implementing and observing. Finally, phase three, *reflection*, covers steps five and six, evaluation and transition (Kuhne and Quigley 1997). The relationship between the six steps and three phases is displayed in Figure 21.3.

Phase one involves three key preliminary steps: (1) developing an *understanding* of a problem, (2) *planning* an action research project, and (3) determining the *measurements* to be used. Developing an understanding of the problem involves conducting extensive interviews with members of the group in order to bring out their perceptions of the problem and its possible cause. In collaborative research such as this, the researcher's perception of the problem is not nearly as important as the participants' view of it. After all, the researcher may not know if he or she is a part of the problem. Gathering this information may involve brainstorming with participants and other researchers, exploring the published professional literature, and, often, simply observing the group. Finally, the researcher and group participants must decide together whether the problem is significant enough to warrant the study.

Defining and planning the project is the second step in phase one of the action research process. The most important part of planning is deciding how to deal with the problem at hand. In a collaborative research activity, this means getting the participants to agree on the intervention program they want applied, organizing the group for action, and agreeing on how the participants are to be involved in the action phase of the process. The result of this step is the generation of a *readiness to accept change* among the members of the group.

Determining the measurements is the third step in phase one. This is the diagnostic stage of action research. In order to know if something has been improved, the researcher must have a *benchmark* from which to measure any change. A benchmark is a clear, comprehensive description of the way things are. It includes specifying what will be measured during the evaluation stage of the action research. In addition to knowing what to measure, it is also necessary to determine *when* to measure. How long should the intervention experiment run before evaluation? There is no set answer to this question; timing is a function of the severity of the problem and the degree of participatory involvement of the participants.

Lewin described this process in his 1947 paper on "Frontiers in Group Dynamics" (in Cartwright 1951, 224): "In discussing the means of bringing

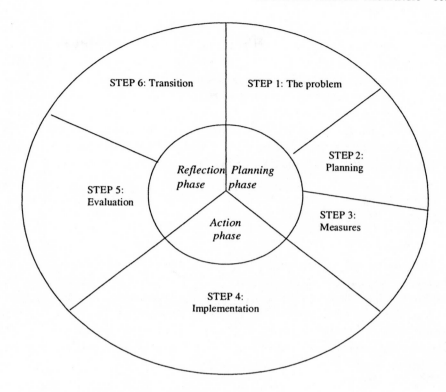

Figure 21.3 **Phases and Steps of Action Research**
Source: Kuhne and Quigley 1997, 281.

about a desired state of affairs one should not think in terms of the 'goal to
be reached' but rather in terms of a change 'from the present level to the
desired one.'"

The single step that makes up phase two, the action phase, of an action
research project is (4) *implementing* the change action. This is the task of the
members of the group, not the researcher. The researcher's role is to function
as a reference point, providing methodological advice if asked, and not as a
leader or instigator of the action. Action research is *participatory* research.
Another important aspect of the researcher's role in this phase is to keep the
group moving according to its initial plan. If the plan turns out to be not an
appropriate intervention or change, the way to meet the group's objectives is
to plan and initiate a second iteration of the entire system. Finally, the researcher must maintain good records of the implementation of the intervention, its effects, and how and in what form changes are generated.

Phase three is the *reflection* part of an action research project. It includes
the last two steps: (5) *evaluating results*, and (6) *transitioning the change into*

the group or organization. Step five may take as long or longer than the actual implementation of the action. All aspects of the data collected before and during the action phase must be studied. The researcher must work closely with group participants to evaluate what the data reveal about the problem and the intervention. This means determining whether the success criteria agreed upon in step three were met and if any tangible gains have taken place. If the problem is resolved, end the project; if not, repeat the cycle. Action research cycles should continue until the desired change is accepted and functioning. Suchman (1967, 177) described what is involved in the evaluation process this way:

> What we evaluate is the action hypothesis that defined program activities will achieve specified, desired objectives through their ability to influence those intervening processes that affect the occurrence of these objectives. . . . An understanding of all three factors—program, objective, and intervening process—is essential to the conduct of [evaluation].

The last phase in the process is evaluating results and *reflecting on the project.* This is an in-depth interpretation of the entire project that includes thinking about what happened and what did not. Did the project produce promising results? Did the observed changes reflect what actually happened? Should another cycle of action research be initiated? Kuhne and Quigley (1997, 34) describe this step as a process of "analyzing outcomes and revising plans for another cycle of acting."

Step six also involves putting together a final report of the entire process for group participants and any other researcher/participant team planning for a similar intervention of their own. Thus, the report must be complete, must be produced in a form that everyone can understand, and must add to theoretical knowledge of change in groups and organizations and the action research process in general.

Case Examples

As you read over these short examples (based on actual cases), ask yourself how action research might play a role in helping the administrators introduce innovation and change into their organizations.

Example 1: Trouble at the Corrections Department

You are a case manager in a state corrections program, attending the university at night to earn your master's degree in public administration. For some time, you and your fellow caseworkers have been expressing more and more dissatisfaction with your working conditions. The former department director kept formal managerial involvement and direction to a minimum, believing that casework required great flexibility in its operating staff. The only formal operational directive governing caseworker activity was: "Case managers are to work with each inmate to implement a correctional and rehabilitation plan that has been developed by staff for the inmate" (Gottfredson 1996). However, because of heavy workloads and staff limitations, correctional plans have been prepared for less than half of the resident population.

Coupled with the difficulties of your job associated with the inmate plan problem is the vagueness of all case managers' official job description. These state only that case managers are to assist in providing rehabilitation programs, help inmates by answering their questions, follow up on problems, and make recommendations on classification decisions.

Recently a new director took over your department. He has proposed a project involving a group of case managers and departmental supervisors to work with an outside consultant to produce a set of behavioral expectations and performance standards for your department. You have been asked to be a member of the group working on the project.

Example 2: Learner Participation in a Homeless Shelter

You have been employed as a literacy instructor at a long-term homeless shelter for women in a town on the outskirts of a large Midwestern city. Residents have their own bedrooms, but share all other common areas. Residents prepare their own meals. After several weeks on your new job, you realize that many of the residents are reluctant to leave their rooms to attend your classes. The literacy program—called Getting Active—includes instruction on life-skill building and can lead to a GED certificate (Kalinosky 1997).

You decide to meet with the director of the center to discuss the problems you are having in reaching all the residents who might benefit from your efforts. With her support, you decide that a research project is needed to determine why some residents are not participating.

To begin, you enlist several former participants who successfully completed the program to form the nucleus of a research advisory committee. These members recruit several nonparticipants to join them in designing a research project. The new advisory committee is scheduled to hold its first meeting tonight.

Example 3: Introducing Innovation

The manager of the city's Office of Budgets and Planning has expressed frustration with the existing cost and performance measurement systems used in this West Coast town of 250,000 residents (Kaplan 1998). For as long as can be remembered, department managers have been using traditional, standard, direct labor-based costing standards in forecasting project costs. They also use a monthly system of financial variance reporting. According to the budget director, the apparent driving force in the city has been: Keep doing things the way we have always done them, and stay on budget!

The manager recently attended a weeklong seminar and workshop on activity-based accounting and balanced scorecard evaluation systems (Kaplan and Norton 1996). At the seminar, participants received a copy of a 1998 article by Kaplan, "Innovation Action Research: Creating New Management Theory and Practice." The manager wonders if an action research project can be used to help the city's department managers accept and adopt innovative costing and performance measurements.

Summary

Action research is a way of initiating *change* in social systems—societies, communities, organizations, or groups—by involving members of the group in the research process. The researcher studies the way the group functions, identifies the problem, and helps the members of the group bring about the needed change that they perceive is right for them.

An emphasis on encouraging citizen participation is one of the reasons that action research is interesting to public administrators. Despite this interest, very little pure action research is conducted directly by or for public administrators. However, the action research approach has become widely accepted among social psychologists, sociologists, social workers, and educators, many of whom plan and conduct research on topics of interest to public administrators and managers of nonprofit organizations.

Today, at least five different models of action research are in use by researchers in the human and administrative sciences: (1) traditional action research, (2) participatory action research, (3) empowerment research, (4) feminist research, and (5) action science or action inquiry.

Suggested Reading

Argyris, Chris, Robert Putnam, and Diana McLain Smith. 1985. *Action Science*. San Francisco: Jossey-Bass.

Geuss, Raymond. 1981. *The Idea of a Critical Theory: Habermas and the Frankfurt School.* Cambridge: Cambridge University Press.

Lippitt, Ronald, Jeanne Watson, and Bruce Westley. 1958. *The Dynamics of Planned Change*. New York: Harcourt, Brace.

Marrow, Alfred J. 1977. *The Practical Theorist: The Life and Work of Kurt Lewin*. New York: Teachers College Press.

Part 6

Qualitative Analysis Methods

22 Analyzing Qualitative Data

The primary building block of all research is *data*. Data can take many different forms and can be gathered in at least five different ways. In their most irreducible forms, they can be quantitative or qualitative. Increasingly, and in more and more disciplines, data exist in *qualitative* form.

Data in any form can be gathered by interviews, questionnaires, overt or covert observation, analysis of documents or artifacts, or the subjective experiences of the researcher (Martin 2000). Regardless of the form they take or how they are gathered, in its raw state data have little or no intrinsic meaning. Data must be *processed*, *analyzed*, and *interpreted* by a researcher before they take on any rational sense.

The *analysis* processes for quantitative and qualitative research data are similar in some ways, but different in others. Similarities include the following (1) data are not just *there*; they must be collected in some way by a researcher; (2) when processed, both quantitative and qualitative data can be used for inference; (3) comparative analyses are used with both data types; and (4) researchers are concerned with both the reliability and the validity of all data.

Quantitative data differ from qualitative data primarily in the way they are tabulated, collated, and processed. Quantitative data are typically computer processed and analyzed with a variety of standard statistical tests. These tests are applied for one or more of the following purposes: (1) to describe a data set, (2) to generate hypotheses through a process of association testing, and (3) to test hypotheses (Fitz-Gibbon and Morris 1987).

Qualitative data, on the other hand, exhibit variety in both form and context. They can also be evaluated and interpreted in a variety of ways. Qualitative data can be words, pictures, artifacts, music scores, and so on. Furthermore, each of the several different analysis approaches has its own underlying purpose, and each often produces a different outcome. This chapter discusses a few of the prevalent ways of analyzing qualitative data, including three separate but similar processing models.

What Is Qualitative Data?

Qualitative data are data that have been gathered during the conduct of interpretive or postpositivist research studies. They exist most often as some sort of narrative. Thus, they can be written text, transcripts of conversations or interviews, transcripts of therapeutic or consultive interviews, records of legal trials, or transcripts of focus group discussions. They can exist as historical or literary documents, ethnographic field notes, diaries, newspaper clippings, or magazine and journal articles. They can also be in the form of photographs, maps, illustrations, paintings, musical scores, tape recordings, films, or any other nonquantitative or quantitative source. Most of the time, however, qualitative research data exists as collections of rough field notes.

Miles and Huberman (1998, 182) suggested that qualitative data exists as "the essences of people, objects, and situations." In their discussion, *essences* refers to the reactions and interpretations that researchers take away from the raw experiences of a research encounter or situation. A researcher must process, analyze, and interpret these essences in order to transform them into a meaningful conclusion.

The following brief statement bears emphasizing: *All data must be analyzed and interpreted before they are meaningful.* All unprocessed and uninterrupted data is usually called *raw data.* Raw quantitative data are the compilation of a set of numbers arranged according to values assigned by a researcher to optional responses to questions or as counts of event occurrences. Raw qualitative data exist most often as a body of unorganized, unstructured field notes or narrative—that is, in the form of words, not numbers.

Components of Qualitative Data Analysis

There are two parts to the interpretation and analysis of qualitative data. The first is *data management*; the second is *data analysis* (Miles and Huberman 1998). Data management includes two important steps. First, managing data begins with organizing the collection process. This includes preplanning, careful selection of the sample or situation to be included in the study, and achieving the researcher's entry into and acceptance by the study group. The researcher must maintain a concise record of the steps and processes taken throughout the study. A précis of this record must be included in the final research report under the heading of *methodology*.

The second step in this process is designing a system for storage of the collected data. In the past, this meant devising a system of index cards, preparing analytical memorandums, and careful categorical coding—in what some analysts referred to as the *clerical* portion of qualitative research. It was laborious and time-consuming. Today, however, computer software programs are increasingly taking the place of this unappealing activity.

A key activity in this half of the management/analysis process is devising a system for retrieving data for comparative analyses and other interpretive activities. It is important to remember the process because some researchers still work this way (Este, Sieppert, and Barsky 1998, 138):

> Only a few short decades ago, QDA [qualitative data analysis] was purely a manual process. Bits of data were copied onto cards, using the traditional technique of cutting and pasting. These cards were filed under appropriate categories generated by the researcher . . . [who] then strove to link the data and connect categories through these physical materials and manipulations, to produce meaningful reflections of the phenomena being studied. The process was a daunting one for researchers. Researchers had to manage overwhelming compilations of material, make analytical decisions that were rarely clear or simple, and work through the tedious and frustrating processes of coding, deriving themes, and building theories.

The second half of the overall process is the actual analysis of data. This phase of the interpretation process also includes three activities: (1) data reduction, (2) data display, and (3) drawing conclusions from the data. First, data reduction is almost always a crucial stage in the interpretation process. It involves selecting the most salient themes and constructs that emerge from the data. Not every bit of data can be its own category; if this were true, the research report would never be written. Qualitative investigations have been known to generate thousands of pages of records. From out of that mass of unconnected narrative, the researcher must choose or devise a conceptual framework. This framework will be constructed of themes, clusters, and summaries.

The second part of the analysis phase is data display. In the chapters on quantitative research methods, this was discussed as the use of descriptive and summary statistics and charts, graphs, and tables to present information. These same graphic displays are often used to present qualitative data. Whatever research approach is followed, the objective is to be able to present findings as an organized, focused collection of pertinent information, out of which a researcher—and a reader—can draw relevant conclusions.

Finally, drawing conclusions forces the researcher to *interpret* the results of the study. It is not enough simply to present the data as they appear, even if they have been effectively organized, categorized, and structured. The research must explain what the data *mean* in relation to the study design and objectives and in terms of their contribution to theory.

Bringing Order to Data: A Nine-Step Process

The analysis and interpretation of qualitative data begins with bringing the raw data into some level of order. First, the researcher identifies and selects a set of relevant *categories* or *classes* in which to sort the data. Comparing the data across categories—a step that is typically used in the testing of hypotheses—often follows the initial comparing phase of the analysis. Strauss and Corbin (1998) called this a process of *conceptualizing*. Conceptualizing means reducing the often bulky amounts of raw data into workable, ordered bits of information that the researcher can manage with confidence. Kvale (1996) described this act of data categorization as a key qualitative research activity that most distinguishes qualitative strategies from quantitative research.

Researchers can best analyze and interpret raw data if they employ some orderly process. Figure 22.1 displays a model of the first of two such processes. This nine-step process for analyzing and interpreting qualitative data has its roots in the threefold grounded theory interpretation models of Strauss and Corbin (1998) and Neuman (2000), and in information provided by Miles and Huberman (1984 and 1994). Each of the nine steps is discussed in detail below.

Step 1: Preliminary Analysis for Patterns and Structure

Order and structure must be brought to all data if they are ultimately to become *information*. Miles and Huberman (1994) refer to order—the patterns or themes in textual qualitative data—as "gestalts" because they pull together a variety of smaller portions of data into larger "wholes."

A key task of the qualitative researcher is sorting and resorting data to identify *patterns*, from which meaning and definition can be established. Finding patterns in the data is a subjective process that often comes naturally to the researcher. Miles and Huberman see this as a potential problem, however, and offer the following caveat:

> The human mind finds patterns so quickly and easily that it needs no how-to advice. Patterns just "happen," almost too quickly. The important thing, rather, is to be able to (a) see *real* added evidence in the same pattern; (b) remain open to disconfirming evidence when it appears. (216)

Step 2: Open Coding to Form Clusters and Identify Themes

A key activity in all qualitative data analysis is *clustering*. This entails putting things that are like each other together into groupings or classes. These may

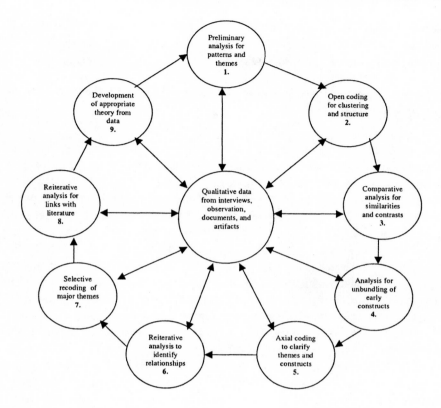

Figure 22.1 **A Nine-Step Process for Analyzing Qualitative Data**

be preexisting classes, although this is not the recommended way to begin. More often, the categories are groupings that the researcher creates from smaller collections of ideas that emerge from the data itself. Coding and categorization go hand in hand during this phase of the analysis.

Strauss and Corbin (1998) and Glaser (1992) identified the coding process that occurs in the first phase of the analysis as open or substantive coding. The goal of this first, open coding process is to begin to form the raw data into meaningful categories with a structure that will guide the researcher in all subsequent analyses and any future gathering of more data.

There are no limits to how many codes are assigned during the open coding phase or to the inclusiveness (breadth) of each. Miles and Huberman (1994, 219) described the process as a necessary task that can be "applied at many levels of qualitative data; at the level of events or acts, of individual actors, of processes, of settings or locales, of sites as wholes."

In qualitative research, usually little or no categorization is done prior to the data being collected. The categorical codes that emerge at this time are taken from the data they embrace. However, the researcher should keep in mind that one of the goals of coding and categorization is the *reduction* of data into more manageable sets.

Step 3: Comparative Analysis for Similarities and Contrasts

Qualitative research studies usually require some comparative analysis of the collected data. In grounded theory research, comparisons are an integral part of the entire analysis process. Both Strauss and Corbin (1998) and Glaser (1992) recommended that comparative analysis should be an integral step in all studies involving qualitative data. Furthermore, they urged that previously gathered data be continuously compared with every bit of new data. Ragin and Zaret (1983) also considered comparative research to be one of the research tactics that distinguish research on social groups. Webb et al. (2000, 5) suggested that, "in all useful measurement, an implicit comparison exists when an explicit one is not visible." Furthermore, they assumed that the goal of all social and administrative science research is to achieve interpretable comparisons.

Neuman (2000) identified comparison as a "central process" in the analysis of all data. In this central role, comparative analysis has two broad objectives: The first is to find cases or evidence that belong together, based on one or more relevant characteristics; the second is to isolate anomalies in the data— events or cases that do not fit a pattern. Similarities enable the researcher to place the data within their proper categories and to develop new categorical codes that embrace the unclassified phenomenon. Anomalies are the distinct characteristics that are central to the research problem; finding distinctive differences in data is like a prospector finding the mother lode.

Miles and Huberman (1994, 254) considered the process of comparative analysis to be a part of their *drawing and verifying conclusions* step in the analysis of qualitative data. Refuting critics whom they accused of considering the act of making comparisons "odious," they responded:

> Comparison is a time-honored, classic way to test a conclusion. We draw a contrast or make a comparison between two sets of things—persons, roles, activities, cases as a whole—that are known to differ is some other important respect. This is the "method of differences," which goes back to Aristotle if not further.

They also offered the following caveats to the use of comparisons:

- Researchers must be sure that their comparisons are the right ones, and that it makes sense to use them in the analysis. "Mindless comparisons are useless."

- Comparisons should extend beyond the data alone. They should also be compared with what the researcher knows about the things being studied.
- Researchers should pause before including a comparison in a research report to ask "How big must a difference be before it makes a difference?" and "How do I know that?"
- With qualitative comparisons, researchers are concerned with the *practical significance* of the data; they cannot apply the statistical significance tests that are available in quantitative studies.

Strauss and Corbin (1998, 73) placed great importance on the activity of comparative analysis. In their opinion, making comparisons is an integral activity that should be used at all steps in the data analysis process. They defined the comparative analysis process as "an analytical tool used to stimulate thinking about properties and dimensions of categories." They considered the act of making comparisons to one of the two tasks that are essential for development of theory in qualitative research; the other essential task is *asking questions*.

Step 4: Analysis for Unbundling of Early Constructs

In this stage the researcher reviews the coded data to determine whether any categorical constructs make better intuitive sense as two or more factors rather than the one originally assigned. "Unbundling" means that each major category should be reexamined to see if it is really two or more categorical constructs. If an unbundling is warranted, care must also be taken to apply the characteristics originally assigned to the category to each of the newly established categories.

Step 5: Axial Coding to Clarify Constructs and Themes

Axial coding affords the researcher a second opportunity to introduce order and structure into the initially coded data. Axial coding can use preestablished codes such as the six categories suggested by Strauss and Corbin (1998), or it can be freely employed without any imposed structure, as Glaser (1992) proposed. Strauss and Corbin added their six categories when they found that the lack of structure at this point made it difficult for beginning researchers to produce clear and cogent theory from the data. Retaining the substantive coding levels, they proposed adding a third, intermediate step in the coding/analysis process. They called this intermediate step "axial coding" (Glaser 1992; Kendall 1999). This step was proposed as a way to demystify the grounded theory process. It requires the researcher to place all the initially open-coded data into these six specified categories: (1) *conditions*, (2) *phenomena*, (3) *context*, (4) *intervening conditions*, (5) *actions/strategies*, and (6) *consequences*.

These categories require the researcher to look for antecedents that lead to the particular event or circumstance, in addition to any resulting consequences. It also forces the researcher to reexamine the strategies and processes involved in both the target organization and the research design.

Step 6: Reiterative Analysis to Identify Relationships

Researchers must establish categories and codes for the major and minor constructs within the data, develop meaningful ideas about the data in context, edit and make critical interpretations, and—perhaps most important—generate ideas and theories from them. A key activity in this process is identifying *relationships* between constructs and groupings. One way to do this is to diagram the data as a set of boxes, circles, arrows, and lines. The "bathtubs and beer barrels" method can be used for this task. Bathtubs (large ovals) are used to represent key ideas, while beer barrels (smaller circles) are used to display antecedents and contributing components or factors, and to indicate effects and consequences. Lines indicate relationships, with arrows showing the direction of the influence or relationship. Diagrams such as these make it clear what sorts of relationships, if any, exist between two or more ideas, patterns, constructs, and groupings. Developing diagrams and relationship charts is an important part of the qualitative analysis procedure.

Another procedure sometimes used for this purpose is as *power* or *influence analysis*. In this process, the researcher first collects data by observing the way people interact or by questioning them on their perceptions of such factors as power and influence in the organization. The researcher then draws a diagram or chart to illustrate the interactions, relationships, and responses to others within a group or other social setting. Examples of graphic displays of this type include context charts, linkage patterns and knowledge flow charts, and role and power charts (Miles and Huberman 1984).

Step 7: Selective Recording of Major Themes

Patterns will usually emerge from the analysis, permitting the researcher to identify salient themes. As the analysis and reanalysis of the mass of collected data continues, it is often possible to merge several themes into a smaller number of categories. In addition to *themes*, these broader themes are sometimes referred to as *constructs*, or *factors*. This process is much like the data reduction statistical process of *factor analysis*, in which the researcher *aggregates* or collects data into a few salient themes. This data reduction or aggregation process makes it much easier to summarize the findings from the research.

Step 8: Reiterative Analysis with Links with the Literature

By the time the research has reached this point in the analysis clear links with the relevant literature in the field should begin to become apparent. The researcher must use this time to clearly show the reader how the collected data connects to or builds upon prior research in this field.

Step 9: Development of Appropriate Theory from Data

A major goal of most research projects is to be able to contribute to the body of knowledge in the intellectual or academic field in which the researcher is working. This means that one or more theories should emerge from the analysis.

A Twelve-Step Process for Analyzing Qualitative Data

Qualitative data gathering and analysis is carried out in a logical sequence of steps. Jones (1996) has organized this sequence into the twelve-step process shown in Figure 22.2. The twelve steps fall into two equal halves, each with six steps: The first half of the process, involving steps 1 through 6, is the *preparatory* half, while steps 7 through 12 constitute the *analysis and report* portion of the analysis procedure.

Part I: Preparing for Qualitative Research

Steps 1 and 2, *Define the research problem* and *establish research objectives*, are the initial activities in all research designs. Step 3, *Do your homework*, means becoming conversant with the full nature of the subject or topic of interest. Interviews with a few key informants and extensive analysis of the relevant literature are the activities often used in this step.

Part I

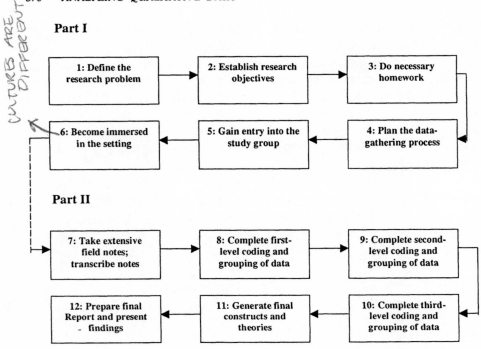

Figure 22.2 **The Twelve Steps of Qualitative Fieldwork, Analysis, and Report Preparation**
Source: Adapted from Newman 2000.

Step 4, *Plan the data-gathering process*, should occur only after the researcher has developed a working familiarity with the subject and study group. The plan should include a preliminary list of the behaviors to be observed, the subjects to be interviewed, the topics to be covered in the interviews, a preliminary coding scheme, and a schedule for each following step in the research process.

Steps 5 and 6, *Gain entry into the group* and *Become immersed in the setting*, are closely related activities; in fact, they often occur simultaneously. While these are more appropriately tasks to use in ethnographic research, they are also important in other qualitative research designs. For example, researchers conducting a study of the operating climate within a government agency must first gain permission of the agency director and the support and compliance of both the managers and the agency staff.

Part II: Analyzing and Reporting

The first activity in the second half of the research process is step 7, *Take extensive field notes*. *Field notes* are the notes, recordings, reminders, and other subjective reporting that the researcher records while observing behaviors or interviewing respondents. Not surprisingly, they are the records produced during the process of conducting *field research*. Field research is what is done when researchers want to know something about people, understand behaviors, or describe a group of people who interact in some way (Neuman 2000). Field notes are the detailed written reports and/or diagrams or pictures of what the researcher sees and hears. The term used to describe the required detail needed in field notes is "thick description." Finally, field notes should be written down or transcribed on a regular basis, as soon as possible after the phenomenon occurs.

Taking good field notes is not easy; the researcher must make a conscious effort to devote the time and effort necessary to produce good notes because, without them, the final report of the research can be only second-rate. Preparing field notes can be a boring, laborious task that requires self-discipline to be done correctly. The notes contain extensive descriptive detail drawn from memory. Researchers must make it a daily habit—better yet, a *compulsion*—to write their notes every day and to begin to transcribe them immediately after leaving the field. Field notes must be neat and organized because "the researcher will return to them over and over again. Once written, the notes are private and valuable. A researcher treats them with care and protects confidentiality" (Neuman 2000, 363).

An example of how difficult it can be to listen to informants in the field (that is, to gather data) and then to transcribe those narratives into meaningful field notes can be found in Jurich's (2001, S152) story of her lengthy field research project with Native Americans on a South Dakota reservation. She explained her methodological difficulties this way:

> I listened to stories during the day and late into the night, often falling asleep long before conversations were ended. I learned early on that questions were likely to be considered interrogation, intrusive, and were not a frequent form of interaction. So I asked few questions. . . . The stories would get summarized in [my] notebooks. . . . I worked hard to listen and remember, to record as completely as I could the substance of what was said. More often, though, the field notes were thick descriptions of my own experiences of going places and engaging in the practices of reservation life, describing social interaction and processes that were part of my daily life.

Once field notes are transcribed into organized records of the researcher's observations or interviews, they must then be put to a preliminary, interpretive analysis. This occurs during steps 8 through 11. Analysis is an ongoing process that begins during the first venture into the field experience, continues until a final set of codes, categories, and constructs is established, and ends with production of the final report of the research. Miles and Huberman

(1994) recommended employing a series of reporting guides or worksheets to ensure that this portion of the process is complete. These include the following: (1) a contact summary, (2) a summary of each document analyzed in the study, (3) first-, second-, and third-level coding and grouping of constructs, patterns, and factors discovered in the data, and (4) a final detailed summary of the site in which the activities, behaviors, and events were studied.

First-Level Coding

Step 8, *Complete first-level coding and grouping of data*, begins with preparation of contact summaries and a summary of each document, if any, analyzed for the study. The contact summary is usually nothing more than a single sheet that contains answers to a set of focusing or summary questions about each subject contacted in the study. It often includes demographic information, indications of relative position in the group under study, and other material. It is used to ensure continuity in the treatment of responses from all contacts.

The document summary is applicable only when documents of any type are acquired for analysis at the research site. The purpose of this guide is to establish a record of the document's significance and how it relates to observations, interviews, or final analysis.

First-level coding is done to develop the initial descriptive codes around which all subsequent data will be organized or grouped. These codes are abbreviations that establish descriptive categories or groupings in the data. Miles and Huberman (1994, 56) have defined a *code* as "an abbreviation or symbol applied to a segment of words—most often a sentence or paragraph of transcribed field notes—in order to *classify* the words." Codes should be considered as *categories*. As such, they are *retrieval* and *organizing devices* that allow the analyst to spot quickly, pull out, then cluster all the segments relating to the particular question, hypothesis, concept, or theme. Clustering sets the stage for analysis.

Second-Level Coding

Second-level, or *pattern coding* takes place in step 9 of the analysis process. Second-level coding involves establishing *interpretive codes*. Here, the researcher goes beyond simple description and begins to form interpretive labels for categories of behaviors. The goal at this point is to be able to read repeating patterns in the data.

Third-Level Coding

Step 10 involves *third-level*, or *thematic development coding* (also called *memoing*). Memoing refers to producing preliminary or partial summary reports for the personal use of the researcher or research team. These might, for example, be used to summarize a pattern or a theme in the data and even be incorporated wholesale into the final analysis. At the third analysis level, the researcher begins to establish *explanatory* codes that link larger groups of patterns into what are called *themes*. These are the major constructs that will make up the central structure under which the final analysis will occur and be recorded.

Step 11, the final activity in the coding and analysis process, is a brief description of the events, members, circumstances, and other relevant information that can serve as both a summary of the data-gathering experience and a memory-jogger during the preparation of the final report.

The last step in this 12-step process—just as in any other type of research project—is to combine the notes, constructs, patterns, and themes, along with the researcher's analysis and synthesis, into some form of *research report.* This important twelfth step in the qualitative research process is not simply putting the researcher's field notes together in one cover. Rather, it involves a number of important activities (Neuman 2000, 395):

> Assembling evidence, arguments, and conclusions into a report is always a crucial step; but more than in quantitative approaches, the careful crafting of evidence and explanation makes or breaks [qualitative] research. A researcher distills mountains of evidence into exposition and prepares extensive footnotes. She or he weaves together evidence and arguments to communicate a coherent, convincing picture to readers.

Analysis of Ethnographic Study Data: Six Phases

Ethnography is the study of groups of people in the settings in which they live, work, and/or play (see Chapter 20). To gather ethnographic data, researchers must gain entry into a social setting, earn and maintain the trust of members of the group, and observe and write narratives of everything that they see, hear, and feel.

Ethnographic data is the content of the researcher's field notes, while ethnographic *narratives* are the researcher's descriptions of the interplay of individuals in groups and how that interaction is influenced by the culture of the group or organization. The information contained in field notes consists of "rich descriptions" of the people, settings, and events observed by the participant researcher. It may also be tape recordings of subjects' life histories, opinions, dreams, and so on as well as photographs, drawings, films, videotapes, artifacts, or written documents. Ethnographers use descriptions of these physical objects in their reports of social interactions.

Before setting a single word to paper, an ethnographer may have amassed hundreds of pages of notes, rough illustrations of relationships, and other descriptive narrative. Making sense of this mass of data by bringing order, structure, and explanation to it has long been the most laborious and tedious task of ethnographic research (Emerson, Fretz, and Shaw 1995). The model displayed in Figure 22.3 reveals the detailed nature of the steps followed in the analysis of ethnographic data.

The processes identified in the model are shown as individual activities. However, in actual practice, some are best carried out in conjunction with others. Collectively, they take place in these six analytical phases that culminate in the writing of the research report:

Phase 1   Reflective Contemplation
Phase 2   Interpretive Questioning
Phase 3   Open Coding and Interpretive Memoing
Phase 4   Identification of Salient Themes in the Data
Phase 5   Focused Coding and Interpretive Memoing
Phase 6   Final Analytical Contemplation to Generate Theory

Phase 1: Reflective Contemplation

Once the data-collecting activity is complete, many researchers like to step away from their material to pause for a while and simply think about what they saw, heard, and took away from the experience. This is the act of reflective contemplation. During this quiet time away from the study site and data collection, ideas, insights, and preliminary interpretations are free to gestate in the mind of the researcher. After a brief period away from the data—away too long and data will be lost from memory—the researcher returns to the data collection and begins a full reading of the material from beginning to end. This experience is likely to give the researcher the first 'big picture" of everything that has occurred during the research study.

Phase 2: Interpretive Questioning

Interpretive questioning is the process of making marginal notes or comments on separate pages for guidance in the continuation of reading and interpreting. It begins during the first complete reading of field notes that follows reflective contemplation about what has been experienced and accomplished during the data gathering. These questioning notes guide the development of structure and organization and suggest groupings and self-directive, subsequent open coding of the data. The following examples are typical questions that might be asked at this time (Emerson, Fretz, and Shaw 1995, 146):

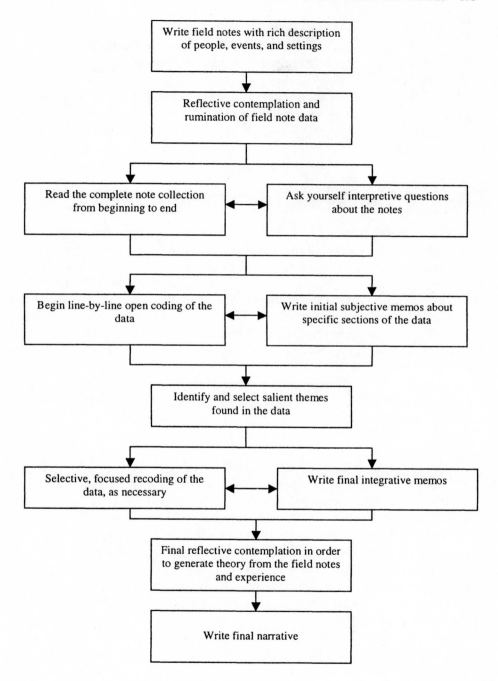

Figure 22.3 **A Model of the Ethnographic Data Analysis Process**

- What are people doing in this setting?
- What are they trying to accomplish? What are they avoiding?
- How, exactly, do they go about these behaviors?
- What sorts of things do people say to each other?
- How do people understand what is going on in their group or society?
- What assumptions guide their behavior?
- What was going on here? What did I learn about these people when I made the notes?
- Why did I include this information?

Phase 3: Open Coding and Interpretive Memoing

This process also begins during the initial full reading of the data collection. The researcher writes identifying words or phrases to describe the portions of data that made up relevant categories or classes of phenomena. The codes themselves should be detailed enough to remind the researcher of what categories they apply to, without having to resort to looking up the meaning of a code in a reference file every time it appears. Also, it is important to remember that codes should emerge from the data itself; they are not artificial constructs created by the researcher. An example of a set of code phrases used in a qualitative study is displayed in Table 22.1 (page 384).

Table 22.1 was developed from a research study designed to identify the attitudes of small business owners about exporting (McNabb, Barnowe, and Nordi 1989). The code phrases listed in column 2 were developed from responses to sentence completion items included in the interviews. The statements in column 3 are abbreviated examples of larger statements offered by respondents.

Both quantitative and qualitative data-gathering processes were used in this study. Qualitative methodology consisted of construction techniques (stories from supplied cartoon situations) and sentence completion techniques. These projective techniques were employed to draw out the personal perceptions and attitudes of owners. These techniques force the respondent to respond in a manner that reflects his or her own need/value system.

The second part of this analysis phase is *interpretive memoing*. "Memoing" can be found in most research data analyses. In the open coding step, memos are written to record the insights and ideas that come to the researcher during the initial, top-to-bottom reading of the data collection. They may serve as suggestions for further analysis, references to relevant literature, personal reminders, subjective opinions, preliminary evaluations, or any such purpose. They should not be considered the final word on the data; the researcher still has much analytical work to do.

Together, initial, open coding and memoing set the stage for the remainder

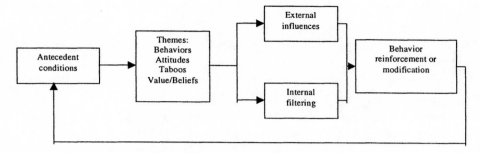

Figure 22.4 A Hypothetical Illustration of Linkages Between Themes and Other Factors

of the analysis. At this stage in the process, however, it is important to remember that this is just the first pass through the data; changes are to be expected to occur at every subsequent phase. The need for flexibility at this stage is highlighted in the following statement:

> [I]nitial coding and memoing require the [researcher] to step back from the field setting to identify, develop, and modify the broader analytic themes and arguments. Early on [however], these efforts should remain flexible and open. (Emerson, Fretz, and Shaw 1995, 157)

Phase 4: Identification of Salient Themes in the Data

In this phase of the analysis, the researcher returns to a broader view of the data collection in order to discern the core, recurring themes in the research data. At the same time, any linkages discovered between themes and constructs should be pointed out. Figure 22.4 illustrates how themes are shown to be linked to antecedent conditions, as well as to resulting consequences and transformations. At the conclusion of this step, the researcher may elect to sort the field notes and/or memos into new groups that reflect the selected themes. This step can also be done during the final coding and memoing phase.

Phase 5: Focused Coding and Interpretive Memoing

Focused coding—also called *selective coding*—is what Emerson, Fretz, and Shaw (1995) described as the product of a "fine-grained, line-by-line analysis of the notes." As one of the last steps in the data analysis process, it often results in preparation of an outline of a first draft of an ethnographic narrative.

Table 22.1

A Table Showing How Qualitative Responses Can Be Placed into Relevant Categories

#	Category code	Examples of responses	ID
1	Worries about exporting to Pacific Rim	• Spending a lot of money and getting no sales in return • Korea, Japan, and Taiwan firms copy our ideas • Money; getting paid; low profit margins	RIM
2	Getting American products to China	• Lots of red tape • Too difficult for small rewards • Lack of transportation or marketing infrastructure	CHI
3	Finding markets in Australia/NZ	• Buyers there go through brokers (making my costs too high) • They are just like any customer here; buyers there fax us directly with purchases • Believe they would buy from us if they knew about us or our products	AUN
4	Difficulties with customers in Korea	• Can't find proper agents/brokers • Can't get paid; very high import tariffs • Product knockoffs; copyright/trade infringements	KOR
5	Why U.S. products don't sell in Asian markets	• We're not good at promoting them against world competition • They are racists and too nationalistic • U.S. products are too expensive and too low in quality	US
6	Why don't participate in trade shows in Japan	• Have never tried it • Incredibly frightening thought; it is difficult and expensive • Do it regularly now; very good opportunity	JAP
7	Generic troubles with selling in Taiwan	• Takes lots of time; they won't commit • Tough to meet their price requirements; low labor costs there • Lack of knowledge about the country; don't know the language	TAI
8	Reactions to "Hong Kong is a good market"	• Agree that it's good now, but for how long? • Don't have contacts there • Don't sell as much as we could or should	HON

| 9 | Generic problems with shipping to Asia | • Either profitable or miserable; nothing in between
• Extremely complicated
• Is easy, straightforward; as smooth as importing from there | ASIA |
| 10 | Small companies getting paid for sales in Asia | • No different than any other market
• Use LCs but is a slow process; demand pay before shipping goods | MON |

Source: McNabb, Barnowe, and Nordi 1989.

The purpose of focused coding is to begin to integrate the final categories into a coherent whole that addresses the central issue or issues of the study. It may include unbundling of previously formed categories, the formation of entirely new categories, or making no change whatsoever. It brings the researcher to a point where no new categories, characteristics, or relationships emerge from the data (Strauss and Corbin 1998).

Integrative memoing also takes place during the open coding phase. Integrative memos are the concrete manifestations of the researcher's thinking process at this stage. They are used to justify the decisions made during the selection of salient themes. Furthermore, memoing is done to provide a record on any conclusions, revisions, or insights that emerge from the second run-through of the data. Integrative memos may follow a single concept though the mass of data, connecting it with other categories as required, or they may serve to integrate two or more concepts into a larger whole. Integrative memos that chronicle the background information of the study should also be written. These help to set the stage for analytical narrative writing, as well as providing a record of the researcher's role in the investigation.

Strauss and Corbin (1998) described three analytical tools that can facilitate the final integration process: (1) writing a storyline, (2) applying diagrams and other graphic display techniques, and (3) reviewing and re-sorting the open memos.

A *storyline* is nothing more than a subjective summary of the project in the words of the researcher, without referring back to the data or memos. It should flow as a freely written narrative, a life history of the project. At this point, details of the research are not critical; they can be inserted later. The overall purpose is to enable the researcher to take an "omniscient author" view of the experience, writing what he or she believes occurred, its meaning, and its relevance. The storyline is not the final interpretive ethnographic narrative, however. It should be considered just another interpretation guide for the researcher.

Diagrams and other graphic displays have long been important analysis tools. Miles and Huberman (1994, 1998) offered important guidance in the use of diagrams, including descriptions and graphic examples of several different approaches. They warned, however, that diagrams and other graphic displays should never be used in an analysis without a description of the content of the display. They described the integrative capability of diagrams in the following terms:

> The display helps the writer see patterns; the first text [i.e., the first draft] makes sense of the display and suggests new analytic moves in the displayed data; a revised or extended display points to new relationships and explanations, leading to more differentiated and integrated text, and so on. Displays beget analyses, which then beget more powerful, suggestive displays. (1998, 189)

Preparing diagrams and other graphic representations of ideas and their interrelationships is a valuable process for several reasons. First, it forces the researcher to step back from the complexity of the data to take a broader view of the study in its entirety. Second, it forces the researcher to establish collective constructs that embrace a variety of ideas and categories. And third, it forces the researcher to examine relationships among themes, constructs, and events.

Reviewing and re-sorting memos is a third way of arriving at a final integration of the data. Recall that memos are subjective notes prepared by the researcher during the review of the data. They contain the conclusions, questions, possible integrations, and perceived connections of themes and constructs as seen by the researcher. In one sense, then, they can be considered a reduced data set. Some researchers use this opportunity to re-sort their memos into new categories that emerged from selective coding of the open-coded data. This provides a possible final structure and organization to guide the researcher in writing the final report.

Phase 6: Final Analytical Contemplation to Generate Theory

The final step in the analysis of ethnographic research data is to reach closure by generating theory that is grounded in the study and its setting. While the concepts are similar, the theory generated by ethnographic research is not the same as the grounded theory method first described by Glaser and Strauss (1967) and modified by Strauss and Corbin (1998). Ethnographers do not "discover" theory in their data. Rather, they create theory during each and every step of their fieldwork and analysis (Emerson, Fretz, and Shaw 1995, 167). For ethnographers, theory generation occurs during the "reflexive" interplay between theory and data. Ethnographers introduce theory at every point in their studies. Emerson, Fretz, and Shaw identified the key objective of this interactive process in the following way: "The goal of fieldwork . . . is to generate theory that grows out of or is directly relevant to activities occurring in the setting under study."

Computer Analysis of Qualitative Data

There has been a dramatic growth in the use of computers in research and the availability of analysis software in the past several decades (Tak, Nield, and Becker 1999; Este, Sieppert, and Barsky 1998; Richards and Richards 1998; Miles and Huberman 1994; Weitzman and Miles 1995). In some research settings, technology has simplified the many necessary but time-consuming and often boring tasks of the data analysis process. However, qualitative researchers have not universally accepted them.

Although today's computer programs are capable of processing large volumes of text material and records, sorting and indexing the data, and retrieving information from a variety of different directions, few researchers have used the qualitative data analysis programs that are presently available (Richards and Richards 1998). Instead, most data coding, sorting, categorizing, and analysis are still done the way they have been done for more than a hundred years—by hand.

This section provides a brief introduction to the concept of computer analysis, using a single program package for an illustration. Readers who seek more information about these programs are encouraged to refer to several published reviews, such as *Computer Programs for Qualitative Data Analysis* by Weitzman and Miles (1995). Miles and Huberman (1994) included a valuable point-by-point comparison of a dozen or more commercially available analysis programs in their text on qualitative data analysis. Richards and Richards (1998) provided a useful introduction to the theoretical underpinnings of computer software programs for analyzing qualitative data, but without evaluating many specific programs.

In the taxonomy of analysis software suggested by Richards and Richards, software is divided into two broad classifications: (1) general-purpose software packages, and (2) special-purpose software developed specifically for data analysis. General-purpose packages include standard word processing programs, database management systems, and text-search software. Richards and Richards identified five categories of special-purpose software:

- Code-and-retrieve software
- Rule-based, theory-building systems

- Logic-based systems
- Index-based systems
- Conceptual, or semantic, network systems

Of these, the two approaches that seem to offer the most promise at this time are logic-based systems and conceptual network systems. Richards and Richards provided an extensive review of a logic-based system they authored, NUD*IST (*Non-numerical Unstructured Data Indexing, Searching, and Theorizing*).

NUD*IST allows the user to code themes and categories by simply attaching labels to segments of the text (Tak, Nield, and Becker 1999). Like a majority of the systems discussed by Richards and Richards, NUD*IST is built around a code-and-retrieve facility. It has been expanded to include a number of different optional processes—a feature that may turn out to be one of the program's greatest faults. Richards and Richards (1998, 237) offered this caveat about their program:

> NUD*IST appears, compared with the other systems described here, as a rather awkward hybrid, containing features of code-and-retrieve, ways of handling production-rule and other types of conceptual-level reasoning, conceptual representations alternative to conceptual network systems, and database storage facilities, all interacting through interlocking tools. . . . And, perhaps most important, the software offers many ways for a researcher never to finish a study. . . .

Despite the potentially confusing complexity of NUD*IST, it has become one of the most, if not the most, popular computer software programs for analysis of qualitative data. It is particularly popular in education, nursing and other medical studies and some sociological applications. It seems to be used less often in ethnographic studies, and is hardly ever seen in public administration research. Despite its slow adoption, a few innovators in public administration and nongovernment organization research have started to test its capabilities.

The second software program to receive special mention by Richards and Richards was the conceptual network system ATLAS/ti. Thomas Mühr developed ATLAS in Germany during the 1980s, when most of the work on analysis software was under way. ATLAS is built on a code-and-retrieve foundation, to which has been added an excellent memoing capability; codes can be assigned to memos as well as to the original text. Its distinguishing feature, however, is its ability to create conceptual graphic displays that show relationships and linkages. According to Richard and Richards (1998, 240): "Allied with ATLAS's sophisticated text-retrieval system, the graphs support subtle exploration of text via a visually immediate interface that relates the text to the systems or theories in the [setting] being studied."

In conclusion, the application of special-purpose software packages for qualitative data analysis is probably here to stay. As more and more professional researchers discover the capabilities of the packages and more students are exposed to them in their research methods classes, this growth in use should accelerate. As of today, however, because of their complexity—due in large part to their extensive capabilities—most researchers still analyze their data using traditional, minimal techniques and processes.

Summary

Conducting any qualitative research is a time-consuming, complicated, and often confusing task. One of the most problematic components of the process is the task of analyzing qualitative data.

The *analysis* processes for quantitative and qualitative research data are similar in some ways, but different in others. Similarities include the following: (1) data are not just *there*; they must be collected in some way by a researcher; (2) when processed, both quantitative and qualitative data can be used for inference; (3) comparative analyses are used with both data types; and 4) researchers are concerned with both the reliability and validity of all data.

Quantitative data differ from qualitative data primarily in the way they are tabulated, collated, and processed. Quantitative data are typically computer processed and analyzed with a variety of standard statistical tests. These tests are applied for one or more of the following purposes: (1) to describe a data set, (2) to generate hypotheses, and (3) to test hypotheses.

Qualitative data, on the other hand, exhibit variety in both form and context. They can also be evaluated and interpreted in a variety of ways. Qualitative data can be words, pictures, artifacts, music scores, and so on. Furthermore, each of the several different analysis approaches has its own underlying purpose, and each can produce a different outcome.

Qualitative data are data that have been gathered during the conduct of interpretive or postpositivist research studies. It can be written text, transcripts of conversations or interviews, transcripts of therapeutic or consultive interviews, records of legal trials, transcripts of focus group discussions, historical or literary documents, ethnographic field notes, diaries, newspaper clippings, or magazine and journal articles. It can also be in the form of photographs, maps, illustrations, paintings, musical scores, tape recordings, films, or any other nonquantitative or quantitative source. All data must be analyzed and interpreted before they are meaningful.

There are two parts to the interpretation and analysis of qualitative data.

The first is *data management*; the second is *data analysis*. Many different techniques and strategies have been developed for analyzing qualitative data; three are discussed in this chapter. The first is a nine-step process; the second follows twelve steps divided into two halves. The third was developed by anthropologists for analyzing ethnographic data.

Advances in computer software have resulted in a number of special-purpose software packages for analyzing qualitative data. Two popular programs discussed briefly here are NUD*IST and ATLAS/ti. Researchers studying public administration and nongovernment organization management topics have been slow to adopt these new approaches for analysis, but are now doing so in greater numbers.

Suggested Reading

Denzin, Norman K., and Yvonna S. Lincoln, eds. 1998. *Collecting and Interpreting Qualitative Materials.* Thousand Oaks, CA: Sage.

Emerson, Robert M., Rachel I. Fretz, and Linda L. Shaw. 1995. *Writing Ethnographic Fieldnotes.* Chicago: University of Chicago Press.

Jones, Russell A. 1996. *Research Methods in the Social and Behavioral Sciences.* Sunderland, MA: Sinaur Associates.

Miles, Matthew B., and A. Michael Huberman. 1994. *Qualitative Data Analysis.* 2d ed. Thousand Oaks, CA: Sage.

Mühr, Thomas. 1991. "ATLAS/ti: A Prototype for the Support of Text Interpretation." *Qualitative Sociology* 14: 339–347.

Neuman, W. Lawrence. 2000. *Social Research Methods.* 4th ed. Boston: Allyn and Bacon.

Qualitative Solutions and Research. 1997. *QSR NUD*IST 4 User Guide.* 2d ed. Thousand Oaks, CA: Scolari.

23 Analyzing Texts, Documents, and Artifacts

Sources of research data include people, their words and actions, publications, material culture, and any item or symbol that communicates a message of any kind. Data-gathering methods range from watching how people act; asking them questions about their opinions, attitudes, or perceptions; reading what they have written; watching their movements; listening to their songs and other sounds; rummaging through their garbage; examining their tools and toys; deciphering their signs, symbols, or facial expressions—the list can go on and on. This chapter discusses some of the ways that researchers go about examining textual material, cultural artifacts, body language, and similar types of written and unwritten communications, records, documents, signs, and symbols.

For convenience, these different sources of research data can be grouped into four broad categories. The first is *written texts*—books, periodicals, narratives, reports, pamphlets, and other published materials. Collectively, this group of sources includes most if not all of the mass media. Research using these sources is often called *library research*, or *desk research*.

The second category is *formal and informal documents*; it includes personal messages and assorted types of archival information, such as personal notes and memos, government records and vital statistics, and other informal written materials, including e-mail. The third category of sources is made up of the wide variety of *nonwritten communications*—graphic displays (graphs, tables, charts), photographs and illustrations, tools and other artifacts, and films and videotapes. The final category includes all *nonverbal signs and symbols*. Among these are the silent messages in body language, facial expressions, gestures, music and dance, animal sounds and behavior, and even noise.

Researchers employ a variety of analytical tools and methods in their study of texts, symbols, and artifacts. Among these are *hermeneutics, content analy-*

sis, *meta-analysis*, *semiotic analysis*, *proxemics*, *kinesics*, *discourse analysis*, *site surveys*, and more. Table 23.1 displays the relationship between various sources of data and methods used in their analysis. The analytical approaches used most often in public and nonprofit organization research are the formal literature review; archival analysis; meta-analysis; hermeneutic analysis of textual material; semiotic analysis; content, discourse, and narrative analysis; and analysis of material culture. Each of these will be discussed in greater detail in the following pages.

Another way to categorize these research approaches might be to look at the formal literature review, meta-analysis, hermeneutics, semiotics, and content analysis, as *methods*, and archives, texts, artifacts, and signs and symbols as *sources* of research data. This chapter is structured along these lines, with the discussion of textual sources first discussed in a section on the literature search process. Narrative and discourse analyses are discussed in the content analysis section.

Analysis of Texts As Data

In public administration and nonprofit organization research, if not in research in all of the social and administrative sciences, library-based research draws on documents of all types as the source of data. It is, in this aspect, the opposite of the field research methods that have been discussed to this point. These types of library or desk research projects are common in such fields of inquiry as philosophy, social theory, law, and history, which rely almost exclusively upon documents as their key source (Denscombe 1998). Library research is also important in public administration research, with many studies drawing upon legislative archives for data.

From the researcher's point of view, literature or documentary research can be grouped into three key classes. The first is the traditional *literature review* that is or should be a part of all scientific research. A key purpose of the literature review is to provide background information that can then be used to design a complete research project.

The second strategy is called *archival studies*. In substance similar to a standard literature review, the archival study draws upon public and private formal documents, records, and other material of a historical nature for data. They may or may not be stored in a library. When they are, they are generally not open for general access or circulation.

The third approach is known as a *meta-analysis* design. In this approach, researchers use other studies as subjects for analysis. Meta-analysis is a quantitative technique for summarizing other investigators' research on a topic; as such, it uses the literature as a source of data in its own right.

Table 23.1

The Relationship Between Sources, Examples, and Study Methods

Source	Examples	Analysis methods
Written texts	• Professional literature • Mass media • Narratives • Books and stories	Hermeneutics Content analysis Narrative analysis Meta-analysis Literature review
Informal documents and records	• Archival information • Government reports • Vital statistics • Records, documents • Notes and memos	Hermeneutics Content analysis Archival analysis Semiotics
Nonwritten communications and material culture	• Photos and drawings • Films and videos • Tools and artifacts • Graphs and tables	Semiotics Discourse analysis Hermeneutics Site surveys
Nonverbal signs, symbols, and other communications	• Body language • Gestures • Music and dance • Nonverbal sounds • Signs • Noise	Semiotics Proxemics Kinesics

The Literature Review

A crucial early step in the design and conduct of all research is a thorough investigation of the relevant literature on the study topic, the research question, and the methodology followed by others who have studied the same or similar problems. Called a *review of the relevant literature* or, simply, a *literature review*, the process has been defined as "a systematic, explicit, and reproducible method for identifying, evaluating, and interpreting the existing body of recorded work produced by researchers, scholars, and practitioners" (Fink 1998, 3).

Purposes for the Literature Review

Different authors have identified many different purposes for the literature review. Denscombe (1998), for example, saw the literature review serving three fundamental purposes: First, it shows those who read the research findings that the researcher is aware of the existing work already done on the topic. Second, it clearly identifies what the researcher believes are the key issues, crucial questions, and the obvious gaps in the field. Third, it establishes a set of guiding signs that allow readers to see which theories and principles the researcher used to shape the research design and analysis (Denscombe 1998).

Despite the critical importance of the literature review, some researchers skip this step entirely in the mistaken belief that theirs is a "unique" study problem, or if they do look into the literature of the study topic, field, or discipline, they often take a wrong approach. The literature review is not intended to be just a summary of the articles and books that were read. Nor should a literature review be a list of the authors with whom the researcher agrees or disagrees. The good literature review has a greater purpose than this; it is a source of data in its own right (Denscombe 1998). Piantanida and Garman (1999) proposed a list of five purposes for the literature review. Among the most meaningful strategic purposes to which the literature review can be put are the following:

- The review can *trace the historical evolution* of the study problem or key issues, themes, or constructs pertaining to the problem.
- The review can provide a schematic of the *different schools of thought* that have developed or are developing with regard to the study problem.
- The review can examine the study problem from several *different disciplines* (for example, looking at welfare reform from the point of view of social work and of economics).
- The review can examine the positions of *different stakeholder-groups*, such as public administrators, citizen groups, and nonprofit organizations.
- The review can trace *different conceptual schools of thought* that have emerged over time and that may be currently taking opposing or conflicting views in the literature.

These are only a few of the many approaches for a literature review; the important thing to remember about this list is that *these approaches and strategies are not mutually exclusive*. A good literature review can achieve many goals at the same time. Lang and Heiss (1984) identified two key purposes for reviewing the related literature. First, it hones the researcher's attack on a specific study problem, and second, it provides a point of reference to use when discussing and interpreting the findings of the research. Specifically, a well-conducted literature review can do all of the following:

- Set specific limits for subsequent research
- Introduce the researcher to new and different ways of looking at the problem
- Help the researcher avoid errors and omissions in planning the study
- Suggest new ideas
- Acquaint the researcher with new sources of data and, often, totally different ways of looking at an issue

A formal literature review should follow an organized series of steps. The action model portrayed in Figure 23.1 has been developed from several sources, but owes a special debt to the contributions of Arlene Fink (1998). The model begins with an encouragement to researchers to study all their options before embarking on their journey through the literature. This means that all potential sources should be considered. Limiting a literature search to a quick perusal of the Internet or a run through a single CD-ROM database is not the way to conduct a thorough, scientific review of the literature. The second step in the literature review process is made up of three equally important activities. The researcher must establish some basis for selecting articles (content criteria) and establish methodological criteria. Examples of such criteria include:

1. Should the studies all be qualitative or quantitative?
2. Should they all be about the same size?
3. Should the samples discussed all have been randomly selected?

These decisions will be based on the study question and may change somewhat when the search itself—the third activity in this step—is underway. Identifying high quality studies to include in the analysis follows establishment of selection criteria.

The collected research must then be read in detail. As this occurs, relevant categories of information should begin to stand out. These categories must be coded, with the pertinent information copied onto cards or worksheets. Repeated salient themes in the literature should be recorded; these often serve as discussion points during the writing of the final research report. Detailed analysis begins at this point. As this point the researcher often continues by writing interpretive memos that summarize the material and allow the researcher to comment on the content. These memos are sometimes carried into the final report with little or no revision.

During the next-to-last stage in the process, the researcher is encouraged to record all the important bibliographic information on the source documents. This usually includes information about the author(s), the discipline in which

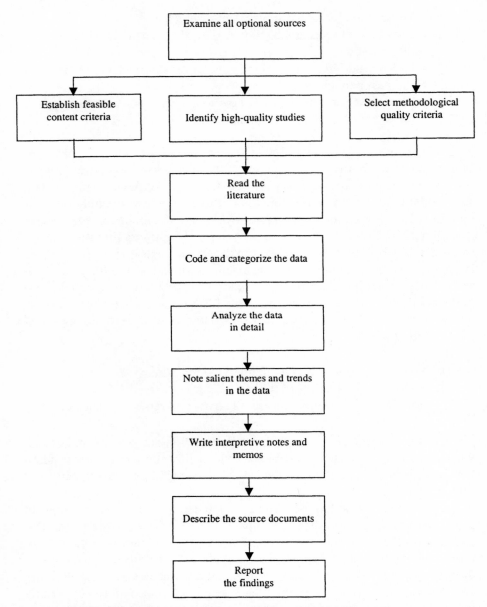

Figure 23.1 **A Model of the Steps in a Literature Review Process**

they did their research, all information about the source, and any connections to other sources that have been or might be also investigated. The last step in the process is preparing and presenting a report of the research findings.

Document Research Using Archival Data

Archives, long thought to be of interest only to librarians, have lately come to be recognized as rich sources of research material in the social sciences, including public administration. They are particularly valuable as a source for cross-checking interview and narrative study data. In this way they contribute to improved validity through triangulation—using several different approaches in a research study. While it is certainly possible for bias and dishonesty to exist in archival data, they are less susceptible to some types of error, including researcher error.

Archival records include a wide variety of sources and types of data. The following is only a partial list of archival sources of research data:

- Private letters and collections
- Political and judicial documents
- Voter registration lists
- The Congressional Record
- Actuarial records (e.g., vital statistics)
- Records of quasi-governmental agencies (weather reports)
- The mass media
- Professional and academic journals
- Company and organization records
- Personal histories
- Published and unpublished documents, etc.

Archivists collect, organize, and store documentary evidence of events, operations, correspondence, and organizational functioning, thereby performing a valuable service for historians and social science researchers. However, gaining access to archives can sometimes be problematic. If the reaction of one of America's leading archivists, T.R. Schellenberg, is any indication, a guiding principle of archival science might be *a place for everything and everything in its place.* One implication that can be taken away from Schellenberg is: *And that is where it should stay.*

Researchers, by the very act of researching archival data, must often synthesize, reorganize, restructure, and condense archival data in order to interpret their meaning. Schellenberg grudgingly admitted this fact, but believed that researchers could not really be trusted to leave things the way they found them. He blamed this on their lack of knowledge of the archival profession, though he forgave them for their ignorance (Schellenberg 1984, 152):

> If historians (and other social scientists) fail to preserve the evidential values of records by insisting on a violation of the principle of provenance, their action may

be attributed to their ignorance of the archival profession, about which they are expected to know very little, and may for this reason be excused.

Despite Schellenberg's condescending and biased attitude about the purpose of collections, he was indeed making a valid point—one that everyone should remember: As researchers, we all owe future investigators the same right to access to the original archival data that we expect. Therefore, researchers must always treat archives with care and leave them in the state we would like them to be in when we find them.

The Running Record

Webb et al. (2000) group the many sources into just two broad classes or types of archives: the *running record* (essentially all types of public documents, artifacts, and mass media), and the *episodic and private record* (discontinuous types that are usually not a part of the public record).

Running record archives are the continuous, ongoing records of society. The first thing that comes to mind when we think about this source is the extensive body of vital statistics and other records kept by all levels of governments and the mass media. However, it also includes actuarial records of insurance companies, recorded votes of political officeholders, government budgets, and the like. Like the second type of archive records, these data can exist as words, numbers, pictures, graphic displays, the residue of human activity, and society's refuse.

Public administration researchers are often particularly concerned with political and judicial records, including speeches by candidates, officeholders, and their supporters and opponents, voting records, judicial decisions (including minority opinions), and other similar records. Researchers may also be interested in legislators' seniority, party majorities, committee assignments, scales that measure political philosophy, events, or legislative emphasis during times of economic or political stress, and many other such phenomena. For example, a study conducted in the State of Washington evaluated legislative effectiveness under stress as measured by the number and scope of bills passed during two periods when a tie existed in the lower house.

Webb et al. (2000) also identified the mass media as an important source of archival data. Citing a number of different studies, they concluded that carefully selected media could clearly serve as a record of the values of society at a given period.

Webb also alerted the researcher to two classes of potential bias that can creep into public records—*selective deposit* and *selective survival.* Artifacts survive in nature because they are not consumed, not eroded away, and not combined into other artifacts and thus lost to view or memory. For example, ceremonial stones, decorative stone facings, and similar components of Greek and Roman structures have been removed over the centuries to be incorporated into the baser constructions of later generations. Temples have become stables.

Changes in political administrations usually result in the filing away and delivery to archival storage of volume after volume of written records. Potentially damaging or embarrassing records somehow get misplaced, "accidentally" removed from the archival record. In other instances, well-meaning historians or social science researchers may be charged with bringing order to a body of unorganized archival records. In the process, they often "edit" the raw data, unwilling to leave it as they found it. What survives may be what that researcher believed was important. Also, records of events tend to be grouped together, thereby blurring the real contextual time structure of events. The phenomenon is visible today in the decay evident in many inner cities. Buildings are abandoned, their materials removed and used for other purposes. What remains for later generations to read is far different from the record as it was originally laid down.

Researchers are encouraged in such instances to fall back on the tried and true practice of *triangulation*, validating the remaining archival record by using other sources. These include written records prepared by visitors from other cultures, biographies and histories, others' interpretations of the time, and, for phenomena in the not too distant past, the remembrances of participants in the events.

An example of triangulation design in which archival data played a role is the Monopoli and Alworth (2000) study involving Navaho World War II veterans. Four surviving tribal members were part of a panel who participated in a 1950s Thematic Apperception Test (TAT) study of attitudes and opinions of Native Americans. The surviving subjects were interviewed and the data compared with archival records of the original study. In addition to the benefits of a longitudinal design, the researchers were also able to identify some biasing errors in the earlier study results that might not have come to light with the use of the archival data in only the modern study.

Another example of triangulation in an archival design involved a comparison of official written histories with daily reports of speeches, paid announcements, and published articles appearing in the regional mass media of the period (McNabb 1968). The study subject was the conflict between advocates of public ownership of electrical power generation and distribution, and those representing the large holding-company forces of investor-owned utilities led by the Samuel Insull group of utilities. The battle began in earnest shortly before World War I, eventually becoming one of the last great causes of the Progressive Movement in the United States.

Episodic and Private Archives

It is important to remember that episodic and private record archives are, first, private data. Furthermore, they are usually not as accessible as public records. They tend to be stored for shorter periods and are often destroyed after a set period of time. This accounts for one of the major differences between these two broad classes of archives: it is often not possible to perform longitudinal analyses on private archival data.

Episodic archives can be grouped into three broad classes: company records, institutional records, and personal documents. Company information, such as sales records, has long been used to measure the popularity of, preference for, and loyalty toward a product, event, idea, or service. It is also used to measure the effectiveness of advertising and government informational communications programs. Institutional records are the files of companies, organizations, agencies, and institutions. They can be used to measure job stress by providing evidence of absenteeism, tardiness, turnover, and labor union grievances, for example. They can also be used to evaluate agency effectiveness by measuring customer complaints and the content of suggestion programs. Personal records such as letters, memos, collections, artwork, and other possessions are usually the concern of historians and as such have little application for research in public administration.

A Word of Caution Concerning Archives

Caution is advised in the use of archival materials because of the potential distortion that can exist in personal archives (Webb et al. 2000). Low-paid clerical workers often indifferently keep archives with no stake in the accuracy of their product. Because record keepers may feel that the saved material has little value, it may be stored haphazardly. It may be years if not decades before the material is again examined; therefore, their diligence or lack thereof seldom comes to light. When a researcher appears on the scene, however, there is a tendency for their interest to be revitalized, with the unfortunate result of some altering or even destruction of recorded data.

Archive research involves a way of looking at published or previously prepared material and also defines the types of materials that are examined. While this approach to the investigation of archival records of all types can serve as an excellent source of pertinent data for many studies in public administration and nonprofit organization management, it is not without its disadvantages. This final warning was provided by Webb et al. (2000, 84):

> For all their gains [i.e., advantages], however, the gnawing reality remains that archives have been produced for someone else by someone else. There must be a

careful evaluation of the way in which the records were produced, for the risk is high that one is getting a cutrate version of another's errors.

Nontextual Archives: Physical Traces

Physical evidence is another information source that might be considered "archival evidence." Archival evidence consists of any historical record that was saved or stored for future reference. It is most often written material and can be in the form of notes, letters, reports, and any other historical data. According to Webb et al. (2000), physical evidence is probably the least used source of data in the social and administrative sciences. However, it does hold what they called "flexible and broad-gauge potential." They identified two broad classes of physical evidence:

1. *Erosion measures*—the degree of selective wear or erosion that occurs over time, such as using the rate of wear in museum floor tiles as a measure of exhibit popularity.
2. *Accretion measures*—the degree to which materials collect over time. There are two subclasses of accretion measures: (1) *remnants*—only one or a few traces are available for study, and (2) *series*—an accumulative body of evidence remains.

The major advantage of physical evidence is its inconspicuousness. It is, indeed, a *silent* measure of change. What is measured is generated without the subject's knowledge of its use by investigators. This circumvents the problems that arise from the subject's awareness of being measured and removes the bias that comes from the measurement process itself becoming a part of the phenomenon. With all types of physical traces, and particularly when the phenomenon still occurs, index numbers are generated for comparisons, rather than the specific measurements themselves.

Performing a Meta-Analysis of Text Materials

Examining the literature of a study topic has been shown to have many purposes. First, it allows the researcher to frame his or her study in light of what others have investigated previously. Second, it can provide insights and new ideas regarding the study problem. Third, it can suggest new ways of examining the problem or conducting analysis of the gathered data. A meta-analysis is a fourth purpose for analysis of existing literature on a topic, method, or conclusions.

Lipsey and Wilson (2001) defined *meta-analysis* as a type of survey research in which previously prepared research reports, instead of poeple, are the subjects of analysis. Meta-analyses are used in order to summarize and compare the results of many different studies; other researchers have produced most if not all of these other studies. Meta-analysis is an excellent way of establishing the state of research findings on a subject—it provides the researcher with the "big picture," rather than simply another discussion of one or a few parts of the question, problem, or issue.

Meta-analysis can be applied only to empirical research reports—that is, studies that employed primary research and data gathering. Neither qualitative studies nor studies that summarize a set of other studies can be used in a meta-analysis. Although experiments are not a requirement, many empirical research reports have followed an experimental design.

Advantages and Disadvantages of Meta-Analysis

Lipsey and Wilson (2001) identified four important advantages of the meta-analysis research design. First, the complete process of establishing a coding scheme and criteria for selecting studies (a survey protocol), reading the study reports, coding the material, and subjecting it to a rigid statistical analysis imposes a discipline on the researcher that is sometimes missing in qualitative summarizations and comparative analyses. Second, the process results in greater sophistication in summarizing research, particularly when compared with qualitative summary attempts. The application of common statistical tests across all the studies can correct for wide differences in sample size, for example. Third, meta-analysis may enable the researcher to find effects or associations that other comparative processes miss. Finally, it provides a way to organize and structure diverse information from a wide variety of study findings.

Meta-analysis is not without its disadvantages, however. A few of the criticisms that have been cited for the method include the following:

1. The large amount of effort and expertise it requires is an often cited disadvantage of the method. Properly done, a meta-analysis takes considerably more time than a conventional qualitative research review; many aspects of the method require specialized knowledge, particularly in the selection and computation of appropriate "effect sizes" (i.e., the statistic chosen for comparison across all the studies).

2. Meta-analysis may not be sensitive to some important issues, including but not limited to the social context of the study, theoretical

influences and implications, methodological quality, design issues, and procedures.

3. The mix of studies (an *apples and oranges* issue) combined into larger groups may hide subtle differences seen in individual studies.
4. Finally, inclusion of studies that are methodologically weak can detract from the findings in strong studies.

Lipsey and Wilson admit the validity of these criticisms, but are convinced that the strengths of the method far outweigh any such disadvantages.

How to Do a Meta-Analysis

Fink (1998, 216) has recommended the following series of seven steps for conducting a meta-analysis:

Step 1. Clarify the objectives of the analysis.
Step 2. Set explicit criteria for including and excluding studies.
Step 3. Justify the methods used for searching the literature.
Step 4. Search the literature using a standardized protocol for including and excluding studies.
Step 5. Devise a standardized protocol to collect data from each study, including study purposes, methods, and outcomes (i.e., effects measured).
Step 6. Describe in detail the statistical method for pooling results.
Step 7. Report the results of the comparative analysis, including conclusions and perceived limitations.

A slightly longer, but possibly more informative, list of steps can be discerned by combining ideas from Lipsey and Wilson's seminal manual on the method with Fink's later review. This summary procedure model is displayed in Figure 23.2.

State the Topic or Question

This step provides the framework upon which all subsequent steps in the process follow. An example question statement for a meta-analysis might be: How have mandatory sentencing guidelines affected the number of repeat arrests for crimes in which a weapon was involved?

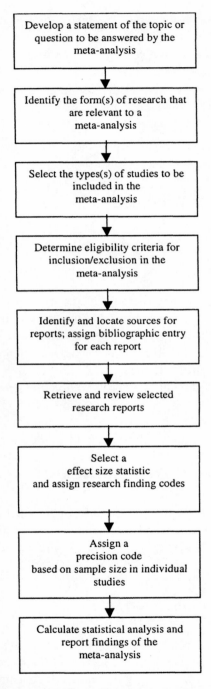

Figure 23.2 **Steps in a Meta-Analysis Research Design**
Source: Information from Lipsey and Wilson 2001; Fink 1998.

Identify the Form(s) of Research Relevant to a Meta-Analysis on the Topic

The "forms" are the types of analysis conducted in the individual research studies—for example, studies that report treatment/control group experiments or focus on correlations between two or more variables. Another example is a standard two-sample comparison study. In the mandatory sentencing example, a typical form would be studies that compare mean rates of arrests or length of sentences before mandatory sentencing, and then a repeat of the study after imposition of sentencing minimums. This is a typical pre- and posttreatment comparison or hypothesis testing research design. The test statistic for the next step could be t-test scores or p-values of comparisons.

Select Types of Studies to Be Included in the Analysis

This decision step is similar to the step above, but refers to the statistical tests used. Four types of tests are regularly used in meta-analyses: (1) central tendency descriptions (such as mean scores), (2) pregroup/postgroup hypothesis test studies, (3) other group contrasts, either pure experiments or nonexperimental grouping comparisons (for example, comparing gender or age groups), and (4) studies employing regression analysis.

Determine Eligibility Criteria

In this step the researcher chooses topics upon which to base a decision about including the study in the meta-analysis. Examples of criteria often used include (1) the distinguishing feature of a study (what made writing about it worthwhile), (2) research subjects (i.e., types or characteristics of respondents used in the study), (3) key variable(s), (4) research designs, (5) cultural and/or linguistic range, (6) time frame involved, and (7) type of publication.

Identify and Locate Sources of Research Reports

At this stage the researcher must apply the decision criteria established in the previous step. Lipsey and Wilson urged that the researcher develop a meticulous accounting system so that each study is assigned its own detailed bibliographic entry and its own identification number in order to facilitate future cross-referencing and to ensure that reports are assigned to their appropriate comparison group. A brief description of the subject report should also be prepared at this time.

Sources and listings for research reports include review articles, references in other studies, computer databases, bibliographies, professional and academic journals, conference programs and proceedings, correspondence with researchers active in the field, government agencies, the Internet, colleges and universities, professional associations, and others.

Retrieve and Review Eligible Research Studies

This step involves several activities: First, the researcher must find bibliographic references to potentially eligible studies and, second, obtain a copy of the study for screening. If it is considered to be eligible, it must be coded for inclusion in the meta-analysis.

Select an Effect Size Statistic for Use with the Entire Sample of Reports

In a meta-analysis, a single research finding is a statistical representation of the relationships among the variable(s) of interest. This statistical representation is the effect size statistic that will be used in comparative analysis during the meta-analysis. Research findings in the subject reports are test statistics; each must be coded as a value on the same effect size statistic. This must be the same statistic across the entire sample of reports. For example, if the effect size statistic is the correlation between two or more variables, the variables in all the reports must have been measured at the same level (nominal, ordinal, or interval), with the same correlation statistic employed (Pearson's r, Spearman's rho, the chi-square-based phi or Cramer's V). Similar restrictions apply for other statistical measures that might be selected. Table 23.2 displays some of the effect size statistics used in meta-analysis (Lipsey and Wilson 2001).

Assign a Precision Code for Each Research Report

A precision code is similar to a weighting system. It is based upon the sample size employed in each subject report. For example, a study in which a sample size of 500 was tested can be expected to be considerably more precise than one in which the sample size was, say, only 5—or even 50. The statistical calculations used in meta-analysis take these precision weights into effect, thus correcting for possible error associated with small samples. The greater the perceived reliability, the greater should be the precision code value assigned to the study.

Finally, researchers must keep in mind that there are two parts to a meta-

Table 23.2

Effect-Size Statistics Used in Meta-Analysis

Type of relationship	Type of statistical analysis
One-variable relationships	• Proportions (percentages) • Arithmetic means

Two-variable relationships
  a. Pre-post contrasts
  b. Group contrasts
	• Unstandardized mean gain
	• Standardized mean gain
	• Unstandardized mean difference
	• Standardized mean difference
	• Proportion difference

Association between variables	• Correlation analysis • Regression analysis
Multivariate relationships	• Multivariate relationship tests

Source: Adapted from Lipsey and Wilson 2001.

analysis coding process. The first part is the information that describes characteristics of the subject report; this is the "study descriptor" portion of coding. Study characteristics include the methods, the measures, sample characteristics and size, constructs developed, treatments given, and the like. The second part of the coding protocol covers information about the empirical findings contained in the report; this is the "effect sizes" portion of the coding, together with the precision code for each study. Effect sizes, for example, are the statistical values that indicate the association between variables.

Calculate and Report Findings

The first section of this chapter discussed documentary data as a source of data that researchers turn into information. The following section begins a discussion on some of the ways that researchers actually conduct analyses of texts. Texts include signs and symbols, as well as artifacts and other facets of material culture. Methods such as *hermeneutics*, *semiotics*, and *content analysis* will be discussed.

Hermeneutic Analysis of Text Material

Hermeneutics is a method of analyzing all types of data (particularly written texts) according to a set of principles that requires the analyst to decipher the meaning of the text (1) through the eyes and intent of the writer or creator of the text or artifact, (2) according to the time frame existing at the time of the writing, and (3) considering the political and cultural environmental influences existing at the time of the creation of the text or artifact.

Hermeneutics owes its long history of interpretive applications to the analysis of, first, religious texts, and second, legal documents and written administrative rulings (Gadamer 1975, 1986; Bauman 1992; Alejandro 1993). The term originates from the Greek word *hermeneutikós*, which means the act of explaining—"making clear" or clarifying the obscure (Bauman 1992).

Hermeneutic analysis requires that the researcher take a holistic, or "contextualist" approach to analysis of a problem. The meaning of a text or social phenomenon that is analyzed hermeneutically depends on the whole—that is, the text, the author(s), *and* the context. Meaning cannot be deciphered without understanding the context as well as the text or phenomenon (Wachterhauser 1986).

Hermeneutics is a way of clarifying the meaning of a text by interpreting it *historically*. It looks upon a text as the "medium which links human subjects (i.e., writers of textual material) to their world and to their past . . . it involves identification with the intentions and situation of the [writer]" (Moore 1990, 94). Maas (1999), writing about the hermeneutic analysis of religious texts, explained this two-part focus by describing both a *material* and a *formal* object for the process. The material object is the text or other document that is being explained; the formal object is deciphering the sense of the author at the time the text was written.

Hermeneutic analysis is particularly relevant when studying historical documents, such as past legislation, the records of discourse that occurred over legislative or administrative hearings, and similar applications. In this way, public administration hermeneutics deals with government texts or documents as its material object, with the deciphering of the intent of the framers at the time of the text's creation (i.e., passage or implementation) as its formal object. Thus, legislation that might seem silly today has the potential to be interpreted as logical and meaningful in the light of events and circumstances at its enactment.

Principles of Hermeneutics

Several key principles underlie the hermeneutical analysis process. First, *all thought is derived from language and follows the same laws that regulate language.* A writer uses the traditions and conventions of his or her time and particular circumstances, including the same rhetorical logic, the same sequence of ideas, and the same rules of grammar in use at the time of the text's creation. Therefore, the analyst who wishes to fully understand the writer and correctly interpret the writer's words must first understand the author's meaning *at the time and place of the writing*. The interpreter must know the context of the text: the writer's language, train of thought, and psychological and historical condition at the time of the writing. Hence, the first principle of hermeneutics is this (Maas 1999, 3): "Find the sense of a book by way of its language (grammatically and philogically) by way of the rules of logic . . . and by way of the writer's mental and external condition (at the time of writing)."

Several other principles follow from this first principle of hermeneutics. Hermeneutic analysis presupposes that the analyst (1) has knowledge of both the grammar and historical evolution of the language in which the work is written, (2) is familiar with the laws of logic and rhetoric, and (3) has knowledge of psychological principles and the facts of history (of the time the work was written).

Hermeneutic Analysis of Nontext Phenomena

Although it is used most often as a method for analyzing texts, hermeneutics is applicable to more than this; it is a broadly based theory of interpreting all creations of humankind. Henrietta Moore (1990, 99), describing philosophy's contributions to hermeneutic theory and application, wrote:

> [The] theory of [hermeneutic] interpretation may be extended beyond the written text to encompass other human phenomena which can be said to have textual characteristics. One such phenomenon is meaningful action . . . and action is understood when it can be explained why the individual acted as [he or she] did, and thus can only be explained when a reason or motive for the action can be adduced.

Moore saw that the problem of analyzing meaningful action is at the very heart of much of the research and philosophical speculation in the social sciences, including public administration:

> In the hermeneutic tradition . . . this problematic is approached through the understanding that the social world is made up of individuals who speak and act in meaningful ways; these individuals create the social world which gives them their identify and being, and their creations can *only be understood through a process of interpretation*. [Thus], all human phenomena are susceptible to interpretation. (111; emphasis mine)

Richardson (1995, 1) also commented on the application of hermeneutic analysis to phenomena other than textual materials, although admitting a sense of puzzlement over the fact:

> Hermeneutics has come forward as that comprehensive standpoint from which to view all the projects of human learning. For those of use who have been puzzled by

the new intellectual dominance of hermeneutics, the key is that the term no long refers to the interpretation of texts only but encompasses all the ways in which subjects and objects are involved in human communication . . . hermeneutics or interpretation has come to be regarded as shorthand for all the practices of human learning.

Roberto Alejandro applied hermeneutic analysis to public administration issues in his book *Hermeneutics, Citizenship, and the Public Sphere.* He described the key contributions to hermeneutics of German philosopher Hans-Georg Gadamer (*Truth and Method*, 1990). Alejandro discussed two key principles: First, all humans are born into their own tradition, but, because we are all "interpretive beings," we are always working to achieve understanding and interpretation. Second, hermeneutics assumes that mankind's relation to the world is "fundamentally and essentially" made through language (Alejandro 1993, 34–35).

Meaning and Emphasis in Hermeneutics

Hermeneutics holds that there is always a plurality of meanings available for every human phenomenon. Meaning is not something that just exists; every reader must interpret it. Interpretations vary from reader to reader and can be understood only in the light of historical, social, and linguistic traditions. According to Alejandro (1993, 36):

> Interpretation is always a construction of meaning, which is what distinguishes the scientists' endeavor from hermeneutics' purpose. The scientist seeks certainty; hermeneutics seeks clarity. This clarity is anchored in the principle that the construction of meaning that interpretation makes possible is not arbitrary; it is not the outcome of the pure will of the interpreter. The construction of meaning has to consider the boundaries provided by the text (or phenomenon) itself as well as the background provided by the traditions that made it possible.

Bauman (1992, 12) also commented on this difference in emphasis. Because social phenomena—the subject matter of public administration research—are ultimately acts of human beings, they must be understood in a different way than by simply explaining. Men and women do what they do on purpose. True understanding can occur only when we know the purpose, the intent of the actor, his or her distinctive thoughts and feelings that lead up to an action. "To understand a human act . . . [is] to grasp the meaning with which the actor's intention invested it . . . [this is] essentially different from [the goal] of natural science."

In terms of its importance for research on questions in public administration and nonprofit organizations, hermeneutics provides a new way of looking at public issues. The hermeneutic approach assumes that the "constant of history" exists in the mind of every individual and that citizens' actions are inescapably influenced by their beliefs, traditions, and historical events. In the words of Vincent Descombes (1991, 254), *there can be no understanding without interpretation* (author's emphasis).

The Hermeneutic Circle

The process of hermeneutic analysis is less a method than it is a philosophical approach to scientific inquiry. By this is meant that, counter to traditional scientific epistemology that focuses first on explaining and then predicting, the hermeneutic approach is concerned with *interpretation in order to understand*. Achieving understanding, according to Bauman (1992, 17), means following a circular approach "toward better and less vulnerable knowledge."

This path to understanding is called the *hermeneutic circle.* It means beginning by interpreting a single part of the whole, then reevaluating and restating the interpretation in light of information about the time and intent of the event or text. Only then does one move to the next part—again searching the context for greater enlightenment. Merrell (1982, 113) added to understanding of this process by describing the way the analysis moves from the whole to its parts and back to the whole: "When written texts are broken down into isolated segments, those segments can then be relatively easily juxtaposed, compared, and contrasted. That is, they can be subjected to analysis by means of which consciousness of condensed and embedded wholes can be increased."

Understanding of parts thus builds on the greater understanding. With each of the parts assessed and reassessed in this way—in a circular analytic process that Bauman described as being "ever more voluminous, but always selective"—full understanding emerges at last.

An Application of Hermeneutic Analysis

Mercier (1994, 42) described how he used the hermeneutic method to examine organizational culture. In his opinion, a hermeneutical analysis of an organization is particularly valuable when management is considering a major shift in strategy. He concluded that a good hermeneutic analysis helps members of the organization recognize that their choices are not as limited as they once believed. Mercier proposed that hermeneutic analysis take place in the following brief sequence of steps:

1. Identification of a "spirit" or central point in an organization's culture ("spirit" refers to what might also be called the *defining characteristic* of the organization)

2. Explanation and interpretation of some of the other puzzling or contradictory elements of the organization through this central point
3. And finally, identification of hard and/or historical elements—related to factors in the environment—that have caused or dramatically influenced the defining characteristic

In a final word on the hermeneutic method, Wachterhauser (1986, 12) left researchers the following warning, referring to the principle of hermeneutic analysis that establishes and validates many different possible interpretations of a text: "There are no fundamental, underlying 'Truths.' Rather, the rationalistic ideal of discovering a set of self-evident 'foundational' truths from which all legitimate knowledge-claims would follow by strict logical inference is impossible to achieve."

Semiotics: The Analysis of Signs and Symbols

Semiotics is a relatively modern interpretive science that emerged during the middle and last half of the twentieth century as a way of describing how meaning is derived from text, language, and social actions as symbols. The primary social action of interest was initially limited to *language*—in both its written and spoken forms. However, semiotics was soon applied to analysis of things other than texts, but which could be "read" as text.

Social structure, ritual and myth, material culture, including art and tools: these all became the subject of research into the meaning of their signs and symbols. Today, semiotics is used as a way of interpreting all types of verbal and nonverbal signs and symbols, regardless of the discipline.

The Meaning of Semiotics

Nöth (1990), writing on the history of the science of semiotics, identified four underlying disciplines that have contributed to the development of the Western semiotic tradition—*semantics* (including the philosophy of language), *logic*, *rhetoric*, and *hermeneutics*. Other disciplines that helped forge modern semiotics include linguistics, aesthetics, poetics, nonverbal communication, epistemology, and the human sciences in general.

Many definitions of semiotics have been proposed; most relate it in some way to the interpretation of signs and symbols (Peirce 1962; Barthes 1968; Eco 1976; Sebeok 1976; Hodder 1982; Silverman 1983; Nöth 1990; Manning and Cullum-Swan 1998). For example, Nöth (1990, 49) drew upon previous definitive work to give semiotics the following broadest possible definition— although later in her *Handbook of Semiotics* Nöth referred to semiotics as simply "the science of meaning" (103):

[The science of signs] has for its goal a general theory of signs in all their forms and manifestations, whether in animals or men, whether normal or pathological, whether linguistic or nonlinguistic, whether personal or social. Semiotics is thus an interdisciplinary approach.

Manning and Cullum-Swan (1998, 251–252) were just as brief in their proposed definition, but took a slightly different approach, referring to semiotics simply as "the science of signs." They defined a *sign* as "anything that represents or stands for something else in the mind of someone." This definition has two parts: first, an *expression* (such as a word, a sound, a symbol, or the like), and second, a *content*, which is what completes the sign by giving it meaning. Offering another interpretation, Silverman (1983, 14) defined a sign as:

something which stands to somebody for something in some respect or capacity. It addresses somebody, that is, it creates in the mind of that person an equivalent sign, or perhaps a more developed sign . . . the sign stands for something, its object. It stands for that object, not in all respects, but in reference to a sort of idea, which I sometimes call the *ground*.

Perhaps the most complete definition of what constitutes a sign was provided by Eco (1976, 16), who defined a sign as "*everything* [his emphasis] that, on the grounds of a previously established social convention, can be taken as *something standing for something else.*"

Forms of Signs

Signs come in many different forms. Sebeok (1976) grouped the many different types of signs into six broad classifications: signals, symptoms, icons, indexes, symbols, and names. Semiotics pioneer John Peirce, however, developed the most widely used classification system, in 1962. He grouped signs into just three classes: icons, indices, and symbols. An icon is a sign that signifies its meaning by qualities of its own. An index communicates its meaning by being an example of its intended sign, such as a weathercock or a yardstick. Peirce considered the symbol to be a synonym for a sign.

Semiotic methodology can be used for either theoretical or applied research studies. The key thing to remember is that the focus of semiotics research should always be on determining the *meaning of signs and symbols*, regardless of the form in which they are encountered.

Researchers do not simply study signs; they focus instead on the *links* between the things that signs represent and the people for whom they have meaning. Symbols are not a reflection of society; rather, they play an active role in forming and giving meaning to social behavior (Hodder 1982). Thus, in order to really understand social behavior, the researcher must begin by interpreting the *contextual* meaning of the signs and symbols of the society.

Public administration researchers may use semiotics in any research involving verbal or nonverbal communication. Table 23.3 contains an extensive list of fields and study types that Eco (1976, 9–14) believed belong to the field of semiotics. By extension, they may be of interest to public administration and nonprofit organization researchers as well. They are listed here as illustrations of the wide applicability of semiotics research.

A Final Word of Caution About Signs

Christopher Tilley (1989, 186), primarily an anthropologist, offered this final caveat regarding the interpretation of signs:

> Meaning . . . resides in a system of relationships between signs and not in the signs themselves. A sign considered in isolation would be meaningless. Furthermore, the meaning of a sign is not predetermined, but is rather of cultural and historical convention. Consequently, it does not matter how a signifier appears, so long as it preserves its difference from other signifiers.

Content Analysis

Content analysis is a quantitative method of analyzing the content of written documents, transcripts of films, videos and speeches, and other types of written communication (Denscombe 1998). It has been defined as *"any technique for making inferences by objectively and systematically identifying specified characteristics of messages"* (Holsti 1969, 14).

The main advantage of content analysis is that it provides the researcher with a structured method for quantifying the contents of a qualitative or interpretive text, and does so in a simple, clear, and easily repeatable format. Its main disadvantage is that it contains a built-in bias of isolating bits of information from their context. Thus, the contextual meaning is often lost or, at the least, made problematic. Furthermore, content analysis has great difficulty in dealing with *implied* meanings in a text. In these situations, interpretive (hermeneutic) analysis may be more appropriate, with content analysis supplementing the primary analysis method.

Content analysis is best used when dealing with communications in which the messages tend to be clear, straightforward, obvious, and simple. The more that a text relies on subtle, intricate meanings, the less able is content analysis to reveal the full meaning of the communication. Thus, content analysis is used most often to *describe attributes of messages*, without reference to the intentions of the message sender or the effect of the message on the receiver

Table 23.3

Examples of Semiotic Research Applications

Research focus	Description of content
1 Aesthetic texts	Analysis of the aesthetic import of textual material
2 Codes of taste	Present in the culinary and enology fields; how tastes communicate certain images
3 Cultural codes	Behavior and values systems, including etiquette, cultural systems, and social organization of groups and societies
4 Formalized languages	"Languages" of statistics, chemistry, engineering, psychology, etc.
5 Kinesics and proxemics	Movement, gestures, special relationships
6 Mass communications	Coding, sending, receiving, interpreting messages
7 Medical semiotics	Signs and symptoms of the illness they indicate and other symbols forwarded by a patient
8 Musical codes	Musical signs with explicit denotative meanings, such as trumpet calls in the military; music that conveys selected emotional or conceptual meanings, such as tone poems
9 Natural languages	Studies in logic, philosophy of language, etc.
10 Olfactory signs	The "code of scents"; important in atmospherics
11 Paralinguistic sounds	Sounds without linguistic features, such as grunts, growls, etc.
12 Plot substructure	Mythology, mass communication drama and novels, etc.
13 Rhetoric	An early contributor to the field of semiotics; models of oral persuasion, argument, etc.
14 Systems of objects	From architecture to objects in everyday use
15 Tactile communication	Communication systems of the blind, as well as such behaviors as the kiss, embrace, slap on the shoulder, and caress
16 Text theory	The study of text as a "macro unit"; text as a whole unit
17 Visual communication	Graphic displays, advertisements, brands, and trademarks
18 Written languages	Includes unknown languages, secret codes, ancient alphabets, cryptography, etc.
19 Zoosemiotics	Communications behavior of nonhumans

Source: Adapted from Geo 1976.

(Denscombe 1998, 169; Holsti 1969, 27). Counting how many times in a speech a candidate denigrates the character of a political opponent is an example of content analysis.

The major purpose of all content analysis is to be able to make inferences about one or more variables uncovered in a text. It accomplishes this by systematically and objectively analyzing either the content of the text, the process of communication itself, or both (Sproull 1988). Content analysis takes place in the nine-step process displayed in Figure 23.3.

The first step in the content analysis process should be a familiar one by now: Establish objectives for the research process. This means determining *in advance* of the research what the researcher wants to accomplish by its conduct. Next, assuming that the researcher has some familiarity with the larger issues and/or themes at stake in the phenomenon, a list should be made of the *variables* that are to be counted in the text. Variables are not the same as words; rather, they tend to be constructs that describe or refer to broader complex issues of behavior or attitude. This list is clearly embedded in the study objectives.

Once the researcher has decided what to look for and where to look for it, he or she must then establish a system for coding the content items and determining how they are going to be counted and recorded. The texts themselves are then collected.

Holsti (1969) recommended that at this time researchers should draw a random sample of the materials for a pilot test of the study. The pilot test will provide important clues as to the relative effectiveness of the research design. For example, since the variables of interest are established before measurement takes place, there is a possibility that the variables are not treated significantly in the sample of sources chosen. In that case, the researcher would have to go back and identify new variables for the study.

The final steps in the study involve conducting statistical analysis on the measurements. When possible, these should include correlation analysis and simple hypothesis testing.

Complementary Tools: Narrative and Discourse Analysis

Content analysis is related to several similar research designs, among which are *narrative analysis* and *discourse analysis*. A *narrative* is an oral or written exposition that typically describes the events in a person's life. A *discourse* is either an oral or written communication designed to inform, rather than entertain. The term "discourse" is often used to identify an *exchange* of communication between two or more speakers or writers.

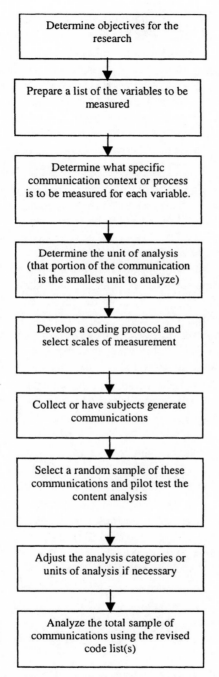

Figure 23.3. **Steps in Content Analysis Research Design**
Source: Adapted from Holsti 1969; Sproull 1988; and Denscombe 1998.

Narratives have been formally defined as "a means of representing or reca-pitulating past experience by a sequence of ordered sentences that match the temporal (time) sequence of the events which, it is inferred, actually occurred" (Labov, cited by Cortazzi 1993, 43). A *narrative analysis* is a *qualitative* ap-proach to the interpretation of texts and, as such, is often used to augment a quantitative analysis of content. Noting the mutually supportive roles of the various methods, Holsti (1969, 11) reminded researchers that:

> The content analyst should use qualitative and quantitative methods to supplement each other. It is by moving back and forth between these approaches that the inves-tigator is most likely to gain insight into the meaning of his [sic] data. . . . It should not be assumed that qualitative methods are insightful, and quantitative ones merely mechanical methods for checking hypotheses. The relationship is a circular one; each provides new insights on which the other can feed.

Narratives are a record of events that have significance for both the narra-tor and his or her audience (a researcher, for example). Narratives are for-mally structured; they have a beginning, a middle, and an ending. Furthermore, they are organized according to a set of distinct structures with formal and identifiable characteristics (Cortazzi 1993; Coffey and Alkinson 1996).

Cortazzi adapted the narrative evaluation or analysis model developed by Labov and Waletsky. Table 23.4 summarizes the model. Labov's purpose for developing the model was to illustrate how informal styles of narrative (speech) correlate with a number of extant social characteristics. The specific docu-ments selected for analysis might be newspaper stories, speeches at local ser-vice clubs, or official records such as the *Congressional Record.*

Manning and Cullum-Swan (1998) described several different approaches to the analysis of narratives, among which are *Russian formalism* and *struc-tural methods* such as *top-down* or *bottom-up* approaches. Russian formalism emphasizes the role that form plays in conveying meaning in a narrative. It has been used to analyze the form that Russian fairy tales follow, for ex-ample. Each tale follows a similar, simple structure. The same approach has been used to examine myths, poetry, and fiction.

Top-down approaches analyze the narrative text according to a set of cul-turally established rules of grammar and exposition. These methods are used extensively in education. Bottom-up methods, on the other hand, use ele-ments in the text to build a structure for analyzing the whole. This is the approach followed most often in ethnographic research.

In 1934, Karl Bühler (cited in Merrell 1982) provided an early framework of narrative and discourse analysis that is still relevant today. Bühler saw three main functions for a language. First, it must be *expressive*: The message must serve to convey the emotions or thoughts of the user of the language. Second, it must serve a *signaling* or *stimulative* function: The message must

Table 23.4

The Labov/Cortazzi Six-Part Narrative Evaluation Model

Structural element	Comment	Questions
Abstract		What was this about?
Orientation	Establishes the situation	Who? What? When? Where?
Complication	Major account of the events that are central to the story	Then what happened?
Evaluation	High point of the analysis	So what?
Result	Outcome of the events or resolution of the problem	What finally happened?
Conclusion	Returns to the present	[Finish of the narrative]

stimulate an expected response by the receiver. And third, it must have a *descriptive* function: The user of the language must be able to use it to describe a particular state of affairs in ways that convey the full picture. Others have added additional functions; the most important of these is an *argumentative* or *explanatory* function, by which language users present alternative thoughts, views, or propositions to the descriptive messages (Merrell 1982, 116).

Discourse Analysis of Communications

Discourse analysis is a method of analyzing oral or written communications in order to identify the formal structure of the message while at the same time keeping a *use-of-the-language* purpose in mind. It can be applied to the same types of messages, texts, and documents that are appropriate for content analysis, albeit for a different purpose. Discourse analysis is strongly associated with the analysis of linguistic structures in the message or text. Potter and Wetherell (1994, 48) referred to this point in their discussion of three particularly pertinent features of discourse analysis:

1. Discourse analysis is concerned with talk and texts as "social practices." It examines both the linguistic content—that is, the meaning and the topics discussed—in a message as well as the features of language form, such as grammar and cohesion.
2. Discourse analysis has a "triple concern" with the themes of *action*, *construction*, and *variability* in the message.

3. Discourse analysis is concerned with the rhetorical or augmentative organization of texts and talks.

Finally, the objective of discourse analysis is to take the focus of analysis away from questions of *how* a text version relates to reality in order to ask instead how the version is designed to compete successfully with one or more alternative versions. The following five rules direct discourse analysis:

- Variation in theme and message is to be used as a lever in analysis.
- The discourse must be read and analyzed in minute detail.
- A key effort in the analysis is the search for rhetorical organization.
- Accountability: Whether or not the points made are supported?
- Finally, discourse analysis requires cross-referencing with other studies.

Examining Material Culture: Finding Meaning in Artifacts

The study of material culture—the tools and other artifacts that are created, used, and left behind by society—is closely related to the science of semiotics. While it owes a great debt to the science of archaeology, it is not restricted to the search for meaning among the shards and bones of ancient civilizations. Artifact analysis is a modern science as well; modern archeologists also study the garbage dumps of modern society.

According to archaeologist Ian Hodder (1982), artifact analysis involves a process that begins with the interpretation of signs and symbols, making it a legitimate target for both hermeneutic and semiotic analysis approaches. He defined the term *symbol* as the word used to refer to an object or social situation in which a "direct, primary or literal meaning also designates another indirect, secondary and figurative meaning."

Hodder (1998) identified the key problem affecting the interpretation of artifacts as the need to locate them within the contexts of their creation, while at the same time interpreting them within the context of the modern researcher. By the very act of being interpreted, the artifact is removed to a new and different context, thus bringing decisive interpretation into question. Potentially, many meanings are possible; the researcher must decide not which is best, but which is most probable. Also related to this problem is the fact that material culture, because it often lasts a long time, either takes on or is given new meanings the longer it is separated from its primary producer. While the artifacts typically retain their original form, their meaning changes: "Material items are continually being reinterpreted in new contexts" (Hodder 1982, 120).

Tilley (1990) also commented on the need to look beyond the individual "piece" of material culture itself when deciphering its meaning: "To understand material culture we have to think in terms that go beneath the surface appearances to an underlying reality. This means that we are thinking in terms of relationships between things, rather than simply in terms of the things themselves." Tilley (1989, 188) urged public administration researchers to remember that the "interpretation of the meaning and significance of material culture is a contemporary activity. The meaning of the past does not reside in the past, but belongs in the present."

The Interpretation of Material Culture

The interpretation of artifacts requires that the researcher function in a scientific environment that is halfway between the past and the present. Interpretation also involves comparing different examples of material culture. This makes the interpretation process problematic, at best. The physical evidence under study is often not what the researcher expected—it has, as Hodder (1998, 121) has noted, "the potential to be patterned in unexpected ways." Furthermore, because physical evidence cannot "talk" directly to the researcher, it forces the analyst to evaluate and enlarge his or her own experience and worldview.

At all stages of the evaluation of material culture—from identifying categories and attributes to what Hodder called the "understanding of high-level social processes" (Hodder 1982)—the researcher must work at three levels of interpretation simultaneously:

1. The researcher must understand the *context* within which artifacts are deemed to have similar meanings.
2. Inseparable from understanding the context is the *identification of similarities and differences* in the artifacts. By showing that people responded the same way to similar stimuli, the researcher identifies patterns.
3. While working with the first two levels of interpretation, the researcher must also establish their relevance in terms of historical theories regarding the data.

Hodder (1982, 122) cautioned that interpreters of material culture should not let themselves be locked into a theory simply because it is fashionable at the time of the research: "Observation [of material culture] and interpretation are theory laden, although theories can be changed in confrontation with material evidence in a dialectical fashion." In a final word of warning, he discussed controversies over what is seen as a major weakness of artifact analysis: the lack of a method for confirming interpretive conclusions. For all researchers working with material culture, Hodder proposed two processes to satisfy the critics of interpretation:

> Perhaps the major difficulty is that material culture, by its very nature, straddles the divide between a universal and natural science approach to materials and a historical, interpretive approach to culture. There is thus a particularly marked lack of agreement in the scientific community about the appropriate bases for confirmation procedures . . . the twin struts of conformation are coherence and correspondence.

As has been shown, material culture interpretation methods involve the simultaneous processes of these three activities: (1) definition of the context of the artifact at its time of creation, (2) identification of patterns of similarities and difference, and (3) the use of relevant theories of social and material culture. The researcher's conclusions must present a coherent picture of the interpretation of the artifacts and at the same time establish a corresponding relationship between the artifacts, their context, and the interpretive conclusion.

Summary

This chapter discussed some of the ways that researchers go about examining texts, cultural artifacts, body language, and similar types of written and unwritten communications, records, documents, signs, and symbols. The different sources of research data were grouped into four broad categories. The first category is *written texts*, which include books, periodicals, narratives, reports, pamphlets, the mass media, and other published materials. Research using these sources is often called *library research*, or *desk research*. The second category is *formal and informal documents*; it includes personal messages and assorted types of archival information, such as personal notes and memos, government records and vital statistics, and other informal written materials, including e-mail. The third category is the wide variety of *nonwritten communications*, including graphic displays (graphs, tables, charts), photographs and illustrations, tools and other artifacts, and films and videotapes. The fourth category includes all *nonverbal signs and symbols*: body language, facial expressions, gestures, music and dance, animal sounds and behavior, and even noise.

Researchers employ a variety of analysis tools and methods in their study of texts, symbols, and artifacts. Among these are *hermeneutics*, *content analysis*, *meta-analysis*, *semiotic analysis*, *proxemics*, *kinesics*, *discourse analysis*, *site surveys*, and more. The analysis approaches used most often in public and nonprofit organization research are the formal literature review; archival analysis; meta-analysis; hermeneutic analysis of textual material; semiotic analysis; content, discourse, and narrative analysis; and material culture.

Suggested Reading

Alejandro, Roberto. 1993. *Hermeneutics, Citizenship, and the Public Sphere.* Albany: State University of New York.

Banks, Marcus. 2001. *Visual Methods in Social Research.* London: Sage.

Cook, Michael. 1986. *The Management of Information from Archives.* Aldershot, UK: Gower.

Fink, Arlene. 1998. *Conducting Research Literature Reviews.* Thousand Oaks, CA: Sage.

Fink, Deborah. 1989. *Process and Politics in Library Research.* Chicago: American Library Association.

Hodder, Ian. 1982. *Symbols in Action.* Cambridge: Cambridge University Press.

Holsti, Ole R. 1969. *Content Analysis for the Social Sciences and Humanities.* Reading, MA: Addison-Wesley.

Lipsey, Mark W., and David B. Wilson. 2001. *Practical Meta-Analysis.* Thousand Oaks, CA: Sage.

Tilley, Christopher, ed. 1990. *Reading Material Culture.* Oxford: Basil Blackwell.

Webb, Eugene J., Donald T. Campbell, Richard D. Schwartz, and Lee Sechrest. 2000. *Unobtrusive Measures.* rev. ed. Thousand Oaks, CA: Sage.

Part 7

Preparing and Presenting Research Findings

24 Organizing and Structuring the Research Report

Once research data has been collected, tabulated, and analyzed, the researcher must then organize the information and choose a structure for presenting the findings of the study and the conclusions. There are many different ways to do this. One way is to use a *chronological* organization. A second approach is to move *from the general to the specific* or *from the specific to the general*. The researcher could use the points in the *definition of the study question or the research hypotheses* as a discussion structure, starting a paragraph with a point or a hypothesis, then using material from the literature to show how the point is applied in practice. Many other approaches are also possible.

There are no ironclad rules to follow when deciding how to organize research findings and present ideas. However, it is recommended that the report writer avoid jumping around from one point to another with no underlying plan. Remember: A fundamental goal of your writing is that it be *read*. For that to happen, it must be *interesting and readable*. This requires adopting a structure and sticking to it.

Ways to Organize the Research Report

The key step in organizing and presenting ideas is to select a *point of view*. This involves deciding how to structure the paper so that the ideas flow smoothly from section to section. The chances of the paper being read can often be improved by following a simple, standard structure and by using a writing style consistent with the writing in that field of study. Later, if the researcher tries to publish a research paper, the format *must* meet the specific structure and style requirements of the selected journal. For now, concentrate on meeting as many of the following requirements as possible.

Points of View for Research Reports

Different disciplines in the social and administrative sciences and the humanities recommend a variety of ways to structure or organize written reports. A valuable overview of some of the different directions or points of view that researchers can take when planning and writing reports of their findings has been suggested by Sorrels (1984, Chapter 6), who lists these seven different points of view (or "patterns") that are often chosen:

1. The *indirect pattern*, which moves from factual parts to a general conclusion
2. The *direct form*, which reverses indirect order, moving from a general conclusion to the facts that support it
3. A *chronological pattern*, which takes the reader through an order of events, such as a sequence of dates
4. A *spatial pattern*, which moves the reader from one department or location to others in a logical sequence
5. An *analytical organization*, in which the whole is separated into its parts, with each part addressed completely before moving onto the next part
6. A *comparative pattern*, in which parts of a whole are compared point by point
7. A *ranked method*, in which portions of the paper are presented in the order of their importance or impact, either ascending or descending orders

Barzun and Graff (1970, 262–263) suggested that the research report should lead the reader through a logical, chronological progression of the material. They offered this single-case analysis of an organization as an example. The example illustrates a strategy that is followed in many if not most qualitative research reports. The chronological list of topics begins with the founding of the organization and ends with an outlook for its future:

1. The founding of the company
2. Success and the first twenty years
3. Cracking at the seams (growth)
4. The big lawsuit (problems)
5. Reorganization: New management and new projects
6. Expansion through subsidiaries
7. The complete empire (the modern firm)
8. Research and charitable enterprises (ethics considerations)
9. Present performance and outlook for the future

---

1. Title page

2. Abstract

3. Introduction or rationale for the study

4. Review of the literature examined for the study

5. Discussion of the methodology used for the study

6. Complete discussion of the results or findings

7. Conclusions and recommendations

8. Detailed list of the references and/or sources cited

9. Appendices

Figure 24.1 **Nine Major Components of a Research Report**

Sections of the Final Research Report

Written research reports contain, at most, nine or ten parts or sections. These are usually organized in the manner presented in Figure 24.1. However, it is also important to remember that not all papers and reports follow this format, and not all include every one of the parts.

The following section includes a brief discussion of each of the major report components. Please keep in mind that this represents a summary or compendium of many different report style recommendations. As they scan published papers and books, researchers are likely to encounter a host of variations on this list of components. Keep in mind that most researchers and business writers in general do not regularly follow any one style or format for their reports, but allow themselves some *flexibility*. With this flexibility in mind, the format and style presented here have been designed to meet most key writing requirements and can be safely followed in most instances.

Notice that this list does not include any mention of charts, tables, graphs, illustrations, drawings, models, or other graphic communication tools. That is because these tools are not limited to any one section. Naturally, graphic items are seldom if ever found on the title page or in the abstract or references. However, there is nothing to say that they cannot be used in any or all of the other sections. When used correctly, graphic tools greatly improve the ability of a report to communicate. They allow the researcher to present detailed information *clearly*, *succinctly*, and *at a glance*, regardless of where they are used in the report.

The Title and Title Page

The title is one of the most important components of a paper. It should leap off the page, grabbing the reader's attention. This does not mean that it should be "cute." In fact, always avoid using anything that smacks of being cute. Never use slang in your writing. If for some reason slang must be used for special effect, for example, it should always be set off in quotation marks or in italics.

Most students and beginning researchers tend to use titles that are too general or that do not say anything about what the research or assignment involves. For example, this is not an appropriate title, even if it is true: "A Report in Compliance with the Research Assignment of February 2."

Do not make the title too long; eight or ten words ought to be the maximum. On the other hand, do not be terse (abruptly brief). Research papers are not newspaper stories; short, tricky headlines as titles are not appropriate—even if they are explained in the first section of the paper.

Components of a Good Title

Good titles should contain four key components.

1. The topic of the study
2. The specific application or dimension of the topic studied (Innovations, Revisions, Results, Effects, Use of, New Ways of, etc.)
3. The agency, location, people, industry, or other such relevant focus
4. Key methodology used (qualitative, quantitative, etc.)

The purpose of the title is to tell the reader what the paper is about—and to capture the reader's interest so that the full finished product is examined. For example, say that a researcher has examined a state agency accused of practices that are destructive to the environment. The research report might be titled "Environmental Actions of a State Agency." But that's not good enough. Readers need to know what kinds of actions were studied, why they were important enough to study, and why a report has been written. Who really cares? A better title, then, might be "A Review of Reports of the Environmentally Destructive Logging Practices of the State Bureau of Water Resources."

The topic of the paper, the first component, is the environment. The specific dimension studied is environmentally destructive logging practices. The organization is the State Bureau of Water Resources. The methodology is a review of published reports. A *review* is a secondary literature research strategy. The researcher studies the issue by reading all available information about the bureau and the topic and then presents a synthesis of that information in the research report. This *qualitative research* method is known as a literature review.

It is a good idea to include the research *method* followed in the title of the final report. Some examples of titles for reports of these types of studies include the following:

Examples of Titles for Qualitative Studies

- "Use of Community Meetings to Impose Public Attitudes"
- "Measuring Public Confidence in Mutual Funds"

Examples of Titles for Quantitative Studies

- "A Factor Analysis of Consumer Attitudes About Smoking"
- "A Time Series Study of Minority Hiring Data"

Finally, the title page should include the title of the paper, the name of the author or authors (usually in alphabetical order based on the first letter of the last name), and any other relevant information. Examples of title pages for a typical class term paper (Figure 24.2) and for a thesis for a master's degree (Figure 24.3) follow.

The Abstract

The *abstract* is a concise summary of the research study and report. It is placed at the top of the first page of the paper, immediately below the title and before the introduction section. While most reports are typed double-spaced, the abstract is usually typed single-spaced and indented five spaces on both sides of the paper.

Typically, the abstract ranges from 100 to 200 words. In some journals, such as the *Journal of Marketing Channels*, instructions for authors call for the abstract to be less than 100 words. Whatever length, in this short space the abstract must inform readers what was done, how it was done, the most significant results or findings, and what readers will find when they read the entire paper.

Abstracts are found in all professional journal articles and in the long-form listing of papers included in such CD-ROM databases as *ABI-Inform* and oth-

THE TITLE OF THE REPORT

by
Author's Name

Name of the group, team, or organization
Name of the parent agency
Submission date of the report

Figure 24.2 Components of a Title Page for a Research Report

**THE PRIVATE vs. PUBLIC POWER FIGHT IN SEATTLE,
1930–1934**

A Study of the Efforts of Three Daily Newspapers
to Influence Public Opinion

by

David E. McNabb

*A thesis submitted in partial fulfillment of the requirements for the degree of
Master's of Arts in Communications*

University of Washington
Seattle, Washington

Figure 24.3 Title Page for a Master's Degree Thesis
Source: McNabb 1968.

ers. Abstracts contain enough information to accurately inform the researcher of the key ideas in a paper, while also encouraging the researcher to read the full paper.

In a report prepared for internal distribution, such as a study done for management or a consultant's recommendation report, the abstract is replaced by a slightly longer summary that is called an *executive summary*. While abstracts follow normal sentence construction, the executive summary may be presented in outline or "bulleted" form. The executive summary is often made into an overhead transparency and used to guide an audience through an oral presentation of the paper. The executive summary is seldom used for classroom reports.

A Sample Abstract

In the 122-word abstract shown in Figure 24.4, the authors tell the audience that the paper is about a survey of the perceptions and attitudes on environmental and social issues held by students in Canada, Taiwan, and the United States. It explains who the members of the sample were and provides a rationale for conducting the research. A brief suggestion of the results is also included.

The Introduction

In the formats of some professional journals, this section may be called the *background* section. In others it is referred to as the *rationale for the study*. In some journals, the section may have no label or headline; the writer just begins with the writing. Most public administration and administrative science journals continue to use the *introduction* label.

The purpose of the *introduction* section is to explain to the reader in some detail what the study and paper are all about. Beyond this, there are few specific rules about what goes in the introduction, only suggestions. The researcher might wish to think about the following ideas before writing the introduction for the report or paper.

The introduction section is where readers are introduced to the full scope of the study topic. It includes background information on the topic or situation, the researcher, funding agencies, if any, and any other relevant preliminary information. It is the place to state why the topic was selected and to list the steps taken in developing the study. The introduction explains how or why the study was first considered and what the researcher hoped to learn by studying this particular topic.

The introduction sometimes includes a brief discussion of key items of the literature so that readers can see how the research relates to other work done

ABSTRACT

This paper presents findings of a cross-cultural survey of university students' perceptions of the importance of environmental and social issues, and of programs to deal with these issues. Students in undergraduate courses in Canada, Taiwan, and the United States were surveyed. The study grew out of discrepancies seen in various cultures' priorities for resolving environmental problems. The researchers developed a list of 45 environmental and/or social problems and 20 statements about how organizations deal with environmental problems. The findings supported the propositions that different countries have different ideas about global environmental problems, that more international cooperation is needed, and management education must include more comprehensive discussions of environmental problems to prepare researchers to function in the sustainable-growth economies of the future.

Figure 24.4 **An Abstract for a Research Report**

on this topic. Special care must be taken to avoid simply repeating what others have written, however. It is important that the researcher *interprets* others' reports and indicates how they relate to the new study.

The introduction is the first place where writing should begin to sparkle. This section must be carefully written and rewritten. It is the first chance to hook the people who are in a position to judge your research and writing.

The following statement from the "Information for Contributors," which appears in every issue of the *Academy of Management Review* (*AMR*), emphasizes the importance of careful presentation of the researcher's ideas:

> Manuscripts submitted will be judged primarily on their substantive content, but writing style, structure, and length also will be considered. Poor presentation is sufficient reason for reviewers to reject a manuscript. Clarity and logical presentation are necessary; also, a provocative, challenging orientation that stimulates debate is appreciated, assuming professionalism is maintained.

To summarize, the introduction section should include the following:

- A brief (no more than one or two paragraphs) review of the background of the study
- A statement explaining why the topic was selected

- If appropriate, a brief introduction to other research on the subject
- An indication of what will be presented in the pages to follow
- Any additional information that logically could be considered as an introduction to the research project, study, topic, or paper.

Review of the Literature

The section that follows the introduction is the *review of the literature*. It should contain the majority of your analysis of what other researchers and authors have said about the topic. This is where the results of the library and/or Internet investigation are presented. Since everything included in this section comes from the work of others, the researcher must be careful to always cite sources; the person who did the work first *must* be given credit for their work.

For research papers that follow a document analysis strategy, this section might more appropriately be called the *discussion section*. For example, for a paper about how managers in public organizations exercise one or more aspects of good leadership, all data might come from already published sources, such as one or more broadly focused management journals like *Business Week*, *Harvard Business Review*, or similar sources on CD-ROM or the Internet. Once this step is complete, the researcher might then carry out a more extensive search of the public administration literature for specific articles on the managers in the public sector. This is not as difficult as it sounds because good managers tend to get lots of attention in the media.

The researcher may include introductory paragraphs defining the topic and variables in question; in this example it means describing specific leadership traits. Then, the literature that addressed each of the traits might be examined. Or the researcher might be asked to prepare a more structured study that involves observing leadership traits as exhibited by managers in the researcher's own organization.

The method of gathering this data may be either qualitative, quantitative, or a combination of the two research methods. In this situation, the literature search can provide suggestions about what traits might be more important than others, how leadership traits are or might be measured, and other relevant foundation material.

Research and Theory

Developing new ideas and concepts requires that a researcher first have a thorough grounding in *existing* theory. This comes from a comprehensive review of the literature on the topic. Sources may be personal interviews with experts. They may be from the extensive body of domestic and international professional and/or occupational literature or from current and past textbooks. Or they may be from other published materials such as newspapers, encyclopedias, yearbooks, and opinion pieces by other scholars, or from material prepared expressly for and carried only on the Internet.

To summarize this discussion, the review of the literature (or discussion section in a shorter paper) should do the following:

- Review earlier work done in the field
- Explain how earlier work relates to this investigation
- Give examples of directions being taken by other investigators
- Give a sense of continuity or closure to the work
- For a shorter paper, it may provide the body of the researcher's ideas and results of the study.

Methodology

Sometimes called *research methods*, or *methods and materials*, or simply the *methods* section, this is the part of the report which finally and fully explains how the work was done. In research studies, this section describes in some detail how data was collected and processed.

Was the study completely a library study? Was the research limited to a study of Internet sources? If so, why? Was a custom-designed questionnaire developed, or was an existing questionnaire used for the survey? Why? Was the data gathered by observation? If so, was the researcher functioning as a full participant or as unobtrusive bystander? Did the research involve conducting a series of personal interviews? Was an experiment designed and carried out? These are only a few of the many different ways to gather information. The method chosen will depend upon the nature of the study problem, the relevant study variables, and the resources available to the researcher.

Methods and Data Differences

It might be worthwhile here to briefly review one of the key differences in data as they relate to study methodology. This is the *primary-secondary data* dichotomy. *Primary* data are data that the researcher generates; they can be considered specific to the research project at hand. An example is the collective responses to the questions in a questionnaire (also called a *survey instrument*) that are acquired from a sample of subjects. *Secondary* data, on the other hand, are data that were collected by someone else for a different purpose. Examples include published economic or demographic statistics. Typically, secondary data are cheaper and quicker to gather. Primary data tend to be the more reliable of the two data types. There are a place and a purpose for both. If the study involves a library or Internet research for a short paper, it will mean gathering second-ary data exclusively. If the research study requires conducting an experiment to evaluate citizens' responses to public service announcements, it means gathering primary data.

When gathering secondary data, remember that every source of informa-tion used must be identified in the paper. This means including a complete bibliographic citation, including page numbers for actual quotes included in the paper (page numbers should *not* be used with source citations when they are paraphrased).

Research can mean studying published books and articles in the library or checking sources over the Internet. It can require examining artifacts or ob-serving behavior in the field. It can involve developing a set of questions and asking people to respond to a questionnaire. Or it can require carefully de-signing and conducting an experiment with human subjects. In every case, the researcher must describe exactly what was done and how it was done. That information goes here, in the *methods* section of the research paper.

The Results or Findings Section

Once readers have been told what was researched and how it was done, it is time to tell them what the research revealed—what it accomplished. Some-times this section is called the *discussion section*; sometimes it is labeled simply *results* or *findings*. Whichever, this is where readers are shown the results of the effort; in the process, it explains the reasons for conducting the research in the first place.

This information must be presented clearly, factually, simply, and without editorial comment. This section is not the place for the researcher to intro-duce opinions or reactions; conclusions, judgments, or evaluations of the in-formation should not be interjected into this section of the report. The job of the author is simply to *explain what the data* reveal—nothing more.

Do not "editorialize" about the data in this section. Remain cool and objec-tive; simply "tell it like it is." Avoid negative opinions; don't say a manager was "really stupid." However, it is possible to describe the behavior that makes you or others think that he or she was. Let your readers make their own evalu-ations and conclusions; never tell them how to think.

First Person or Third Person?

Typically, quantitative reports are written in the third person, while qualita-tive study reports may be written in either the first person or third person. It is a good thing to get in the habit of using the form used most often in your field of interest or study. For example, authors are strongly encouraged to avoid using the first person pronoun ("I") in reports on business or economics research, whereas many public administration journals include papers written in both forms. The topic and research methodology followed should dictate the form to use.

As a rule of thumb, however, it is difficult to get into trouble when writing clearly and objectively in the third person format. However, it is also important to know that many instructors require that personal opinions be included in class writing in order to encourage students to develop critical thinking skills. Whenever the issue comes up, it is best to comply with one of the first requirements of all writing in organizations: Write for your audience. To summarize, here are some key points for the *results* section of the paper:

- Third person is the preferred style for business and economics papers; public administration papers are written in either first or third person format.
- Unless specifically asked for your opinion, do not give it in the results section; it goes in the conclusions section.
- Do not editorialize about the study results in the findings section.
- Remain cool and objective.
- Avoid negative opinions; let the readers come to their own conclusions.
- Use clear, objective writing.

Is It "Style" or Is It "Format"?

The words *style* and *format* are often used interchangeably to refer to the way a paper is put together. They shouldn't be. They mean different things. *Format* refers to the way the research paper is structured or organized. It includes headings, subheads, and the order of the components of the paper. *Style*, on the other hand, refers to the choice of words and sentences used in the report. It includes punctuation and grammar.

Format often varies from discipline to discipline, journal to journal, and with the purpose of the paper. Sometimes, when people talk about style they are referring to the *writing rules* endorsed by organizations like the American Management Association or the University of Chicago. At other times, they mean the subjective, creative, artistic part of writing: selecting words that sparkle, using the active rather than the passive voice, using a variety of sentence lengths.

What kinds of textbooks and articles do you hate to read? A volume with sentences that ramble on forever; one with huge seas of black or gray type that put you to sleep because the author refused to paragraph, did not use headings or subheads, or did not perk up the text with illustrations or graphics? Those that offend you because they either talk down to you or assume you have twenty years' experience in the field and so understand complicated or esoteric jargon that the author insists on using? Most people prefer textbooks and articles that can be easily read and understood. These are the examples to use as models for your own writing. Good writing *can* be learned, just as poor writing can be avoided!

Conclusions and/or Recommendations Section

Writing a research report is much like writing a speech. In both cases, the writer selects a topic, finds something out about the topic, and then writes about it. The writer closes with a summary and shares conclusions about the process with an audience. People who teach speech making have reduced this process to a three-part structure: (1) tell your audience what you are going to tell them, (2) tell them, then (3) tell them what you told them.

In a sense, we have been following these directions as we moved from section to section in this chapter. In the introduction section of a report, readers are told what the research and report are going to be about. The methodology section describes the way the data were gathered and processed. The results section presents the main body of research findings. Now is the time to wrap things up by telling the audience what was learned from the research.

A good *conclusions* section can be one of the most valuable components of a paper (Markman, Markman, and Waddell 1989)—part summary, part conclusion, and part recommendations. This section can be used for several different purposes.

First, it provides an opportunity to summarize the main ideas gleaned from the literature and also permits repeating the critical findings from experimental research. Second, it allows the researcher to *interpret* the findings and to present a subjective interpretation in his or her own words. In a good public administration paper, this may be the only place where the researcher can be "original." To this point, the writing remained completely objective. Only the *facts* were reported.

Finally, the conclusions section gives the researcher a chance to prove to the readers that the research idea, design, and project were valid and "worth the doing." Now, however, the researcher must explain what it all means. To do this well requires the researcher to finally be creative, analytical, and persuasive. At the same time, the author tries to influence the audience or to convince them that the presented interpretation is the "right" one.

This section should begin with a brief summary of the research, present the researcher's interpretation, and close with the implications of the findings or with recommendations.

To summarize, the conclusions section should:

- Summarize the main ideas
- Say what these ideas mean
- Include a personal interpretation of the findings (the researcher's *opinions*)
- Convince readers that the research was worth the effort
- Make recommendations, if necessary, to the reader

References (Bibliography) Section

In the references the writer identifies all sources of information. Typically, there are two parts to this section: (1) the location of the information used in the study, and (2) an alphabetically listed compilation of all sources cited, studied, or examined during the work.

The first part of this section is known as the *notes* or *sources cited* and can be presented in the report as *endnotes*, *footnotes*, or *in-text citations*. Notes are presented in chronological order as they appear in the paper, from the first to the last. In-text citations are included in the body of the paper; they appear as the source information is used.

The second part is the *references* or *bibliography*, which contains complete bibliographic information about all sources used in the study. Many different bibliographic styles are used in research writing. It is usually best to follow the style used by the most influential writers in the field or the "best" journal in the discipline.

Writers may use footnotes, endnotes, or in-text citations to inform readers of the location of their information sources. "Location" information is needed for others to either replicate the study or test for flaws. For papers of ten or twelve pages, authors are no longer required to use endnotes or footnotes. This does not mean that authors can use the work of others as their own. Doing so is *plagiarism*, and plagiarism is theft. The practice is unethical, immoral, and, in most cases, illegal. At some universities and colleges, students can be expelled for plagiarism.

What it does mean is that the citations issue can be dealt with by placing the author's last name and the date of publication in parentheses at the beginning or end of the passage describing that work. This is called an in-text citation. The in-text citation method is growing in popularity; most publications and organizations prefer that this method be used exclusively. It is the method used throughout this book.

The *references* section of the research paper must include a complete bibliographic entry for every source used in the research. If a source has been examined for the study but not used, it is not necessary to include it in the bibliography.

The information used as background for a research project can come from published books; periodicals (magazines, newspapers, journals); interviews or surveys; films; electronic sources such as the Internet; government or company brochures, reports, or pamphlets; television programs; and other sources. There are a variety of rules governing how to list these sources, both as notes and references.

In the past, some stylebooks called for both notes and references to be included. Today, however, in-text citations are usually substituted for endnotes or footnotes. Most periodicals require in-text citations instead of endnotes or footnotes, together with a formal bibliography at the end of the paper.

The Appendix

The *appendix* is the last component of a research paper. This word has two plural forms: *appendixes* or *appendices*; you may use the one you prefer. The appendix is where to place any attachments that relate to the paper but that cannot or should not be placed in the body of the paper itself. Examples include a brochure or advertisement, a copy of the questionnaire used in a research study, a complicated mathematical table, or a copy of an article from a magazine, journal, or newspaper.

There are no limits to what can or what should be included in the appendixes. The wide variety of materials that could qualify suggests that there is no one rule or special format to follow for appendixes. Style manuals with recommendations pertaining to the appendix tend to agree with the following conclusions, however:

- Research papers for public administration, business, or economics seldom require an appendix or appendixes.
- When they are used, they should be attached after the bibliography.
- While it is not completely necessary, a single title page (with the label *Appendix*) should be placed before all the attached material.
- Only the number of the appendix title page is noted in the table of contents.
- When more than one appendix is used, the word *Appendixes* is placed in the table of contents and on the section title page.
- More than one appendix may be labeled: Appendix A, Appendix B, Appendix C, etc.

Summary

Both format and style were discussed in this chapter. *Format* refers to the logical way papers and reports are structured or organized. *Style* refers to the choice of words, how words are used in sentences, and how sentences are formed into paragraphs. It includes punctuation and grammar. A related aspect of style is the form used to present references and works cited in the paper.

This chapter also discussed the sections that are included in most research project reports. Research reports are often organized to include nine major components. These include (1) the title and title page; (2) an abstract; (3) an introduction or rationale for the study; (4) a review of the literature; (5) a discussion of the methodology used for the study; (6) the major section of the report, a complete discussion of the results produced by the study, often called the *findings section*; (7) the conclusions and/or recommendations; (8) references; and (9) appendixes, if any.

Suggested Reading

Barzun, Jacques, and Henry F. Graff. 1970. *The Modern Researcher.* Rev. ed. New York: Harcourt, Brace, and World.

Baugh, L. Sue. 1995. *How to Write Term Papers and Reports.* Lincolnwood, IL: VGM Career Horizons.

Becker, Howard S. 1986. *Writing for Social Scientists.* Chicago: University of Chicago Press.

Williams, Joseph M. 1990. *Style: Toward Clarity and Grace.* Chicago: University of Chicago Press.

25 Writing the Research Report*

When editors talk about style, they mean either one or all of these writing features: (1) the author's choice of words and sentences, (2) the author's employment of the basic rules of grammar and punctuation, or (3) the mechanics of footnotes, endnotes, in-text citations, and bibliographic (reference) notations. This chapter is about the third component of style: *notes*, *citations*, and *reference notation*. It is also a brief introduction to several of the most commonly used notation styles, those recommended by the Modern Language Association (MLA), the American Psychology Association (APA), and the University of Chicago (Chicago style). Style references in several disciplines are also explained.

Formats for Endnotes and Footnotes

Endnotes, footnotes, and in-text citations are tools used to show readers where the researcher found information. Footnotes are placed on the bottom of the page on which the material they referred to is introduced. An identifying number or symbol is placed at the end of the material to which the footnote applies and repeated at the beginning of the reference information. Superscript is the preferred font for the notations; [1] is an example of superscript. Endnotes are footnotes placed at the end of the paper, just before the bibliography.

Both endnotes and footnotes allow the researcher to include additional or parenthetical information that is not otherwise considered part of the regular flow of the paper. They may contain personal observations, comments, or

---

*Please be aware that this is only partial information that is useful only for writing research reports. When writing books or journal articles, you should follow the preferred style of the specific publisher.

questions about the sources. The may also be *asides*—information that adds to the understanding or fuller appreciation of a point in the paper itself. However, their primary purpose is to tell the reader the source of the ideas. Unless the ideas are exclusively the researcher's, their source must always be cited.

Endnote and footnote entries are made in numerical order, from the first to the last. The first time a source is mentioned, a complete bibliographic entry is included using the same format required for a complete bibliography. If the end- or footnote is not a citation but rather additional or parenthetical information, it should be written using complete sentences with proper punctuation. With end- or footnotes, the complete citation is included in only the first note. After the first entry, all subsequent entries use only the author's last name. The Latin phrases *Ibid.* and *Op. cit.* are hardly ever used in research reports or any scientific writing and should be avoided.

Formats for In-Text Citations

Today, the preferred way of noting sources in the body of a paper is the in-text citation method. It is easy and quick to use. The citations appear in parentheses within the text as they occur in the paper. If several sources are listed within the same parentheses, they should be placed in chronological order. They consist of the author's last name and the year of publication, without commas or periods, unless followed by a page number. Page numbers are added if a direct quote is used; place a comma between the date and page number.

Say, for example, that you are writing a paper about religion and business. One of your sources discusses parables in modern business literature. If you use an idea found in the source but express it in your own words (i.e., you paraphrase), you need not place it in quotation marks. At the end of your reference to that work, you must add the following notation: (McNabb 2000). Beyond this, no end- or footnote notation is required. However, if you quote from the work, you must add the page number after the date, thus: (McNabb 2000, 223). The work itself would be listed in your bibliography this way (or in some other accepted form):

Armstrong, Jack E. 2000. *Biblical Parables in Modern Business Writing.* Sioux City, IW: Reality Publishing.

Use of Notes in Large Reports

For large papers and research reports (forty pages or longer), some editors suggest that it is better to use footnotes or endnotes instead of in-text citations. However, if the paper is to be published in a professional journal, the system required by the journal must be used. If it is a paper for a class, follow the instructor's requirements. Here is a good rule of thumb to follow: If the paper is shorter than twenty or so pages, do not use endnotes or footnotes; if the paper is longer than twenty pages, you may use endnotes or footnotes. Other than this, use them if doing so makes the paper éasier to read or understand.

Tips for Using Sources

Here are some tips for documenting the sources in a research report.

- In the bibliography, arrange citations in alphabetical order according to the last name of the first author or the name of the publishing organization if no author is listed.
- List in the bibliography only the sources you have cited in the paper.
- Use author's initials or first name and middle initial, following the style used in your discipline.
- Put the date of publication immediately after the author's name.
- Capitalize only the first word of an article or book chapter title. Do not put the title in quotation marks. (This style varies from publisher to publisher).
- Italicize (or underline of you do not have access to italic font) the titles of journals and/ books.
- In in-text citations for direct quotes, include the page number after the year; separate the year and page number with a comma and a space.
- Multiple works by the same author in the same year should be distinguished by letters (1999a, 1999b, 1999c, etc.).

Bibliographic Style

Most style manuals group source materials into three broad categories: (1) books, (2) periodicals (magazines, journals, newspapers), and (3) miscellaneous, including pamphlets, brochures, annual reports, letters, interviews, films, and other sources. Today, a fourth category has been added: *electronic sources*. These include the World Wide Web, CD-ROMs, and miscellaneous electronically accessed databases.

A word of caution: There is a lack of agreement on the best or most appropriate way to list citations. Almost every discipline has its own format. It is up to you to determine which format is accepted or preferred in the organization for which the paper is written; follow that style. Considerable disagreement also exists on citation formats for electronic sources. Several different citation guides are listed in this chapter; one is the *Columbia Guide to Online Style* (1998), published by Columbia University Press.

In the following pages are examples of citation styles recommended by the MLA, the APA, and the University of Chicago's *Manual of Chicago Style*. These are the three "standard" styles recommended for writers. However, some academic disciplines and professions use styles that differ somewhat from any of the three standard styles. Public administration, business, and economics publications usually follow format requirements established or promoted by their respective professional associations. Communications courses also have format requirements of their own; they often follow a newspaper style established by either the Associated Press (AP) or United Press International (UPI). Citation formats for papers written for natural sciences also vary somewhat from the three major styles. This chapter also includes mention of some style requirements for government, business, and economic disciplines. Included are styles approved for management, marketing, accounting and finance, human resources, public administration, and economics. Professional societies for each of these disciplines have adopted styles that they require for all writing in their professional journals. And not all societies in the profession have identical style requirements. The following is a summary of style information:

- Most style manuals group sources into three categories: books, periodicals, and miscellaneous.
- Today, a fourth category is also used: electronic sources.
- These three major styles are the standard forms in use (often with some variation): MLA, APA, and Chicago.
- Some disciplines recommend using either Associated Press (AP) style or United Press International (UPI) style.
- There are many different ways to cite sources: Use *one* and stick to it.
- Never create your own style; never mix styles within the same paper.
- Style manuals have been written for many occupations. Find the one used in your industry or discipline and use it for all your writing.

Standard Style Requirements

MLA Style

According to the Modern Language Association of America (MLA), all sources included in a bibliography include three main components: author(s), title, and publication information. All other style formats are in agreement with these requirements; they differ, however, in the way and the order in which the elements are presented. MLA requires that this source section of a report be a separate page or pages titled " Works Cited." In citing books using MLA style, an entry can include most (but seldom all) of the following information:

1. Name(s) of authors

2. Title of the entry, if a part of a book
3. Title of the book
4. Name of the editor, translator or compiler, if appropriate
5. Edition of the work
6. Name(s) or number(s) of the volume(s) used, if a multivolume work
7. Name of the series, if part of a series of books
8. Place of publication (city)
9. Name of the publisher
10. Date of publication
11. Page numbers, if quoted or if the work is part of a compendium
12. Any other relevant bibliographic information and/or annotation

In addition to the above parts, twelve or more types of book listings are described in the MLA style manual. These range from books with a single author to multiple or unknown authors. Also included are compilations by editors, various editions or volumes in a series, parts of books, the forward or preface, encyclopedias, and dictionaries. Only a few of the most commonly encountered versions are listed here. When the name of a book's author is not known, the title of the book or journal is substituted.

MLA style calls for two spaces between citation components (e.g., between the author's name and title of the work). If you do not have access to an italic typeface for the title, underline it instead. Do not indent the first line of each bibliography or note listing; instead, indent the *second* and each subsequent line five spaces.

Use double space or space-and-a-half for all listings. MLA also recommends omitting short labels like "Press," "Co.," "Corp.," and "Inc." after the name of the publisher. An exception to this rule is for books printed by university presses: Instead of typing "Oxford University Press," use "Oxford UP." Some specific example are shown below.

Books

1. Books with one author:
   Aldershot, Benjamin B. *Writing for Fun and Profit.* Chicago: Winslow, 1997.
2. Books with two or more authors:
   West, Barbara A., and Janet C. Lagerquist. *Principles of Qualitative Research.* London: Oxford UP, 1998.
   (Only the first author is listed last name first; separate the names of two or more authors by commas.)
3. Books with editors:
   Andreeson, Elizabeth, ed. *Strategies for Competing after 2000.* Homewood, IL: Business Books, 1999.

4. Author with an editor (article in an anthology):

   Marshall, Jay B. "From Cottage to Factory." *Wool and the Industrial Revolution in Britain.* Ed. James B. Galloway. Liverpool: Liverpool UP, 1990. 87–102.

   (Note that the title of the article or chapter in this book is in quotation marks; the book's editor comes after the book title, with "Ed." (for "Edited by") before the editor's name; the pages of the article or chapter are separated from the date by a period.)

5. Books, second or later edition:

   Smith, Alfred E. *Principles of Management.* 6th ed. San Jose: Lighthouse, 1998.

6. Article in an encyclopedia:

   "Ethics." *Encyclopedia Britannica.* 15th ed. 1995.

Periodicals (Magazines, Journals, and Newspapers)

Several different terms are used here to refer to what are commonly known as magazines, or what libraries call periodicals. Periodicals appear as often as daily or as seldom as once or twice a year. They may be of general or special interest. They may carry news of an industry, a career field, or research or new developments in a discipline. Because the articles usually go into some depth on a specific idea, problem, or question, they are excellent sources of information for papers. Most but not all periodicals include the name of the author(s) and titles or headlines for each of the articles.

Newspapers are published daily, weekly, every one or two weeks, or monthly. Not all newspaper articles include the author's name (the author's name is sometimes called a *byline*). Newspaper articles are usually current; they include what is news *today*. However, most of the time they do not go into much depth. Exceptions are the *Wall Street Journal* and the Sunday edition of the *New York Times.*

A reference listing of a periodical article must include the name of the author, title of the article, name of the periodical, month and year of publication, and page numbers. Newspaper article citations also include the day of publication and section, if available. If the article is broken into two or more sections—for example, starting on pages 33 to 40 and continued on pages 101–105, use 33+, not 33–105. Following are some of the most commonly used ways to present source citations:

1. Article in a weekly publication:

   Serenski, Sergi V. "Cost Accounting Is Sexy." *Business Week* 22 February 1998: 35–36.

2. Article in a monthly or quarterly journal:

   Rice, Jerry B. "Tracking the Cost of Professional Football Admissions." *Journal of Accounting* (January 1991): 64–72.

(Substitute the season for the month for quarterly publications; for example: Spring 1991.)
3. Unknown author:
   "Boeing Employment Cuts Go Deep." *Time* 3 December 1998: 20–21.
4. Article in a newspaper:
   Sorenson, Theodore X. "Microsoft Foes Throw Rocks at Windows."
      Tacoma News-Tribune 5 October 1999: B1.
   (The article appeared on the first page of the B section of this day's paper.)

Other Sources

1. A government pamphlet or brochure, no author listed:
   U.S. Dept. of Agriculture. *Regulations for Applying Pesticides.*
      Washington: GPO. 1990.
   ("GPO" is the U.S. Government Printing Office, where most federal publications are published and distributed.)
2. Company pamphlet, brochure, or annual report:
   The Boeing Co. *1997 Annual Report.* Seattle: The Boeing Co., 1998.
3. Unpublished (Ph.D.) dissertation or (M.A.) thesis:
   McNabb, David E. "Segmenting the Market for Post-Secondary
      Education." Diss. Oregon State U, 1980.
4. A personal letter:
   LeBlank, Peter A. Letter to the author. 25 June 1997.
5. A personal interview:
   Jones, Edward S. Personal interview. 30 January 1996.
6. Published proceedings of a conference:
   Sepic, F. Thomas, and David E. McNabb. *Organization Climate and
      an Organization's Readiness for Change.* Proc. of Western Decision
      Sciences Institute, 1994, Reno, Fullerton: Cal-State Fullerton U,
      1994.

Electronic Sources

Today, researchers and authors are turning to electronic sources for much if not most of their secondary information. Changes in these sources are occurring rapidly; the World Wide Web and online databases are rapidly becoming preferred sources for research information. However, until recently no provision was made for citing electronic sources. Style guides still do not agree upon the preferred format(s) to use for the World Wide Web (WWW) and other electronic sources.

The following recommendations are from James-Catalao's *Researching on the World Wide Web* (1996), Harnack and Kleppinger's (1997) manual:

ONLINE! A Reference Guide to Using Internet Sources, and Li and Crane's (1996) publication, *Electronic Styles: A Handbook for Citing Electronic Information.*

A citation for a Web source must include as much of the following information as is available: author's name, title of the piece, date it was placed on the Web, address and other retrieval information, and date that the user accessed the article. The following recommendations have been adapted to comply with MLA style requirements.

1. World Wide Web sources:
   U.S. Dept. of Labor. "The Occupational Safety and Health Act of 1970 (OSH Act)." *Small Business Handbook: Safety and Health Standards.* November. http://www.dol.gov/dol/asp/public/programs/handbook/osha.htm. 2 December 1998.
   Gillmor, Dan. "Nader May Be the True Microsoft Threat." 27 October 1997. http://www.computerworld.com. 23 November 1998.
2. An e-mail source:
   McNabb, David E. *Students' Attitudes on Environmental Issues.* 4 November 1998. Available from Prof. Samuel Goldberg: sgoldberg@oregonstateu.edu.

APA Style

The American Psychological Association (APA) prefers that authors use in-text citations with references to an end-of-paper "Works Cited" section. This applies for all papers, regardless of length. All source listings should include the name of the author(s), title of the work, and publication information. Page numbers are required for all direct quotes. Publication dates are placed in parentheses immediately after the author's name. APA style is recommended in many business administration research and writing programs.

As with MLA style rules, APA style requires you to *underline* a title if you do not have access to an italic typeface. Do not indent the first line of a listing; instead, indent the second and each subsequent line *three* spaces (MLA required a five-space indentation). *All* authors' names must be listed—never use *et al.*

All names must be inverted (listed last name first). If there is no author's name, alphabetize the listing by the first word of the title (except for short words such as "the," "a," or "an.")

Capitalize only the first word of article titles in book, journals, and newspapers (except for proper nouns). Do not put quotation marks around the titles.

Use double space or space-and-a-half for listings. APA also allows but does not require you to drop short labels as "Press," "Co.," "Corp.," and "Inc." after the name of the publisher. Books printed by university presses are usually typed out in full, thus: Oxford University Press.

Periodical citations include the name(s) of the author(s), date of publication, title or headlines of the articles, and name of the periodical; use initial capital letters for periodical title names (e.g., *Business Week, Journal of Macroeconomics, Journal of State and Local Government*). Volume and issue numbers, when available, are also included, appearing just before page numbers.

Chicago Style

The editorial staff of the University of Chicago Press, a major publisher of works by academic authors, printed its first Manual of Style for writers in 1906. Since that time, the manual has gone through at least fourteen revisions, with more on the way. The Chicago Manual of Style describes the use of both footnotes and in-text citations. A full bibliographic listing is required in the end-of-work references section.

When available, all listings should include the name of the author(s), title of the work, and publication information. Page numbers are required for all direct quotes. For notes, publication dates are placed at or near the end of the listing, immediately before the page numbers (see *Chicago Manual of Style*, Chapter 15).

For bibliographic listings, only the first author's name should be inverted (listed last name first); others are listed first name, middle initial, last name. If there is no author's name, alphabetize the listing by the first word of the title. *All* authors' names must be listed. Capitalize the first letter of *all* words in book, journal, and newspaper titles. Put quotation marks around the titles of journal articles. Chicago style requires titles of journals and books to be in italics.

Chicago style requires these items to be listed in the following order in citations of books:

- Name of the author or authors, editors, or institution responsible for the writing of the book.
- Full title of the book, including subtitle
- Series, if any
- Edition if not the first
- Publication city
- Name of the publisher
- Date of publication

Periodical citations should include as many of the following as possible:

- Name(s) of the author(s)
- Title of the article
- Name of the publication
- Volume (and number) of the periodical
- Date of the volume or of the issue
- Page numbers of the article

The following information for electronic sources has been adapted to come as close as possible to Chicago style guidelines. Electronic sources must include as much of the following information as is available:

1. Known author:
   - Name(s) of author(s)
   - Date that the piece was placed on the Web
   - Title of the piece (including edition number, if not the original)
   - Type of medium
   - Producer (optional)
   - Available: supplier or database identifier or number
   - Date that the user accessed the article
2. Unknown author:
   - Title (edition)
   - Type of medium
   - Year
   - Producer
   - Available: supplier or database identifier or number
   - Access date

Other Style Manuals

Many different style manuals offer help in writing. Although varying in their recommendations, they all serve a common purpose, to serve as a guide to the "proper" way to present a written report. Some of the manuals are slim pamphlets; others are full-size books. Some manuals give suggestions and rules for all aspects of researching; others are only guides to citing sources.

The following is a partial list of available style manuals; most can be found in any college of university library.

General

- *The Complete Guide to Citing Government Information Sources: A Manual for Writers and Librarians*

- *Electronic Styles: A Handbook for Citing Electronic Information*
- *The Little, Brown Guide to Writing Research Papers*
- *The McGraw-Hill Style Manual*
- *Manual for Writers of Term Papers, Theses and Dissertations* (Kate Turabian)
- *A Manual of Style: U.S. Government Printing Office*
- *Prentice Hall Handbook for Writers*

For Specific Disciplines

- Environment and Earth Sciences: *Suggestions to Authors of the Reports of the United States Geological Survey.* (Originally an internal USGS document, this manual has been made available to the public and serves as a guidebook for all writing in the earth sciences.)
- Education: *Journal Instructions to Authors: A Compilation of Manuscript Guidelines from Education.*
- Computer Topics: *Electronic Styles: A Handbook for Citing Electronic Information.*
- Journalism: *A Broadcast News Manual of Style; UPI Stylebook* (United Press International); *AP Stylebook* (Associated Press).
- Law: *The Bluebook: A Uniform System of Citation.*
- Psychology: *Publication Manual of the American Psychological Association* (this is the APA Style Manual).
- Social Science: *Writing for Social Scientists: How to Start and Finish Your Thesis, Book or Article.*

Requirements for Public Administration Research Reports

The style recommendations of the American Society for Public Administration can be found in such journals as the *State and Local Government Review.* This journal uses the *Chicago Manual of Style* system for in-text citations.

1. Cover page: The cover page includes the title of the paper and the author's name, position, and organizational affiliation (for a class paper, the course number and name). At the top of the first page only the title is repeated.
2. Abstract: An abstract of no more than 100 words should be placed on the first page between the title page and the start of the paper's text.
3. Headings: The introduction section does not have a heading. Do not number any headings or subheadings. Headings are typically used for the Findings and Conclusions sections. Other headings may be used at the discretion of the author.

4. Summary: Papers should *not* end with a summary section. If relevant, a summary may be included in the author's conclusion section.

5. Tables, graphs, figures: When the paper is distributed within an organization, the tables, graphs, and figures should be inserted at the appropriate spots in the paper itself. When the paper is sent to a journal for publication, tables, graphs, and figures should be attached as separate sheets at the end. Authors must explain all tables, graphs, and figures in the body of the paper itself. All tables, graphs, and figures *must* be numbered and titled, with a descriptive legend. Titles, column headings, captions, and so on must be clear and to the point. When the paper is submitted to a journal, tables are often numbered with Roman numerals (e.g., Table IX). For papers distributed within an organization, either Roman numerals or Arabic numbers may be used. Figures must be numbered with Arabic numerals (e.g., Figure 9). Each figure must have a title followed by a descriptive legend. The figure's title should be part of the caption.

6. Endnotes: Authors should avoid the use of notes as much as possible. If notes must be used, they should be numbered sequentially. A list of endnotes typed on a separate page must be placed before the references section.

7. Citations: In the body of the paper, use the *Chicago Manual* format for in-text citations: Jones and Smith (1997) found that. . .
If the in-text citation deals with a quotation, the page number must be added after the date of publication, separated by a comma: (Jones and Smith 1997, 25).

8. References: The references section should include only works cited in the text, typed on a separate page(s) under the heading "References." References are listed alphabetically according to the last name of the first author. The first line of the citation should be flush left; all other lines are to be indented three spaces. Do not number the entries.

The following examples should be followed for reference listings:

1. Books:
For single works by an author or authors, use the following format:
Rouge, Anna M., and Marvin O. Johnson. 1994. *Governing the Ungovernable City.* San Bruno, CA: Mathematics Press.

For more than one work by the same author, list the works in order of publication (earliest first). Use a three-em dash in place of the author's name. If subsequent works have different second or more authors, continue to list them chronologically after the first notation of the principal author. Examples:

Lee, Brian, and Elizabeth Chung. 1994. etc.

————, and Susan H. Arden. 1996. *Training for Quick Advancement.* Tacoma, WA: University of Puget Sound Press.

————. 1997. *Development in the Central City.* Roseburg, OR: City Press.

2. Books with an editor (collective works):

Rom, Charlene D., and William D. Brown. 1997. Health programs in the inner city. In *Medical Delivery Systems Today*, Richard E. Keating and John P. MacDonough, eds. Seattle: University of Washington Press.

3. Periodicals:

Pearl, Andrew O. 1995. Measuring organizational climate in public safety organizations. *American Journal of Political Science* 17 (Winter): 101–110.

Note that only the first word in the article title is capitalized; all words in the periodical title begin with a capital letter. Titles are not set apart by quotation marks. Periods separate sections. The volume number but not month of issue is included; a colon separates the volume number from the page numbers.

Finance and Economics Research Reports

The *Journal of Macroeconomics* and the *Journal of Economic Perspectives* are examples of finance periodicals that follow style requirements established by the American Finance Association (AFA). This style is based on the then-current edition of the Chicago Manual of Style. Examples of style requirements can be found in the *Journal of Macroeconomics*, among others.

Organizational Management Reports

Papers written on management and many public administration topics usually follow style requirements established by the American Academy of Management. Examples and guidelines for authors can be found in the Academy of Management Review and other periodicals published by the academy (PO Box 3020, Briarcliff Manor, New York, 10510–8020).

Professional organizations often ask that all papers be double-spaced and typed in a plain twelve-point typeface (font). If it is impossible to italicize in the paper, underlining is allowed. Boldface type should be used for the title and headings. Tables should be typed in the same font used for the body of the paper. A title page is required. An abstract of seventy-five or fewer words should be included under the title near the top of the second page. The abstract should include the purposes for the research, any theoretical basis for the hypotheses, analyses, major results, and implications of the findings.

Summary

Today, almost all publications follow the in-text citation model. The citation includes the authors' last names and the publication year of the reference in parentheses. For works with two authors, both names should be used every time the work is cited. For three or more authors, all the authors' names are used only the first time the reference is cited.

All references used in the paper should appear in a separate section at the end of the report but before any appendixes, tables, or figures. This section starts on a new sheet, continuing the pagination used in the body of the paper. The word "References" should be centered, boldfaced, at the top of the section. All references should be double-spaced.

Citations should be in alphabetical order by the last name of the author or first author in multiple-author works or by the organization for a corporate author (e.g., *Seattle Times*). When more than one work by the same author or authors is used, the most current one is listed first. If there are two or more works with the same publication date, lower-case letters are used to distinguish them (1987a, 1987b, 1987c).

Reference listings use authors' last names and initials. Additional authors of a work are also presented with the last name first followed by their initials. Italicize titles of publications (underline if unable to use italic type font). The references format used in this work is a modified version of Chicago Style.

Suggested Reading

Fowler, H. Ramsey, and Jane E. Aaron. 1995. *The Little, Brown Handbook.* 6th ed. New York: HarperCollins.

Gibaldi, Joseph, and Walter S. Achtert, eds. 1988. *MLA Handbook for Writers of Research Papers.* New York: Modern Language Association of America.

Hacker, Diana. 1992. *A Writer's Reference.* 2d ed. Boston: Bedford Books.

Strunk, William, Jr., and E.B. White. 1979. *The Elements of Style.* 4th ed. Boston: Allyn and Bacon.

University of Chicago. 1993. *The Chicago Manual of Style.* 14th ed. Chicago: University of Chicago Press.

References

Abdellah, Faye G., and Eugene Levine. 1994. *Preparing Nursing Research for the 21st Century.* New York: Springer.

Achinstein, Peter. 1997. "Concepts of Science: A Philosophical Analysis." In *The Way of Science,* ed. Frank E. Egler, 40–47. New York: Hafner.

Adler, Patricia A., and Peter Adler. 1998. "Observational Techniques." In *Collecting and Interpreting Qualitative Materials,* ed. Normal K. Denzin and Yvonna S. Lincoln, 79–109. Thousand Oaks, CA: Sage.

Alasuutari, Pertti. 1995. *Researching Culture: Qualitative Method and Cultural Studies.* London: Sage.

Alejandro, Roberto. 1993. *Hermeneutics, Citizenship, and the Public Sphere.* Albany: State University of New York.

Ammons, David N., Charles Coe, and Michael Lombardo. 2001. "Performance-Comparison Projects in Local Government: Participants' Perspectives." *Public Administration Review* 61, no.1 (January/February): 100–110.

Annells, Merilyn. 1996. "Grounded Theory Method: Philosophical Perspectives, Paradigm of Inquiry, and Postmodernism." *Qualitative Health Research* 6, no. 3 (August): 379–394.

Argyris, Chris, Robert Putnam, and Diana M. Smith. 1985. *Action Science.* San Francisco: Jossey-Bass.

Arneson, Pat. 1993. "Situating Three Contemporary Qualitative Methods in Applied Organizational Communication Research: Historical Documentation Techniques, the Case Study Method, and the Critical Approach to Organizational Analysis." In *Qualitative Research: Applications in Organizational Communications*, ed. Sandra L. Herndon and Gary L. Kreps, 159–173. Cresskill, NJ: Hampton Press.

Bailey, Mary T. 1994. "Do Physicists Use Case Studies? Thoughts of Public Administration Research." In *Research in Public Administration: Reflections on Theory and Practice*, ed. Jay D. White and Guy B. Adamss, 183–196. Thousand Oaks, CA: Sage.

Banks, Marcus. 2001. *Visual Methods in Social Research.* London: Sage.

Barnet, Sylvan. 1993. *Critical Thinking, Reading, and Writing.* Boston: St. Martin's Press.

Barnett, Marva T. 1987. *Writing for Technicians* (3d ed.). New York: Delmar.

Barthes, Roland. 1968. *Elements of Semiology.* Annette Lavers and Colin Smith, trans. New York: Hill and Wang.

Barzun, Jacques, and Henry F. Graff. 1970. *The Modern Researcher* (rev. ed.). New York: Harcourt, Brace and World.

Bauman, Zygmunt. 1992. *Hermeneutics and the Social Sciences.* Aldershot, UK: Gregg Revivals.

Berg, Bruce L. 1995. *Qualitative Research Methods for the Social Sciences.* Needham, MA: Allyn and Bacon.

Bernard, H. Russell. 1995. *Research Methods in Anthropology* (2d ed.). Walnut Creek, CA: Alta Mira.

———. 1994. "Methods Belong to All of Us." In *Assessing Cultural Anthropology*, ed. Robert Borofsky, 168–179. New York: McGraw-Hill.

———. 1988. *Research Methods in Cultural Anthropology.* Beverly Hills, CA: Sage.

Blyler, Nancy. 1998. "Taking a Political Turn: The Critical Perspective and Research in Professional Communications." *Technical Communication Quarterly* 7, no. 1 (Winter): 33–53.

Borofsky, Robert, ed. 1994. *Assessing Cultural Anthropology.* New York: McGraw-Hill.

Brookfield, Stephen D. 1988. *Developing Critical Thinkers.* Milton Keynes, UK: Open University.

Boskoff, Alvin. 1972. *The Mosaic of Sociological Theory.* New York: Crowell.

Box, Richard C. 1992. "An Examination of the Debate Over Research in Public Administration." *Public Administration Review* 52, no. 1 (January/February): 62–69.

Brase, Charles S., and Corrine P. Brase. 1999. *Understandable Statistics: Concepts and Methods.* (6th ed.) Boston: Houghton Mifflin.

Bredemeier, Harry C., and Richard M. Stephenson. 1967. "The Analysis of Culture." In *The Study of Society*, ed. P.I. Rose, 119–133. New York: Random House.

Brewer, Gene A., James W. Douglas, Rex L. Facer II, and Laurence J. O'Toole Jr. 2000. "Determinants of Graduate Research Productivity in Doctoral Programs of Public Administration." *Public Administration Review* 59, no. 5 (September/October): 373–382.

Brookfield, Stephen D. 1988. *Developing Critical Thinkers.* Milton Keynes, UK: Open University Press.

Button, Graham, ed. 1991. *Ethnomethodology and the Human Sciences.* New York: Cambridge University Press.

Cartwright, Dorwin, ed. 1951. *Field Theory in Social Science: Selected Theoretical Papers by Kurt Lewin.* New York: Harper and Row.

Cassell, Catherine, and Gillian Symon, eds. 1997. *Qualitative Methods in Organizational Research.* Thousand Oaks, CA: Sage.

Ceram, C.W. 1984. *Gods, Graves and Scholars.* E.B. Garside and Sophie Wilkins, trans. Harmondsworth, UK: Penguin.

Cleary, Robert E. 1992. "Revisiting the Doctoral Dissertation in Public Administration: An Examination of the Dissertations of 1990." *Public Administration Review* 52 (January/February): 55–61.

Coffey, Arman, and Paul Alkinson. 1996. *Making Sense of Qualitative Data.* Thousand Oaks, CA: Sage.

Cohen, Ronald. 1973. "Generalizations in Ethnography." In *A Handbook of Method in Cultural Anthropology*, ed. Raoul Naroll and Ronald Cohen, 31–50. New York: Columbia University Press.

Columbia University. 1998. *Columbia Guide to Online Style.* New York: Columbia University Press.

Comstock, Donald E., and Russell Fox. 1993. "Participatory Research as Critical Theory: The North Bonneville, USA, Experience." In *Voices of Change: Participatory Research in the United States and Canada*, ed. Peter Park, Mary Brydon-Miller, Budd Hall, and Ted Jackson, 103–124. Westport, CT: Bergin and Garvey.

Cook, Deborah. 1991. "Rereading Gadamer: A Response to James Risser." In *Gadamer and Hermeneutics*, ed. Hugh J. Silverman, 106–116. London: Routledge.

Cook, Michael. 1986. *The Management of Information from Archives.* Aldershot, UK: Gower.

Cook, Ronald G., and David Barry. 1995. "Shaping the External Environment: A Study of Small Firms' Attempts to Influence Public Policy." In *Business and Society* (December): 1–18.

Cooper, Charles W., and Edmund J. Robins. 1962. *The Term Paper: A Manual and Model* (3d ed.). Stanford, CA: Stanford University Press.

Cooper, Terry L. 1998. *The Responsible Administrator: An Approach to Ethics for the Administrative Role* (4th ed.). San Francisco: Jossey-Bass.

Cortazzi, Martin. 1993. *Narrative Analysis.* London: Falmer Press.

Cozzetto, Don A. 1998. "Quantitative Research in Public Administration: A Need to Address Some Serious Methodological Problems." *Administration and Society* 26, no. 3 (November): 337–343.

Creswell, John W. 1994. *Research Design: Qualitative and Quantitative Approaches.* Thousand Oaks, CA: Sage.

Cunningham, J. Barton. 1995. "Strategic Considerations in Using Action Research for Improving Personnel Practices." *Public Personnel Management* 24, no. 4 (Winter): 515–540.

Dastmalchian, A., P. Blyton, and R. Adamson. 1991. *The Climate of Workplace Relations.* London: Routledge.

Davidson, Larry, David A. Stayner, Stacy Lambert, Peter Smith, and William H. Sledge. 2001. "Phenomenological and Participative Research on Schizophrenia." In *From Subject to Subjectivity: A Handbook of Interpretive and Participatory Methods,* ed. Deborah L. Tolman and Mary Brydon-Miller, 163–179. New York: New York University Press.

Davis, Whitney. 1989. "Towards an Archeology of Thought." In *The Meaning of Things: Material Culture and Symbolic Expression,* ed. Ian Hodder, 202–209. London: HarperCollins Academic.

deLaine, Marlene. 2000. *Fieldwork, Participation and Practice: Ethics and Dilemmas in Qualitative Research.* London: Sage.

Denhardt, Katherine G. 1988. "The Management of Ideals: A Political Perspective on Ethics." *Public Administration Review* 49: 187–193.

Denison, Dwight V., and Robert Eger III. 2000. "Tax Evasion from a Policy Perspective." *Public Administration Review* 60, no. 2 (March/April): 163–172.

Denzin, Norman K, and Yvonna S. Lincoln. 1998. *Strategies of Qualitative Inquiry.* Thousand Oaks, CA: Sage.

———. 1994a. "Entering the Field of Qualitative Research." In *Handbook of Qualitative Research,* ed. Norman. K. Denzin and Yvonne. S. Lincoln, 1–34. Thousand Oaks, CA: Sage.

———. 1994b. *Handbook of Qualitative Research.* Thousand Oaks, CA: Sage.

Denscombe, Martyn. 1998. *The Good Research Guide.* Buckingham, UK: Open University.

DePoy, Elizabeth, and Ann Hartman. 1999. "Critical Action Research: A Model for Social Work Knowing." *Social Work* 44, no. 6 (November): 560–570.

Descombes, Vincent. 1991. "The Interpretation of Texts." In Gadamer and Hermeneutics, ed. High J. Silverman, 247–268. London: Routledge.

Dood, Janet S., ed. 1986. *The ACS Style Guide: A Manual for Authors and Editors.* Washington, DC: American Chemical Society.

Dusche, Richard A. 1994. "Research on the History and Philosophy of Science." In *Handbook on Research in Science Teaching and Learning,* ed. Dorothy L. Gabel, 443–465. New York: Macmillan.

Duveen, Gerard. 2000. "Piaget, Ethnographer." *Social Science Information* 39, no. 1 (March): 79–97.

Eco, Umberto. 1976. *A Theory of Semiotics.* Bloomington: Indiana University.

Einspruch, Eric L. 1998. *An Introductory Guide to SPSS for Windows.* Thousand Oaks, CA: Sage.

Eisner, Elliot W. 1997. "The New Frontier in Qualitative Research Methodology." *Qualitative Inquiry* 3, no. 2 (September): 259–274.

Emerson, Robert M., Rachel I. Fretz, and Linda L. Shaw. 1995. *Writing Ethnographic Fieldnotes.* Chicago: University of Chicago Press.

Este, David, Jackie Sieppert, and Allan Barsky. 1998. "Teaching and Learning Qualitative Research with and without Qualitative Data Analysis Software." *Journal of Research on Computing in Education* 31, no. 2 (Winter): 138–155.

Fay, Brian. 1975. *Social Theory and Political Practice.* London: Allen and Unwin.

Fernandez, Sergio, and Ross Fabricant. 2000. "Methodological Pitfalls in Privatization Research: Two Cases from Florida's Child Support Enforcement Program." *Public Productivity and Management Review* 24, no. 2 (December): 133–144.

Fetterman, David M. 1989. *Ethnography: Step by Step.* Newbury Park, CA: Sage.

Fink, Arlene. 1998. *Conducting Research Literature Reviews.* Thousand Oaks, CA: Sage.

Fischler, Raphael. 2000. "Case Studies of Planners at Work." *Journal of Planning Literature* 15, no. 2 (November): 184–195.

Fitz-Gibbon, Carol Taylor, and Lynn Lyons Morris. 1987. *How to Analyze Data.* Newbury Park, CA: Sage.

Fletcher, Roland. 1989. "The Messages of Material Behavior: A Preliminary Discussion of Nonverbal Meaning." In *The Meaning of Things: Material Culture and Symbolic Expression*, ed. Ian Hodder, 33–40. London: HarperCollins Academic.

Flick, Uwe. 1999a. "Qualitative Methods in the Study of Culture and Development: An Introduction." *Social Science Information* 38, no. 4 (December): 631–658.

———. 1999b. "Social Constructions of Change: Qualitative Methods for Analyzing Developmental Processes." *Social Science Information* 38, no. 4 (December): 625–629.

Folz, David H. 1996. *Survey Research for Public Administration.* Thousand Oaks, CA: Sage.

Fong, Margaret L. 1992. "When a Survey Isn't Research." *Counselor Education and Supervision* 31, no. 4 (June): 194–196.

Fowler, H. Ramsey, and Jane E. Aaron. 1995. *The Little, Brown Handbook* (6th ed.). New York: HarperCollins.

Fox, Richard G. 1977. *Urban Anthropology: Cities in Their Cultural Settings.* Englewood Cliffs, NJ: Prentice Hall.

Fredericksen, Patricia, and Rosanne London. 2000. "Disconnect in the Hollow State: The Pivotal Role of Organizational Capacity in Community-Based Development Organizations." *Public Administration Review* 60, no. 3 (May/June): 230–239.

Freedman, Paul. 1960. *The Principles of Scientific Research* (2d ed.). London: Pergamon.

Gabel. Dorothy. 1995. An Introduction to Action Research. Presidential address at National Association for Research in Science Teaching Annual Meeting, San Francisco, April 24. <<www.phy.nau.edu>> (November 14, 2000).

Gadamer, Hans-Georg. 1990. *Truth and Method* (2d ed.). New York: Crossroads.

———. 1986. "Text and Interpretation." In *Hermeneutics and Modern Philosophy*, ed. Bruce R. Wachterhauser, 377–396. Albany: State University of New York.

———. 1975a. "Hermeneutics and Social Science." *Cultural Hermeneutics* 2: 307–316.

———. 1975b. *Truth and Method.* Joel Weinsheimer and Donald G. Marshall, trans. London: Sheed and Ward.

Garofalo, Charles, and Dean Geuras. 1999. *Ethics in the Public Sector: The Moral Mind at Work.* Washington, DC: Georgetown University Press.

Garrick, John. 1999. "Doubting the Philosophical Assumptions of Interpretive Research." *International Journal of Qualitative Studies in Education* 12, no. 2 (March/April): 147–157.

Garson, G. David, and Samuel Overman. 1983. *Public Management Research in the United States.* New York: Praeger.

Geertz, Clifford. 1973. *The Interpretation of Cultures: Selected Essays.* New York: Basic Books.

Geuss, Raymond. 1981. *The Idea of a Critical Theory: Habermas and the Frankfurt School.* Cambridge: Cambridge University Press.

Gibaldi, Joseph, and Walter S. Achtert. 1988. *MLA Handbook for Writers of Research Papers.* New York: Modern Language Association of America.

Gill, Jeff, and Kenneth J. Meier. 2000. "Public Administration Research and Practice A Methodological Manifesto." *Journal of Public Administration Research and Theory* 10, no. 1 (January): 157–199.

Gill, John, and Phil Johnson. 1991. *Research Methods for Managers.* London: Chapman.

Glanz, Jeffrey. 1999. "A Primer on Action Research for the School Administrator." *Clearing House* 72, no. 5 (May/June): 301–305.

Glaser, Barney G. 1999. "The Future of Grounded Theory." (Keynote address at the Fourth Annual Qualitative Health Research Conference, Vancouver, BC, February 1998). *Qualitative Health Research* 9, no. 6 (November): 836–845.

———. 1992. *Emergence vs. Forcing: Basics of Grounded Theory Analysis.* Mill Valley, CA: Sociology Press.

Glaser, Barney G., and Anselm L. Strauss. 1967. *The Discovery of Grounded Theory: Strategies for Qualitative Research.* Chicago: Aldine.

Golden, M. Patricia, ed. 1976. *The Research Experience.* Itasca, IL: Peacock.

Goss, Robert P. 1996. "A Distinct Public Administration Ethics?" *Journal of Public Administration Research and Theory* 6, no. 4 (October): 573–598.

Gottfredson, Gary D. 1996. "The Hawthorne Misunderstanding (and How to Get the Hawthorne Effect in Action Research)." *Journal of Crime and Delinquency* 33, no. 1 (February): 28–49.

Gubanich, Alan A. 1991. *Writing a Scientific Paper.* Dubuque: Kendall/Hunt.

Gummesson, Evert. 1987. *Qualitative Methods in Management Research.* Newbury Park, CA: Sage.

Gurman, Pamela J., ed. 1997. *Written Communications Resources Digest.* Needham Heights, MA: Simon and Schuster.

Gustavsen, Bjorn. 1996. "Action Research, Democratic Dialogue, and the Issue of 'Critical Mass' in Change." *Qualitative Inquiry* 2, no. 1 (March): 90–104.

Haig, Brian. 1996. "Grounded Theory as Scientific Method." *Philosophy of Education Society Yearbook.* <<http://www.ed.uiuc.edu/EPS>> (November 2, 2000).

Hall, Wendy A., and Peter Callery. 2001. "Enhancing the Rigor of Grounded Theory: Incorporating Reflexivity and Relationality." *Qualitative Health Research* (March): 257–272.

Hanson, N.R. 1958. *Patterns of Discovery: An Inquiry into the Conceptual Foundations of Science.* Cambridge: Cambridge University Press.

Harnack, Andrew, and Eugene Kleppinger. 1997. *ONLINE! A Reference Guide to Using Internet Sources.* New York: St. Martin's Press.

Harper, Douglas. 1998. "On the Authority of the Image: Visual Methods at the Crossroads." In *Collecting and Interpreting Qualitative Materials*, ed. Norman K. Denzin and Yvonna S. Lincoln, 130–149. Thousand Oaks, CA: Sage.

———. 1986. "Text and Interpretation." In *Hermeneutics and Modern Society*, ed. Brice Wachterhauser, 377–396. Albany: State University of New York.

———. 1975. "Hermeneutics and Social Science." *Cultural Hermeneutics* 2 (May): 307–316.

Harvey, Don, and Donald R. Brown. 1996. *An Experiential Approach to Organizational Development* (5th ed.). Upper Saddle River, NJ: Prentice Hall.

Hedges, Alan, and Sue Duncan. 2000. "Qualitative Research in the Social Policy Field." In *Qualitative Research in Context*, ed. Laura Marks, 191–215. Henley-on-Thames, UK: ADMAP.

Hodder, Ian. 1998. "The Interpretation of Documents and Material Culture." In *Collecting and Interpreting Qualitative Materials*, ed. Norman K. Denzin and Yvonna S. Lincoln, 110–129. Thousand Oaks, CA: Sage.

———. 1989a. *The Meaning of Things: Material Culture and Symbolic Expression.* London: HarperCollins Academic.

———. 1989b. "Post-Modernism, Post-Structuralism and Post-Processual Archeology." In *The Meaning of Things: Material Culture and Symbolic Expression*, ed. Ian Hodder, 64–78. London: HarperCollins Academic.

———. 1982. *Symbols in Action.* Cambridge: Cambridge University Press.

Holsti, Ole R. 1969. *Content Analysis for the Social Sciences and Humanities.* Reading, MA: Addison-Wesley.

Houston, David J., and Sybil M. Delevan. 1990. "Public Administration Research: An Assessment of Journal." *Public Administration Review* 50 (November/December): 674–681.

Hughes, John, and Wes Sharrock, eds. 1997. *The Philosophy of Social Research* (3d ed.). London: Longman.

Imms, Mike. 2000. "The Theory of Qualitative Research." In *Qualitative Research in Context*, ed. Laura Marks, 1–15. Henley-on-Thames, UK: ADMAP.

Jacques, Elliott. 1951. *The Changing Culture of a Factory: A Study of Authority and Participation in an Industrial Setting.* London: Tavistock Institute.

James-Catalao, Cynthia N. 1996. *Researching on the World Wide Web.* Rocklin, CA: Prima.

Janesick, Valerie J. 1994. "The Dance of Qualitative Research Design." In *Handbook of Qualitative Research*, ed. Norman. K. Denzin and Yvonne. S. Lincoln, 209–219. Thousand Oaks, CA: Sage.

Jones, Russell A. 1996. *Research Methods in the Social and Behavioral Sciences* (2d ed.). Sunderland, MA: Sinauer.

Jurich, Katarin. 2001. "Getting the Story Straight: Grounded Theory, Hermeneutics and the Practice of Fieldwork on the Plains of South Dakota." *Sociological Perspectives* 43, no. 4: S149–162. (EBSCO-Host. Available. August 3, 2001.)

Kalinosky, Kathy. 1997. "Action Research and Learner Participation in a Homeless Shelter." *New Directions for Adult and Continuing Education* 73 (Spring): 52–55.

Kaplan, Robert S. 1998. "Innovation Action Research: Creating New Management Theory and Practice." *Journal of Management Accounting Research* 10: 89–119.

Kaplan, Robert S., and David P. Norton. 1996. *The Balanced Scorecard*. Boston: Harvard Business School Press.

Kassarjian, Harold H. 1974. *Handbook of Consumer Behavior*. Upper Saddle River, NJ: Prentice Hall.

Kaufman, Herbert. 1960. *The Forest Ranger: A Study in Administrative Behavior*. Baltimore: John Hopkins University Press.

Keller, Julia. 1998. "Cyber-Goofs Point Out Need for Fact Checking." *Seattle Times*, December 27, p. C-2.

Kelley, Kevin T. 1996. *The Logic of Reliable Inquiry*. Oxford: Oxford University.

Kendall, Judy. 1999. "Axial Coding and the Grounded Theory Controversy." *Western Journal of Nursing Research* 21, no. 6 (December): 743–758.

Kennedy, X. J., and Dorothy M. Kennedy. 1987. *The Bedford Guide for College Papers*. New York: St. Martin Press.

Kidder, Louise H. 1986. *Research Methods in Social Relations*. New York: Holt, Rinehart and Winston.

King, Cheryl S., Kathryn M. Feltey, and Bridget O. Susel. 1998. "The Question of Participation: Toward Authentic Public Participation in Public Administration." *Public Administration Review* 58, no. 4 (July/August): 317–326.

King, James R. 1999. "Am Not! Are Too! Using Queer Standpoint in Postmodern Critical Ethnography." *International Journal of Qualitative Studies in Education* 12, no. 5 (September/October): 473–491.

Kiniry, Malcolm, and Mike Rose, eds. 1990. *Critical Strategies for Academic Writing*. Boston: Bedford Books.

Klein, Heinz K., and Michael D. Myers. 1999. "A Set of Principles for Conducting and Evaluating Interpretive Field Studies in Information Systems." *MIS Quarterly* 23, no. 1 (March): 67–98.

Kluckholm, Clyde. 1967. "The Study of Culture." In *The Study of Society*, ed. P.I. Rose, 74–93. New York: Random House.

Konecki, Krysztof. 1997. "Time in the Recruiting Search Process by Headhunting Companies." In *Grounded Theory in Practice*, ed. Anselm Strauss and Juliet Corbin, 74–93. Thousand Oaks, CA: Sage.

Kornblum, William. 1996. "Introduction." In *In the Field: Readings on the Field Research Experience* (2d ed.), ed. Carolyn D. Smith and William Kornblum, 1–7. Westport, CT: Praeger.

Kuechler, Manfred. 1998. "The Survey Method." *American Behavioral Scientist* 42, no. 2 (October): 178–200.

Kuhne, Gary W., and Allen Quigley. 1997. "Understanding and Using Action Research in Practice Settings." *New Directions for Adult and Continuing Education* 73 (Spring): 23–40.

Kuhns, Eileen, and S. V. Martorana, eds. 1982. *Qualitative Methods for Institutional Research*. San Francisco: Jossey-Bass.

Kumar, Ranjit. 1996. *Research Methodology*. London: Sage.

Kvale, Steiner. 1996. *Interviewing: An Introduction to Qualitative Research*. Thousand Oaks, CA: Sage.

Lan, Zhiyong, and Kathleen K. Anders. 2000. "A Paradigmatic View of Contemporary Public Administration Research." *Administration and Society* 32, no. 2 (May): 138–166.

Lang, Gerhard, and George D. Heiss. 1997. *A Practical Guide to Research Methods* (6th ed). Lanham, MD: University Press of America.

Lasswell, Harold D. 1953. "Why Be Quantitative?" In *Reader in Public Opinion and Communication*, ed. Bernard Berelson and Morris Janowitz, 265–272. Glendoe, IL: Free Press.

Lastrucci, Carlo L. 1967. *The Scientific Approach: Basic Principles of the Scientific Method.* Cambridge: Schenkman.

LeCompte, Margaret D., and Jean J. Schensul. 1999. *Designing and Conducting Ethnographic Research.* Walnut Creek, CA: AltaMira Press.

Lee, Thomas W. 1999. *Using Qualitative Methods in Organizational Research.* Thousand Oaks, CA: Sage.

Leedy, Paul D. 1974. *Practical Research: Planning and Design.* New York: Macmillan.

Lehmann, Donald R. 1985. *Market Research and Analysis* (2d ed.). Homewood, IL: Irwin.

Leiter, Kenneth. 1980. *A Primer on Ethnomethodology.* New York: Oxford University Press.

Lenkowsky, Leslie, and James L. Perry. 2000. "Reinventing Government: The Case of National Service." *Public Administration Review* 60, no. 4 (July/August): 298–307.

Lessor, Roberta. 2000. "Using the Team Approach of Anselm Strauss in Action Research: Consulting on a Project in Global Education." *Sociological Perspectives* 43, no. 4 (Winter): S133–148.

Lester, James D., Sr., and James D. Lester Jr. 1992. *The Research Paper Handbook.* Glenview, IL: Scott Foreman.

Lewin, Kurt. 1948. *Resolving Social Conflicts* New York: Harper Collins.

Lewicki, R.J., R.D. Bowen, D.R. Hall, and F.S. Hall. 1988. *Experiences in Management and Organizational Behavior* (3d ed.). New York: Wiley.

Li, Xia, and Nancy B. Crane. 1996. *Electronic Styles: A Handbook for Citing Electronic Information.* Medford, NJ: Information Technology Today.

Lincoln, Yvonna S. 1997. "From Understanding to Action: New Imperatives, New Criteria, and New Methods for Interpretive Researchers." *Theory and Research in Social Education* 26. no. 1 (Winter): 12–29.

Lindzey, Gardner. 1961. *Projective Techniques and Cross-Cultural Research*: New York: Appleton-Century-Crofts.

Linz, Juan J. "Ecological Analysis and Survey Research." 1980. In *Quantitative Ecological Analysis in the Social Sciences*, ed. Mattei Dogan and Stein Rokkan, 91–131. Cambridge, MA: Massachusetts Institute of Technology.

Lippitt, Ronald, Jeanne Watson, and Bruce Westley. 1958. *The Dynamics of Planned Change.* New York: Harcourt, Brace.

Lipsky, Michael. 1969. *Street-Level Bureaucracy.* New York: Sage.

Lipsey, Mark W., and David B. Wilson. 2001. *Practical Meta-Analysis.* Thousand Oaks, CA: Sage.

Locke, Karen. 1996. "Rewriting the Discovery of Grounded Theory After 25 Years?" *Journal of Management Inquiry* 5, no. 3 (September): 239–246.

Maas, A.J. 1999. "Hermeneutics." Janet Grayson, trans. In *The Catholic Encyclopaedia, Vol. 7.* Online edition: <<http.//www.newadvent.org/cathen/0/2/1anum>> (August 8, 2000).

Malhotra, Naresh K. 1999. *Marketing Research: An Applied Orientation* (3d ed.). Upper Saddle River, NJ: Prentice Hall.

Manning, Peter K., and Betsy Cullum-Swan. 1998. "Narrative, Content, and Semiotic Analysis." In *Collecting and Interpreting Qualitative Materials*, ed. Norman K. Denzin and Yvonna S. Lincoln, 246–273. Thousand Oaks, CA: Sage.

March, James. 1977. "Administrative Practice, Organizational Theory, and Political Philosophy: Ruminations on the Reflections of John M. Gaus." *Political Science and Politics* 30, no. 4: 689–698.

Margulies, N., and J. Wallace. 1973. *Organizational Change: Techniques and Applications.* Glennview, IL: Foreman.

Markman, Roberta H., Peter T. Markman, and Marie L. Waddell. 1989. *10 Steps in Writing the Research Paper* (4th ed.). New York: Barron's Educational Series.

Marks, Laura. 2000. *Qualitative Research in Context.* Henley-on-Thames, UK: ADMAP.

Marrow, Alfred J. 1977. *The Practical Theorist: The Life and Work of Kurt Lewin.* New York: Teachers College Press.

Marshall, Catherine, and Gretchen B. Rossman. 1999. *Designing Qualitative Research* (3d ed.). Thousand Oaks, CA: Sage.

Martin, Lana A. 2000. "Effective Data Collection." *Total Quality Management* 11, no. 3 (May): 341–345.

Maxwell, Joseph A. 1996. *Qualitative Research Designs: An Interactive Approach.* Thousand Oaks, CA: Sage.

Maykut, Pamela, and Richard Morehouse. 1994. *Beginning Qualitative Research: A Philosophic and Practical Guide.* London: Falmer Press.

McCurdy, Howard E., and Robert E. Cleary. 1984. "Why Can't We Resolve the Research Issue in Public Administration?" *Public Administration Review* 44 (January/February): 49–55.

McDaniel, Carl Jr., and Roger H. Gates. 1993. *Contemporary Marketing Research.* Fort Worth, TX: West.

McDonald, Gael. 2000. "Business Ethics: Practical Proposals for Organizations." *Journal of Business Ethics* 25, no. 2/2 (May): 169–184.

McNabb, David E. 1968. The Private vs. Public Power Fight in Seattle, 1930–1934. Unpublished master's thesis. Seattle: University of Washington.

———. 1991. Shaping the 18th-Century Consumer Society: The *London Post* and *General Advertiser*, 1734–1809. Proceedings of the 16th Annual European Studies Conference, October, Omaha, Nebraska.

McNabb, David. E., and F. Thomas Sepic. 1995. "Culture, Climate, and Total Quality Management: Measuring Readiness for Change." *Public Productivity and Management Review* 18, no. 4: 369–385.

McNabb, David, E., J. Thad Barnowe, and Richard Nordi. 1989. Small Business Managers' Perceptions of Pacific Rim Market Opportunities. Proceedings, Pan Pacific Conference VI, May, Sydney, Australia.

McNabb, David E., F. Thomas Sepic, and J. Thad Barnowe. 1999. *Organizational Climate Survey.* Tacoma, WA: Pacific Lutheran University.

McWilliam, Carol L. 1996. "Creating Understanding That Cultivates Change." *Qualitative Inquiry* 2, no. 2 (June): 151–176.

Meacham, Shuaib J. 1998. "Threads of a New Language: A Response to Eisenhart's 'On the Subject of Interpretive Review.'" *Review of Educational Research* 68, no. 4 (Winter): 401–407.

Melia, Kathy M. 1996. "Rediscovering Glaser." *Qualitative Health Research* 6, no. 3 (August): 368–379.

Mercier, Jean. 1994. "Looking at Organizational Culture Hermeneutically." *Administration and Society* 261 (May): 28–47.

Merrell, Floyd. 1982. *Semiotic Foundations.* Bloomington: Indiana University.

Merriam, Saran B., and Edwin L. Simpson. 1984. *Guide to Research for Educators and Trainers of Adults.* Melbourne, FL: Krieger.

Merton, Robert K. 1967. "Research and Sociological Theory." In *The Study of Society*, ed. P.I. Rose, 35–48. New York: Random House.

Miles, Matthew B., and A. Michael Huberman. 1998. "Data Management and Analysis Methods." In *Collecting and Interpreting Qualitative Materials,* ed. Norman K. Denzin and Yvonna S. Lincoln, 179–210. Thousand Oaks, CA: Sage.

———. 1994. *Qualitative Data Analysis: A Sourcebook of New Methods* (2d ed.). Beverly Hills, CA: Sage.

———. 1984. *Qualitative Data Analysis: A Sourcebook of New Methods.* Beverly Hills, CA: Sage.

Miller, Delbert C. 1991. *Handbook of Research Design and Social Measurement* (5th ed.). Newbury Park, CA: Sage.

Miller, Gerald J., and Marcia L. Whicker, eds. 1999. *Handbook of Research Methods in Public Administration.* New York: Dekker.

Miller, Steven I., and Marcel Fredericks. 1996. *Qualitative Research Methods: Social Epistemology and Practical Inquiry.* New York: Lang.

Mitchell, Jerry. 1998. "Ethical Principles for Public Administration Research." In *Teaching Ethics and Values in Public Administration Programs*, ed. James Bowman and Donald Menzel, 305–320. Albany: State University of New York Press.

Mitchell, Marilyn L. 1998. *Employing Qualitative Methods in the Private Sector*. Thousand Oaks, CA: Sage.

Monopoli, John, and Lori L. Alworth. 2000. "The Use of the Thematic Apperception Test in the Study of Native American Psychological Characteristics: A Review and Archival Study of Navaho Men." *Genetic, Social and General Psychology Monographs* 126, no. 1 (February): 43–79.

Montgomery, D.C. 1991. *Design and Analysis of Experiments* (3d ed.). New York: Wiley.

Moore, Henrietta. 1990. "Paul Ricoeur: Action, Meaning, Text." In *Reading Material Culture: Structuralism, Hermeneutics, and Post-Structuralism*, ed. Christopher Tilley, 85–120. Oxford: Blackwell.

Morse, Janice M. 1994. "Designing Funded Qualitative Research." In *Handbook of Qualitative Research*, ed. Norman K. Denzin and Yvonna S. Lincolns, 220–235. Thousand Oaks, CA: Sage.

Munhall, Patricia L., and Carolyn J. Oiler. 1994. *Nursing Research: A Qualitative Perspective*. Norwalk, CT: Appleton-Century-Crofts.

Myers, M.D. 1997. "Qualitative Research in Information Systems." *MIS Quarterly* 21, no. 2 (June): 241–242. *MISQ Discovery*: <<http://www.misq.org/misqd961/world/>> (April 28, 1999).

Nakano, Lynne Y. 2000. "Volunteering as a Lifestyle Choice: Negotiating Self-Identity in Japan." *Ethnology* 39, no. 2 (Spring): 93–107.

Naroll, Raoul, and Ronald Cohen, eds. 1973. *A Handbook of Method in Cultural Anthropology*. New York: Columbia University Press.

Narotzky, Susana. 2000. "The Cultural Basis of a Regional Economy: The Vega Baja del Segura in Spain." *Ethnology* 39, no. 1 (Winter): 1–14.

Neef, Nancy A., Brian A. Iwata, and Terry J. Page. 1986. "Ethical Standards in Behavioral Research." In *Research Methods in Applied Behavior Analysis: Issues and Advances*, ed. Alan Poling and R. Wayne Fuqua, 233–263. New York: Plenum Press.

Neuman, W. Lawrence. 2000. *Social Research Methods: Qualitative and Quantitative Approaches*. Boston: Allyn and Bacon.

Northrop, Alana, and Kenneth L. Kraemer. 1982. "Contributions of Political Science and Public Administration to Qualitative Research Methods." In *Qualitative Methods for Institutional Research*, ed. Eileen Kuhns and S. V. Martorana, 43–54. San Francisco: Jossey-Bass.

Norusis, Marija J. 2000. *SPSS for Windows Base System User's Guide*. Chicago: SPSS Inc.

Nöth, Winfried. 1990. *Handbook of Semiotics*. Bloomington: Indiana University.

Novak, Joseph D., and D. Bob Gowin. 1984. *Learning How to Learn*. Cambridge: Cambridge University Press.

Oliver, Paul. 1997. *Teach Yourself Research for Business, Marketing and Education*. Chicago: NTC Publishing Group.

Oppenheim, A.N. 1992. *Questionnaire Design, Interviewing, and Attitude Measurement* (rev. ed.). New York: St. Martin's Press.

Organ, Dennis W., and Thomas S. Bateman. 1991. *Organizational Behavior* (4th ed.). Homewood, IL: Irwin.

Orlans, Harold. 1967. "Ethical Problems in the Relations of Research Sponsors and Investigators." In *Ethics, Politics, and Social Research*, ed. Gideon Sjoberg. Cambridge, MA: Schenkman.

Oskamp, Stuart. 1977. *Attitudes and Opinions*. Englewood Cliffs, NJ: Prentice Hall.

O'Sullivan, Elizabethann, and Gary R. Rassel. 1995. *Research Methods for Public Administrators* (2d ed.). White Plains, NY: Longman.

Patton, Michael Q. 1990. *Qualitative Evaluation and Research Methods* (2d ed.). Newbury Park, CA: Sage.

Pechenik, Jan A. 1987. *A Short Guide to Writing about Biology*. New York: HarperCollins.

Peirce, John R. 1962. *Symbols, Signals, and Noise*. London: Hutchinson.

Pelto, Pertti J. 1970. *Anthropological Research: The Structure of Inquiry.* Cambridge, UK: Cambridge University Press.

Pernanen, Kai. 1993. "Research Approaches in the Study of Alcohol-Related Violence." *Alcohol Health and Research World* 17, no. 2: 101–108.

Perry, James L., and Kenneth L. Kraemer. 1986. "Research Methodology in the *Public Administration Review,* 1975–1984." *Public Administration Review* 46 (May/June): 215–226.

Peters, Thomas J., and Robert W. Waterman. 1982. *In Search of Excellence: Lessons from America's Best Run Companies.* New York: Harper and Row.

Peterson, Karen S. 2001. "Would I Lie to You?" *USA Today,* July 5, p. 8D.

Petrick, Joseph A., and John F. Quinn. 1997. *Management Ethics: Integrity at Work.* Newbury Park, CA: Sage.

Pfiffner, John M. 1940. *Research Methods in Public Administration.* New York: Ronald Press.

Phillips, Bernard S. 1976. *Social Research: Strategy and Tactics* (3d ed.). New York: Macmillan.

Phillips, Denis C. 1987. *Philosophy, Science, and Social Inquiry.* Oxford: Pergamon.

Piantanida, Maria, and Noreen B. Garman. 1999. *The Qualitative Dissertation.* Thousand Oaks, CA: Sage.

Poister, Theodore H. 1978. *Public Program Analysis: Applied Research Methods.* Baltimore: University Park Press.

Poister, Theodore H., and Richard H. Harris Jr. 2000. "Building Quality Improvement Over the Long Run: Approaches, Results, and Lessons Learned from the PennDOT Experience." *Public Productivity and Management Review* 24, no. 2 (December): 161–176.

Potter, Jonathan, and Margaret Wetherell. 1994. "Analyzing Discourse." In *Analyzing Qualitative Data.* ed. Alan Bryman and Robert B. Burgess, 47–66. London: Routledge.

Punnett, Betty J., and Oded Shenkat. 1996. *Handbook for International Management Research.* Cambridge, UK: Blackwell.

Quigley, B. Allen, and Gary W. Kuhne. 1997. "The Role of Research in the Practice of Adult Education." *New Directions for Adult and Continuing Education* 73 (Spring): 3–22.

————. 1997. *Creating Practical Knowledge Through Action Research: Posing Problems, Solving Problems, and Improving Daily Practice.* San Francisco: Jossey-Bass.

Rabin, Jack, W. Barkley Hildreth, and Gerald J. Miller, eds. 1989. *Handbook of Public Administration Research.* New York: Dekker.

Racker, Efraim. 1997. "A View of Misconduct in Science." In *Research Ethics,* ed. Deni Elliott and Judy E. Stern, 34–51. Hanover, NH: University Press of New England.

Raelin, Joseph A. 1997. "Action Learning and Action Science: Are They Different?" *Organizational Dynamics* 26, no. 1 (Summer): 21–35.

Ragin, Charles, and David Zaret. 1983. "Theory and Method in Comparative Research: Two Strategies." *Social Forces* 61, no. 3 (March): 731–754.

Reason, Peter. 1998. "Three Approaches to Participative Inquiry." In *Strategies of Qualitative Inquiry,* ed. Norman K. Denzin and Yvonna S. Lincoln, 261–291. Thousand Oaks, CA: Sage.

Reisman, David. 1979. "Ethical and Practical Dilemmas of Fieldwork in Academic Settings: A Personal Memoir." In *Qualitative and Quantitative Social Research,* ed. R.K. Merton, J.S. Coleman and P.H. Rossi, 210–231. New York: Free Press.

Reynolds, Paul D. 1979. *Ethical Dilemmas and Social Science Research.* San Francisco: Jossey-Bass.

Richards, Thomas J., and Lyn Richards. 1998. "Using Computers in Qualitative Research." In *Collecting and Interpreting Qualitative Materials,* ed. Norman K. Denzin and Yvonna S. Lincoln, 211–245. Thousand Oaks: Sage.

Richardson, Frank C., and Blaine J. Fowers. 1998. "Interpretive Social Science." *American Behavioral Scientist* 41, no. 4 (January): 465–495.

Richardson, Kurt A. 1995. "Postmetaphysical Hermeneutics: When Practice Triumphs Over Theory." *Premise* 2, no. 8 (September 27): 8–19.

Roberts, Carol A. 1999. "Drug Use Among Inner-City African American Women: The Process of Managing Loss." *Qualitative Health Research* 9, no. 5 (September): 620–639.

Robinson, Viviane M.J. 1994. "The Practical Promise of Critical Research in Education." *Educational Administration Quarterly* 30, no. 1 (February): 56–77.

Robrecht, Linda C. 1995. "Grounded Theory: Evolving Methods." *Qualitative Health Research* 5, no. 2 (May): 169–178 (EBSCO-Host. Available August 3, 2001).

Rodgers, Robert, and Nanette Rodgers. 1999. "The Sacred Spark of Academic Research." *Journal of Public Administration Research and Theory* 9, no. 3 (July): 473–492.

Rohr, John A. 1998. *Public Service, Ethics, and Constitutional Practice.* Lawrence: University Press of Kansas.

Rosenthal, Robert, and Ralph L. Rosnow. 1991. *Essentials of Behavioral Research* (2d ed.). New York: McGraw-Hill.

Rothman, Jack. 1974. *Planning and Organizing for Social Change: Action Principles from Social Science Research.* New York: Columbia University.

Rutgers, Mark R. 1997. "Beyond Woodrow Wilson: the Identity of the Study of Public Administration in Historical Perspective." *Administration and Society* 29, no. 3 (July): 276–300.

Schein, Edgar H. 1985. *Organizational Culture and Leadership.* San Francisco: Jossey-Bass.

———. 1996a. *Organizational Culture and Leadership* (2d ed.). San Francisco: Jossey-Bass.

———. 1996b. "Culture: The Missing Concept in Organization Studies." *Administrative Science Quarterly* 41 (June): 229–240.

Schellenberg, James A. 1978. *Masters of Social Psychology.* Oxford, UK: Oxford University Press.

Schellenberg, T.R. 1984. "Archival Principles of Arrangement." In *Modern Archives Reader,* ed. Maygene F. Daniels and Timothy Walch, 63–86. Washington: National Archives and Records Service.

Schmuck, Richard A. 1997. *Practical Action Research for Change.* Arlington Heights, IL: SkyLight.

Schwab, Donald P. 1999. *Research Methods for Organizational Studies.* Mahwah, NJ: Erlbaum.

Schwandt, Thomas A. 1997. *Qualitative Inquiry: A Dictionary of Terms.* Thousand Oaks, CA: Sage.

Scott, Judy E. 2000. "Facilitating Interorganizational Learning with Information Technology." *Journal of Management Information Systems* 17, no. 2 (Fall): 81–114.

Seaman, Catherine C., and Phyllis J. Verbonick. 1982. *Research Methods* (2d ed.). New York: Appleton-Century-Crofts.

Sebeok, Thomas A. 1976. *Contributions to the Doctrine of Signs.* Lanham, MD: University Press of America.

Seech, Zachary. 1993. *Writing Philosophy Papers.* Belmont, CA: Wadsworth.

Selltiz, Claire, Lawrence S. Wrightman, and Stuart W. Cook. 1976. *Research Methods in Social Relations.* New York: Holt, Rinehart and Winston.

Selznick, Philip. 1949. *TVA and the Grass Roots: A Study in the Sociology of Formal Organization.* Berkeley: University of California Press.

Shahariw-Kuehne, Valerie. 1998/1999. "Building Intergenerational Communities Through Research and Evaluation." *Generations* 22, no. 4 (Winter): 82–88.

Shaughnessy, John J., and Eugene B. Zechmeister. 1994. *Research Methods in Psychology* (3d ed.). New York: McGraw-Hill.

Shelly, Gary B., Thomas J. Cashman, and Misty E. Vermatt. 1995. *Microsoft Office: Introductory Concepts and Techniques.* Danvers, MA: Boyd and Fraser.

Silverman, Eric K., and Clifford Geertz. 1990. "Toward a More 'Thick' Understanding." In *Reading Material Culture: Structuralism, Hermeneutics, and Post-Structuralism,* ed. Christopher Tilley, 121–159. Oxford: Blackwell.

Silverman, Hugh J. 1991. *Gadamer and Hermeneutics.* London: Routledge.

Silverman, Kaja. 1983. *The Subject of Semiotics.* Oxford: Oxford University.

Small, Stephen A. 1995. "Action-Oriented Research: Models and Methods." *Journal of Marriage and the Family* 57, no. 4 (November): 941–956.

Smith, Carolyn D., and William Kornblum, eds. 1996. *In the Field: Readings on the Field Research Experience* (2d ed.). Westport, CT: Praeger.

Smith, Charles B. 1981. *A Guide to Business Research*. Chicago: Nelson-Hall.

Soni, Vidu. 2000. "A Twenty-First Century Reception for Diversity in the Public Sector: A Case Study." *Public Administration Review* 60, no. 5 (September/October): 395–408.

Sorrels, Bobbye D. 1984. *Business Communications Fundamentals*. New York: Macmillan.

Sproull, Natalie L. 1988. *Handbook of Research Methods*. Metuchen, NJ: Scarecrow Press.

Stack, Carol. 1996. "Doing Research in the Flats." *In the Field: Readings on the Field Research Experience* (2d ed.), ed. Carolyn D. Smith and William Kornblum, 21–25. Westport, CT: Praeger.

Stake, Robert E. "Case Studies." 1994. In *Handbook of Qualitative Research*, ed. Norman. K. Denzin and Yvonne. S. Lincoln, 236–247. Thousand Oaks, CA: Sage.

Stallings, Robert A., and James M. Ferris. 1988. "Public Administration Research: Work in PAR, 1940–1984." *Public Administration Review* 48 (January/February): 580–587.

Stein, Harold, ed. 1952. *Public Administration and Policy Development: A Case Book*. New York: Harcourt, Brace and World.

Stivers, Camilla. 2000. "Public Administration Theory as a Discourse." *Administrative Theory and Praxis* 221 (March): 132–139.

Stone, Eugene F. 1978. *Research Methods in Organizational Behavior*. Santa Monica: Goodyear.

Strauss, Anselm, and Juliet Corbin. 1998. *Basics of Qualitative Research* (2d ed.). Thousand Oaks, CA: Sage.

———. 1990. *Basics of Qualitative Research*. Thousand Oaks, CA: Sage.

———, eds. 1997. *Grounded Theory in Practice*. Thousand Oaks, CA: Sage.

Stringer, Ernie, ed. 1999. *Community-Based Ethnography: Breaking Traditional Boundaries of Research, Teaching, and Learning*. Mahwah, NJ: Erlbaum.

Strunk, William, Jr., and E.B. White. 1979. *The Elements of Style* (3d ed.). Boston: Allyn and Bacon.

Suchman, Edward A. 1967. *Evaluative Research: Principles and Practice in Public Service and Social Action Programs*. New York: Russell Sage Foundation.

Suppe, Frederick. 1988. "The Structure of a Scientific Paper." *Philosophy of Science* 65 (September): 381–405.

Tak, Sunghee H., Margaret Nield, and Heather Becker. 1999. "Use of a Computer Software Program for Qualitative Analyses—Part 1: Introduction to NUD*IST (N1)." *Western Journal of Nursing Research* 31, no. 1 (February): 111–118.

Taxpayers for Common Sense (TFCS). 2001. "Senator William Proxmire and the History of the Golden Fleece Award." <<http.//www.taxpayer.net/proxmire.html>> (July 7, 2001).

Thompson, James R. 2000. "Reinvention as Reform: Assessing the National Performance Review." *Public Administration Review* 60, no. 6 (November/December): 508–521.

Tibbetts, Arn. 1987. *Practical Business Writing*. Boston: Little, Brown.

Tilley, Christopher. 1989. "Interpreting Material Culture." In *The Meaning of Things: Material Culture and Symbolic Expression*, ed. Ian Hodder, 185–194. London: HarperCollins Academic.

———, ed. 1990. *Reading Material Culture: Structuralism, Hermeneutics, and Post-Structuralism*. Oxford: Blackwell.

Tolman, Deborah L., and Mary Brydon-Miller, eds. 2001. *From Subjects to Subjectivities*. New York: New York University Press.

Turner, Roy, ed. 1974. *Ethnomethodology: Selected Readings*. Harmondswork, UK: Penguin.

Van Evera, Stephen. 1997. *Guide to Methods for Students of Political Science*. Ithaca, NY: Cornell University Press.

Velasquez, Manuel. 1998. *Business Ethics: Concepts and Cases* (4th ed.). Upper Saddle River, NJ: Prentice Hall.

Wachterhauser, Brice. 1986. "History and Language in Understanding." In *Hermeneutics and Modern Philosophy*, ed. Brice Wachterhauser, 5–61. Albany: State University of New York.

Waddington, David. 1997. "Participant Observation." In *Qualitative Methods in Organiza-*

tional Research, ed. Catherine Cassell and Gillian Symon, 107–122. Thousand Oaks, CA: Sage.

Walizer, Michael H., and Paul L. Wienir. 1978. *Research Methods and Analysis: Searching for Relationships*. New York: Harper and Row.

Walker, Robert, ed. 1985. *Applied Qualitative Research*. Aldershot, UK: Gower.

Wasson, Chester R. 1965. *Research Analysis for Marketing Decision* [sic]. New York: Appleton-Century-Crofts.

Waterston, Alice. 1999. *Love, Sorrow, and Rage: Destitute Women in a Manhattan Residence*. Philadelphia: Temple University Press.

Webb, Eugene J., Donald T. Campbell, Richard D. Schwartz, and Lee Sechrest. 2000. *Unobtrusive Measures* (rev. ed.). Thousand Oaks, CA: Sage.

Weitzman, Eben A., and Matthew B. Miles. 1995. *Computer Programs for Qualitative Data Analysis: A Software Sourcebook*. Thousand Oaks, CA: Sage.

Whelan, Robert K. 1989. "Data Administration and Research Methods in Public Administration." In *Handbook of Public Administration Research*, ed. Jack Rabin, W.B. Hildreth, and G.J. Miller, 657–682. New York: Dekker.

White, Jay D. 1986. "Dissertations and Publications in Public Administration." *Public Administration Review* 46 (May/June): 227–239.

———. 1999. *The Narrative Foundations of Public Administration Research*. Washington, DC: Georgetown University Press.

White, Jay D., and Guy B. Adams, eds. 1994. *Research in Public Administration*. Thousand Oaks, CA: Sage.

Whiting, Beatrice, and John Whiting. 1973. "Methods for Observing and Recording Behavior." In *A Handbook of Method in Cultural Anthropology*, ed. Raoul Naroll and Ronald Cohen, 282–315. New York: Columbia University Press.

Williams, Terry. 1996. "Exploring the Cocaine Culture." *In the Field: Readings on the Field Research Experience* (2d ed.), ed. Carolyn D. Smith and William Kornblum, 27–32. Westport, CT: Praeger.

Wilson, James Q. 1989. *Bureaucracy: What Government Agencies Do and How They Do It*. New York: Basic Books.

Yeager, Samuel J. 1989. "Classic Methods in Public Administration Research." In *Handbook of Public Administration*, ed. J. Rabin, W.B. Hildreth, and G.J. Miller, 683–793. New York: Marcel Dekker.

Yin, Robert K. 1994. *Case Study Research: Design and Methods* (2nd ed). Thousand Oaks, CA: Sage.

———. 1984. *Case Study Research: Design and Methods*. Beverly Hills, CA: Sage.

Zikmund, William G. 1994. *Research Methods*. Fort Worth, TX: Dryden.

Index

About the Author

After a career that has included stints in municipal and state public adminis-tration and business management, **David E. McNabb** turned to a second pro-fession in academia and advanced to the rank of professor during nearly twenty years on the Business Administration faculty at Pacific Lutheran University. Professor McNabb has earned degrees from California State College at Ful-lerton, the University of Washington, and Oregon State University. He has taught a variety of public and private administration courses, both in the United States and abroad (in Latvia, Bulgaria, Germany, the United Kingdom, Italy, France, and Belgium). He is currently a thesis advisor for The Evergreen State College MPA program and a visiting faculty member in the Entrepre-neurship and Administration program. Professor McNabb is also a visiting professor at the Stockholm School of Economics–Riga. He continues to teach graduate and undergraduate courses for military personnel under University of Maryland's University College–European Division. McNabb is the author of nearly fifty peer-reviewed conference papers and articles. He has also con-tinued to serve the community as a member of the Seattle, Washington, Citi-zens' Advisory Committee on Solid Waste Management; the Kirkland, Washington, Central Business District Advisory Committee; and the Port of Tacoma, Washington, International Trade Association.